CORNEILLE

CORNEILLE

BY

P. J. YARROW

SENIOR LECTURER IN FRENCH IN THE
UNIVERSITY OF EXETER

LONDON
MACMILLAN & CO LTD
NEW YORK · ST MARTIN'S PRESS
1963

MACMILLAN AND COMPANY LIMITED
St Martin's Street London WC2
also Bombay Calcutta Madras Melbourne

THE MACMILLAN COMPANY OF CANADA LIMITED
Toronto

ST MARTIN'S PRESS INC
New York

PRINTED IN GREAT BRITAIN

TABLE OF CONTENTS

INTRODUCTION

No full-length study is available in English of the great French dramatist, Corneille, whom at least two French critics have called 'notre Shakespeare'. Even in French, though the list of books and articles devoted to him is long, there is no completely satisfactory up-to-date general study. And yet such a study is badly needed, for Corneille has long been neglected and imperfectly appreciated.

It is possible to suggest several reasons for this. His output was large — thirty-two plays in all — and human sloth is only too prone to dismiss as negligible a large part of the output of a prolific writer. Moreover, his plays were written over a long period, from 1629 to 1674, a period during which social and political changes brought about a considerable revolution in taste. Thus, by the end of his life, his early comedies were no longer understood and appreciated. Further, during the last fifteen years of his literary career, Corneille had ceased to be in tune with the taste of the public; and works, however good, which do not meet with immediate success, often take a long time to be rediscovered — as the fortunes of Stendhal and Barbey d'Aurevilly show. Hence, already in the latter half of the seventeenth century, Corneille had come to be regarded only as the author of some half dozen plays.[1]

Now, to be remembered for only part of one's work may be an advantage. No doubt Lesage, Prévost and Murger gain by being remembered for only one novel each. Sometimes, however, not only is popular taste unjust, but it leads to a distorted and imperfect appreciation of what is remembered. Balzac, for example, cannot be fully appreciated unless his work is read as a whole. In the case of Corneille, concentration on a few works has certainly hindered appreciation of the variety of his genius, and fostered sweeping generalizations and clear-cut formulas which have

---

[1] Boileau, *VIIe Réflexion sur Longin*; La Bruyère, *Des Ouvrages de l'Esprit*.

blinded readers and audiences to his richness and subtlety. And there are two further reasons why such unjust generalizations and formulas have become current. One is the rivalry between Corneille and Racine, which led to the vogue of *parallèles* between the two writers, a vogue which dates from the second half of the seventeenth century, but which still seems to survive in France. Inevitably such parallels attempted to sum up their characteristics in simple, contrasting formulas;[1] but clear-cut antitheses of this type are not the best way of appreciating literary works: literary criticism should be a subtle and flexible instrument. The other is the *Querelle des Anciens et des Modernes*. In this heated controversy which raged in the closing years of the seventeenth century, Racine, along with Boileau and La Bruyère, maintained the superiority of the ancients; while the value of the moderns was asserted by Fontenelle and the *Mercure Galant*, the co-editors of which were Donneau de Visé and Thomas Corneille. Now, since Thomas Corneille was Corneille's brother and Fontenelle his nephew, and since Racine was on the other side, it was inevitable that disparagement of Corneille should become a weapon in the literary controversy.

In France, according to a recent critic,[2] the admirers of Corneille are forced on to the defensive. And although one might have imagined his work to be more akin to English taste than that of Racine, his reputation has long stood lower in this country than his rival's.

In the following pages, an attempt will be made to study Corneille's plays in their entirety, to show their variety and subtlety, to relate them to their age, and to approach them without preconceived notions — either about the nature of Corneille's art, or about the nature of comedy and tragedy: for Corneille has also suffered to some extent from the fact that the distinction made in the seventeenth century between comedy and tragedy does not altogether coincide with modern ideas on the subject. The parallel

---

[1] Critics have always seemed to find it hard to like one of the two poets without being unfair to the other.

[2] L. Herland, *Corneille par lui-même*, 1954, p. 63.

with Racine will be avoided completely. Above all, the attempt will be made to read Corneille as he himself wished to be read:

> je vous demande pour sa lecture un peu de cette faveur qui doit toujours pencher du côté de ceux qui travaillent pour le public, avec une attention sincère qui vous empêche d'y voir ce qui n'y est pas, et vous y laisse voir tout ce que j'y fais dire.
>
> (*Sophonisbe, Au Lecteur*)

ACKNOWLEDGMENTS

THE pages on Chimène and Pauline in Chapter 8, originally forming part of articles published in the *Modern Language Review* and *French Studies* respectively, appear here, with modifications, by kind permission of the Editors of these journals.

PART I

The Age of Corneille

Chapter One

ORDER AND DISORDER
IN THE AGE OF CORNEILLE

The seventeenth century in France is an age of striking contrasts. It is an age of refinement and of coarseness; it allowed women to play an important part in social life, but completely disregarded their wishes where matrimony was concerned. It united extreme religious austerity with a considerable degree of free-thought and immorality. Sexual freedom in private life was accompanied by a growing prudery in literature, by an increasing dislike of allusions to sex or even to the human frame at all in stage plays. The age which carried to perfection the classical tragedy of Corneille and Racine delighted at the same time in ballets, operas, comédies-ballets and machine-plays which are the very antithesis of classical tragedy.

The greatness of the seventeenth century, its particular characteristics, are due precisely to these contrasts, to the tension between so many apparently contradictory tendencies. Three basic tensions, in particular, go far to explain the age of Corneille: (1) The tension between the forces of order and those of disorder, between the centripetal and the centrifugal tendencies of the age, which helps to explain the character of the people of the time — the people, that is to say, who went to see the plays of Corneille, to please whose taste those plays were written, from whom he derived his knowledge of human nature, and whose lives provided the material for his situations and his plots; (2) The tension between Reason and Faith, which helps to explain their outlook; and (3) The tension between baroque and classicism, which helps to explain their taste, their art, their literature.

*   *   *

The whole history of France is an alternation of order and disorder, of periods of strong, central government and of anarchy; but in the first half of the seventeenth century, order and disorder succeeded each other with more rapidity than ever before. The assassination of Henry IV was followed by rebellions of disaffected nobles and Huguenots. Richelieu re-established the power and prestige of the monarchy, but only at the cost of a long series of wars at home and abroad; and a constant series of conspiracies, risings and revolts shows the strength of the forces opposed to him and the insecurity of his achievement. After Richelieu, came Mazarin and the Fronde, the last fling of the rebels and the malcontents, and then France accepted with relief the absolute government of Louis XIV. But even Louis XIV's authority was not complete: risings and rebellions were frequent throughout his reign, and his will was not always law.

The age of Corneille was thus a restless, turbulent age — an age of wars, intrigues, rebellions, conspiracies, invasions; an age of violence and disorders of all kinds; an age in which all classes — turbulent nobles, peaceable bourgeois, wretched peasants — were prepared to resort to arms to assert their rights or call attention to their grievances. The nobles fought the crown; the Queen Mother, Maria de' Medici, waged war against her own son, Louis XIII; the Huguenots fought the Catholics. It was an age of instability. Henry IV was assassinated by Ravaillac; Concini, Maria de' Medici's favourite, was put to death by the officer sent by Louis XIII to arrest him; plots threatened the lives of Richelieu and Mazarin. Striking reversals of fortune were witnessed — Louis XIII's favourite, Cinq-Mars, was executed for conspiring against Richelieu and signing a treaty with Spain; the Fronde brought the arrest of three princes of the blood, the exile of

Mazarin, the spectacle of the King's cousin, Mademoiselle, defending Orléans against the royal troops and even turning the guns of the Bastille against her royal cousin's army, and finally the desertion of the greatest French general, Condé, to the enemy. In 1661, the wealthy and powerful surintendant des finances, Foucquet, was arrested and imprisoned for life. Nor were such happenings confined to France. In England, Guy Fawkes and his confederates tried to blow up the Houses of Parliament; the Duke of Buckingham was assassinated; Charles I was executed, and his family sought refuge in France. The King of Bohemia lost his throne at the outbreak of the Thirty Years' War; Wallenstein was murdered; Christina of Sweden abdicated; and, in 1665, the Queen of Poland — a French princess — was forced by a Swedish invasion to take refuge in Silesia.

This instability did not escape the notice of contemporaries. 'Qui aurait eu l'amitié du roi d'Angleterre, du roi de Pologne et de la reine de Suède, aurait-il cru manquer de retraite et d'asile au monde?' asks Pascal. And, referring to Henrietta Maria, Charles I's wife and a French princess, Mme de Motteville writes:

> Cette princesse, après avoir été la plus heureuse des femmes, et la plus opulente de toutes les reines de l'Europe, avec trois couronnes qu'elle avait sur la tête, fut réduite en tel état, que pour faire ses couches,[1] il fallut que la Reine [of France] lui envoyât Madame Péronne sa sage-femme, et jusques aux moindres choses qui lui étaient nécessaires.

The fall of Chavigny in 1648 prompts her to reflect on the paradox of life:

> Il se vit humilié dans ce même lieu où il avait commandé, et réduit à cette dure nécessité de souffrance, par les ordres de l'homme du monde qu'il croyait lui être le plus obligé. Voilà cette diversité qui se trouve pour l'ordinaire dans la fortune des hommes qui sont appelés à la faveur.

La Rochefoucauld dwells at length on the paradoxes of his century in one of his *Réflexions diverses*.

The lives of the lower orders of society were no less liable to excitements and reversals of fortune than those of the great. It was

---

[1] The occasion was the birth of Princess Henrietta in Exeter, 1644.

not uncommon for the porters of the Parisian theatres to be murdered by those seeking to enter without paying; and in 1638 members of the parlement and the chambre des comptes came to blows in Notre-Dame over a question of precedence. In the provinces the people often suffered from the tyranny and the exactions of the nobles. Sometimes the governor exploited his position without scruple, like the maréchal de La Ferté, of whom it was said that 'l'on n'a jamais tant volé et pillé province comme celui-là a fait'. Sometimes lesser nobles tyrannized their estates or their district — such as Beaulieu-Picart, of whom Tallemant des Réaux says:

> il faisait apparemment [i.e. openly] la fausse monnaie, rançonnait ses paysans, mais les exemptait des gens de guerre, troquait ses chevaux, et avait trois fois plus de train qu'il n'en pouvait nourrir en vivant en homme de bien.

Auvergne was particularly lawless, and in 1665 a special tribunal, the Grands Jours d'Auvergne, was sent down to deal with some of the unruly nobles. Fléchier, who accompanied it, wrote an account of the cases it tried. His book is full of stories of nobles who extorted money or forced labour from their peasants and who beat, murdered or imprisoned those who resisted.

The lower classes suffered, too, from the depredations of the troops. Soldiers were undisciplined. Bussy-Rabutin, for example, imprisoned in the Bastille because his men had been guilty of highway robbery and salt-smuggling, felt aggrieved because at the time he himself had been absent from his regiment, chasing after a woman. With this standard of discipline and responsibility, it is not surprising that the armies of the time, whether hostile or not, caused much suffering. The Fronde brought untold misery to the peasants: wherever troops passed, they raped women and girls, not sparing even nuns, tortured and murdered the wretched inhabitants, carried off or wantonly destroyed their property, and desecrated churches. Here, for instance, is an eye-witness account of the behaviour of the royal troops in the village of Marle:

> en un moment les 3.000 hommes se saisissent des 60 maisons, où ils se font traiter à discrétion et avec toutes les inhumanités indicibles,

depuis le 20 janvier jusqu'au 24, qu'ils en sortent; pendant lequel temps ils pillent et emportent tous les meubles, grains et autres choses qui se trouvent aux maisons, sans presque y rien laisser, battent, outragent et excèdent leurs hôtes afin de les faire abandonner, les dépouillent en la rue et en plein jour, violent quantité de filles et de femmes, brûlent cinq ou six maisons et plusieurs bâtiments, rançonnent certains habitants pour leur rendre leurs femmes, retiennent un petit enfant à l'âge de six mois un fort long temps sans le rendre à sa mère quoiqu'il mourût presque de faim, et menacent de l'embrocher, si elle ne leur donne ce qu'elle n'avait pouvoir de faire.[1]

Instability, violence, suffering, sudden reverses of fortune — these constitute one aspect of the age. But there is another. It was an age of growing centralization; the court and the capital were playing an increasingly important part in the life of France. Feudalism, though its institutions remained, was breaking down, and real power was passing more and more into the hands of the middle classes. The nobles, impoverished by inflation, were looking more and more to the King for financial support and tending more and more to leave their estates and seek their fortune at court. The social life of the capital was, in consequence, becoming more and more vigorous, and the seventeenth century was a period of great salons, of growing feminine influence, of increasing refinement of taste and manners, of *préciosité*, of psychological analysis and linguistic discussion, of gallantry and intellectual interests.

To the fact of being poised between order and disorder, between anarchy and civilization, between violence and refinement, the seventeenth century owes many of its characteristics. Refinement, centralization and social order had not yet weakened individualism: self-reliance and strength of character were still necessary for survival. Life in the seventeenth century was, in fact, rather like life under the Revolution, as Chateaubriand describes it in his *Mémoires*:

Les moments de crise produisent un redoublement de vie chez les hommes. Dans une société qui se dissout et se recompose, la lutte des

---

[1] Quoted by A. Feillet, *La Misère au temps de la Fronde et Saint Vincent de Paul*, 5th edition, 1886, p. 459.

B

deux génies, le choc du passé et de l'avenir, le mélange des mœurs anciennes et des mœurs nouvelles, forment une combinaison transitoire qui ne laisse pas un moment d'ennui. *Les passions et les caractères en liberté, se montrent avec une énergie qu'ils n'ont point dans la cité bien réglée.*

Such was life in the seventeenth century, though it was soon to change. Already in the eighteenth century we find Diderot, in the *Neveu de Rameau*, complaining of 'cette fastidieuse uniformité que notre éducation, nos conventions de société, nos bienséances d'usage, ont introduite', and Mirabeau saying nostalgically:

> En taillant ce diamant, un lapidaire malhabile lui a ôté quelques-unes de ses plus vives étincelles. Au moyen âge, que dis-je? encore sous Richelieu, le Français avait la *force de vouloir*.[1]

*   *   *

'Les passions et les caractères en liberté': that is precisely what we find in the age of Corneille. The people of the age give an impression of great vigour, robustness, bluffness and individuality. In the pages of Tallemant des Réaux and the memorialists, *characters* abound in all their variety — rogues, naïfs or simpletons, *extravagants* and eccentrics.

Forthrightness, often combined with humour or wit, is a characteristic of the time; for the contemporaries of Corneille were no respecters of persons. The Bishop of Belley — the novelist, Camus — once preached a sermon before Louis XIII's brother on the theme that good intentions are not enough:

> Par exemple, Monseigneur, on dira quand vous n'y serez plus, car les princes meurent comme les autres hommes, M. d'Orléans avait les meilleures intentions du monde; mais il n'a jamais rien fait qui vaille.

Gaston d'Orléans did not take offence. On another occasion, seeing Gaston sitting between two of his cronies, the same bishop, in the course of his sermon, as if addressing Christ, said: 'Je vous vois là, mon Seigneur, entre deux brigands.' The duc de Condé, the father of the great Condé, was admonished in the parlement one day for interrupting the debate. 'Enfin ne savez-vous pas que

---

[1] Quoted by Stendhal in *Le Rouge et le Noir*, epigraph to Ch. LXIII.

je suis prince de sang?' he asked. 'Oui, monsieur,' retorted the president, 'nos registres en sont chargés.' Meeting Voiture at Rueil in 1644, Anne of Austria, then Regent, asked him what he was thinking about; without hesitation he replied with an impromptu poem alluding to her amours with the Duke of Buckingham:

> Je pensais, car nous autres poètes
> Nous pensons extravagamment,
> Ce que dans l'humeur où vous êtes,
> Vous feriez si dans ce moment
> Vous avisiez en cette place
> Venir le Duc de Bokingham?
> Et lequel serait en disgrâce
> De lui ou du père Vincent?

Even towards the King there was no subservience. When M. de Turin, a lawyer of the parlement, had to judge a lawsuit between M. de Bouillon and M. Bouillon la Mark for the possession of the city of Sedan, Henry IV sent for him and told him that he wanted the former to win.

'Hé bien, Sire,' lui répondit le bonhomme, il n'y a rien de plus aisé; je vous l'enverrai, vous le jugerez vous-même.' Quand il fut parti, quelqu'un dit au Roi: 'Sire, vous ne connaissez pas le personnage, il est homme à faire ce qu'il vous vient de dire.' Le Roi sur cela y envoya, et on trouva le bonhomme qui chargeait les sacs sur un crocheteur.

A gentleman in the reign of Henry IV, annoyed that he was not allowed to drive into the courtyard of the Louvre, had his own castle in Burgundy built without a carriage-entrance, saying: 'Si le Roi ne veut pas que j'entre chez lui en carrosse, il n'entrera pas non plus en carrosse chez moi.' When the bailli de Valençay, who commanded a vessel at the siege of La Rochelle, had to give Louis XIII lunch on board, he had a dish of mouldy biscuits and another of cod served with pea soup. The King laughed: 'Sire,' said Valençay, 'quand on nous payera mieux, nous vous ferons meilleure chère.' — Louis XIII seems to have been willing to put up with a good deal of blunt speaking from his courtiers. When he missed a ball at rackets, Nogent punningly called out: 'Ah!

vraiment, voilà un beau Louis le Juste!' In 1620, Bassompierre, being received coldly by Louis XIII, asked him point-blank: 'Sire, me faites-vous la mine à bon escient, ou si vous vous moquez de moi?' Some years later, after he had been sent to Spain as ambassador, Bassompierre told the King how he had entered Madrid on a mule. 'Oh! la belle chose que c'était,' said the King, 'de voir un âne sur une mule!' 'Tout beau, Sire,' retorted Bassompierre, 'c'est vous que je représentais.'

Strong-minded, masculine women were not rare, either. Mme de Chasteau-Gay fought a duel with a lover of whom she was jealous and lost her life in an attack upon some neighbouring gentlemen with whom she had a quarrel, although she and her supporters were outnumbered by three to one. Her sister fought a duel with her own husband and used to amuse herself by snuffing candles with musket shots. Mme de Saint-Balmont used to dress as a man, wearing a skirt over her breeches, and slew or captured four hundred men with her own hands. Mme de la Guette, 'la Saint-Balmont de la Brie,' was a good horsewoman and loved the sound, not only of drums and fanfares of trumpets, but of guns. Her *fermeté d'âme* was such, she tells us, as to cause her to prefer warfare to more feminine activities:

> Si je suivais ma fantaisie,
> Je m'en irais dans les combats,
> Avec un fort grand coutelas,
> Faire une étrange boucherie.

She did not hesitate to intervene in a quarrel between her father and her husband:

> Je me mis au-devant de mon père pour lui servir de bouclier et découvris ma poitrine; puis je dis à mon mari, qui avait l'épée nue: 'Donne là-dedans; il faut que tu me tues, avant que tu fasses la moindre chose à mon père;' et tout d'un coup je lui sautai au collet et lui arrachai son épée qu'il n'eut pas de peine à me lâcher, lui étant impossible de me résister en quoi que ce fût, car il m'aimait trop pour cela. Je jetai l'épée par la fenêtre, et j'emportai mon mari entre mes bras hors de la salle; puis je fermai la porte.[1]

[1] Doubts have been cast on the authenticity of Mme de la Guette's *Mémoires*. Even if they were justified, which is by no means certain, she would be a representative figure.

Pontis tells us that, Créquy having seized a castle which belonged to Monravel, it was besieged by Mme de Monravel. When Créquy sent reinforcements, she stood on the bridge, saying that 'ils ne passeraient point qu'ils ne lui marchassent sur le ventre; que c'était à eux à voir s'ils la voulaient écraser, parce qu'elle ne partirait pas de la place.' They withdrew. And Tallemant relates that a certain Fontenay Coup-d'Epée, whose mistress would not admit him to her house, effected an entrance by means of a petard, but was received by the lady with a brace of pistols.

Life in a turbulent age tended to bring out such qualities as will-power, resolution, courage and daring, fortitude, and the sense of honour.

For Richelieu, politics is a combination of reason and will, and he describes his ideal minister thus:

> De la capacité et de la probité naît un si parfait accord entre l'entende-ment et la volonté qu'ainsi que l'entendement fait choisir les meilleurs objets et les moyens les plus convenables pour en acquérir la possession, la volonté sait aussi les embrasser avec tant d'ardeur qu'elle n'oublie rien de ce qu'elle peut pour parvenir aux fins que l'entendement s'est proposé.

And Descartes makes resolution the second of his four provisional maxims of conduct. But it was not only in theory that will-power and resolution were important: there are plenty of examples in real life. Historians speak of Richelieu's iron will. Pascal, with his insistence on subduing the flesh and his ability to distract his attention from his neuralgia by solving geometrical problems, is another such. The capacity of Sully and Colbert for work is an-other form of the same thing: Colbert worked for fifteen or sixteen hours a day; 'c'est la volonté,' he said, 'qui donne le plaisir à tout ce que l'on doit faire, et c'est le plaisir qui donne l'application.'

People prided themselves on their ability to overcome their passions. Anne of Austria, on Mazarin's advice, treated Richelieu's relatives generously after his death; according to Mme de Motte-ville, besides being convinced of the wisdom of Mazarin's counsel, she had the pleasure 'de se vaincre elle-même dans son ressenti-ment'. In Retz, will-power took the form of hypocrisy — 'le seul vice qui soit aussi pénible, aussi difficile qu'une vertu'.[1] Like Stendhal's Julien Sorel, he decided what conduct would best enable him to make his way in the Church and resolved to suit his behaviour to his ambition. Mademoiselle, who had always detested Condé, tells us that when, during the Fronde, her father, Gaston d'Orléans, resolved to try to free Condé, who had been imprisoned by Mazarin, she determined to overcome her unreasonable aversion. And, writing in her *Mémoires* of Condé's subsequent release, she notes:

> La nouvelle de la sortie de M. le Prince du Havre réjouit tout le monde; elle me réjouit doublement, je l'étais de sa sortie, et *de connaître par elle le pouvoir que j'avais sur moi d'avoir passé, dès que je l'avais voulu, de la haine à l'amitié.*

Similarly, one day after the Fronde, during her exile from Paris, she passed within sight of the city and observed with pride that she could behold it without a pang; she congratulates herself on being 'si maîtresse de moi-même'. Louis XIV overcame his passion for Marie Mancini, and prided himself in later life on never allowing his love affairs to influence his policy.

> S'il arrive que nous tombions malgré nous dans quelqu'un de ces égarements, il faut du moins observer deux précautions que j'ai toujours pratiquées et dont je me suis fort bien trouvé.
> La première, que le temps que nous donnons à notre amour ne soit jamais pris au préjudice de nos affaires [. . .]
> Mais la seconde considération, qui est la plus délicate et la plus difficile à conserver et à pratiquer, c'est qu'en abandonnant notre cœur, il faut demeurer maître absolu de notre esprit; que nous séparions les tendresses d'amant d'avec les résolutions de souverain; que la beauté qui fait nos plaisirs n'ait jamais la liberté de nous parler de nos affaires, ni des gens qui nous y servent, et que ce soient deux choses absolument séparées.

Of the courage and fortitude of the people of the age — which is another manifestation of their will-power and self-mastery — there are many examples. At the siege of Suze in 1629, Bassompierre and some sixty nobles were covered with earth by a

---

[1] Barbey d'Aurevilly.

cannonade. Bassompierre tells us that he looked at his companions: 'je n'en aperçus pas un qui fît aucun signe d'étonnement, non pas même d'y prendre quasi garde.' Mazarin met his end bravely; and both Anne of Austria and Louis XIV bore their last, painful illnesses with great fortitude. Fléchier tells of a young woman condemned to death, who, when the executioner offered to save her life by marrying her, retorted disdainfully:

> La mort que je vais recevoir de toi me paraît mille fois plus douce que la vie que je mènerais avec toi. Que si tu sens encore quelque bon mouvement pour moi, exécute promptement les ordres de la justice, et ne me laisse pas vivre plus longtemps malheureuse de t'avoir plu.

Mme de Brinvilliers, the poisoner, was remarkable for the courage she displayed after her arrest and under torture. Her confessor, Pirot, wrote of her:

> Elle était naturellement intrépide et d'un grand courage ... Son âme avait d'elle-même quelque chose de grand, d'un sang-froid aux accidents les plus imprévus, d'une fermeté à ne s'émouvoir de rien, d'une résolution à attendre la mort et à la souffrir même s'il eût été nécessaire.

On being taken to the chamber where three buckets of water were standing ready to be poured down her throat, she found it in her to jest, saying, according to Mme de Sévigné: 'C'est assurément pour me noyer; car de la taille dont je suis, on ne prétend pas que je boive tout cela.'

Pride — self-confidence, the consciousness of one's own worth — is perhaps a form of self-protection in an uncertain world; it was at any rate a common enough quality in the seventeenth century. The duc d'Aumont was nicknamed Tarquin-le-Superbe on account of his intolerable pride. Retz, says La Rochefoucauld, 'avait de l'orgueil et de la fierté'. The comte d'Harcourt, at the siege of Turin, when his companions called some soldiers who were fleeing from a sortie of the enemy cowards, retorted: 'Non, non, ils sont braves gens; mais c'est qu'ils ne m'ont pas à leur tête.' And when, during the *affaire des poisons*, the duc de Luxembourg was accused of having entered into a pact with the devil in order to marry his son to Louvois's daughter, he replied: 'Quand Matthieu de Montmorenci épousa la veuve de Louis-le-Gros, il ne s'adressa point au diable, mais aux états-généraux, qui déclarèrent que, pour acquérir au roi mineur l'appui des Montmorencis, il fallait faire ce mariage.'

But what better example could one find than Mademoiselle? Mademoiselle, indeed, full of pride in her birth, her rank and her achievements, wanting to marry the Emperor and scornful of such lesser suitors as the King of Portugal and the prince of Wales ('mon cœur le regardait du haut en bas aussi bien que mes yeux'), seems the very personification of pride. Relating how the marriage with the Emperor fell through, she remarks: 'Je puis dire sans vanité, que Dieu qui est juste n'a pas voulu donner une femme telle que moi à un homme qui ne me méritait pas.' A report that the prince of Wales had been thinking of marrying Mlle de Longueville evokes the comment: 'Pour moi, je lui ai fait la justice de ne le pas croire, persuadée qu'un homme qui a songé à moi ne se rabattrait pas à Mademoiselle de Longueville.'[1] Again, mentioning a proposal that she should marry the prince of Savoy, she writes:

> L'on verra par tout ce que j'ai écrit par ces Mémoires, que je n'ai eu aucune envie de me marier, à moins que de trouver des grandeurs qui fussent conformes à ma naissance, et à la juste ambition qu'elle me devait donner. Je n'ai guères rien compris qui pût l'égaler, et avec cela l'imagination vive que Dieu m'a donnée, me poussait toujours dans l'excès: ainsi je ne pouvais être touchée que d'un grand mérite, ou d'une grande élévation, et je ne trouvais ni l'un ni l'autre dans M. de Savoie.

Narrating her forcible entry into Orléans during the Fronde, she describes the gate through which she entered the city as 'cette illustre porte, et qui sera tant renommée par mon entrée'. And when she had entered, she roundly told the magistrates that 'lorsque des personnes de ma qualité sont dans un lieu, elles y sont

---

[1] Bussy-Rabutin tells us in his *Mémoires* that he tried to make Mlle de Romorantin jealous by paying court to another lady; but his stratagem was unsuccessful. 'Elle me dit bien fièrement qu'un cœur était indigne d'elle, qui au sortir de ses mains s'était profané un moment au service d'une petite dame de province.'

les maîtresses, et avec assez de justice'. She herself admirably sums up her character in a sentence: 'Dieu m'a fait naître dans une grande élévation, il y a proportionné mes sentiments, et on ne m'en a jamais vu de bas, Dieu merci.'

For examples of pride in less exalted ranks, we might turn to Port-Royal. M. Singlin, for instance, hearing that Mme de Guéménée had complained of his lack of attentions to her, re-marked: 'Je serais bien éloigné de voir ces personnages-là, à moins qu'elles ne me demandassent ou que quelque nécessité ne m'y engageât.' But there is no need to look further than Corneille himself. His pride is evident in the well-known *Stances à Marquise*:

> Pensez-y, belle Marquise,
> Quoiqu'un grison fasse effroi,
> Il vaut bien qu'on le courtise,
> Quand il est fait comme moi.

And when his friends pointed out some of his minor failings to him, he would answer, with a smile, 'Je n'en suis pas moins pour cela Pierre de Corneille.'

The motive force of these people — often, at least — was a sense of honour and duty, a love of *gloire* and distinction. It is on the grounds of honour that Richelieu in his *Testament politique* rejects Machiavelli:

> Puisque la perte de l'honneur est plus que celle de la vie, un grand prince doit plutôt hasarder sa personne même et les intérêts de son État que de manquer à sa parole, qu'il ne peut violer sans perdre sa réputation et par conséquent la plus grande force des souverains.

Similarly, Mademoiselle, mentioning some dubious conduct on the part of Mme de Chatillon, adds:

> Quoi que l'on puisse dire, je ne saurais croire que les personnes de qualité s'abandonnent au point que les médisants disent qu'elle a fait. Quand on n'aurait pas son salut en vue, l'honneur du moins est à ma fantaisie si beau, que je ne comprends pas comment on peut le mépriser.

And, in practice, in a conflict between inclination and duty or honour, the latter frequently won — as when, during the Fronde, the duc de Saint-Simon, governor of Blaye, despite his hatred of Mazarin and his affection for Condé, remained loyal to the government:

> Son esprit [says Mme de Motteville] eut de la peine à se déterminer à faire du mal au Prince de Condé; mais le devoir l'emportant sur tout le reste, il demeura ferme dans le service du Roi, et fit ce qu'un homme d'honneur se doit à soi-même.

The sense of honour was often reinforced by the desire for glory, the impulse to win distinction by some extraordinary exploit. A minister of state, says Richelieu, needs 'un honnête aiguillon de gloire, sans lequel les plus capables et les plus gens de bien demeurent souvent sans se signaler par aucune action avantageuse au public'. Retz enunciates as a maxim that:

> Les plus grands dangers ont leurs charmes pour peu que l'on aperçoive de la gloire dans la perspective des mauvais succès; les médiocres n'ont que des horreurs quand la perte de la réputation est attachée à la mauvaise fortune.

Anne of Austria, accused of corresponding with Spain, suggested that La Rochefoucauld should carry her and Mlle de Hautefort off to Brussels, a project which filled him with enthusiasm:

> Quelque difficulté et quelque péril qui me parussent dans un tel projet, je puis dire qu'il me donna plus de joie que je n'en avais eu de ma vie: j'étais en un âge où on aime à faire des choses extraordinaires et éclatantes, et je ne trouvais pas que rien le fût davantage que d'enlever en même temps la Reine au Roi, son mari, et au Cardinal de Richelieu, qui en était jaloux, et d'ôter Mlle de Hautefort au Roi qui en était amoureux.

It came to nothing; nevertheless in practice *gloire* seems to have provided a stimulus to daring or fortitude. When Bassompierre dissuaded Condé from an imprudent advance, he was told: 'Je vois bien que vous êtes de la cabale des autres, qui me veulent détourner d'acquérir de la gloire et faire perdre un grand service.' During the Fronde, after the arrest of Broussel, the chancellor Séguier was ordered to go down to the parlement to preside. Though his friends warned him of the danger and tried to deter

him, he was sustained by the desire for *gloire*, according to Mme
de Motteville:

> Il vit des mêmes yeux que les autres le danger où il s'exposait; mais
> cette âme trop attachée à la faveur ne le fut point à l'amour de la vie:
> il préféra à cette crainte l'avantage de faire une action qui fût au-
> dessus du commun; et, comme la Reine même l'avait jugée néces-
> saire, il voulut y aller, sans montrer aucune marque de faiblesse.

Mme de Motteville also relates that the maréchal du Plessis, who,
in winning two victories, had lost two sons, told her that he was
more sensible of the victories than of his double bereavement,

> me faisant entendre que ce qui regarde notre honneur et notre gloire
> nous ˋparaît plus propre, et nous est plus cher, que nos enfants, que
> nous ne saurions aimer que comme d'autres nous-mêmes, au lieu que
> nous aimons bien moins nous-mêmes que notre honneur, pour
> lequel nous nous sacrifions tous les jours.

This attitude is very close to that of old Horace in Corneille.[1]

The seventeenth century, however, is a complex period, and
we must not exaggerate one aspect of it at the expense of the other.
The desire for *gloire* or honour was not always successful in
overcoming human weakness or passion. La Rochefoucauld was
hardly seeking *gloire* when he tried to choke Retz between the
two leaves of a door during the Fronde; and Mme de Motteville
tells us how Mlle de Rohan married M. de Chabot, whose rank
was far inferior to her own, though not without a struggle:

> L'honneur, ce fantôme si puissant, qui donne et ôte la réputation des
> honnêtes gens, plutôt selon le bruit du plus grand nombre, que
> selon la véritable justice, l'a fait souventes fois renoncer à l'amitié

---

[1] 'S'il est vrai qu'un grand donne plus à la fortune lorsqu'il hasarde une vie destinée à
couler dans les ris, le plaisir et l'abondance, qu'un particulier qui ne risque que des jours
qui sont misérables, il faut avouer aussi qu'il a un tout autre dédommagement, qui est la
gloire et la haute réputation. Le soldat ne sent pas qu'il soit connu, il meurt obscur et dans
la foule; il vivait de même, à la vérité, mais il vivait; et c'est l'une des sources du défaut de
courage dans les conditions basses et serviles. Ceux, au contraire, que la naissance démêle
d'avec le peuple et expose aux yeux des hommes, à leur censure et à leurs éloges, sont
même capables de sortir par effort de leur tempérament, s'il ne les portait pas à la vertu; et
cette disposition de cœur et d'esprit, qui passe des aïeuls par les pères dans leurs descendants,
est cette bravoure si familière aux personnes nobles, et peut-être la noblesse même.' (La
Bruyère, *Caractères*) — Montesquieu, in the *Lettres persanes*, talks of 'cette passion
générale que la nation française a pour la gloire'.

dont elle était touchée [. . .] Enfin, malgré ses combats, la fierté de
cette illustre héritière fut abattue, et sa raison fut chassée comme
importune.

Moreover, if *gloire* is sometimes associated with duty and
honour, at other times they are distinct. Mme de Nemours
criticizes Mme de Longueville for sacrificing everything to her
gloire, while having a wrong conception of *gloire*, so that she was
left with only 'la vaine imagination de l'avoir cherchée où elle
était'. During the Fronde, the duc de Bouillon hanged an innocent prisoner as an act of reprisal.

Cette action [says Mme de Motteville] fut louée de ceux qui ont
pour maxime qu'il ne faut point être tyran à demi, et que les grands
hommes ne sauraient soutenir de hautes entreprises, s'ils ne sont
capables des grands crimes, comme des grandes vertus; les unes
étant quelquefois nécessaires pour soutenir les autres.

She herself deplores this point of view as un-Christian; but it
existed. Retz is an example of one who thought scruples incompatible with greatness. He tells us in his *Mémoires* that, though
duty required him to be loyal to the court, *gloire* pulled him in the
opposite direction:

ce qui acheva d'étouffer tous mes scrupules fut l'avantage que je
m'imaginai à me distinguer de tous ceux de ma profession par un
état de vie qui les confond toutes [. . .] j'abandonnai mon destin à
tous les mouvements de la gloire.

Finally, as one reads, in the memoirs of the time, of licentious,
brutal nobles, who did not hesitate to cheat at cards, to take unfair
advantage of an adversary in a duel, to be dishonest in money
matters and leave their debts unpaid, even to forge money, one
realizes that there were many for whom honour and *gloire* can
have meant little. Indeed, we find contemporaries complaining
that people are indifferent to *gloire*. Nervèze, in his *Guide des
Courtisans* (1606),[1] laments:

Tout le soin s'en va aux parements et bienséances extérieures du
corps, dont les appétits altèrent ceux de l'âme, et s'opposent à tout

[1] Quoted by M. Magendie, *La Politesse mondaine et les théories de l'honnêteté en France,
au XVIIᵉ siècle, de 1600 à 1660*, vol. I, pp. 342–3.

ce qui sent sa magnanimité; de sorte que vivant sous une humeur nonchalante au bien et active à la vanité, ces jeunes cavaliers s'endurcissent aux voluptés; au lieu que l'amour de la gloire les devrait embraser!

Balzac, in his dissertation on *Gloire*, complains that disinterested ambition and the passion for *gloire* belonged to the youth of the world, whereas nowadays no one cares for anything but money; and Mme de Motteville similarly claims that 'l'ambition déréglée, et l'avarice, sont les plus belles vertus des plus grands seigneurs et des plus honnêtes gens du siècle'. In everything the *grand siècle* has its reverse side.

*   *   *

'Les passions et les caractères en liberté'.... In this age of sturdy independence and robust individuality, passions were strong and indeed often took extravagant forms. Pontis claims that the death of Louis XIII afflicted him to such an extent that for nearly three months he was almost out of his mind, 'ne sachant à qui m'en prendre de cette mort, cherchant tous les jours mon Roi, et ne le trouvant plus, ce qui me réduisit presque au désespoir.' Mme de Sévigné describes herself as sobbing for five hours after the departure of her daughter in 1671.[1] Lovers felt no less deeply. Givry, abandoned by the princesse de Conti, went and got himself killed at the siege of Laon (1594). The cardinal de la Valette, repulsed by the princesse de Condé, shut himself up in a plague hospital. When the great Condé (then still duc d'Enghien) departed for the army, he could not take leave of Mlle de Vigean without shedding tears; on one occasion he swooned.

With such people, living in a society in which the law was not always enforced and in which one consequently had to fend for oneself, it was inevitable that individuals should be inclined to take the law into their own hands. Those in authority did not always discourage this tendency. Tallemant relates, for instance, that

[1] Cf., too, the violence of Mme de la Guette's grief on the deaths of her mother and her husband. An unexpected visit from her husband caused such a transport of emotion that she could not sleep for three whole months afterwards.

after the murder of Concini Louis XIII remarked to a young
man: 'Tu n'en oserais faire autant à ton oncle, l'abbé de la Couronne, qui couche avec ta mère.' Piqued, the young man had his
uncle murdered; but, says Tallemant, 'comme le Roi l'aimait, on
n'osa poursuivre.'

Weapons were drawn easily, and quarrels often led to violence.
A M. d'Anguittard fired upon four pilgrims who had failed to
salute him. They beat him with their staves and left him for dead.
A gentleman of Aix shot his neighbour's peacock which had
flown into his garden; the neighbour, with fifty friends, broke into
his house and did as much damage as he could; the first gentleman's friends rallied to his support and a pitched battle was
narrowly averted. Love and jealousy were the cause of many acts
of violence. Tallemant tells of a French gentleman in Turin who,
being unsuccessful in wooing a lady who lived opposite him,
borrowed a couple of falconets from the governor of the citadel
and, from an attic window, turned them on her house to persuade
her to surrender. A lawyer's wife, Mme de Montaigne, a member
of the essayist's family, cut off the nose of a female client of her
husband's in a fit of jealousy. Coustenan was killed by a peasant
— 'plus sensible que ne sont d'ordinaire cette sorte de gens,' says
Tallemant — whose wife he had raped and whipped. Sons tried
to punish their mothers' lovers; husbands murdered the lovers of
their guilty wives, sometimes their wives too. Fléchier tells us of
a M. d'Espinchal who, believing his wife to have been unfaithful
with a page, gave her the choice between a pistol and a cup of
poison, and castrated the page. If we mention M. d'Espinchal, it
is because, finding Auvergne too hot to hold him, he took refuge
in Paris and lived, until the death of the duc de Guise, in a house
'qui avait une entrée dans l'hôtel de Guise'. In other words he
must have been a near neighbour of Corneille, who lived in the
hôtel de Guise from 1662 until the duke's death two years later.

Violence did not, of course, always go so far as murder.
Beatings were common. Masters and mistresses beat their servants, who sometimes retaliated. The duc d'Aumont struck a
maître d'hôtel, who had refused to lend him money, so hard that

he died four days later. Mme de Vervins whipped a maidservant to death. The princess Palatine records, as something exceptional, that she only saw Louis XIV beat two men. But it was not only menials who were beaten. The duc de Guise had a doctor beaten for mocking him in some verses he had written. The maréchal de Vitry was put in the Bastille for beating the Archbishop of Bordeaux. Bautru, a diplomat in the service of Richelieu, was so much beaten that one day when he visited the Queen carrying a stick, the prince de Guéménée commented: 'il porte le bâton comme Saint-Laurent porte son gril: c'est la marque de son martyre.' Literary controversies often ended with the stick or the threat of the stick. In 1628, Balzac had Javersac beaten on account of his *Discours d'Aristarque à Nicandre*. Corneille was threatened with a beating in the *Querelle du Cid*; so were Boileau and Racine in the controversy over *Phèdre*. At Leyden, Haute-Fontaine, who had failed to obtain a chair of philosophy, unphilosophically administered 'cent coups de poing' to his successful rival.

Swords were drawn easily and duels common, fought often on slight pretexts. Bussy-Rabutin's first duel was fought for something an uncle of his was alleged to have said. Gibes, disputes of any kind — between two people wanting the same lodging or claiming the *haut du pavé* — might lead to a duel; and not merely the principals fought, but also their seconds and supporters, a practice of which Montaigne complains in his *Essais*. L'Estoile estimated in his journal that between 1589 and 1607, four thousand gentlemen had lost their lives in duels, and 940 gentlemen were killed during the Regency of Anne of Austria. Nor were duels confined to the nobility or to professional soldiers. Gombauld boasted of having fought two in an hour. Voiture fought four — 'de jour et de nuit, au soleil, à la lune et aux flambeaux,' says Tallemant, the last being fought in the grounds of the Hôtel de Rambouillet. Men passed naturally from a duel to ordinary social life. Bussy-Rabutin remarks in his *Mémoires*:

> Rien ne fut plus galant pour Jumeaux [his second] et pour moi que cette journée: le matin nous nous battons, nous avons tous deux l'avantage, et le soir nous venons danser un ballet avec des dames.

Duelling brought a man distinction, as Lord Herbert of Cherbury found in 1608:

> All things being ready for the ball, and every one being in their place, and I myself next to the Queen,[1] expecting when the dancers would come in, one knocked at the door somewhat louder than became, as I thought, a very civil person. When he came in, I remember there was a sudden whisper among the ladies, saying *C'est Monsieur Balagny*, or, It is Monsieur Balagny; whereupon also I saw the ladies and gentlewomen one after another invite him to sit near them, and, which is more, when one lady had his company a while, another would say, You have enjoyed him long enough, I must have him now; at which bold civility of theirs, though I were astonished, yet it added unto my wonder, that his person could not be thought at most but ordinary handsome; his hair, which was cut very short, half grey, his doublet but of sackcloth cut to his shirt, and his breeches only of plain grey cloth. Informing myself by some standers-by who he was, I was told that he was one of the gallantest men in the world, as having killed eight or nine men in single fight, and that for this reason the ladies made so much of him, it being the manner of all Frenchwomen to cherish gallant men, as thinking they could not make so much of any else with the safety of their honour. This cavalier, though his head was half grey, he had not yet attained the age of thirty years [. . .]

Abductions and elopements, too, were frequent occurrences. Tallemant tells of a wife of fifteen carried off on horseback by her lover, and of a girl of eleven abducted and married by her own brother-in-law. Bussy-Rabutin's unsuccessful attempt to abduct Mme de Miramion is of interest. She was a wealthy widow, whose confessor wrote to Bussy to say that she was willing to marry him, that her parents were opposed to the match, and that she would be 'bien aise que je lui aidasse, par une violence apparente, à dire oui'.

> Je compris qu'elle voulait que je l'enlevasse, et ce conseil me surprit beaucoup; néanmoins me venant de la part d'un bon religieux, qui ne me paraissait avoir d'autre intérêt en cette affaire que l'avantage et la satisfaction des parties, je ne me balançai pas à le suivre.

At this time (1648), Bussy was serving in Condé's army, but

[1] Marguerite de Navarre.

military discipline was no obstacle. He consulted Condé, who offered his help, gave him a despatch to carry to the court as a pretext for leaving the army, and placed an estate of his own at his disposal as a refuge. Bussy, then, with five friends waylaid the lady's coach and forcibly escorted it away. She, however, was unwilling and had to be sent home. She even had the bad taste to go to law, but a letter from Condé to her relatives put a stop to that. Condé, while still duc d'Enghien, had already aided and abetted the comte de Chatillon in carrying off Mlle de Bouteville — who, however, unlike Mme de Miramion, was willing.

* * *

The seventeenth century, especially in its first half, gives the impression of being a romantic, cloak and dagger age. We read, for example, of Retz making a treaty with the duchesse de Bouillon and signing it with his own blood. When Anne of Austria was suspected of being in correspondance with Spain, she agreed to send Mme de Chevreuse a copy of the *Hours* bound in green if all was well, and a copy bound in red if it was advisable for her to leave the country. Naturally the red copy was sent by mistake and Mme de Chevreuse fled. The turbulence and the duelling of the age gave many opportunities for the display of romantic gallantry — as when, one night in Paris, the maréchal de Guébrian, hearing the clash of swords outside his lodging, went down,

> et, voyant un homme assez mal accompagné attaqué de plusieurs autres, [. . .] se met du côté du plus faible et le tire de leurs mains: c'était le baron du Bec que le marquis de Praslin [. . .] assassinait par jalousie; car ils étaient rivaux, et le Baron était mieux traité que lui.

Bassompierre's illegitimate son, La Tour, acting as second and finding his opponent to be a man who had lost the use of his right arm, had his own right arm bound behind his back and still beat his opponent.

Gallantry and love affairs played an important part in the life of the time and sometimes influenced the actions of statesmen and generals. Buckingham was believed to have declared war on

c

France simply to further his love for Anne of Austria.[1] Richelieu was another *soupirant* of Anne's and, though his advances were not favourably received, Louis XIII's jealousy nearly led, according to La Rochefoucauld, to his dismissal. The duc de Guise,[2] whom Mme de Motteville describes as 'le véritable portrait de nos anciens paladins', wrote to Mazarin, after his expedition to Naples:

> ni l'ambition, ni le désir de m'immortaliser par des actions extra-ordinaires, ne m'a embarqué dans un dessein si périlleux que celui où je me trouve; mais la seule pensée, que faisant quelque chose de glorieux, de mieux mériter les bonnes grâces de Mlle de Pons, et d'obtenir par l'importance de mes services, que la Reine con-sidérant davantage, et elle, et moi, je pusse, après tant de périls et de peines, passer doucement avec elle le reste de mes jours.

Disguises, a common enough feature in the seventeenth-century theatre, were frequently assumed in real life. During the Fronde, it was often necessary to conceal one's identity. Retz and La Rochefoucauld both disguised themselves on occasion; so did Condé when, in 1652, he made his adventurous journey across France from one army to another. Going to Paris in 1650 in order to confer with the duc de Nemours, Bussy-Rabutin took a lodging 'sous un nom bizarre dans le quartier de Sainte-Gene-viève' where he fell ill. 'Le duc de Nemours me venait voir en chaise sans livrée,' he says, 'et ma femme de même.' His mother died and he had to return to Bussy to set his affairs in order:

> Mais comme le duc de Vendôme, qui commandait alors en Bour-gogne, était fort alerte, je me déguisai. Je pris une perruque noire, je me mis un emplâtre sur un œil, et m'étant ainsi rendu méconnaissable à moi-même, je partis avec Launay-Lyais, lui faisant le maître, et moi portant la valise derrière mon cheval.

But it was not only during the Fronde or for military purposes

---

[1] See p. 237. — Anne of Austria gave Buckingham some diamond tags (*ferrets*). The Countess of Carlisle cut them off his dress at a ball, in order to send them to Richelieu as proof of the Queen's guilty love. Buckingham closed the ports to prevent the Countess from leaving the country, and had copies of the tags made and sent to Anne. Dumas uses this episode in the *Trois Mousquetaires*.

[2] Corneille lived in his house from 1662 to 1664, and Thomas Corneille dedicated *Timocrate* to him. According to Voltaire, when people saw him walking with Condé, they would remark: 'Voilà les héros de l'histoire et de la fable.'

that people assumed disguises. Even the grave *solitaires* of Port-Royal were accustomed to incognitos and disguises in times of persecution. Sainte-Marthe leaped over the wall to administer the sacraments to the sequestered nuns within; M. de Singlin visited his flock disguised as a doctor, squaring his conscience by saying that after all he *was* a doctor of souls; Arnauld took refuge in the Hôtel de Longueville, wearing secular dress, with a large wig on his head and a sword at his side. Women dressed as men, too. The Duke of Lorraine's sister, when the King's troops were besieging Nancy in 1632, left the town in man's attire in order to go and marry Gaston d'Orléans; and Mme de Chevreuse assumed man's apparel to escape the clutches of Richelieu.

Many disguises were assumed for love affairs. One of Bussy-Rabutin's mistresses was with difficulty dissuaded from serving him disguised as a page. Anne de Gonzague, the sister of Marie de Gonzague who married the King of Poland, dressed as a man to go and join her lover, the Archbishop of Reims, in Brussels. Mme de Chappes one day met her brother-in-law, M. d'Aumont, 'déguisé en minime sur le chemin de Picardie.' She recognized him, however, because he rode too well and was too well-mounted: he was on his way to Flanders to see a lady. Montausier, the elder brother of Mme de Rambouillet's son-in-law, dressed as a capuchin monk in order to enter a besieged town in Piedmont to visit a lady whom he loved. In 1661, Lauzun, so Mme de La Fayette tells us, accompanied the princess of Monaco to her principality, disguised 'tantôt en marchand, tantôt en postillon;' and the comte de Guiche used to visit Henriette d'Angleterre disguised as a female fortune-teller.

The seventeenth century, moreover, was an age of heroism and bravado, of romantic, undisciplined, irresponsible daring. At Saint-Venant, in 1638, La Rochefoucauld tells us:

> vingt-cinq ou trente volontaires de qualité soutinrent seuls, sur une digue, tout l'effort des ennemis, et les repoussèrent quatre ou cinq fois, à coups d'épée, jusques dans les barrières de leur camp.

We frequently read of officers — even generals — rashly exposing themselves to the fire of the enemy (it was thus that Sully won the friendship of Grillon), or vying to be first in attack, or to have the post of danger. At the siege of La Rochelle, in 1627, Bassompierre undertook to construct a fort in the face of the enemy with what were regarded as grossly inadequate forces and refused an offer of reinforcements. The following anecdote of Lord Herbert of Cherbury about the siege of Jülich in 1610 is typical of many others:

> One day Sir Edward Cecil and myself coming to the approaches that Monsieur de Balagny had made towards a bulwark or bastion of that city, Monsieur de Balagny, in the presence of Sir Edward Cecil and divers English and French captains then present, said, *Monsieur, on dit que vous êtes un des plus braves de votre nation, et je suis Balagny, allons voir qui faira le mieux* — 'They say you are one of the bravest of your nation, and I am Balagny, let us see who will do best;' whereupon leaping suddenly out of the trenches with his sword drawn, I did in the like manner as suddenly follow him, both of us in the meanwhile striving who should be foremost, which being perceived by those of the bulwark and cortine opposite to us, three or four hundred shot at least, great and small, were made against us. Our running on forwards in emulation of each other, was the cause that all the shots fell betwixt us and the trench from which we sallied. When Monsieur de Balagny, finding such a storm of bullets, said, *Par Dieu il fait bien chaud* — 'It is very hot here;' I answered briefly thus: *Vous en ires premier, autrement je n'iray jamais* — 'You shall go first, or else I will never go;' hereupon he ran with all speed, and somewhat crouching, towards the trenches. I followed after leisurely and upright, and yet came within the trenches before they on the bulwarks or cortine could charge again; which passage afterwards being related to the Prince of Orange, he said it was a strange bravado of Balagny, and that we went to an unavoidable death.

*   *   *

The age of Corneille is characterized both by refinement and coarseness. The seventeenth century was an age of great salons, of growing feminine influence, of *préciosité* and the *honnête homme*. As time wore on, impropriety was largely banished from the theatre, and violent action and bloodshed ceased to be shown on the stage. In social life, ceremonious politeness was the rule; questions of precedence loomed large, and it was important to assign to each guest the exact type of chair which etiquette required. Conversation in the salons was gallant and often concerned with the subtle analysis of character or passion. This, for instance, was the type of conversation favoured by Mme de Longueville and her circle at the beginning of the Fronde, according to Mme de Nemours:

> Quoiqu'ils eussent pourtant tous beaucoup d'esprit, ils ne l'employaient que dans les conversations galantes et enjouées, qu'à commenter et à raffiner sur la délicatesse du cœur et des sentiments: ils faisaient consister tout l'esprit et tout le mérite d'une personne à faire des distinctions subtiles, et des représentations quelquefois peu naturelles là-dessus.

The précieuses preached Platonic love and favoured long and elaborate courtships.

But that is only one side of the picture. Underneath the polish and the civilization, passions were strong, and the contrast between the formal politeness of the age and the real feelings concealed beneath or revealed in a burst of forthrightness is often portrayed, with great dramatic effect, by Corneille, as well as by Molière and Racine. Moreover, we must not overlook the filthy streets, the coarse table manners, the widespread sexual immorality, or the considerable strain of insensibility, cruelty and brutality. Tallemant tells us of a M. de Vaubecourt who, when he took prisoners, made his son, a boy of ten, kill them, to accustom him to bloodshed. Mme de la Guette sent her nine-year-old son to the wars. Louis XIII was insensible to the sufferings of prisoners and amused himself by counterfeiting the grimaces of the dying. Criminals were broken on the wheel, burned alive, tortured.[1] The treatment of the peasants by the troops of both sides during the Fronde, of the Protestants of the South by Louis XIV's dragoons at the end of the century, was merciless.

An aspect of the lack of refinement of the age which should be

---

[1] Dorchain, in his book on *Corneille*, points out that, from his room in the rue de la Pie at Rouen, Corneille must have heard the shrieks of the victims in the place du Vieux-Marché hard by, 'car c'est sur la place du Vieux-Marché que se dressent alors, sans parler du pilori où l'on expose, l'échafaud où l'on décapite, où l'on écartèle, où l'on roue' (p. 18).

borne in mind when one is considering a poet who wrote comedies, is that its sense of humour was often somewhat crude. Richelieu, for example, liberally rewarded a page for making a poor pun. It happened on this wise: he had a page who excelled at punning, and asked him one day if he could make a pun on the name of M. de Lansac.

'Monseigneur, il me faut une pistole, sans cela je ne saurais équivoquer.' [. . .] Le Cardinal lui en donne donc une. Le petit page la met dans sa poche et dit '*Pistole Lansac*' (pistole en sac). Le Cardinal la trouva si plaisante qu'il lui en fit donner dix.[1]

The seventeenth-century sense of humour seems to have been very much inclined to run to practical jokes. When Louis XIII's *grand-maître de la garde-robe*, the marquis de Rambouillet, who was somewhat short-sighted, was dressing him, the King used to amuse himself by stretching out his feet instead of his hands and, on one occasion, his bottom instead of his head. Richelieu concealed thorns under the saddle of a canon of the Sainte-Chapelle, and played a somewhat heartless trick on the Bishop of Chartres, a man of notorious dishonesty. Richelieu secretly gave him a piece of rich cloth, telling him to have a suit made of it; the same evening, he told his servants that the cloth was missing and set them searching for it: so that when M. de Chartres arrived some days later in his new clothes, the servants thought that he had stolen the cloth. Mlle de Gournay sent Racan a copy of one of her works and he decided to call on her to thank her. Unfortunately, two of his friends had visited her that day already, each claiming to be Racan, so that the real Racan, when he arrived, was turned out ignominiously.[2] Several instances are recorded of hostesses putting before their guests meals that they could not eat, and then taking them into another room where a repast more to their taste was served.

Such practical jokes sometimes verged on cruelty. Mme de Rambouillet, reading quietly in her room, turned round to find two bears behind her, secretly introduced by Voiture; she

---

[1] Not far short of £100 of our money.
[2] This episode was made into a play by Boisrobert.

retaliated by having a freshly composed sonnet of his printed and bound in an old volume to make him think that he had inadvertently been guilty of plagiarism. At the Hôtel de Rambouillet, too, the comte de Guiche's clothes were taken in overnight to make him believe that over-indulgence in mushrooms had made him swell. An even more unkind form of the same joke was played on Marie-Anne Mancini, then six years old, by her uncle, Mazarin, and Anne of Austria. Her clothes were taken in from time to time to make her believe that she was pregnant, and one morning she awoke to find a baby in her bed. 'Ce qui avait été d'abord un passe-temps domestique, devint à la fin un divertissement public pour toute la cour,' relates her sister. Richelieu frightened Abra de Raconis by getting a ventriloquist to make a mysterious voice address him, saying:

> Je suis l'âme de ton père qui souffre il y a longtemps en purgatoire, et qui ai eu permission de Dieu de te venir avertir de changer de vie. N'as-tu pas honte de faire la cour aux grands, au lieu d'être dans les églises?

The trick was so effective that even Richelieu, according to Tallemant, was slightly ashamed of himself.[1]

*   *   *

Tallemant des Réaux tells us of one of Mme de Montbazon's sisters who wanted to live in Paris but had no relatives there. She took up her abode with the superior of the Hospitalières of the Place Royale.

> Là, pour voir du monde, elle recevait les gens dans la salle des malades; et l'on voyait cette fille toute couverte d'or dans un lieu où un malade rend un lavement, l'autre change de linge; l'un tousse, l'autre crache; celui-ci crie, et celle-là se confesse.

There we have no bad image of the age of Corneille. With its refinement and its coarseness, its splendour and its crudity, its delicacy and its bluntness, it is a great age; and it is perhaps precisely to those contradictions, to the tension between those apparently irreconcilable aspects, that it owes its robust vigour and its greatness.

[1] Similarly, Mme Cornuel appeared before her husband in the guise of a ghost.

Chapter Two

REASON
AND FAITH

In the mental outlook of the seventeenth century, the basic tension is between the scepticism, the rationalism, the spirit of inquiry inherited from the Renaissance, on the one hand, and the religion of the Counter-Reformation on the other — for it was not until the seventeenth century that the Counter-Reformation spread to France, where the decisions of the Council of Trent were first promulgated in 1615.

The rationalism of the seventeenth century shows itself in several ways. In the first place, *libertins* or free-thinkers, who did not believe in God, who were sceptical of miracles and the immortality of the soul, and whose moral code was based on nature, were by no means rare.[1] Vanini was burnt in 1619 for his book, *De admirandis Naturae reginae deaeque mortalium arcanis;*[2] and Jean Fontanier was strangled and burnt at the stake two years

---

[1] The scepticism of the *libertins* was based partly on reason (which showed the absurdity of certain beliefs), partly on mistrust of reason derived from Montaigne. Since human reason provides no certain answer to our questions, universal doubt is the only sensible attitude. Mistrust of reason could also, of course, lead to the conclusion that divine revelation should be accepted without question. — One might indeed argue that the fundamental cleavage of the seventeenth century is not so much between faith and reason as between faith in reason and mistrust of reason, with sceptics and believers in both camps.

[2] When the sentence was read to Vanini, he is said to have remarked: 'Pour Dieu, je n'en crois point; pour le roi, je ne l'ai offensé; pour la justice, que le diable l'emporte, s'il y a des diables au monde.'

later. But such sentences, though they discouraged the open expression of irreligious views in writing, did not stop *libertinage* itself, and all through the century we find plenty of *libertins* — poets such as Malherbe or Théophile de Viau who was banished for his impiety in 1625; the novelist, Sorel; philosophers and scholars such as La Mothe le Vayer, Gabriel Naudé, Gassendi; Bernier, the oriental traveller and friend of La Fontaine; Ninon de Lenclos; Saint-Evremond. Haudessens used to say that he had eighty-one religions, each as good as the other. Bois-Yvon denied the immortality of the soul, refused to confess himself on his death-bed, and said that his thirty remaining sous were to hire porters to carry his body to the refuse-dump. 'Dieu', he said, 'est si grand seigneur, et moi si petit compagnon que nous n'avons jamais eu de communication ensemble.'

Libertins were less discreet than one might have expected. Des Barreaux narrowly escaped stoning when he tore the cap off a priest who was carrying the sacred host, saying that it was insolent of him to be covered in the presence of his creator. Roquelaure, with some kindred spirits, says Tallemant, 'dit la messe dans un jeu de paume, communia, dit-on, les parties honteuses d'une femme, baptisa et maria des chiens, et fit et dit toutes les impiétés imaginables.' He was arrested, and when someone observed that he had God against him, he replied: 'Dieu n'a pas tant d'amis que moi dans le Parlement.' His friend, Romainville, being ill, a cordelier came to confess him. Roquelaure levelled a gun at him, saying: 'Retirez-vous, mon père, ou je vous tue: il a vécu chien, il faut qu'il meure chien.'[1] One day during the Fronde, Fontrailles, Vitry, Matha and Brissac drew their swords and charged a procession, shouting 'Voilà l'ennemi!' at the crucifix. The songs they sang at table, according to Retz, 'n'épargnaient pas toujours le bon Dieu.'

The indiscretion of the *libertins* often aroused the superstitious fears of the populace. When the vines were blighted by frost, for example, the peasants thought that this was a judgment on Des Barreaux's atheism and attacked the house in which he was

[1] But Roquelaure repented on his own death-bed and confessed himself.

staying. Mme de Sévigné describes the scenes that followed the death of another *libertin* in 1672:

> Il ne voulut point se confesser, et envoya tout au diable, et lui après: son corps est en dépôt à Saint-Nicolas; le peuple s'est mis dans la tête que son âme revient la nuit tout en feu dans l'église; qu'il crie, qu'il jure, qu'il menace; et là-dessus ils veulent jeter le corps à la voirie, et assassiner le curé qui l'a reçu. Cette folie est venue à tel point, qu'il a fallu ôter le corps habilement de la chapelle, et faire venir la justice pour défendre de faire insulte au curé.

Another form of rationalism, stoicism — the attempt of the reason to rise superior to the blows of fortune — springs from the Renaissance admiration for the ancient classics, and was strengthened by the troubled condition of France in the late sixteenth and in the seventeenth centuries. It is expressed in the writings of philosophers, such as Montaigne, Charron, Du Vair, and Descartes. The third maxim of the *morale provisoire* given in Descarte's *Discours de la Méthode* and elaborated in the *Traité des Passions* (1649), is to

> tâcher toujours plutôt à me vaincre que la fortune, et à changer mes désirs que l'ordre du monde, et généralement de m'accoutumer à croire qu'il n'y a rien qui soit entièrement en notre pouvoir que nos pensées, en sorte qu'après que nous avons fait notre mieux touchant les choses qui nous sont extérieures, tout ce qui manque de nous réussir est au regard de nous absolument impossible.

But stoicism is not merely found in the writings of moralists and philosophers. For Richelieu, an essential quality of a minister of state is the ability to bear calumny and adversity. For the hero of Sorel's novel, *Francion*, stoicism is an essential ingredient of genuine nobility:

> Etre noble, ce n'est pas savoir bien piquer un cheval, ni manier une épée, ni se panader avec de riches accoutrements, [. . .] c'est avoir une âme qui résiste à tous les assauts que lui peut livrer la fortune, et qui ne mêle rien de bas parmi ses actions.

Stoicism is not merely a literary attitude; it is part of the way of life of the age. It has two main aspects: detachment from worldly goods, and impassivity in the face of suffering. When Mme de

Motteville believed herself to be on the point of being involved in a friend's disgrace, she tells us that

> il me passa dans l'esprit que les biens qu'on possède à la cour, et même dans la faveur quand j'en avais eu, ne sont point de véritables biens qui soient dignes de notre estime; que peut-être mon éloignement malgré moi, me jetant dans la solitude, me serait un plus véritable bonheur; et que ce n'en est pas un de demeurer dans un lieu où il est presque impossible de se sauver des faiblesses qui font autant de peine que de dépit à ceux qui sont assez illuminés pour les connaître.

Mme de la Guette's lands were pillaged during the Fronde by the Lorrainers, who did 60,000 francs' worth of damage:[1] 'Je puis dire,' she writes, 'que tout cela ne me toucha nullement, n'ayant jamais eu d'attache au bien et en ayant fait un mépris toute ma vie.' On another occasion, learning that her house was on fire:

> Je dis à M. Molé: 'Allons, Monsieur, nous en aurons le passe-temps comme les autres.' Je n'en eus aucune émotion, ayant toujours été insensible à toutes sortes de pertes de biens. M. Molé me présenta la main, et je m'y en allai aussi gaiement que si ç'avait été quelque bonne fête.

Fortitude, impassivity in the face of suffering and setbacks is a feature of the age. The Chancellor Séguier, being dismissed from his office in 1650, 'fit ce que les hommes s'efforcent de faire en de pareilles occasions,' says Mme de Motteville, 'qui est de recevoir avec fermeté les rudes coups du malheur, et de l'infortune.' The duc de Beaufort, though his arrest in 1643 was an unexpected blow, showed no sign of surprise or dismay, and 'fit bonne mine dans son malheur'. Condé suffered his arrest in 1650 'sans nulle marque de chagrin, ayant le visage serein, et tranquille'. He, his brother Conti, and his brother-in-law Longueville, spent their first night of captivity playing cards together

> avec gaieté et beaucoup de repos d'esprit. Le Prince de Condé, raillant le Prince de Conti et le Duc de Longueville, leur dit mille choses agréables; ce qui témoignait assez la fermeté de son courage, et que s'il avait paru ému, et s'il avait tant de fois inutilement

---

[1] A franc or livre was roughly worth a modern English pound.

demandé à voir la Reine et le Ministre, la vivacité de son esprit et la force de ses passions, y avaient plus de part que sa faiblesse.[1]

(Mme de Motteville)

Foucquet, says Mme de Sévigné, arranged to have advance news of his sentence brought to him, saying that, provided he had half an hour to prepare himself, he was 'capable de recevoir sans émotion tout le pis qu'on lui puisse apprendre'.

Even death caused no tremor. Cinq-Mars did not expect to be executed, but when sentence of death was pronounced, 'une chose si dure et si peu attendue ne lui fit pourtant témoigner aucune surprise. Il fut ferme, et le combat qu'il souffrait en lui-même ne parut point au-dehors,' says Tallemant. He went to his death bravely:

Il alla à la mort sans qu'on s'aperçût d'aucune émotion. Il s'habilla le jour de son supplice comme s'il eût voulu aller chez le Roi, et sa fermeté parut à la sérénité de son visage.

(Mme de Motteville)

Quite apart from *libertinage* and stoicism, reason played a considerable part in the life of the age. The philosophy of Descartes is based on reason; and in the importance Descartes attached to reason he is typical of his age. For Richelieu, reason is the only guide; hence, feminine influence in politics is bad, women being swayed by their passions, whereas 'la raison est le seul et le vrai motif, qui doit animer et faire agir ceux qui sont dans l'emploi des affaires publiques.' Elsewhere in the *Testament politique* he writes:

La lumière naturelle fait connaître à un chacun que, l'homme ayant été fait raisonnable, il ne doit rien faire que par raison, puisqu'autrement il ferait contre sa nature et par conséquent contre Celui même qui en est l'auteur.

Reason played a great part in Pascal's life, and his sister tells us that 'il agissait toujours par principes, en toutes choses; son esprit et son cœur, faits comme ils étaient, ne pouvaient pas avoir d'autre conduite'.

---

[1] But contrast Marillac who, when he was arrested, 'ne ferma point du tout l'œil pour dormir, et il ne fit autre chose que se promener, que crier, que se plaindre, qu'écrire des lettres, et les déchirer après les avoir écrites, tant était grande l'agitation de son esprit.'

(Pontis)

Reason was often regarded as a safer guide than inclination. In this connection, the story of Sully's marriage is of interest. He was 'grandement amoureux' of Mlle de Saint-Mesmin; nevertheless, he resolved to marry Mlle de Courtenay, of whose virtue, beauty, wealth and birth he had heard,

> la raison pouvant plus sur vous,[1] qui avez toujours tenu pour maxime, que celui qui veut acquérir de la gloire et de l'honneur, doit tâcher à dominer ses plaisirs, et ne souffrir jamais qu'ils le dominent, que tant de bonnes chères que vous receviez de cette belle fille.

One day in 1583, Sully put up at an inn and found both ladies there. This meant that he had to make his choice there and then, for if he visited one lady first, the other would be mortally offended. Mlle de Saint-Mesmin's younger sister came down and urged him to call on her sister; but M. de La Font advised him to see her rival: 'Monsieur, tournez votre cœur à droit, car là vous trouverez des biens, une extraction royale, et bien autant de beauté lorsqu'-elle sera en âge de perfection.' He immediately went and paid his respects to Mlle de Courtenay, who became his wife the following year. Tallemant has a somewhat similar story about Patru, who was in love with a married woman. When her husband died, Patru told her that he could not in fairness go on seeing her, 'car s'il l'épousait, il la mettait mal à son aise, et s'il ne l'épousait pas, il la perdait en l'empêchant de se remarier.' She tried to make him change his mind by arousing his jealousy.

> Elle allait à l'église avec une foule de petits galants. Il m'a avoué que cela lui brûlait les yeux, et qu'il n'a en sa vie si mal passé son temps que de voir qu'une des plus belles personnes du monde, et dont il était aussi amoureux qu'on pouvait être, le souhaitait si ardemment, et de ne pouvoir jouir d'un si grand bonheur. Il en eut la fièvre: sa raison fut pourtant la maîtresse, et il ne vit jamais depuis Mme l'Evesque chez elle.

Mademoiselle says firmly that love is a bad thing, and that reason is the only sound basis for marriage. The unhappy married life of Frontenac and his wife prompts her to this comment:

---

[1] Sully's *Œconomies royales* are written in the second person.

Pour moi j'étais fort étonnée de voir cela, j'avais toujours eu grande
aversion pour l'amour, même pour celui qui allait au légitime, tant
cette passion me paraissait indigne d'une âme bien faite: je m'y con-
firmai davantage, et je compris bien que la raison ne suit guères ce
qui est fait par passion, que la passion cesse bientôt, et qu'elle n'est
jamais de longue durée, que l'on est fort malheureux le reste de ses
jours, quand c'est pour une action de cette durée où elle engage
comme le mariage, et que l'on est bienheureux, quand on veut se
marier, que ce soit par raison; même quand l'aversion y serait, je
crois que l'on s'en aime davantage après.

* * *

But however rational an age, the age of Corneille was also deeply
religious. Indeed, what is Cartesianism, the characteristic contri-
bution of the age to philosophy, but the fusion of reason and
faith? It was an age of religious revival, of monastic reform, of
good works and pious foundations — the age of Saint François
de Sales, of Bérulle, the founder of the Oratoire, and Olier, who
founded the seminary of Saint-Sulpice, of Monsieur Vincent, of
mère Angélique and the *solitaires* of Port-Royal, of the secret
society, the *Compagnie du Saint-Sacrement*.

It was an age of saints and martyrs. The Jesuit missionaries in
Canada died bravely for their faith. Isaac Jogues and Antoine
Daniel, who were martyred in 1648, and Jean de Brébeuf, who
was killed the following year, had all three taught at the Jesuit
college of Rouen, Corneille's school, and it is likely that he knew
them or of them and followed their fortunes. Jogues's avowed
ambition was to be a martyr; and though he was horribly tortured
by the Indians in 1642, he did not flinch, but went back amongst
them. Jean de Brébeuf bore the most atrocious and protracted
tortures with the utmost fortitude. In France, the *solitaires* and
nuns of Port-Royal resisted persecution bravely. Sœur Angélique
de Saint-Jean steadfastly refused to sign the formulary, despite
weeks of solitary confinement and deprivation of the sacraments;
and Arnauld was described by an eighteenth-century admirer as

un homme, au milieu d'une persécution continue, supérieur aux
deux grands mobiles des déterminations humaines, la crainte et

l'espérance, un homme détaché, comme le plus parfait anachorète, de toutes vues d'intérêts, d'ambition, de bien-être, de sensualité, qui, dans tous les temps, ont formé les recrues de tous les partis.

Basically, everyone in the seventeenth century was more or less convinced of the truth of the Christian religion; even the free-thinkers, however sceptical, could not altogether overcome their upbringing and the force of habit — as the atheist in Pirandello's story instinctively recites the Ave Maria in a moment of danger. Hence, conversions were frequent, occurring whenever anything drew the attention of people to the need for religion or to the seriousness of life. The most distinguished people, one's intimate friends, even *libertins*, were liable to be converted or turn devout — like the duc de Ventadour, who founded the *Compagnie du Saint-Sacrement*, or Antoine Lemaître, the distinguished barrister who became the first of the *solitaires* of Port-Royal, or Pascal, or the Prince de Conti and his wife, or Louise de la Vallière. Mademoiselle d'Epernon, as Mademoiselle puts it, 'préféra la couronne d'épines à celle de Pologne': the death of the chevalier de Fiesque, whom she honoured with 'une tendre et honnête amitié', turned her thoughts away from worldly matters; and, when it was proposed to marry her to the brother and heir-presumptive of the King of Poland, she feigned an illness, was ordered to take the waters at Bourbon, and on the way entered a Carmelite convent (1648). Mademoiselle herself, having set her heart upon marrying the Emperor, resolved to be devout like him; and after pretending to be devout for a time, she became so genuinely religious, she tells us, that for a week she was determined to renounce all ambition and become a nun. Rancé, celebrated as the reformer of La Trappe, on which he imposed a harsh discipline, and who inflicted greater hardships on himself than on others, was originally a worldly abbé, the friend of Retz and the lover of Mme de Montbazon. Shaken by her death, he went into retreat on his estate at Véretz and became converted; and, after the death of Gaston d'Orléans, he finally made up his mind to enter the monastery. Even when there was no definite conversion, it was common to turn devout in later life — like

Anne of Austria, Mme de Longueville, Gaston d'Orléans, Bussy-Rabutin, Racine, Louis XIV.[1]

Such conversions were, of course, not always permanent. Descartes criticizes people with 'l'esprit bas et faible' who

> passent souvent fort promptement de l'extrême impiété à la superstition, puis de la superstition à l'impiété, en sorte qu'il n'y a aucun vice ni aucun dérèglement d'esprit dont ils ne soient capables.

This type did in fact exist. Bocquillot and Pontchâteau, two of 'ces messieurs' of Port-Royal, oscillated several times between piety and worldliness before finally settling down in the convent. Mme de Villedieu, after an unedifying career, was shocked by the sudden death of a friend and entered a convent where her piety won the general esteem, until the nuns learned of her past life and turned her out. She was received into the house of a sister of her own and gradually returned to her old ways. Mme de Guéménée was another such.

> Elle a des saillies de dévotion, puis elle revient dans le monde. Elle fit ajuster sa maison de la Place-Royale.[2] Monsieur le Prince lui disait: 'Mais, madame, les Jansénistes ne sont donc point si fâcheux qu'on dit, puisque tout ceci s'ajuste avec la dévotion. Voici qui est le plus beau du monde; je crois qu'il y a grand plaisir à prier Dieu ici.' [...] Toute dévote qu'elle était, quand on disputa le tabouret à Mlle de Montbazon, qui est aujourd'hui dans le monde, elle dit que pour l'intérêt de sa maison elle serait capable de jouer du poignard.
>
> (Tallemant)

Conversions were usually followed by austerities — the lash, belts with iron spikes, and the like. At Port-Royal, Monsieur Hamon ate the dogs' food, giving his own to the poor, and wore rags; Pontchâteau stopped changing his shirt and acted as gardener; Mlle d'Elbeuf, a grand-daughter of Henri IV, mended

---

[1] Molière's Célimène points out that this is a normal effect of age:

> Il est une saison pour la galanterie;
> Il en est une aussi propre à la pruderie.
> On peut, par politique, en prendre le parti,
> Quand de nos jeunes ans l'éclat est amorti:
> Cela sert à couvrir de fâcheuses disgrâces.

[2] The one in which Victor Hugo lived later.

the nuns' shoes; and Monsieur de Gibron served as cook to the servants, feeling that any other employment was too good for him. When Pascal had to meet company, he was afraid lest he should enjoy the conversation:

> L'esprit de mortification [relates his sister] [. . .] lui inspira d'avoir une ceinture de fer pleine de pointes et de la mettre à nu sur sa chair [. . .] Il le fit, et lorsqu'il s'élevait en lui quelque esprit de vanité, ou qu'il se sentait touché du plaisir de la conversation, il se donnait des coups de coude pour redoubler la violence des piqûres, et se faire ensuite ressouvenir de son devoir.

Even the easy-going La Fontaine, after his conversion, wore hair-shirts and scourged himself.

On the other hand, it was an age of contrasts; and, if there were many *dévots* practising austerities and many saintly bishops and priests, many clerics were worldly, loose-living, even irreligious. The abbess of Maubuisson used to swear by the fourteen children 'qui avaient tourné dans ses flancs'. One of Mme de Rambouillet's daughters was an abbess who lived with her novices in furnished rooms in Paris and led a merry life. Bussy-Rabutin's Mlle de Romorantin was proud of being a Cardinal's daughter. The Bishop of Nantes is described by Tallemant as a 'grand jureur, grand débauché, grand batteur et le plus méchant voisin du monde'. The Bishop of Clermont, Joachim d'Estaing, was another lady's man; on one occasion, when his canons had closed the doors of the cathedral against him, he forced his way in with a battering ram. The Archbishop of Reims, who combined libertinage with the episcopal rank, did not atone for a bad life on his death-bed:

> On disait qu'il était mort en tenant un chapelet de marrons pour tout chapelet, et que comme son confesseur lui représentait qu'il faudrait rendre compte à Dieu, il écouta longtemps, et puis il lui dit tout bas à l'oreille: 'Le diable emporte celui de nous deux qui croit rien de tout ce que vous venez de dire!' (Tallemant)

Finally, to complete this brief sketch of the mentality of the seventeenth century, it is necessary to add that it was not only religious and rational, but also credulous and superstitious. 'Que

D

penser,' asks La Bruyère towards the end of the century, 'de la magie et du sortilège?' And he goes on:

> La théorie en est obscure, les principes vagues, incertains, et qui approchent du visionnaire; mais il y a des faits embarrassants, affirmés par des hommes graves qui les ont vus ou qui les ont appris de personnes qui leur ressemblent. Les admettre tous ou les nier tous apparaît un égal inconvénient, et j'ose dire qu'en cela, comme dans toutes les choses extraordinaires et qui sortent des communes règles, il y a un parti à trouver entre les âmes crédules et les esprits forts.

The belief in alchemy, astrology, diabolic possession, dreams, magic and the occult was widespread. Bernier says that the eclipse of the sun on August 12, 1654, made people buy a drug against the eclipse, hide indoors or in their cellars, and take refuge in churches; and, according to Bayle and Fontenelle, the appearance of a comet in the same year had a like effect. Mme de la Guette, fearing rabies, went to Paris to be touched by the chevalier de Saint-Hubert, because 'depuis qu'on en a été touché on est hors de danger des bêtes enragées'. Father Joseph recommended to Richelieu a père Du Bois, who claimed to be able to transmute metals into gold; and, in the Louvre, in the presence of the King, he duly converted — or appeared to convert — two musket balls into fine gold. Henry IV, on the birth of his son, had his horoscope read. Mme de la Guette, while her husband was in Italy, dreamed of him one night and concluded that she would see him next day; he did in fact arrive unexpectedly. Several religious reformers were stimulated by dreams — Mme Martin and Mme de Peltrie, for example, who helped to evangelize Canada.

Fléchier tells us of a man accused of magic, one of whose valets deposed that 'il lui avait donné des caractères qui le faisaient quelquefois élever de terre, lorsqu'il était à l'église, à la vue de tout le monde'. He also tells us of a couple unable to consummate their marriage because of witchcraft: a farmer who had a grudge against them had cast a spell by means of a hazel twig:

> L'ayant partagé en deux, il l'avait attaché à une cheville du même bois, et [. . .] il avait prononcé trois fois une invocation magique qui fait peur, et que je n'oserais redire.

Sully records the appearance in the forest of Fontainebleau in 1598 of a 'fantôme [. . .] devancé d'une meute de chiens et environné d'un grand bruit de chasse, toutes lesquelles choses s'évanouissaient lorsque l'on pensait s'en approcher ou le questionner'. He tells us, too, that the deaths of the wife of the connétable and of Mme de Beaufort in 1599 were widely believed to be the work of the devil, who had called upon them to seek payment for services rendered. A party which included Retz, Turenne and Voiture, one night took a procession of black Augustine friars to be a procession of devils. The interrogation of the sorceress, Mme Voisin, and her associates in 1679, showed that the very greatest in the land were in the habit of resorting to sorceresses and fortune-tellers for the purchase of love philtres and black masses: the maréchal de Luxembourg was accused, for example, of having asked the devil to carry away his wife, and Mme de Montespan of having had black masses celebrated over her naked body in order to win back the love of Louis XIV.

Neither religion nor free-thought excluded superstition. In 1599, Marthe Brossier counterfeited diabolic possession and had a considerable following among the clergy. At Loudun in the thirties an ecclesiastical court was convinced that Sœur Jeanne des Fleurs had the names of saints written in her hand and condemned Urbain Grandier to the stake for causing nuns to be possessed of the devil. Pascal and Port-Royal accepted the miracle of the Holy Thorn. Indeed, religion sometimes verged on superstition — as when the nuns of Port-Royal placed a letter to God in the coffin of a dead sister to be delivered on arrival, or M. de Montbazon, on the point of seducing his *concierge*'s daughter, made her get out of bed to say her prayers first. Bussy-Rabutin, on the other hand, was something of a *libertin*, but he was not without superstitious fears. In 1640, he was staying with the comtesse de Busset:

> Je couchais dans une grande chambre, d'où sitôt que j'étais au lit, le page sortait et fermait ma porte à la clef. Cette maison était faite comme celles qu'on représente où il revient des esprits; de sorte que moi, qui les crains sans les croire, je me mettais la tête sous la

couverture dès que j'étais couché, tant pour m'échauffer plus tôt, que pour m'ôter les moyens de rien entendre qui me pût faire peur.

Un soir qu'à mon ordinaire, je m'étais enfoncé dans le lit, j'entendis quelque temps après un grand bruit à ma porte, et s'étant ouverte, j'ouïs marcher quelqu'un dans ma chambre. La peur qu'on ne me vînt égorger me donnait envie de lever la tête; mais la crainte de voir quelque fantôme me retenait. Enfin comme on ouvrit brusquement les rideaux de mon lit, je ne pus m'empêcher de regarder, et je vis six femmes que je ne connaissais point, les unes avec des flambeaux allumés et les autres avec de grands bassins pleins de viandes froides et de confitures qu'on mettait sur la table.

Il me souvint dans ce moment de ces contes qu'on fait aux enfants, de collations servies comme cela par des gens inconnus, et puis des bras, des têtes, des jambes et tout le reste du corps qui tombent par la cheminée, dont il se forme des personnes qui, après avoir bu et mangé, disparaissent. Tout cela me passait dans la tête, lorsque je vis entrer trois demoiselles de ma connaissance, suivies de la comtesse qui était en déshabillé fort élégant; je ne fus pas encore tout à fait rassuré, car je crus que des esprits pouvaient avoir pris ces ressemblances pour me mieux tromper. Mais lorsque la comtesse se mit à rire, je la trouvai si jolie que, quand même ç'aurait été un démon, je m'y serais apprivoisé.

In short, whether Corneille is making his characters reason lucidly or showing the limitations of reason, whether he makes them be tormented by dreams and oracles or bear suffering with impassivity, whether he is depicting the religious fervour of a Polyeucte or a Théodore or the scepticism of a Sévère, whether he shows the magic spells of a Medea or the sudden conversions of a Pauline and a Félix, he is very much a man of his age.

Chapter Three

BAROQUE
AND CLASSICISM

The third basic tension of the seventeenth century is between baroque and classicism.

The baroque age in France is roughly the period from 1580 to 1660, though many baroque characteristics are inherited by the writers of the classical period. It is the age of the Counter-Reformation, an age, in other words, which had lost the first flush of the enthusiasm for inquiry of the Renaissance, which had seen the consequences of unrestrained inquiry, which knew both civil war and religious war, and which, in consequence, was trying to combine the spirit of the Renaissance with reform of the Church. Baroque, says V. L. Tapié, is 'l'héritier à la fois de la Renaissance et de l'idéal religieux du Concile. Il devait découvrir ce qui dans la première, favorisait le succès du second'. It is an age which, with plenty of vitality and exuberance, is nevertheless characterized by a fundamental uncertainty and a desire to bolster up its beliefs by every possible means: uncertainty, over-emphasis — most of the characteristics of baroque literature and art can be traced back to one or other of these complementary aspects. Baroque, says Gonzague de Reynold, 'est le contraire d'un art tranquille. Il pèche par excès de dynamisme et manque de mesure, par excès de gestes et de mouvements, manque de calme et d'équilibre.'

A sense of the impermanence of things is one of the most common features of the literature of the period. The macrocosm and the microcosm are seen as ever-changing, as fluid and unstable.

> Le monde n'est qu'une branloire perenne. Toutes choses y branlent sans cesse: la terre, les rochers du Caucase, les pyramides d'Egypte, et du branle public et du leur. La constance même n'est autre chose qu'un branle plus languissant.
>
> (Montaigne)

Man, argues Montaigne, can never know reality, because both he and it are in a state of flux; nor can he ever learn from history, since nothing is ever the same: 'Il n'est aucune qualité si universelle en cette image des choses que la diversité et variété.'

The world is full of vicissitudes — empires fall, the mighty are dispossessed, the humble exalted. Montaigne devotes an essay to the subject, *Il ne faut juger de notre heur qu'après la mort*.

> Depuis que l'homme vient au monde,
> Jusqu'à l'heure de son trépas,
> Mille malheurs lâchent la bonde,
> Inséparables de ses pas:
> Il n'a félicité qui dure,
> Et celui se peut dire heureux,
> A qui la fortune moins dure,
> Ne montre un front trop rigoureux,

says the chorus of Hardy's *Scédase*; and Racan's *Bergeries* ends with the lines:

> Ce n'est point en cela qu'est le contentement,
> Tout se change ici-bas de moment en moment,
> Qui le pense trouver aux richesses du monde
> Bâtit dessus le sable, ou grave dessus l'onde,
> Ce n'est qu'un peu de vent que l'heur du genre humain,
> Ce qu'on est aujourd'hui, l'on ne l'est pas demain,
> Rien n'est stable qu'au Ciel, le temps et la fortune
> Règnent absolument au-dessous de la lune.

Tristan's Page Disgracié remarks that 'on aperçoit en toutes choses une vicissitude perpétuelle, et [. . .] selon les secrètes et justes lois de la divine providence, les petites fortunes sont élevées et les

grandes sont anéanties,' and sees his own life as 'un merveilleux tableau de l'inconstance des choses'. 'Oh, que la plupart des beaux objets sont fragiles!' he laments.

The idea that the world is governed by fortune recurs over and over again. For Montaigne, success and failure are the work of fortune, and it is wiser to trust to fortune than to one's own foresight. Fortune delights in bringing sudden adversity:

> Tandis que d'un Tyran l'arrogance excessive
> Jette ses feux soudains, le Sort rit à ses vœux,
> Son choc comme un torrent traverse impétueux
> Les passages plus forts, son Empire se monte
> Degré dessus degré d'une façon trop prompte:
> Mais si le vent se tourne et d'un tour seulement
> Donne à ce grand amas le moindre ébranlement
> Tout fond en un clin d'œil, et la brèche première
> Abolit du surplus la mémoire dernière.
>
> (Schelandre, *Tyr et Sidon*, 1608)

> en un moment la fortune se change,
> Fait rire bien souvent ceux qu'elle a fait pleurer,
> Et soumet sa malice à qui peut l'endurer.
>
> (Mairet, *Sophonisbe*)

> Plus la fortune élève, et plus elle est à craindre.
> Les biens qu'elle nous fait, sont des biens apparents;
> Le principe et la fin en sont fort différents:
> La volage se rit, l'inconstante se joue;
> Et notre heur ne dépend que d'un branle de roue.
>
> (Scudéry, *Le Prince déguisé*)

Writers of memoirs, too, like to point out the vicissitudes of fortune. Bassompierre, relating how, in his youth, he set out to fight the Turks and ended up by fighting the Pope, concludes that 'la fortune est la plupart du temps maîtresse et directrice de nos actions;' and Tristan's page sees himself as a 'jouet des passions des astres et de la fortune'. Quotations of this kind could be multiplied indefinitely; but one further passage should be quoted from *Tyr et Sidon*, because it shows the connection between the conviction of the impermanence of human happiness and the detachment of the stoics:

Mais qui veut reconnaître
Que nos jours sont bornés, et qu'on n'avise rien
Qui ne soit périssable en ce rond terrien,
Qui sait que du serpent la rondeur infinie
Rend des plus durs remparts la hauteur aplanie,
Celui ne fonde point son appui tellement
Sur un homme fragil qu'en son ébranlement
Il tombe quand et lui[1] désolé sans remède,
Mais plus modestement ses amis il possède
Et ses biens les plus chers, s'imaginant toujour
Que, puisqu'ils sont du monde, il les doit perdre un jour:
Lors, après les élans de soudaine tristesse
(Dont la raison si tôt ne peut être maîtresse)
Il rentre en ses esprits, laissant tout à loisir
Adoucir et miner son mordant déplaisir.[2]

The world is the plaything of fortune; and baroque writers love to point out the freaks of fortune, the vagaries of fate, the paradoxical nature of the universe. Montaigne delights in paradox — in pointing out that diametrically opposed means produce the same result, that the same cause may provoke both laughter and tears, that evil means may lead to a good end, that men appreciate only what is out of their reach, that extremes meet. The paradox of human nature is the central theme of Pascal's *Pensées*. In drama, paradoxical situations are frequent, and are always commented upon. In *Tyr et Sidon*, for instance, there is the captor-captive:

Pourquoi dans cette cour, de façon familière
Hanta le prisonnier qui me tient prisonnière?

And in Mairet's *Sophonisbe* that of the queen who loves her enemy, and that of the victor-vanquished:

Dieux! faut-il qu'un vainqueur expire sous les coups
De ceux qu'il a vaincus?

The situation of the lover who scorns the girl who loves him and is scorned by the girl he loves occurs over and over.

Car je fuis qui me suit, j'aime qui me méprise,

[1] = with him.
[2] The belief in fortune is condemned by Descartes (*Traité des Passions*, § 146).

says a character in Desmarets de Saint-Sorlin's *Visionnaires*, but many parallels to the line could be found. Sometimes the world is seen not merely as paradoxical, but as completely topsy-turvy or mad. Hardy's Scédase reproaches Jupiter with not having punished the ravishers and murderers of his daughters:

> Tel acte en ta présence impuni, montre bien,
> Que l'univers n'a point de chef qui le régisse,
> Que tout roule au hasard, sans ordre, et sans justice,
> Que les plus vertueux sont les plus outragés . . .

Even if the world is not regarded actually as mad, the writer often delights in envisaging a world gone mad.

Si cela se fait, le monde ira à rebours: les quêteurs seront honteux, les Espagnols modestes, les Allemands sobres, et tout ira sens dessus dessous.

> L'aigle aura l'âne pour compagne,
> Le bœuf et le gourmand pourceau
> Feront le plongeon dans l'eau,
> Et la mouche prendra l'yraigne;
> Plus ne nous produira la terre
> Ni herbe, ni feuilles, ni fleurs;
> L'arc-en-ciel sera sans couleurs,
> Et la paix aimera la guerre;
> Le printemps sera sans verdure,
> L'été sans épis et chaleurs,
> L'automne sans des raisins mûrs,
> Et l'hiver sans glace et froidure.
>
> . . . .
>
> Plutôt se taira la cigale,
> Et la grenouille fuira l'eau,
> Que ne soit d'une putain sale
> L'amant plumé jusqu'à la peau.

(Larivey, *Les Tromperies*)

So, too, in *Tyr et Sidon*:

> Moi je verrai plutôt rebrousser le Jordan
> Jusqu'au cédreux sommet du Palestin Liban,
> Je verrai le brandon qu'à Delphes on adore
> Se lever au Ponant, se coucher à l'Aurore,
> Je verrai les clous d'or du plus haut firmament

Vaguer comme animaux au plus bas élément,
Et plutôt je verrai cette ronde machine
Se refondre en Chaos d'une guerre intestine,
Qu'avoir si lâchement le cœur épouvanté . . .

Théophile's ode, *Un corbeau devant moi croasse*, similarly evokes a sinister, topsy-turvy world, and Sorel's Francion, in Book III, describes at length a fantastic dream.[1]

Man is no less paradoxical than the world about him; he is seen as a mass of contradictions, inconsistent, ever-changing.

Si je parle diversement de moi, c'est que je me regarde diversement. Toutes les contrariétés s'y trouvent selon quelque tour et en quelque façon. Honteux, insolent; chaste, luxurieux; bavard, taciturne; laborieux, délicat; ingénieux, hébété; chagrin, débonnaire; menteur, véritable; savant, ignorant, et libéral et avare, et prodigue, tout cela, je le vois en moi aucunement, selon que je me vire; et quiconque s'étudie bien attentivement trouve en soi, voire et en son jugement même, cette volubilité et discordance.   (Montaigne)

He preaches one thing and practises another.

Baroque heroes experience the vicissitudes of fortune and pass rapidly from one state to its contrary:

Quand je songe [says Francion] aux aventures qui me sont arrivées ce jour-ci, je me représente si vivement l'instabilité des choses du monde qu'à peine me puis-je tenir d'en rire [. . .] Il n'y a pas longtemps que j'étais couvert d'habillements somptueux, et maintenant j'ai une cape de pèlerin. Je couchais sous les lambris dorés des châteaux, et je ne couche plus qu'aux fossés sans aucun toit. J'étais sur des matelas de satin, bien piqués, et je me suis trouvé dedans une cuve pleine d'eau, pensez pour y être plus mollement. Je me faisais traîner dans un carrosse assis sur des coussinets, et voici que je suis encore trop heureux d'avoir pu trouver une méchante charrette où je me vautre dedans la paille [. . .]

Francion is amused; more often the hero is bewildered:

Je ne sais qui je suis
Dans ce dédale obscur de peines et d'ennuis . . .
                              (Du Ryer, *Alcimédon*)

[1] Cf., in Shakespeare, Hamlet's 'Doubt truth to be a liar,' or Ulysses's description of chaos in *Troilus and Cressida*, I, 3, or the seventeenth-century song, 'If all the world were paper'.

Je doute qui je suis, je me perds, je m'ignore;
Moi-même je m'oublie et ne me connais plus.

(Rotrou, *Amphitryon*)

He loses his sense of identity, thinks he is in a dream.

Man is changeable, inconstant and paradoxical like his lot and the world about him. He, too, is ever-changing: 'Certes,' says Montaigne, 'c'est un sujet merveilleusement vain, divers et ondoyant, que l'homme. Il est malaisé d'y fonder jugement constant et uniforme.' He describes the mass of men as 'stupide, basse, servile, instable et continuellement flottante en l'orage des passions diverses qui la poussent et repoussent: pendant toute d'autrui,' and asks: 'Quand serai-je à bout de représenter une continuelle agitation et mutation de mes pensées, en quelque matière qu'elles tombent?' So changeable are men that — so Montaigne points out — they cannot feel one emotion at a time; restlessness and irresolution are their dominant qualities. They love change, and their opinions and customs, their tastes and fashions vary: 'Combien diversement jugeons-nous des choses? combien de fois changeons-nous nos fantaisies?' Movement is the natural state of man. 'Notre vie n'est que mouvement,' says Montaigne;[1] and Francion agrees:

> mon naturel n'a de l'inclination au mouvement, je suis toujours en une douce agitation [. . .] mon souverain plaisir c'est de frétiller, je suis tout divin, je veux être toujours en mouvement comme le Ciel.

Inconstancy in love is a frequent theme. Love, says Montaigne, is by nature fickle: 'c'est contre la nature de l'amour s'il n'est violent, et contre la nature de la violence s'il est constant.' Pascal agrees, though his explanation is different:

> Il n'aime plus cette personne qu'il aimait il y a dix ans. Je crois bien: elle n'est plus la même, ni lui non plus. Il était jeune et elle aussi; elle est tout autre. Il l'aimerait peut-être encore telle qu'elle était alors.

Lyric poets are fond of praising inconstancy — Durand's *Stances à l'inconstance* are a good example; and the drama of the period is

---

[1] Pascal continues Montaigne: 'j'ai connu que notre nature n'était qu'un continuel changement' . . .

full of men and women who transfer their affections with ease
from one person to another. In Hardy's tragi-comedy, *Procris*,
for example, the goddess Aurore is unfaithful to her mortal
husband, Tithon, and becomes enamoured of Céphale. Céphale
disguises himself as a foreign merchant and tries to seduce his own
wife. She does not emerge satisfactorily from this test, and
Céphale considers himself justified in becoming Aurore's lover.
Lovers regularly complain of the fickleness of women, and women
of the fickleness of their lovers:

> ce sexe inconstant, que gouverne la Lune,
> N'a pas de ces désirs la face longtemps une,
> Girouette d'humeur, il change plus souvent,
> Que sur les flots marins ne se change le vent.

(Hardy, Scédase)

> La femme est un roseau qui branle au premier vent
> L'image d'une mer, et d'un sable mouvant;
> Pour vaincre il lui faudrait ne combattre personne:
> Le changement la flatte, et le respect l'étonne.

(Pichou, Les Folies de Cardénio)

Lovers and coquettes are not merely inconstant, but sometimes
erect inconstancy into a philosophy, a way of life — like Fernant
in *Les Folies de Cardénio*:

> Comment voulez-vous vivre et n'aimer qu'une fois,
> Parmi tant de beautés qui nous donnent des lois?
> Quelle fidélité ne rendrait pas les armes
> Aux nouvelles douceurs que produisent leurs charmes,
> Lorsque la jouissance a suivi nos désirs,
> Que l'amour nous exerce en ses plus doux plaisirs,
> Qu'il rend la passion tout à fait assouvie,
> Et le contentement aussi prompt que l'envie?
> Quel esprit peut alors conserver ses ferveurs
> Dans la possession des dernières faveurs?
> Et lorsqu'il s'abandonne à des grâces nouvelles,
> Doit-on pas excuser ses désirs infidèles?
> Cet aveugle démon qui préside aux amants,
> Permet ce doux remède à leurs moindres tourments,
> Et les plus inconstants, dont il voit les exemples,
> Ne sont point rejetés de l'accès de ses temples.

Sometimes representatives of the two philosophies debate the merits of constancy and inconstancy — in *L'Astrée*, for example: but the tradition goes back at least as far as Guarini's *Pastor Fido*.

A fundamental baroque problem is the difficulty, the impossibility of knowing things as they really are. The sense that the world is an illusion is general, and it is accompanied by the feeling that it is hard, if not impossible, to distinguish between illusion and reality. This is one of Montaigne's favourite themes. Our emotions and our imagination, he says, often betray our senses, which in any case are unreliable guides. Hence we cannot know reality:

> Finalement, il n'y a aucune constante existence, ni de notre être, ni de celui des objets. Et nous, et notre jugement, et toutes choses mortelles, vont coulant et roulant sans cesse. Ainsi il ne se peut établir rien de certain de l'un à l'autre, et le jugeant et le jugé étant en continuelle mutation et branle.

Happiness and unhappiness are merely matters of opinion: some flee death, poverty and hardships; others seek them out; 'la fortune fournissant simplement de matière, c'est à nous de lui donner la forme'. Truth and falsehood are indistinguishable: 'La vérité et le mensonge ont leurs visages conformes, le port, le goût et les allures pareilles: nous les regardons de même œil.'[1] Similarly, we cannot know the real man from the appearance; neither actions nor external appearance are a safe indication of the real nature of a man:

> Voilà comment tous ces jugements qui se font des apparences externes, sont merveilleusement incertains et douteux; et n'est aucun si assuré témoin comme chacun à soi-même.

That last phrase, indeed, is the starting point of Montaigne's essays. Moreover, not only are appearances in themselves deceitful, but men are often deliberately hypocritical; they assume a mask: 'et le dedans et le dehors de l'homme est plein de faiblesse

---

[1] Similarly Rotrou's Sosie points out that vice and virtue are a matter of rank:

> Le rang des vicieux ôte la honte aux vices,
> Et donne de beaux noms à de honteux offices.

et de mensonge'. Montaigne is not alone in complaining of the
hypocrisy of his age; hypocrisy is a constant theme in the drama
of the period.

> Puis faites jugement des hommes, par le front,
> Puis vous laissez séduire à ce masque qu'ils ont,
> Puis croyez que la bouche exprime le courage . . .
>
> (Hardy, *Scédase*)

> Es-tu de ces voleurs dont l'injuste dessein
> Nous montre un bon visage, et nous perce le sein?
> Caches-tu le poison sous un front d'allégresse,
> Et portes-tu la mort à qui tu fais caresse?
>
> (Pichou, *Folies de Cardénio*)

And there is a striking account in Retz's memoirs of a visit he
paid to the Queen; he shows in detail how everyone present,
including himself, was dissembling, 'jouait la comédie'.

The heroes of the period often think that they are dreaming.
'Songé-je, ou si je veille?' asks a character in Larivey's *La Veuve*,
and the question recurs in dozens of plays from Larivey to Racine.
Life itself is often likened to a dream. 'Ceux qui ont apparié notre
vie à un songe, ont eu de la raison, à l'aventure plus qu'ils ne
pensaient,' says Montaigne; and Pascal notes that the only difference between waking and dreaming is that there is less continuity
in dreams: 'la vie est un songe un peu moins inconstant.' Descartes
devotes a good deal of space in the *Méditations métaphysiques* to
considering whether we can distinguish between waking and
dreaming.[1]

In the drama of the period, there is a fondness for all those
things that make life appear different from what it really is — for
disguise and feigning, confusion of identity, illusion, double-
entendre, hypocrisy, madness. Disguise is as common in the
French plays of the period as it is in the plays of Shakespeare:
noblemen dress as servants, women as men. Sometimes the hero
is not merely disguised, but unaware of his identity. The ambiguous oracle or the vow which is fulfilled in an unexpected way is

[1] Cf.
>   We are such stuff
> As dreams are made on, and our little life
> Is rounded with a sleep.

another manifestation of the same thing, a form of double-entendre. In Scudéry's *Le Prince déguisé*, for example, the Queen vows that as long as she remains Queen, her enemy shall perish: in fact, she abdicates in order that he may marry her daughter. Here a set of words which appears to mean one thing turns out to mean another; two antithetical meanings have but one expression. We are still in the world of false appearances, as we are, too, with such characters as the boasting soldier, who wears a mask of courage over his real cowardice, or the madman whose delusions are for him as real as other men's reality — which is, after all, only an illusion. The baroque age is an age of great madmen — Don Quixote, Hamlet, Lear. In France, the theme of madness is treated by Pichou in his *Folies de Cardénio* (based on an episode of *Don Quixote*), by Beys in his *Hôpital des Fous* (which depicts the inmates of a madhouse), by Tristan in his *Folie du Sage*, and, one might add, by Desmarets de Saint-Sorlin in his *Visionnaires*, a gallery of portraits of *extravagants* who are certainly on the fringe of madness if they do not all cross the border. Another frequent character in the drama of the period is the magician, who can metamorphose reality or create illusion.

In this bewildering world, human reason is no guide: the baroque writer has no faith in human reason or judgment. One of Montaigne's essays is entitled *De l'Incertitude de notre jugement*, and a good deal of the *Apologie de Raymond Sebond* is a demonstration of the weakness, futility and inadequacy of human reason, a theme to which he returns in Book III, essay no. 11. 'Combien l'humaine raison est un instrument libre et vague,' he says.

> Jamais deux hommes ne jugèrent pareillement de même chose, et est impossible de voir deux opinions semblables exactement, non seulement en divers hommes, mais en même homme à diverses heures. [...] Ses poursuites[1] sont sans terme, et sans forme; son aliment c'est admiration, chasse, ambiguité.

Pascal continues Montaigne in this attack on the human reason, but the point of view is by no means confined to these two writers: it is general.

[1] Those of the human mind.

Votre raison vous trompe, aussi bien que vos yeux,

writes the poet Régnier; and a character in Mareschal's *Le Railleur*, says:

En ce branle mortel la mode nous entraîne;
La raison n'est qu'esclave, et l'autre est une reine.

This anti-rational tendency brings us to the other aspect of baroque, the desire to be reassured. Mistrust of reason may lead to scepticism, but it can also serve faith, as it does ostensibly in Montaigne and certainly in Pascal. The baroque age, influenced by the Counter-Reformation, is an age of affirmation and faith, the age of the Christian epic (Tasso, Milton, Desmarets de Saint-Sorlin). Baroque art is emotional rather than rational; it does not try to reason, but to convince, to impress, to dazzle, to persuade, to entice and seduce, to ravish the senses. It erects sensuously magnificent churches, surrounds majesty with pomp and ceremony, and delights in ostentation. 'Nous [...] n'apercevons la richesse qu'en montre et en pompe. Notre monde n'est formé qu'à l'ostentation,' says Montaigne. It loves the grandiose and the heroic.[1]

Baroque literature likes to astound and surprise, to horrify, to show extreme states of mind, violent and unnatural passions, and deeds of horror. In Hardy's *Scédase*, two gentlemen rape and murder two girls on the stage (we recall *Titus Andronicus*). Incest and revenge are common themes, and a love of cruelty and the macabre is sometimes evident. It has, for example, been argued that Montaigne likes to dwell on the Spanish atrocities in America, even while reprobating them. Théophile, in one of his elegies, describes to his mistress the moment of death,

Quand les sens pervertis sortent de leur usage,
Qu'une laideur visible efface le visage,
Que l'esprit défaillant et les membres perclus,

[1] It has been said that the essential baroque principle is the sense 'of man's power (including the finiteness of such power) in face of the world. Man can accomplish anything — man can accomplish nothing; in these two propositions, that age's human experience is stated in its full polarity'. (C. J. Friedrich, 'Style as the principle of Historical Interpretation,' in the *Journal of Aesthetics and Art Criticism*, vol. XIV, 1955, p. 150.)

En se disant adieu, ne se connaissent plus;
Que, dedans un moment, après la vie éteinte,
La face sur son cuir n'est pas seulement peinte,
Et que l'infirmité de la puante chair
Nous fait ouvrir la terre afin de la cacher.

In Scudéry's *Ligdamon et Lidias*, Ligdamon addresses his mistress thus:

Lorsque le temps vengeur, qui vole diligent,
Changera ton poil d'or en des filons d'argent,
Que l'humide et le chaud manquant à ta poitrine,
Accroupie au foyer t'arrêteront chagrine,
Que ton front plus ridé que Neptune en courroux,
Que tes yeux enfoncés n'auront plus rien de doux,
Et que, si dedans eux quelque splendeur éclate,
Elle prendra son être en leur bord d'écarlate;
Que tes lèvres d'ébène et tes dents de charbon
N'auront plus rien de beau, ne sentiront plus bon,
Que ta taille si droite et si bien ajustée,
Se verra comme un temple en arcade voûtée,
Que tes jambes seront grêles comme roseaux;
Que tes bras deviendront ainsi que des fuseaux;
Que dents, teint et cheveux restant sur ta toilette,
Tu ne mettras au lit qu'un décharné squelette,
Alors, certes, alors, plus laide qu'un démon
Il te ressouviendra du pauvre Ligdamon.

This speech is a variation on the theme of Ronsard's *Quand vous serez bien vieille*; but with the difference that every unpleasant detail of old age is stressed.

Delighting in violent conflicts and strong contrasts, the baroque age was, perhaps, naturally drawn to the theatre. Certainly the theatre flourished — in England and in Spain, as well as in France. And the interest in the theatre is reflected in the fondness for plays which show a play within a play and the stage on the stage — such plays as *Hamlet* and the *Tempest* and the *Knight of the Burning Pestle*, in England; and in France — not to mention Corneille's *Illusion comique* — Gougenot's *Comédie des Comédiens*, Scudéry's play of the same title, and Rotrou's *Saint Genest*, amongst others. The device of showing the stage on the stage and

E

the play within a play corresponds to the love of showing perspective in depth and a picture within a picture of baroque painters.

To the themes mentioned, correspond certain stylistic features. To the love of ostentation corresponds a love of declamation, of hyperbole and bombast. Procris in Hardy's play of that name having been accidentally killed by her husband, she assures him in these words that she holds him innocent:

> Jamais donques Minos, juge de l'Orque noir,
> Devant lequel je suis proche de comparoir,
> Ne me soit exorable, et que jamais Mercure,
> De descendre là-bas mon esprit n'ait cure;
> Qu'il erre après cent ans aux rives d'Achéron,
> Du passage fatal refusé par Charon,
> Si je te tiens coupable en aucune manière,
> Si ce coup désastreux au sort je ne réfère . . .

To the theme of false appearances corresponds the love of double-entendre and of characters talking at cross-purposes. The sense of the paradoxical nature of the world and the love of contrasts is reflected in the fondness for paradox, oxymoron, and startling antitheses. The love of surprise is satisfied by the far-fetched baroque metaphors and conceits in which words are used in the literal and the figurative sense at one and the same time, as in the famous couplet from Théophile's *Pyrame* which Boileau denounced:

> Ha! voici le poignard qui du sang de son maître
> S'est souillé lâchement: il en rougit le traître!

Another example, from a poem of Théophile's, is the couplet:

> Je baignerai mes mains folâtres
> Dans les ondes de tes cheveux.

Another feature of baroque style is the love of puns and plays upon words (we think of Shakespeare once again), and of verbal echoes:

> O mer amère, mère à la mère d'amours . . .[1]
>   (Schelandre, *Tyr et Sidon*)

[1] Cf. Marbeuf's sonnet beginning:

> Et la mer et l'amour ont l'amer pour partage . . .

Rose elle a vécu ce que vivent les roses . . .

(Malherbe)

J'ai veillé pour mon mal, j'ai veillé pour ma honte;
Veillant, je me suis vu; veillant, je vous le conte:
Je me suis de cent coups, veillant, froissé les os;
J'ai veillé malheureux, et trop pour mon repos.

(Rotrou, *Les Sosies*)

* * *

Corneille began to write in a baroque age; but about the same time the tendency we call classicism began to affect the theatre. The rule of the unities was introduced in 1630; and the *Querelle du Cid* led to stricter observance, not only of the unities, but of the principles of *bienséance* and *vraisemblance* as well.

Classicism, with its belief in reason and regularity, its emphasis on order and discipline, its love of the universal and its disregard for the external, the individual and the picturesque, is very different from baroque, though in some ways it is a continuation of it. The *bienséances* correspond to the moral tendency of the Counter-Reformation (the age in which a prurient Pope clad the statues of the Vatican in vine leaves); and codification, it has been observed, is another characteristic of the Counter-Reformation. It was not until after the Council of Trent that the various Italian commentaries of Aristotle which were to influence the French seventeenth-century writers began to appear. With the codification of literature, the Ancients came to be regarded as infallible models — a tendency akin to the assertion of the principle of authority in religion and politics. Classicism may thus be regarded as a reaction against certain aspects of baroque and a continuation of others — just as *L'art pour l'art* and Parnassianism are at once a reaction against Romanticism and a continuation of it.

Be that as it may, there is in most of the prominent writers of the seventeenth century, even those usually labelled classical, a combination of classicism with baroque themes and stylistic devices.

PART II

Corneille's Career
as a Playwright

CHRONOLOGICAL LIST OF
CORNEILLE'S PLAYS[1]

1629	*Mélite*, comédie	
1630–31	*Clitandre*, tragi-comédie	
1631–32	*La Veuve*, comédie	
1632–33	*La Galerie du Palais*, comédie	
1632–33	*La Suivante*, comédie	
1633–34	*La Place Royale*, comédie	
1635	*Médée*, tragédie	
1635–36	*L'Illusion comique*, comédie	
1637	*Le Cid*, tragi-comédie[2]	
1640	*Horace*, tragédie	
1640–41	*Cinna*, tragédie	
1642–43	*Polyeucte*, tragédie	
1643–44	*La Mort de Pompée*, tragédie	
1643–44	*Le Menteur*, comédie	
1644–45	*La Suite du Menteur*, comédie	
1644–45	*Rodogune*, tragédie	
1645–46	*Théodore*, tragédie	
1646–47	*Héraclius*, tragédie	
1649–50	*Andromède*, tragédie	
1649–50	*Don Sanche*, comédie héroïque	
1651	*Nicomède*, tragédie	
1651–52	*Pertharite*, tragédie	
1659	*Oedipe*, tragédie	
1660	*La Toison d'Or*, tragédie	
1662	*Sertorius*, tragédie	
1663	*Sophonisbe*, tragédie	
1664	*Othon*, tragédie	
1666	*Agésilas*, tragédie	
1667	*Attila*, tragédie	
1670	*Tite et Bérénice*, comédie héroïque	
1672	*Pulchérie*, comédie héroïque	
1674	*Suréna*, tragédie	

[1] The dates of most of Corneille's plays up to *Pertharite* are uncertain.
[2] Described as a tragedy in later editions.

Chapter Four

THE COMEDIES

---

§ 1 *Mélite*[1]

Mélite, Corneille's first play, was virtually the first seventeenth-century French comedy. After three poorly attended performances, it enjoyed great success and led to a revival of the genre:

> Le succès en fut surprenant: il établit une nouvelle troupe de comédiens à Paris, malgré le mérite de celle qui était en possession de s'y voir l'unique; il égala tout ce qui s'était fait de plus beau jusqu'-alors, et me fit connaître à la cour.　　　　　(*Examen*)

Not only, however, has the play considerable historical importance, but it is an interesting play in its own right and, like nearly all Corneille's plays, repays rereading.

The very first scene takes us into the heart of the baroque age. The opening lines touch on what are to be the main themes of the play — the paradoxes of fate, the impotence of the human reason, the power of false appearances.[2] Eraste complains that the rigours

---

[1] For *Mélite*, *Clitandre* and *La Veuve*, the text quoted is that of the first editions as published in the series of *Textes littéraires français* (Droz and Giard) by Roques and Lièvre, R. L. Wagner, and Roques and Lièvre respectively. For the other plays, the text used is that of the standard edition by Marty-Laveaux (*Grands Ecrivains de France*). In all cases the spelling has been modernized.

[2] A study of the vocabulary is revealing in this connection. The word *faux* occurs no less than fourteen times, but to it we must add all its numerous synonyms (*vain*, *affété*, *flatteur*, *trompeur*, *frivole*, *traître*, *hypocrite*, *dissimulé*, *secret*, *caché*, *déloyal*, *perfide*,

of his mistress are powerless to cure him of his love; his situation
is a paradoxical one:

> Jamais un pauvre amant ne fut si mal traité,
> Et jamais un amant n'eut tant de fermeté.   (I, 1)

Though he knows that Mélite does not and never will love him,
the magic of her presence overpowers his reason:

> Un seul de ses regards me séduit et me pipe,
> Et d'un tel ascendant maîtrise ma raison,
> Que je chéris mon mal, et fuis ma guérison...

He realizes that any hope that her eye may give him is illusory,
but to no avail:

> Mais ce flatteur espoir qu'il rejette en mon âme,
> N'est rien qu'un vent qui souffle, et rallume ma flamme,
> Et reculant toujours ce qu'il semble m'offrir
> Me fait plaire en ma peine, et m'obstine à souffrir.

Much of the opening scene consists of a debate upon love between
Eraste and Tirsis, the latter upholding hypocrisy and inconstancy
in affairs of the heart and basing his doctrine on the mutability of
things:

> Pauvre amant je te plains, qui ne sais pas encore
> Que bien qu'une beauté mérite qu'on l'adore,
> Pour en perdre le goût on n'a qu'à l'épouser.
> Un bien qui nous est dû se fait si peu priser,
> Qu'une femme fût-elle entre toutes choisie,
> On en voit en six mois passer la fantaisie,
> Tel au bout de ce temps la souhaite bien loin,
> La beauté n'y sert plus que d'un fantasque soin
> A troubler le repos de qui se formalise,
> S'il advient qu'à ses yeux quelqu'un la galantise:
> Ce n'est plus lors qu'un aide à faire un favori,
> Un charme pour tout autre, et non pour un mari.

conteur, menteur, etc.). Similarly, the verb *tromper* is used seven times only, and the noun
change (or *changement*) only five times; but if we list all the various words used in the play
which suggest fickleness or deceit (*flatter, amuser, abuser, trahir, duper, piper, séduire,
falsifier, feindre, cacher, dissimuler, cajoler, ruse, fourbe, imposture, sembler, semblant,
illusion, déguiser, déguisement, trahison, déloyauté, perfidie, supercherie, piperie, duperie,
feinte*), it is clear that these are the key ideas in the play. In addition, the wind is referred to
several times as the image of impermanence.

But it is not merely the first scene, but the whole play that is baroque. At every turn we are met by paradox, by truth masquerading as falsehood, by falsehood turning out to be truth. The main themes of the play are mutability and illusion, themes which are skilfully brought out by the two carefully contrasted pairs of lovers and by the vicissitudes of the action. Neither of the two speakers in the first scene lives up to the principles he professes. Eraste renounces Mélite and is glad to marry Tirsis's sister, Cloris. Tirsis, after his parade of inconstancy, falls promptly and sincerely in love with Mélite (I, 2); and this reversal of attitude is admirably emphasized by the different senses he attaches within a few lines to the word *vérité*. At the end of the first scene, he says to Eraste:

> Allons, et tu verras que toute sa beauté
> Ne me saura tourner contre la vérité,

— where *vérité* means the folly of constancy. In the following scene, he reinforces his praise of Mélite by saying:

> Je me range toujours avec la vérité.

Could anything be more baroque than to show in this way that truth is relative and varies for each of us with our feelings and desires? The change in Tirsis is paralleled by the change in Mélite, who, at the beginning of the second scene is heart-whole, but who is soon to fall in love with Tirsis.

Immediately after this, we are introduced to the contrasting pair of lovers, Philandre and Cloris, whose reciprocal affection is avowed and shortly to culminate in marriage. But, paradoxically, it is this apparently sincere and genuine love which turns out to be false: Philandre, the upholder of fidelity, not merely turns out to be fickle, but deserts Cloris for an illusion, a chimaera — he deserts her in the mistaken belief that Mélite loves him. And Cloris, who at the outset is affectionate —

> pour un baiser
> Crois-tu que ta Cloris te voulût refuser?

— turns out to accept her lover's desertion philosophically:

Un volage me quitte, et je le quitte aussi
Je l'obligerais trop de m'en mettre en souci . . .
. . . .
. . . elle n'a pas gagné, ni moi perdu grand'chose.
Ma perte me console, et m'égaye à l'instant.   (III, 5)

In contrast to this appearance of genuine love which turns out to
be false, it is the love of the apparently inconstant Tirsis and the
apparently frigid Mélite which turns out to be genuine. Philandre
deserts Cloris, and Cloris accepts his desertion with philosophy;
but Tirsis is heart-broken when he falsely believes Mélite to be
false, and Mélite swoons away in a death-like trance when she
falsely believes him dead.

Everywhere we encounter paradox, false appearances, hypocrisy, illusion. The characters of the play frequently discuss the
falseness of appearances. In answer to Eraste's complaints of
Mélite's coldness, Tirsis says that it is common knowledge that
'Mélite pour toi n'eut jamais de mépris'. No, replies Eraste, this is
but a 'vaine apparence':

Son gracieux accueil, et ma persévérance
Font naître ce faux bruit d'une vaine apparence,
Ses dédains sont cachés, encore que continus,
Et d'autant plus cruels que moins ils sont connus.   (I, 1)

(Cloris, however, is not deceived). Mélite and Eraste debate
whether the former's disdain really causes the latter to suffer. His
appearance is proof of the contrary, argues Mélite:

D'ordinaire on n'a pas avec si bon visage
Ni l'âme ni le cœur en tel équipage.

On the contrary, retorts Eraste, appearances are untrustworthy;
the truth is that, in her presence,

Votre divin aspect suspendant mes douleurs
Mon visage du vôtre emprunte les couleurs.   (I, 2)

Paradoxically enough, it is Philandre, so easily taken in by the
forged letters, who warns Tirsis not to trust appearances:

Souvent un visage moqueur
N'a que le beau semblant d'une mine hypocrite.

. . . .

Ecoute, j'en ai vu de toutes les façons.
J'en ai vu qui semblaient n'être que des glaçons
Dont le feu gourmandé par une adroite feinte
S'allumait d'autant plus qu'il souffrait de contrainte:
J'en ai vu, mais beaucoup, qui sous le faux appas
Des preuves d'un amour qui ne les touchait pas
Prenaient du passetemps d'une folle jeunesse
Qui se laisse affiner à ces traits de souplesse
Et pratiquaient sous main d'autres affections,
Mais j'en ai vu fort peu de qui les passions
Fussent d'intelligence avecques le visage.

Glances and sighs, he adds, are no indication of real feeling:

> Ces choses ridicules,
> Ne servent qu'à piper des âmes trop crédules. (III, 2)

Tirsis, believing himself deceived by Mélite, in his inability to decide whether to believe Mélite herself or the letters which Philandre has received from her, feels his brain reeling:

> Je ne sais plus qui croire ou d'elle, ou de sa plume,
> L'un et l'autre en effet n'ont rien que de léger
> Mais du plus, ou du moins, je n'en puis que juger. (III, 3)

He eventually decides to accept the evidence of the letters, which are in fact forgeries. The false news of the deaths of Tirsis and Mélite drives Eraste mad — so that he can no longer distinguish between imagination and reality, believes himself in Hades, takes Philandre for Charon and the nurse for Mélite:

> Votre douleur vous trouble et forme des nuages
> Qui séduisent vos sens par de fausses images,
> Cet enfer, ces combats, ne sont qu'illusion. (V, 2)

Mélite and Cloris talk at cross-purposes in the fourth act — another form of the confusion between reality and illusion. Cloris reproaches Mélite with having preferred an unworthy lover, meaning Philandre. Mélite thinks that she means Tirsis and waxes indignant. The reality is not the same for the two speakers.

There is plenty of hypocrisy and talk of hypocrisy in the play, too. Eraste, the faithful lover, was once as hypocritical in love as Tirsis, whose doctrines remind him that:

> C'est ainsi qu'autrefois j'amusai Crisolite. (I, 1)

Tirsis, having professed the doctrine of hypocrisy, falls genuinely in love, but he remains a hypocrite in friendship and pretends to Eraste that he is indifferent to Mélite:

> Me prépare le Ciel de nouveaux châtiments,
> Si jamais ce penser entre dans mon courage.

Immediately afterwards, however, he soliloquizes:

> En matière d'amour rien n'oblige à tenir,
> Et les meilleurs amis lorsque son feu les presse,
> Font bientôt vanité d'oublier leur promesse. (I, 3)

Mélite, though loved by Tirsis and in love with him, conceals the truth from Eraste: 'l'amour comme lui je méprise,' she assures him ambiguously. Similarly, Philandre is never so firm in his protestations of fidelity to Cloris as when he is on the point of playing her false. To Eraste, who is tempting him to transfer his affections to Mélite, he says:

> J'ai promis d'aimer l'une, et c'est où je m'arrête . . .
> Adieu, des raisons de si peu d'importance
> N'ont rien qui soit bastant, d'ébranler ma constance. (II, 7)

But he tells the bearer of the letter from Mélite sotto voce to return in a couple of hours. Women are all hypocrites, says Philandre; and Cloris tells her brother the same:

> Apprends que les discours des filles mieux sensées
> Découvrent rarement le fonds de leurs pensées,
> Et que les yeux aidant à ce déguisement
> Notre sexe a le don de tromper finement. (III, 4)

Put a brave face on it, is her reaction when she finds herself jilted. And hypocrisy is the lesson which the nurse tries to inculcate in Mélite:

Une fille qui voit, et que voit la jeunesse,
Ne s'y doit gouverner qu'avec beaucoup d'adresse,
Le dédain lui messied, ou quand elle s'en sert,
Que ce soit pour reprendre un amant qu'elle perd . . .

. . . .

Hors ce cas il lui faut complaire à tout le monde,
Faire qu'aux vœux de tous son visage réponde,
Et sans embarrasser son cœur de leurs amours
Leur faire bonne mine et souffrir leur discours,
Qu'à part ils pensent tous avoir la préférence
Et paraissent ensemble entrer en concurrence.
Ainsi lorsque plusieurs te parlent à la fois,
En répondant à l'un, serre à l'autre les doigts,
Et si l'un te dérobe un baiser par surprise,
Qu'à l'autre incontinent il soit en belle prise,
Que l'un et l'autre juge à ton visage égal
Que tu caches ta flamme aux yeux de son rival,
Partage bien les tiens, et surtout sache feindre
De sorte que pas un n'ait sujet de se plaindre
Qu'ils vivent tous d'espoir jusqu'au choix d'un mari . . . (IV, 1)

Confronted with this world of illusion and this hypocritical society, the human reason is impotent.

La raison en tous lieux est également forte,   (I, 1)

says Tirsis — at the precise moment when he is about to show how wrong he is by falling in love in defiance of his principles. Except for this ironical line, practically every time that reason is mentioned in *Mélite*, its weakness is stressed:

d'un tel ascendant maîtrise ma raison,
Que je chéris mon mal, et fuis ma guérison . . .   (I, 1)

Ah! qu'on aime ce joug avec peu de raison!   (I, 1)

Mais que par ces transports ma raison est surprise!   (III, 3)

Mon âme par dépit, tâche d'abandonner
Un corps que sa raison sut si mal gouverner . . .   (III, 3)

Apprends aussi de moi que ta raison s'égare . . .   (III, 4)

Monsieur, que faites-vous? votre raison s'égare . . .   (IV, 6)

Reason cannot distinguish between the true and the false or resist the magic power of appearances. Mélite's eyes are more powerful than Eraste's reason (I, 1); Tirsis, reproached with too readily believing Mélite faithless, pleads in his excuse that

> un juste déplaisir ne saurait écouter
> La voix de la raison qui vient pour le dompter. (V, 5)

Reason, too, is incapable of deciding where true happiness lies: the characters in the play are divided equally into those who urge that one should marry only for money, and those who put love first.

The theme of the omnipotence and the paradoxical nature of fate is developed all through the play. Some paradoxical situations have been mentioned already; and Eraste himself remarks on the paradox that he himself has introduced to Mélite the lover who has won her from him. But the crowning paradox of the play is that Eraste's trick,[1] far from winning Mélite for him, actually serves to bring Tirsis and Mélite together:

> Votre fourbe inventée à dessein de nous nuire
> Avance nos amours au lieu de les détruire,
> De son fâcheux succès dont nous devions périr
> Le sort tire un remède afin de nous guérir. (V, 6)

Thus false appearances actually bring about the triumph of sincerity and truth. Or do they? Is not this triumph itself, perhaps, an illusion? For the play ends with the nurse's threat to disturb the felicity of the two pairs of lovers:

> Vous êtes bien pressés de me laisser ainsi.
> Allez, je vais vous faire à ce soir telle niche
> Qu'au lieu de labourer, vous lairrez tout en friche.

The style also contains a number of baroque features — paradoxical antitheses, like

> ... je chéris mon mal, et fuis ma guérison ... (I, 1)

---

[1] Corneille, in his *Examen*, accuses Eraste's trick of being improbable. In a sense this is so; and yet, in this play in which everything helps to emphasize the power of illusion and the inability of reason to cope with it, it is neither out of keeping with the rest of the play nor unacceptable.

> Me fait plaire en ma peine, et m'obstine à souffrir; (I, 1)

and conceits:

> Ne soyez plus de glace à qui brûle pour vous. (I, 2)

And in the mad scenes, the love of hyperbole appears — Eraste, in fact, in these scenes, anticipates the Matamore of *L'Illusion comique*:

> Vous me connaissez mal, dans le corps d'un perfide
> Je porte le courage, et les forces d'Alcide,
> Je vais tout renverser dans ces royaumes noirs,
> Et saccager moi seul ces ténébreux manoirs,
> Une seconde fois le triple chien Cerbère
> Vomira l'aconit en voyant la lumière,
> J'irai du fonds d'Enfer dégager les Titans,
> Et si Pluton s'oppose à ce que je prétends,
> Passant dessus le ventre à sa troupe mutine
> J'irai d'entre ses bras enlever Proserpine. (IV, 9)

Double-entendre is, of course, frequent.

> De sa possession je me tiens aussi sûr
> Que tu te peux tenir de celle de ma sœur, (III, 2)

says Tirsis, for example, speaking to Philandre, whom he believes to be the faithful lover of his sister, Cloris. Philandre, who is so far from being faithful to Cloris that he is having — or thinks he is having — a secret correspondence with the very Mélite of whose possession Tirsis feels so confident, replies:

> Pour te faire plaisir j'en veux être d'accord,

— a line which clearly means two different things for the two speakers.

Corneille has constructed his play skilfully around a favourite baroque theme, which he has treated in an original way. Another original feature is the vein of realism that one finds in *Mélite*. It is a comedy of manners, giving, as Corneille puts it in the *Examen*, 'une peinture de la conversation des honnêtes gens.' The impression it gives of the youth of the middle classes of 1629, with their gallant badinage, is one of the attractions of the play.

There is realism, too, in the fact that the play seems to have an autobiographical basis. Thomas Corneille tells us that it was written so that Corneille might introduce a sonnet of his own into it; and Fontenelle, Corneille's nephew, says that, like Tirsis, Corneille was introduced by a friend to his mistress, who, like Mélite, came to prefer him to her lover. These statements are not improbable if we remember that Tirsis in the play is a poet, like Corneille; that, like Tirsis, Corneille is traditionally believed to have loved a lady rather above him in station; that Tirsis in a poem written about this time, *Dialogue entre Tirsis et Caliste*, who is afraid lest his mistress should turn from him to make a wealthier match, probably represents Corneille; and that Corneille himself in the *Excuse à Ariste* tells us that it was love which made him turn to poetry:

> J'ai brûlé fort longtemps d'une amour assez grande,
> Et que jusqu'au tombeau je dois bien estimer,
> Puisque ce fut par là que j'appris à rimer.
> Mon bonheur commença quand mon âme fut prise:
> Je gagnai de la gloire en perdant ma franchise.
> Charmé de deux beaux yeux, mon vers charma la Cour;
> Et ce que j'ai de nom je le dois à l'amour.

The last couplet must allude to *Mélite*, which, he says in the *Examen*, first brought him to the notice of the court.[1]

There are touches of another kind of realism, too — of a sense of the material aspects of life, very refreshing after the unreality of the shepherds of the pastoral. For Tirsis, love leads to marriage, a state not to be accepted too readily:

> Et l'Hymen de soi-même est un si lourd fardeau
> Qu'il faut l'appréhender à l'égal du tombeau.
> S'attacher pour jamais au côté d'une femme!
> Perdre pour des enfants le repos de son âme,
> Quand leur nombre importun accable la maison!
> Ah! qu'on aime ce joug avec peu de raison!　　　　(I, 1)

The importance of money is appreciated by all the characters.

---

[1] The situation of a lover presented to a lady by a friend whom he supplants is found in *L'Astrée* and in two tragi-comedies of Hardy, *Gésippe* and *Dorise*.

> Alors [says Tirsis] ne pense pas que j'épouse un visage,
> Je règle mes désirs suivant mon intérêt,
> Si Doris me voulait, toute laide qu'elle est
> Je l'estimerais plus qu'Aminte et qu'Hippolyte,
> Son revenu chez moi tiendrait lieu de mérite:
> C'est comme il faut aimer, l'abondance des biens
> Pour l'amour conjugal a de puissants liens,
> La beauté, les attraits, le port, la bonne mine,
> Echauffent bien les draps, mais non pas la cuisine,
> Et l'Hymen qui succède à ces folles amours
> Pour quelques bonnes nuits a bien de mauvais jours;
> Une amitié si longue est fort mal assurée
> Dessus des fondements de si peu de durée:
> C'est assez qu'une femme ait un peu d'entregent,
> La laideur est trop belle étant teinte en argent.
> Et tu ne peux trouver de si douces caresses,
> Dont le goût dure autant que celui des richesses. (I, 1)

The fact that Mélite is richer than Cloris is one of the reasons which decide Philandre to desert the latter. Cloris suggests that Tirsis can only love Mélite for her money:

> tous [ses] appas sont tellement vulgaires
> Qu'en elle homme d'esprit n'admira jamais rien
> Que le sujet pourquoi tu lui voulais du bien. (III, 4)

Marry for money is the nurse's advice, too:

> cède enfin, puisqu'il faut que tu cèdes,
> A qui payera le mieux le bien que tu possèdes.
>
> . . . .
>
> Eraste n'est pas homme à laisser échapper,
> Un semblable pigeon ne se peut rattraper,
> Il a deux fois le bien de l'autre, et davantage. (IV, 1)

There is, too, realism in the observation of human nature. Corneille, in the *Examen*, takes pride in his originality in this respect:

> On n'avait jamais vu jusque-là que la comédie fît rire sans person-
> nages ridicules, tels que les valets bouffons, les parasites, les
> capitans, les docteurs, etc. Celle-ci faisait son effet par l'humeur
> enjouée de gens d'une condition au-dessus de ceux qu'on voit dans
> les comédies de Plaute et de Térence, qui n'étaient que des marchands.

It has been pointed out that, in fact, Corneille has not completely eliminated stock characters, since there is a nurse in *Mélite*, and Philandre, who is a coward, to that extent continues the traditional *miles gloriosus*. With these trifling exceptions, the characters of the play are interesting, original and drawn from life. The best, perhaps, is Cloris, an attractively delineated portrait of a girl. She is quick-witted and ready with her repartee:

> *Philandre.* Ta beauté te répond de ma persévérance,
> Et ma foi qui t'en donne une entière assurance.
> *Cloris.* Voilà fort doucement dire que sans ta foi
> Ma beauté ne pourrait te conserver à moi.
>
> . . . .
>
> *P.* Regarde dans mes yeux, et reconnais qu'en moi
> On peut voir quelque chose aussi beau comme toi.
> *C.* C'est sans difficulté m'y voyant imprimée.   (I, 4)

She knows how to treat her lover:

> Un baiser refusé lui fera souvenir
> Qu'il faut une autre fois tarder moins à venir.   (II, 5)

She is shrewd and level-headed, and not susceptible to flattery:

> Une fausse louange est un blâme secret,
> Epargne-moi de grâce, et songe plus discret
> Qu'étant belle à tes yeux plus outre je n'aspire.

On the other hand, she has confidence in herself:

> J'ai trop de vanité pour croire que Philandre
> Trouve encore après moi qui puisse le surprendre.   (I, 5)

When she is betrayed by her lover, she retains her good humour, and refuses to take him back when he repents:

> Pour la première fois il me dupe qui veut,
> Mais pour une seconde il m'attrape qui peut.   (V, 5)

She is, perhaps, above all a good sister, quick to perceive that her brother has fallen in love, inquisitive about the name of his mistress, which in fact she is quick to guess, warm-hearted in encouraging him to pursue his suit, and shrewd in her advice.

The realism of the play is an attractive and original feature; but this, of course, does not mean that Corneille owes nothing to his predecessors. His chief debt is not to comic writers, since there is virtually no comedy in the seventeenth century before *Mélite*, but to the pastoral, the chief dramatic genre of the 1620's. Corneille's originality consists, in fact, largely of taking the pastoral and giving it a contemporary setting. The characters of *Mélite*, like those of the pastoral, are concerned exclusively with their love affairs; and like many pastorals, *Mélite* deals with lovers who are separated by a trick played by a jealous rival. In Guarini's *Pastor Fido*, in Racan's *Bergeries*, and in Mairet's *Sylvie*, for example, a lover had been made to believe his mistress unfaithful. Tirsis, who after railing at love, falls in love with Mélite, and Mélite, who is at first cold-hearted —

> Je ne reçois d'amour, et n'en donne à personne,
> Les moyens de donner ce que je n'eus jamais?   (I, 2)

— and then falls in love with Tirsis, are reminiscent of the pastoral. Ever since Tasso's *Aminta* and Guarini's *Pastor Fido*, it had been traditional for a pastoral to contain a frigid shepherd or shepherdess, devoted to the worship of Diana and the pursuit of hunting, who scorns love for most of the play but finally relents. Tirsis in the first scene, too, is reminiscent of the fickle shepherd who appears in many pastorals. Mad scenes, too, were common — in the fifth act of *Sylvie*, for example, we see both a lover and his mistress driven mad from thwarted love, though Mairet does not use the device for comic effect as Corneille does. But though Corneille has taken details from the pastoral, his characters are observed from life, realistically portrayed, and belong to Paris or Rouen, and not to the woods and pastures of an unreal country-side. Moreover, they have been made comic.

For *Mélite* is a genuine comedy in any sense of the word. It is full of light-hearted and witty conversation, and the characters — Mélite and Cloris, with their reasonableness, their teasing, their habit of greeting flattery with common sense, the nurse with her materialistic outlook, the fickle and cowardly Philandre — are suited to a comedy. If the play is not comic in the same way as

Molière's plays, Tirsis's sudden change of attitude in Act I, scenes 2 and 3, and such scenes as Act II, scene 7, in which Philandre receives the first letter from Mélite and begins to waver in his fidelity to Cloris, Act III, scene 2, in which Tirsis and Philandre each believes himself to be the favoured lover of Mélite and which resembles the *scène des marquis* in *Le Misanthrope* (III, 1), the dialogue between Cloris and Philandre in Act III, scene 7, or Act IV, scene 2, in which Cloris and Mélite talk at cross-purposes, are amusing. Acts IV and V are more serious in tone, but they are enlivened by the extravagant madness of Eraste, which provides a touch of fantasy; and the mixture of tones is reminiscent of some of Shakespeare's plays.

Amusing rather than funny, with some admirably drawn characters and lively dialogue, with some touches of lyricism (V, 4), handling skilfully the baroque themes of change, inconstancy and illusion, this first play of Corneille, despite one or two weaknesses or improbabilities in the plot (which Corneille himself points out in his *Examen*) is an original and delightful comedy.

§ 2 *Baroque and classicism in the comedies*

The characteristic features of *Mélite* are found again in the other comedies of Corneille, which indeed have a family resemblance. They all exemplify the compromise between baroque and classicism characteristic of the period.

They treat many of the baroque themes. The baroque philosophy in its most general form is stated by Philiste in *La Veuve*:

> Le monde est un chaos, et son désordre excède,
> Tout ce qu'on y voudrait apporter de remède.
> N'ayons l'œil, cher ami, que sur nos actions,
> Aussi bien s'offenser de ses corruptions
> A des gens comme nous ce n'est qu'une folie.   (III, 3)[1]

[1] The germ of the first scene of *Le Misanthrope* is perhaps contained in this scene; and the close resemblance between the names of the speakers in both has been pointed out — Philiste–Alcidon and Philinte–Alceste.

and by Alcandre in *L'Illusion comique*:

> Ainsi de notre espoir la fortune se joue:
> Tout s'élève ou s'abaisse au branle de sa roue;
> Et son ordre inégal, qui régit l'univers,
> Au milieu du bonheur a ses plus grands revers.　　　(V, 5)

La Place Royale deals with the problem of behaviour in a mutable world and opens with a discussion of two opposing attitudes: Angélique represents constancy, whereas Phylis believes that, since the world is ever-changing, only those who change too, who can adapt themselves to its vicissitudes, can achieve happiness:[1]

> Fasse état qui voudra de ta fidélité,
> Je ne me pique point de cette vanité,
> Et l'exemple d'autrui m'a trop fait reconnaître
> Qu'au lieu d'un serviteur c'est accepter un maître.
> Quand on n'en souffre qu'un, qu'on ne pense qu'à lui,
> Tous autres entretiens nous donnent de l'ennui;
> Il nous faut de tout point vivre à sa fantaisie,
> Souffrir de son humeur, craindre sa jalousie,
> Et de peur que le temps n'emporte ses ferveurs,
> Le combler chaque jour de nouvelles faveurs;
> Notre âme, s'il s'éloigne, est chagrine, abattue;
> Sa mort nous désespère et son change nous tue,
> Et de quelque douceur que nos feux soient suivis,
> On dispose de nous sans prendre notre avis;
> C'est rarement qu'un père à nos goûts s'accommode,
> Et lors juge quels fruits on a de ta méthode.
> 　　Pour moi, j'aime un chacun, et sans rien négliger,
> Le premier qui m'en conte a de quoi m'engager:
> Ainsi tout contribue à ma bonne fortune;
> Tout le monde me plaît, et rien ne m'importune.
> De mille que je rends l'un de l'autre jaloux,
> Mon cœur n'est à pas un, et se promet à tous:
> Ainsi tous à l'envi s'efforcent à me plaire;
> Tous vivent d'espérance, et briguent leur salaire;
> L'éloignement d'aucun ne saurait m'affliger,
> Mille encore présents m'empêchent d'y songer.

---

[1] Cf.
> Che nel mondo mutabile e leggiero,
> Costanza è spesso il variar pensiero.　　　(Tasso)

> Je n'en crains point la mort, je n'en crains point le change;
> Un monde m'en console aussitôt ou m'en venge.
> Le moyen que de tant et de si différents
> Quelqu'un n'ait assez d'heur pour plaire à mes parents?
> Et si quelque inconnu m'obtient d'eux pour maîtresse,
> Ne crois pas que j'en tombe en profonde tristesse:
> Il aura quelques traits de tant que je chéris,
> Et je puis avec joie accepter tous maris.   (I, 1)

Alidor's reasons for not wanting to marry Angélique are similar to those of Tirsis for avoiding marriage. Phylis and Cléandre, who are mutable and adaptable, find happiness. Cléandre undergoes a sudden change of heart and — like Néron in *Britannicus* — falls in love with Phylis on seeing her in tears. The others — Doraste, Alidor, and Angélique — who cannot change, are doomed to unhappiness; and it is logical that Angélique, the most single-minded of all, who at the beginning of the play declares that Alidor has her whole heart, should at the end leave the world altogether and retire into a convent as the only possible refuge from the uncertainty of the world to which she cannot adapt herself:

> Que veux-tu désormais, que peux-tu faire au monde,
> Si ton ardeur sincère et ton peu de beauté
> N'ont pu te garantir d'une déloyauté?   (IV, 8)

Fickleness is nowhere else the main theme of the play, as it is in *La Place Royale*, but it is not absent. In *La Galerie du Palais*, there is Célidée:

> Mon cœur a de la peine à demeurer constant.   (II, 6)

Florame in *La Suivante* paid court to all ladies before Daphnis fixed his wandering affections; and Clarine, in the play within a play in *L'Illusion*, sees fickleness as characteristic of the age:

> au temps où nous sommes,
> Ni l'hymen ni la foi n'obligent plus les hommes:
> Leur gloire a son brillant et ses règles à part;
> Où la nôtre se perd, la leur est sans hasard;
> Elle croît aux dépens de nos lâches faiblesses;
> L'honneur d'un galant homme est d'avoir des maîtresses. (V, 2)

The problem of the falseness of appearances, of knowing the reality underlying appearance, is raised in Corneille's comedies. Clarice faces it in *Le Menteur*:

> J'en verrai le dehors, la mine, l'apparence;
> Mais du reste, Isabelle, où prendre l'assurance?
> Le dedans paraît mal en ces miroirs flatteurs;
> Les visages souvent sont de doux imposteurs:
> Que de défauts d'esprit se couvrent de leurs grâces,
> Et que de beaux semblants cachent des âmes basses! (II, 2)

Alcidon, in *La Veuve*, sees hypocrisy as the vice of the time:

> Je rêvais que le monde en l'âme ne vaut rien,
> Du moins pour la plupart, que le siècle où nous sommes
> A bien dissimuler met la vertu des hommes,
> Qu'à grand'peine deux mots se peuvent échapper
> Sans quelque double sens afin de nous tromper,
> Et que souvent de bouche un dessein se propose
> Cependant que l'esprit songe à toute autre chose. (III, 3)

Hypocrisy and deception are general in Corneille's comedies, certainly. The sub-title of *Mélite* is *Les fausses lettres*, and Rivaille suggests that similarly *La Veuve* might be subtitled *Les Tromperies*, *La Galerie du Palais Les Dissimulations*, and *La Suivante Les Menteurs*. In *La Veuve*, Alcidon, who loves Clarice, pretends to love Doris; Doris on her side pretends to love him; and the scene (II, 5) in which these two insincere lovers converse in terms which at once express their real feelings and seem to express their feigned emotions, is a masterpiece of double-entendre — a particularly subtle form of hypocrisy, in which words which actually tell the truth serve to disguise it.[1] In *La Suivante*, a comedy of falsehood and misunderstandings, both Théante and Florame pay court to Amarante, but really love Daphnis; while Amarante pretends to love Théante, but really loves Florame. Amidst all this feigning, it is amusing to see the mask falling from time to time — as when Théante says to Amarante:

---

[1] Double-entendre is also used by Théante in *La Suivante* (I, 3) and by Philiste in Act V, scene 5 of *La Suite du Menteur* ('Rentrez dans la prison dont vous vouliez sortir.').

> Arrête: nous pourrons nous voir tout à loisir;
> Rien ne le presse.   (II, 8)

but remarks, when she has departed:

> Ami, que tu m'as fait plaisir!
> J'étais fort à la gêne avec cette suivante.   (II, 9)

In the same play, Damis, who poses as the devoted friend of Théante, turns out to be really working for Florame. In *La Galerie du Palais*, Célidée pretends not to love Lysandre; believing her faithless, he pays court to another lady in order to make her jealous. In *La Place Royale*, Cléandre feigns love for Phylis in order to have access to Angélique. In *L'Illusion comique*, Clindor is a hypocrite who makes love both to Isabelle and to her servant and who fools his master, Matamore, to the top of his bent. And what are the boasts of Matamore but a façade to conceal his pusillanimity? Dorante, in *Le Menteur*, is a liar in whose mouth even truth comes to be discredited, so that all distinction between truth and falsehood becomes impossible.

The problem of appearance and reality appears in another form, too, in *Le Menteur* — in the confusion of identity on which the action of the play turns. Dorante learns that the more beautiful of two young ladies is called Lucrèce. Unfortunately, his standard of beauty and that of his informant are different, so that he thinks that he loves Lucrèce, whereas the girl he prefers is called Clarice. The result is that he refuses to marry Clarice in order to be free to marry the girl he loves, who is, of course, none other than Clarice. The fact that Clarice in Act III pretends to be Lucrèce does not lessen his confusion.

The result of the pretences and misunderstandings in these plays is bewilderment in the characters. 'Je ne sais où j'en suis,' says Lucrèce in *Le Menteur*, echoed shortly afterwards by Clarice:

> Je ne sais plus moi-même, à mon tour, où j'en suis.   (V, 6)

Cliton, too, is bewildered by his master's lies, both in *Le Menteur* and in its *Suite*:

> Je ne sais où j'en suis, et deviens tout confus. (*Suite*, I, 6)

Dorante, overcome by Mélisse's love, declares:

> Surpris, charmé, confus d'une telle merveille,
> Je ne sais si je dors, je ne sais si je veille,
> Je ne sais si je vis . . .   (*Suite*, III, 3)

But characters in earlier plays had had the same experience. Happiness makes Chrysante in *La Veuve* say:

> Mon esprit tout confus doute encore si je veille.   (V, 3)

And the misunderstandings in *La Suivante* reduce Amarante, their author, to a state of bewilderment:

> Mon faible esprit s'y perd et n'y peut rien comprendre.   (V, 4)

Indeed, in *La Suivante*, we find something of the baroque sense that the world is paradoxical and mad:

> Pour tromper mon attente et me faire un supplice,
> Deux fois l'ordre commun se renverse en un jour:
> Un jeune amant s'attache aux lois de l'avarice,
> Et ce vieillard pour lui suit celles de l'amour.
>
> Un discours amoureux n'est qu'une fausse amorce,
> Et Théante et Florame ont feint pour moi des feux:
> L'un m'échappe de gré, comme l'autre de force;
> J'ai quitté l'un pour l'autre, et je les perds tous deux.
>
> Mon cœur n'a point d'espoir dont je ne sois séduite:
> Si je prends quelque peine, une autre en a les fruits;
> Et dans le triste état où le ciel m'a réduite,
> Je ne sens que douleurs et ne prévois qu'ennuis.   (V, 9)

It is paradoxical that Amarante's lie in telling Daphnis's father that Daphnis loves Clarimond (when she really loves Florame) should lead Daphnis to believe herself happy; whereas, when her father tells her to marry Florame, she thinks that he is separating her from him and is miserable.[1]

---

[1] 'A l'avant, sous un éclairage plein, un tourbillon de mensonges et de malentendus aveugle non le spectateur qui tient les ficelles et sait le fin mot de l'histoire, mais les personnages eux-mêmes, les jette de surprise en surprise, les confond, les comble un instant de fausses lueurs pour les plonger de nouveau dans les plus étranges événements; ne sachant plus qui croire ni à qui se fier, ils en viennent à douter d'eux-mêmes, de leurs propres paroles, de leurs propres yeux; ainsi poussés, ballottés de mot en mot et d'obscurités en obscurités comme en une partie de colin-maillard, ils entraînent le spectateur dans leur vertigineuse ronde jusqu'à lui faire perdre le souffle.'   (O. Nadal)

La Place Royale is full of paradox. The hero, Alidor, is himself a paradoxical character, who cannot bring himself to marry Angélique, even though he loves her. She agrees to leave her betrothed husband and elope with him, and finds that in fact he intended to marry her to his friend; on which she comments:

> Si j'aime, on me trahit; je trahis, si l'on m'aime.   (IV, 8)

Cléandre, Alidor's friend, runs off with Phylis in mistake for Angélique and falls in love with her. He, too, meditates on the paradoxicality of the event:

> Avez-vous jamais vu dessein plus renversé?
> Quand j'ai la force en main, je me trouve forcé;
> Je crois prendre une fille, et suis pris par une autre,
> J'ai tout pouvoir sur vous, et me remets au vôtre;
> Angélique me perd, quand je crois l'acquérir;
> Je gagne un nouveau mal, quand je pense guérir.
> Dans un enlèvement je hais la violence;
> Je suis respectueux après cette insolence;
> Je commets un forfait, et n'en saurais user;
> Je ne suis criminel que pour m'en accuser.
> Je m'expose à ma peine, et négligeant ma fuite,
> Aux vôtres offensés j'épargne la poursuite.
> Ce que j'ai pu ravir, je viens le demander;
> Et pour vous devoir tout, je veux tout hasarder.   (V, 1)

Alidor similarly ponders on the paradoxical nature of his lot:

> Ainsi tout me succède;
> Ses plus ardents désirs se règlent sur mes vœux:
> Il accepte Angélique, et la rend quand je veux.
> Quand je tâche à la perdre, il meurt de m'en défaire;
> Quand je l'aime, elle cesse aussitôt de lui plaire.
> Mon cœur prêt à guérir, le sien se trouve atteint;
> Et mon feu rallumé, le sien se trouve éteint:
> Il aime quand je quitte, il quitte alors que j'aime;
> Et sans être rivaux, nous aimons en lieu même.
> . . . .
> Les ombres de la nuit m'ont redonné le jour:
> Que j'eus de perfidie, et que je vis d'amour!   (V, 3)

The theme of the uncertainty of human judgment is touched upon in *La Galerie du Palais*:

> Souvent un bon ouvrage a de faibles succès.
> Le jugement de l'homme ou plutôt son caprice
> Pour quantité d'esprits n'a que de l'injustice.   (I, 7)

Corneille develops this theme further in the *Epître* to *La Suivante*, and in the play itself he shows how easily people allow themselves to be deceived and believe what they would like to be true (III, 4–5).

The stage on the stage occurs, in the form of references to earlier plays of the author, in several plays. In *La Veuve*, Alcidon refers to *Mélite* (III, 3); in *La Place Royale*, Alidor quotes Théante of *La Suivante* (III, 4); and in *La Suite du Menteur*, Cliton tells his master that they have both been put in a play, referring to *Le Menteur*:

> On y voit un Dorante avec votre visage;
> On le prendrait pour vous: il a votre air, votre âge,
> Vos yeux, votre action, votre maigre embonpoint,
> Et paraît, comme vous, adroit au dernier point.
> Comme à l'événement j'ai part à la peinture:
> Après votre portrait on produit ma figure.
> Le héros de la farce, un certain Jodelet,
> Fait marcher après vous votre digne valet;
> Il a jusqu'à mon nez et jusqu'à ma parole,
> Et nous avons tous deux appris en même école . . .   (I, 3)

Jodelet in the rôle of Cliton describing how he had seen Jodelet in the rôle of Cliton is like seeing a mirror reflected in a mirror. In *L'Illusion comique*, we do actually see the stage on the stage, and there is a play within a play — or to be precise a play within a play within a play.

L'Illusion differs somewhat from Corneille's other plays, but is no less baroque. The form is baroque:

> Voici un étrange monstre que je vous dédie. Le premier acte n'est qu'un prologue, les trois suivants font une comédie imparfaite, le dernier est une tragédie: et tout cela, cousu ensemble, fait une comédie. Qu'on en nomme l'invention bizarre et extravagante tant qu'on voudra, elle est nouvelle [. . .]

The theme of illusion is here a central one. Not only does a cowardly braggadocio play a considerable part, but there is a magician, and the play, the result of his magical art, is one great illusion. In the last act, a gigantic piece of *trompe-l'œil*, a play within a play and the stage on the stage, what we think we are witnessing is not what we are in fact seeing:

> J'ai pris sa mort pour vraie, et ce n'était que feinte,

says Pridamant. The whole play aims at — and achieves — deception and surprise. It is a captivating, and very baroque, mixture of fantasy, realism, comedy, tragedy, the romanesque and the mock-heroic.

By the side of these baroque features, however, classical characteristics are to be found in the comedies of Corneille. Despite the use of antithesis —

> Je te voudrai du bien de ne m'en vouloir plus.
> (*La Suivante*, II, 2)

— and paradox, puns and occasional word play —

> *Daphnis.* Je crois que vous m'aimez, et c'est en croire plus
> Que n'en exprimeraient vos discours superflus.
> *Florame.* Mes feux, qu'ont redoublés ces propos adorables,
> A force d'être crus deviennent incroyables;
> Et vous n'en croyez rien qui ne soit au-dessous:
> Que ne m'est-il permis d'en croire autant de vous?
> (*La Suivante*, III, 9)

— the style is not baroque. Moreover, though Corneille's first three plays, written before the rules were established — 'je ne savais pas alors qu'il y en eût,' he tells us in the *Examen* to *Mélite* — are not regular, they are not wildly irregular.

> Ce sens commun [he tells us], qui était toute ma règle, m'avait fait trouver l'unité d'action pour brouiller quatre amants par un seul intrigue, et m'avait donné assez d'aversion de cet horrible dérèglement qui mettait Paris, Rome, et Constantinople sur le même théâtre, pour réduire le mien dans une seule ville.
> (*Examen* of *Mélite*)

In *La Veuve* and *La Galerie*, the acts represent five consecutive days, and, as in *Mélite*, the scene changes, but only from one part of Paris to another. And, in *La Suivante*, Corneille was one of the first to introduce the unities and *liaison de scènes* into a comedy; indeed, he went further and made the acts exactly equal in length. The compromise between baroque and classicism, however, is most striking in *L'Illusion comique*, where the rules are technically obeyed, but only if we accept the fact that what we are seeing is the product of the enchanter's art, that we are in a magician's grotto, seeing in a couple of hours events occurring over a period of months in a variety of places.

§ 3 *Realism in Corneille's comedies*

For Corneille, comedy and realism are synonymous: 'La comédie n'est qu'un portrait de nos actions, et de nos discours, et la perfection des portraits consiste en la ressemblance.'[1] His comedies reflect contemporary manners and society — like so much of contemporary art. Even when he uses Spanish sources, as he does in *Le Menteur* and its sequel, he sets his plays in France and adapts his originals accordingly; whereas other dramatists, such as Rotrou or his own brother, Thomas, were content to leave the foreign setting unchanged. One of the attractions of his comedies, therefore, is that they afford many glimpses of seventeenth-century life and society.

Le Menteur gives an impression of Paris:

> *Dorante.* Paris semble à mes yeux un pays de romans.
> J'y croyais ce matin voir une île enchantée:
> Je la laissai déserte, et la trouve habitée;
> Quelque Amphion nouveau, sans l'aide des maçons,
> En superbes palais a changé ses buissons.
> *Géronte.* Paris voit tous les jours de ces métamorphoses:
> Dans tout le Pré-aux-Clercs tu verras mêmes choses:
> Et l'univers entier ne peut rien voir d'égal
> Aux superbes dehors du Palais Cardinal.
> Toute une ville entière, avec pompe bâtie,

[1] *La Veuve, Au Lecteur.*

> Semble d'un vieux fossé par miracle sortie,
> Et nous fait présumer, à ses superbes toits,
> Que tous ses habitants sont des dieux ou des rois. (II, 5)

All is not perfect in this setting, however, and Corneille reminds us of the turbulence of the period and the underworld of thieves:

> Trois filous rencontrés vers le milieu du pont
> Chacun l'épée au poing, m'ont voulu faire affront,
> Et sans quelques amis qui m'ont tiré de peine,
> Contre eux ma résistance eût peut-être été vaine.
>
> *(Galerie du Palais*, I, 9)

> Connaît-on à l'habit aujourd'hui la canaille,
> Et n'est-il point, Monsieur, à Paris de filous
> Et de taille et de mine aussi bonnes que vous?
>
> *(Suite du Menteur*, I, 1)

There are prison scenes in *L'Illusion* and in the *Suite du Menteur*, and, in the latter play, allusions to the rapacity of the police —

> Mon argent fut pour eux le premier criminel;   (I, 1)

and of the law:

> Ah! Monsieur, sans argent est-il de l'innocence?   (I, 1)

In *La Galerie du Palais* is a delightful glimpse of seventeenth-century shopkeepers, cajoling their customers and quarrelling with each other, and these scenes (I, 4–7; IV, 12–14) are full of information about current fashions in dress and literature.[1] In one of them we see a maid being bribed by a *lingère* to secure her mistress's custom. Corneille, indeed, in *La Galerie*, was one of the first to replace the traditional nurse (played by a man) by the contemporary *suivante* (played by a woman); and, in his next play, this new character becomes the central figure. Of equal interest is the scene in *L'Illusion comique* in which we see the actors sharing out their takings after a performance (V, 5) and hear Alcandre's account of the flourishing state of the theatre. *La Galerie du Palais* reminds us that theatre audiences were turbulent:

[1] 'Here for the first time we see three merchants selling their goods in their places of business.'   (H. C. Lancaster)

> m'ayant tenu quelques propos d'ivrogne,
> Nous eûmes prise ensemble à l'hôtel de Bourgogne;[1]   (I, 9)

and the last words of the *Suite du Menteur*, that the *parterre* had to stand:

> Ceux qui sont las debout se peuvent aller seoir,
> Je vous donne en passant cet avis, et bonsoir.

The narrative of Clitandre's adventures in *L'Illusion comique* gives a fascinating picture of certain aspects of contemporary life:

> Il vous prit quelque argent, mais ce petit butin
> A peine lui dura du soir jusqu'au matin;
> Et pour gagner Paris, il vendit par la plaine
> Des brevets à chasser la fièvre et la migraine,
> Dit la bonne aventure, et s'y rendit ainsi.
> Là comme on vit d'esprit, il en vécut aussi.
> Dedans Saint-Innocent il se fit secrétaire;
> Après, montant d'état, il fut clerc d'un notaire.
> Ennuyé de la plume, il la quitta soudain,
> Et fit danser un singe au faubourg saint Germain.
> Il se mit sur la rime, et l'essai de sa veine
> Enrichit les chanteurs de la Samaritaine.
> Son style prit après de plus beaux ornements;
> Il se hasarda même à faire des romans,
> Des chansons pour Gautier, des pointes pour Guillaume.
> Depuis il trafiqua de chapelets de baume,
> Vendit du mithridate en maître opérateur,
> Revint dans le Palais, et fut solliciteur.   (I, 3)

In the *Suite du Menteur* is a detail which brings the seventeenth century very close. Lyse brings some sweets or *confitures* to Dorante in prison and says:

> Acceptez cependant quelque peu de douceurs
> Fort propres en ces lieux à conforter les cœurs:
> Les sèches sont dessous, celles-ci sont liquides.   (II, 6)

But the realism of Corneille is not concerned solely with such external aspects of life: he gives us in his comedies a vivid impression of the life and the talk of the age. And that he is consciously attempting to do so is shown by the preface to *La Veuve*,

---

[1] The *rival* theatre — Corneille's own plays were performed at the Marais.

in which he tells us that the style of the play is 'prose rimée', and by the *Examen*, in which he points out that it has fewer *pointes* than *Mélite* and expresses his aversion for asides. The conversation is easy, varied, natural and familiar. We learn what *honnêtes gens* talk about:

> Le joli passe-temps
> D'être auprès d'une dame, et causer du beau temps,
> Lui jurer que Paris est toujours plein de fange,
> Qu'un certain parfumeur vend de fort bonne eau d'ange,
> Qu'un cavalier regarde un autre de travers,
> Que dans la comédie on dit d'assez bons vers,
> Qu'un tel dedans le mois d'une telle s'accorde! (*La Veuve*, I, 1)

We overhear them discussing the technique of courtship and arguing about the advantages and disadvantages of matrimony. In *La Veuve*, Clarice rallies Philiste on having paid too much attention to two other ladies, and Doris describes a ball she has attended. In *Le Menteur*, Dorante describes a *collation sur l'eau* offered to a lady. In *La Veuve*, we see negotiations for a marriage being conducted, and in the *Suite du Menteur* is an account of the preparations for a wedding. There are plenty of specimens of the gallant badinage of lovers and their ladies, and in *Le Menteur* there is an example of the military talk fashionable in time of war:

> Tout le secret ne gît qu'en un peu de grimace,
> A mentir à propos, jurer de bonne grâce,
> Etaler force mots qu'elles n'entendent pas,
> Faire sonner Lamboy, Jean de Vert, et Galas,
> Nommer quelques châteaux de qui les noms barbares
> Plus ils blessent l'oreille, et plus leur semblent rares,
> Avoir toujours en bouche, angles, lignes, fossés,
> Vedette, contrescarpe, et travaux avancés:
> Sans ordre et sans raison, n'importe, on les étonne;
> On leur fait admirer les baies qu'on leur donne,
> Et tel, à la faveur d'un semblable débit,
> Passe pour homme illustre, et se met en crédit. (I, 6)

To talk of the wars, it was not necessary to have been there:

> Dorante est-il le seul qui, de jeune écolier,
> Pour être mieux reçu s'érige en cavalier?

Que j'en sais comme lui qui parlent d'Allemagne,
Et si l'on veut les croire ont vu chaque campagne;
Sur chaque occasion tranchent des entendus,
Content quelque défaite, et des chevaux perdus;
Qui dans une gazette apprenant ce langage,
S'ils sortent de Paris, ne vont qu'à leur village,
Et se donnent ici pour témoins approuvés
De tous ces grands combats qu'ils ont lus, ou rêvés!   (III, 3)

There is, moreover, an element of social criticism in these comedies. In play after play, Corneille touches on the hard lot of women, married to suit their parents' convenience:

Dure sujétion! étrange tyrannie!
Toute liberté donc à mon choix se dénie!
On ne laisse à mes yeux rien à dire à mon cœur,
Et par force un amant n'a de moi que rigueur:
Il y va cependant du reste de ma vie,
Et je n'ose écouter tant soit peu mon envie;
Il faut que mes désirs toujours indifférents
Aillent sans résistance au gré de mes parents
Qui m'apprêtent peut-être un brutal, un sauvage,
Et puis cela s'appelle une fille bien sage.   (*La Veuve*, IV, 9)

Je sais ce que la force est en un mariage.
Il me souvient encor de tous mes déplaisirs
Lorsqu'un premier hymen contraignit mes désirs . . .
                                        (*Galerie du Palais*, V, 8)[1]

In *La Suivante*, the abuse of parental authority is illustrated by the rather shady bargain by which Géronte gives his daughter to Florame in exchange for the latter's sister. Corneille seems to have felt deeply about the question — quite possibly because his own mistress had been married to a wealthier suitor.

In *La Suivante*, he touches on a kindred question, the misfortune of women whose wealth was unequal to their merits. Amarante, the *Suivante*, complains:

Daphnis me le ravit, non par son beau visage,
Non par son bel esprit ou ses doux entretiens,
Non que sur moi sa race ait aucun avantage,
Mais par le seul éclat qui sort d'un peu de biens.

[1] Cf. *L'Illusion*, III, 1 and 2.

> Filles que la nature a si bien partagées,
> Vous devez présumer fort peu de vos attraits:
> Quelques charmants qu'ils soient, vous êtes négligées,
> A moins que la fortune en rehausse les traits.　　(V, 9)

The desire of so many of the men to win a wealthy wife, lamented
by Amarante, shows Corneille's grasp of realities. Clindor, in
L'Illusion, speaks for several of Corneille's lovers:

> L'amour et l'hyménée ont diverse méthode:
> L'un court au plus aimable, et l'autre au plus commode.
> Je suis dans la misère, et tu n'as point de bien;
> Un rien s'ajuste mal avec un autre rien.　　(III, 5)

Even more important than the glimpses of contemporary
society is the truth to human nature, the psychological realism
of the comedies. That Corneille attached great importance to this
is clear. In the preface to *La Veuve*, he says: 'Tu y reconnaîtras
trois sortes d'amours aussi extraordinaires au théâtre, qu'ordinaires dans le monde;' and in *La Galerie du Palais* he insists that
plays must be based on personal experience:

> *Lysandre.* Et tel parle d'amour sans aucune pratique.
> *Dorimant.* On n'y sait guère alors que la vieille rubrique:
> Faute de le connaître, on l'habille en fureur;
> Et loin d'en faire envie, on nous en fait horreur.
> Lui seul de ses effets a droit de nous instruire;
> Notre plume à lui seul doit se laisser conduire:
> Pour en bien discourir, il faut l'avoir bien fait;
> Un bon poète ne vient que d'un amant parfait.
> *Lysandre.* . . . .
> O pauvre comédie, objet de tant de veines,
> Si tu n'es qu'un portrait des actions humaines,
> On te tire souvent sur un original
> A qui, pour dire vrai, tu ressembles fort mal!　　(I, 7)

In Corneille's comedies, as we might expect from such remarks, there is a good deal of nice observation and delicate
psychology — Eraste's description of Mélite in love, Philiste's
description of a lover, Lysandre's analysis of falling in love, and
Cliton's account of the different kinds of ladies and lovers in

Paris.[1] *La Veuve* is a good example of the delicacy of Corneille's observation, with its careful analysis of the progress of the loves of Clarice and Philiste, the admirable portrayal of the relations between Philiste and his mother and their contrasting attitudes to the question of Doris's marriage, and Doris's unforgettable description of Florange at the ball:

> Ah Dieu! que c'est un cajoleur étrange . . .
> Il m'épargna si bien que ses plus longs propos
> A grand'peine en une heure étaient de quatre mots,
> Il me mena danser deux fois sans me rien dire.
> — Oui, mais après? — Après? c'est bien le mot pour rire,
> Mon baladin muet se retire en un coin,
> Content de m'envoyer des œillades de loin,
> Enfin après m'avoir longtemps considérée,
> Après m'avoir de l'œil mille fois mesurée,
> Il m'aborde en tremblant avec ce compliment,
> 'Vous m'attirez à vous ainsi que fait l'aimant.'
> (Il pensait m'avoir dit le meilleur mot du monde.)
> Entendant ce haut style aussitôt je seconde
> Et réponds brusquement sans beaucoup m'émouvoir,
> 'Vous êtes donc de fer, à ce que je puis voir.'
> Après cette réponse, il eut don de silence,
> Surpris (comme je crois) par quelque défaillance:
> Depuis il s'avisa de me serrer les doigts
> Et retrouvant un peu l'usage de la voix
> Il prit un de mes gants, 'La mode en est nouvelle
> (Me dit-il) et jamais je n'en vis de si belle,
> Vous portez sur le sein un mouchoir fort carré,
> Votre éventail me plaît d'être ainsi bigarré,
> L'amour je vous assure est une belle chose,
> Vraiment vous aimez fort cette couleur de rose,
> La ville est en hiver tout autre que les champs,
> Les charges à présent n'ont que trop de marchands,
> On n'en peut approcher.'
>
> (I, 3

Corneille's characterization, too, is excellent. Apart from one or two relics of stock characters — the nurse in *La Veuve* and the cowardly Théante of *La Suivante* — his characters owe more to observation than to tradition. Of the men, the most interesting,

---

[1] *Mélite*, II, 1; *Veuve*, I, 5; *Galerie*, I, 8 and III, 6; *Menteur*, I, 1.

perhaps — with Alidor in *La Place Royale* — are Philiste in *La Veuve*, Matamore and Clindor in *L'Illusion comique*, and Dorante and Cliton in *Le Menteur* and its sequel, though these last are no doubt primarily the creations of Don Juan de Alarcon. Philiste is a poor man in love with a wealthy woman, whose policy is to bring her to declare her love first; he is upright and loyal to his friend. Matamore is a stock character, but the verve and fancy with which Corneille endows him, his stories of gods and goddesses, his page employed to bring him false messages from kings and queens, his separation of his good looks and his courage —

> Lorsque j'ai ma beauté, je n'ai point ma valeur,   (II, 2)

— give him freshness and originality. His servant, Clindor, is a somewhat shady adventurer, living by his wits, fooling his master to the top of his bent, making love to both mistress and servant, but freely acknowledging that money is his object —

> J'adore sa fortune et tes perfections.   (III, 5)

If anything, the women are superior to the men. They are self-possessed, and meet flattery with common sense, like Isabelle in *L'Illusion* (II, 6) or Hippolyte in *La Galerie*:

> Ne me contez point tant que mon visage est beau:
> Ces discours n'ont pour moi rien du tout de nouveau;
> Je le sais bien sans vous, et j'ai cet avantage,
> Quelques perfections qui soient sur mon visage,
> Que je suis la première à m'en apercevoir:
> Pour me les bien apprendre, il ne faut qu'un miroir;
> J'y vois en un moment tout ce que vous me dites.   (II, 1)

The flattery of an unwelcome suitor meets with short shrift. Hippolyte receives Dorimant with cruel irony:

> Avoir connu d'abord combien je suis aimable,
> Encor qu'à votre avis il soit inexprimable,
> Ce grand et prompt effet m'assure puissamment
> De la vivacité de votre jugement.
> Pour moi, que la nature a faite un peu grossière,
> Mon esprit, qui n'a pas cette vive lumière,
> Conduit trop pesamment toutes ses fonctions

Pour m'avertir sitôt de vos perfections.
Je vois bien que vos feux méritent récompense;
Mais de les seconder ce défaut me dispense. (*Galerie*, II, 1)[1]

Corneille's heroines are self-confident — like the coquettish, sprightly Lyse of *L'Illusion*:

Ce voisinage
Au frère du concierge a fait voir mon visage;
Et comme c'est tout un que me voir et m'aimer,
Le pauvre malheureux s'en est laissé charmer. (IV, 2)

They are witty, like the Lyse of *La Suite du Menteur*; they can tease, like Hippolyte in *La Galerie* (III, 8), or be ironical like Isabelle in *L'Illusion* (II, 4). They are shrewd, intelligent, clear-sighted, like Doris in *La Veuve*, who recognizes Alcidon's hypocrisy, or Amarante in *La Suivante*, who sees through her mistress. They can be spiteful to each other, too, like Daphnis and Amarante in *La Suivante* (III, 10) or Clarice and Lucrèce in *Le Menteur* (IV, 9).

Some are flirts, like Phylis in *La Place Royale*, who, for all her lightheartedness, is a good sister. Some can lose a lover with philosophy or indifference, like Doris in *La Veuve*. Clarice in *Le Menteur* is above all anxious not to be an old maid, but does not much care whom she marries:

[Je] ne suis pas d'humeur à mourir de constance.
Chaque moment d'attente ôte de notre prix,
Et fille qui vieillit tombe dans le mépris:
C'est un nom glorieux qui se garde avec honte ... (II, 2)

Others, on the other hand, are sincere and true in their love, like Angélique in *La Place Royale*:[2]

Vois-tu, j'aime Alidor, et c'est assez te dire.
Le reste des mortels pourrait m'offrir des vœux,
Je suis aveugle, sourde, insensible pour eux;
La pitié de leurs maux ne peut toucher mon âme
Que par des sentiments dérobés à ma flamme.

---

[1] Cf. Isabelle in *L'Illusion*, II, 3.
[2] 'Touchante et sincère, Angélique est avec la Clarice de *La Veuve* une des plus charmantes figures de femme que Corneille ait tracées.' (J. Schlumberger)

> On ne doit point avoir des amants par quartier;
> Alidor a mon cœur et l'aura tout entier;
> En aimer deux, c'est être à tous deux infidèle.   (I, 1)

Isabelle in *L'Illusion* is another such: she is remarkable, in addition, for her determination and her strength of will:

> Je ne vous dirai point où je suis résolue:
> Il suffit que sur moi je me rends absolue.   (III, 8)

Whereas some of Corneille's women profess absolute obedience to their parents — like Doris in *La Veuve* or Célidée in *La Galerie* — she is rebellious, even vindictive. When her lover is about to be put to death, she vows to kill herself and apostrophizes her father thus:

> Ainsi, père inhumain, ta cruauté déçue
> De nos saintes ardeurs verra l'heureuse issue;
> Et si ma perte alors fait naître tes douleurs,
> Auprès de mon amant je rirai de tes pleurs.
> Ce qu'un remords cuisant te coûtera de larmes
> D'un si doux entretien augmentera les charmes;
> Ou s'il n'a pas assez de quoi te tourmenter,
> Mon ombre chaque jour viendra t'épouvanter,
> S'attacher à tes pas dans l'horreur des ténèbres,
> Présenter à tes yeux mille images funèbres,
> Jeter dans ton esprit un éternel effroi,
> Te reprocher ma mort, t'appeler après moi,
> Accabler de malheurs ta languissante vie,
> Et te réduire au point de me porter envie.   (IV, 1)

Faithful or flirtatious, rebellious or docile to parental authority, witty or serious, grave or gay, Corneille's female characters are varied and convincing.

Not only is Corneille an excellent creator of character, but he frequently studies interesting and original states of mind. Célidée, in *La Galerie*, is wearied of her lover's fidelity and resolves to try his constancy by being disdainful to him. She begins to regret her decision no sooner than it is made; regains her love when she finds her lover submissive; and becomes jealous and unhappy when he pretends to be unfaithful. Amarante, the *suivante* in the play of that name, whose mistress attracts her lovers away from her, is jealous, outspoken, and full of bitterness, besides being vain, fickle, and a flirt. In the duel of wits between her and her mistress, there is malice on both sides. Perhaps the most interesting of all is Alidor in *La Place Royale*. Like Célidée, he is weary of his mistress's fidelity, though for a different reason: if only she were less perfect, he might be able to stop loving her:[1]

> Ce n'est qu'en m'aimant trop qu'elle me fait mourir,
> Un moment de froideur, et je pourrais guérir . . .   (I, 4)

His wish is to be free — to confer his love voluntarily, not because he is constrained thereto by his mistress's charms:

> Je veux la liberté dans le milieu des fers.
> . . . .
>   je veux
> . . . .
> Donner quand il me plaît et retirer ma foi.   (I, 4)

He is afraid of marriage — 'ce joug humain, ce passage trompeur, ce supplice éternel,' which is permanent in a changing world — and will only enter into it by an act of free will:

> Je ne me résoudrai jamais à l'hyménée
> Que d'une volonté franche et déterminée,
> Et celle à qui ses nœuds m'uniront pour jamais
> M'en sera redevable, et non à ses attraits . . .   (IV, 1)

Nevertheless, he is incapable of achieving this impossible ambition. After striving to bring about the marriage of Angélique to his friend Cléandre in the interests of his own freedom, he has to admit that love is too strong for him:

> Aussi ma liberté n'a plus rien qui me flatte;
> Le grand soin que j'en eus partait d'une âme ingrate;
> Et mes desseins, d'accord avecque mes désirs,
> A servir Angélique ont mis tous mes plaisirs.   (V, 3)

---

[1] There is a hint of Alidor already in Philandre in *Mélite*:
> Ton bel œil mon vainqueur
> Fait naître chaque jour tant de feux en mon cœur,
> Que leur excès m'accable, et que pour m'en défaire
> Je recherche par où tu me pourras déplaire . . .   (I, 4)

Angélique, however, disgusted with his treatment of her, resolves to enter a convent, and he professes himself content: her decision means that, though he cannot have her, no one else will, so that he retains his freedom and is spared jealousy.

> Je cesse d'espérer et commence de vivre;
> Je vis dorénavant, puisque je vis à moi;
> Et quelques doux assauts qu'un autre objet me livre,
> C'est de moi seulement que je prendrai la loi. (V, 8)

Even when Corneille seems to us to be most fantastic and romantic, he is much nearer to the real life of his age than we might think. If elopements, abductions and duels occur in his comedies, so they do in the life of the time. The magician in *L'Illusion* is a stock character of the pastoral; but the belief in magic, sorcery, soothsaying and alchemy was strong in the seventeenth century. Similarly, even some of the more extravagant characters of the comedies have their counterparts in real life. With Phylis in *La Place Royale*, who boasts:

> D'un million d'amants je puis flatter les vœux, (II, 7)

we might compare Mme de Gironde, who, says Tallemant, 'ne marchait point sans une foule d'amants,' and who 'parlait avec une liberté extraordinaire de sa beauté et de ses *mourants*'. If we are to believe the *Epître dédicatoire* to *La Place Royale*, Alidor in that play was copied from a living model. In any case, Montaigne tells us that 'étant jeune, je m'opposais au progrès de l'amour que je sentais trop avancer sur moi, et étudiais qu'il ne me fût si agréable qu'il vînt à me forcer enfin et captiver du tout à sa merci.' And Fléchier, a generation later, has an anecdote about a M. de Bégon who is a little reminiscent of Alidor. This gentleman vowed eternal love to a lady, who asked him to be faithful to her for a month, until the end of the carnival.

> Il se rendit encore plus assidu qu'il n'avait été; il lui écrivait mille billets doux; il la menait dans toutes les assemblées, et toute la ville attendait le succès d'une passion si connue. Le jour du mardi gras, il lui donna le bal le plus superbe qu'il put; jamais on ne vit tant de profusion et tant de passion qu'en cette rencontre. Il la prit à danser

plusieurs fois, il lui dit cent douceurs devant tout le beau monde qu'il avait prié, et jusqu'à minuit on ne le vit jamais ni plus gai ni plus passionné. Mais tout à coup un laquais qu'il avait laissé en sentinelle lui étant venu dire tout bas que la douzième heure était sonnée, il prit en même temps un air sérieux. Il lui tenait une main et il la rejeta comme avec dépit; il tenait la coiffe de sa maîtresse, et il la laissa tomber avec quelque espèce de mépris; et prenant un air fort indifférent: 'Vous n'aviez demandé mon cœur que pour le reste du carnaval, lui dit-il, voilà le temps, voilà l'amour expiré;' et tirant de sa poche un sonnet qu'il avait préparé à cet effet, il l'exhorta de lire [. . .]

Pendant qu'elle lisait, il quitta l'assemblée et se retira dans la chambre de la collation. Tout le monde fut surpris de ce procédé, et lui, oubliant tout à fait qu'il eût jamais aimé, se mit à la fenêtre pour la voir sortir, et se plaignit de ce qu'il y avait quelqu'un qui prît la peine de la conduire.

Madmen, like Eraste, not only existed but mixed in society. Richelieu's elder brother sometimes thought he was God, and his sister, the maréchale de Brézé, believed her backside was made of glass and would not sit down for fear of breaking it.[1] Guillaume Menant, *secrétaire du roi*, imagined that he spent two or three months every year in the 'néant'. The president Toré, the son of M. d'Emeri, the surintendant des finances, Tallemant tells us, was in love with an 'épingle jaune', which he had caused to be gilded and to which he 'rendait tous les devoirs qu'on peut rendre à une maîtresse'. The comtesse de Suze fell in love with Jesus, and told Ninon that she knew from personal experience that he was dark. Mlle d'Esche's brother went mad from love and for ten years refused to leave his stable. A priest called Dulot also went crazy from love of a woman called Madeleine Quipel:

Et quand une fois il se fut mis à extravaguer, lorsque la lune était au plein il disait que Mme Quipel était dedans. Cette femme avait un fils; il se mit dans la tête que c'était un prophète et qu'il était son précurseur [. . .]   (Tallemant)

It is, perhaps, scarcely necessary to say that cowards were not

---

[1] If the second Duchesse d'Orléans is to be believed, Richelieu was not exempt from the family failing: 'Quelquefois, il s'imaginait être cheval, sautait autour d'un billard, en ruant et hennissant; cela durait une heure: puis ses gens le couchaient [. . .]'

unknown in the seventeenth century,[1] but liars like Dorante take more believing. Nevertheless, they existed. The duc de Guise was a great teller of tall stories. The marquise d'Exidueil persuaded her husband — a crack-brained, gullible man — that a new kind of horse had been discovered which could transport a man from Lorraine to Paris in a day, and that by this means she was carrying on an affair with Louis XIII — he was then in Lorraine and she in Limousin — as a result of which her husband would supplant Richelieu in the King's favour. Subsequently, she was found one day 'sur un lit, les bras pendants, pâle, défigurée, un chien expirant à ses pieds, une écuelle pleine d'un brouet noir'. She said that her husband had poisoned her; but confessed a fortnight later that it was a fiction.

The most extravagant figure in the comedies is Matamore, but even he — although Corneille himself said later that he had no original amongst mankind — had in fact his counterparts in real life. The marquis d'Assigny, in a manner reminiscent of Matamore, used to despatch gentlemen with messages to Richelieu, 'ou du moins on les voyait partir, afin de faire accroire qu'il avait part aux affaires.' A page of his once said:

> Il faut avouer qu'on apprend bien à vivre chez Monsieur. Que penseriez-vous qu'il fait pour nous aguerrir? Il fait que quelqu'un, comme nous venons de nous mettre à table, vient crier: *Aux armes! les ennemis approchent*. Aussitôt chacun sort avec ses armes, et nous courons quelquefois une demi-lieue, jusqu'à ce qu'on nous vient avertir qu'ils se sont retirés. Deux autres gentilshommes et moi sommes toujours auprès de Monsieur, de peur qu'il ne s'engage trop avant parmi les ennemis; aussi nous tient-il pour les plus vaillants. Après nous retournons dîner.   (Tallemant)

The page spoke with such seriousness that it was impossible to tell whether he believed in these imaginary enemies or not. The président de Chevry, who was always boasting of what he would have done, had he been present on such an occasion, is even more like Matamore:

---

[1] Bussy-Rabutin tells us that after the battle of Bléneau (1652), 'un lieutenant d'un régiment de cavalerie de Mépas s'enfuit des environs de Bléneau jusqu'à Cosne-sur-Loire, où il entra si éperdu qu'il avait encore l'épée nue à la main.' He was stopped and taken to Bussy: 'Il n'était pas encore bien remis de sa peur.'

Cette humeur martiale le prenait quelquefois au milieu d'un compte de finance. Un trésorier de France, de mes amis [. . .] m'a dit qu'un jour, travaillant avec lui, il appela Corbinelli, son premier commis, et lui dit d'un ton sérieux: 'M. Corbinelli, faites ôter ces corps de cette cour.' Ce trésorier fut bien étonné; mais Corbinelli s'approchant lui dit: 'Ce sont de ses visions ordinaires, ne laissez pas de continuer' [. . .]

Un homme lui avait gagné trente pistoles; il ne voulait pas les lui payer. 'Il m'a trompé,' disait-il: et il donne ordre à ses gens de le frotter s'il revenait. Cet homme revient, voilà ses gens après, et lui aussi; mais il partit longtemps après les autres; il trouve Mme Pilou, qui avait vu cet homme se sauver. 'Eh bien!' lui dit-il, 'ma bonne amie, n'avez-vous pas vu comme je l'ai frotté?' Il n'en avait pas approché de cent pas. (Tallemant)

§ 4 *Comedy in the comedies*

If *Mélite* is undeniably a comedy, the same cannot be said of all the others. Until *Le Menteur*, Corneille's comedies — like those of his contemporaries — are not always funny from beginning to end; the tone is often far from comic, and the plays sometimes verge on tragedy. A good deal of *La Veuve* is serious in tone; so is *La Suivante*, which ends with the imprecations of Amarante:

> Vieillard, qui de ta fille achètes une femme
> Dont peut-être aussitôt tu seras mécontent,
> Puisse le ciel, aux soins qui te vont ronger l'âme,
> Dénier le repos du tombeau qui t'attend!
>
> Puisse le noir chagrin de ton humeur jalouse
> Me contraindre moi-même à déplorer ton sort,
> Te faire un long trépas, et cette jeune épouse
> User toute sa vie à souhaiter ta mort!

La Place Royale, which ends with the heroine's retiring into a convent, is again serious in tone, and the soliloquies of Angélique (II, 3, IV, 8) and of Alidor (IV, 1, IV, 5) would not be out of place in a tragedy. The same might be said of the *stances* in *La Veuve* (II, 1), of Florame's soliloquy in *La Suivante* (IV, 8), which is

not unlike the *stances* of Rodrigue in *Le Cid*, of Lysandre's
soliloquies in *La Galerie* (II, 9, V, 1).

Cruelle à moi-même,
Parce que j'aime trop j'ai banni ce que j'aime,   (II, 6)

soliloquizes Daphnis in *La Suivante*. It has often been pointed
out, too, that Matamore's speeches in *L'Illusion* at times resemble
those of Rodrigue or the Count in *Le Cid* in tone.

For Corneille, comedy is largely to be identified with realism.
It differs from tragedy in its characters and plot rather than in its
tone. In the *Epître dédicatoire* of *Don Sanche*, for instance, he
affirms that that play is 'une véritable comédie, [. . .] puisqu'on
n'y voit naître aucun péril par qui nous puissions être portés à la
pitié ou à la crainte'; and in the first *Discours*, he says that the
difference between comedy and tragedy

> ne consiste qu'en la dignité des personnages, et des actions qu'ils
> imitent, et non pas en la façon de les imiter, ni aux choses qui servent
> à cette imitation [. . .]
>   La comédie diffère donc en cela de la tragédie, que celle-ci veut
> pour son sujet une action illustre, extraordinaire, sérieuse; celle-là
> s'arrête à une action commune et enjouée; celle-ci demande de
> grands périls pour ses héros: celle-là se contente de l'inquiétude et
> des déplaisirs de ceux à qui elle donne le premier rang parmi ses
> acteurs.

A comedy, then, for Corneille, is primarily a play dealing with
the middle classes and concerned with accurate observation
rather than with arousing laughter. Nevertheless, some of his
comedies — notably *Mélite*, *La Galerie*, *L'Illusion*, *Le Menteur*
and *La Suite du Menteur* — are amusing; and in all there are
traces of the same comic devices as Molière used later.

The light-hearted tone of the conversation and the badinage
are amusing; so are the exuberant fancy of Matamore and of
Dorante, the glibness of Clindor in *L'Illusion*, and the repartee of
Cliton and Lyse in *La Suite du Menteur*. There are occasional
passages of amusing narrative, too, such as Doris's description of
Florange at the ball or Lyse's account of the way in which she
became engaged to the gaoler (*Illusion*, IV, 2). More specifically

comic devices found in the style — all baroque features, incidentally — are double-entendre (e.g. *Veuve*, II, 5) and its close relative, irony (used in *La Place Royale*, for instance, by Alidor in II, 2, and by Doraste in IV, 7), characters talking at cross-purposes (*Suivante*, III, 7 and IV, 2), and puns:

> Ne vous estimez pas quitte pour la quitter.
>
> (*La Suivante*, V, 6)

Repetition, too, is used sometimes with comic effect:

> *Cloris.* Et pour l'amour de vous je n'en ferai que rire.
> *Mélite.* Et pour l'amour de moi vous lui pardonnerez.
> *Cloris.* Et pour l'amour de moi vous m'en dispenserez.
>
> (*Mélite*, V, 5)

It is particularly common in *Le Menteur*. In Act I, scene 5, Alcippe comically echoes Philiste's words:

> *P.* Quoi? sur l'eau la musique et la collation?
> *A.* Oui, la collation avecque la musique.
> *P.* Hier au soir?
> *A.*　　　　　　Hier au soir.
> *P.*　　　　　　　　　　Et belle?
> *A.*　　　　　　　　　　　　　Magnifique.

Cliton uses repetition to reproach Dorante with his untruthfulness: Dorante, having twice assured him that he would be

> de mon cœur l'unique secrétaire,
> Et de tous mes secrets le grand dépositaire,　　(II, 6)[1]

Cliton, when he finds Dorante lying to him again, slyly remarks:

> Quoi? Monsieur, vous m'en donnez aussi,
> A moi, de votre cœur l'unique secrétaire,
> A moi, de vos secrets le grand dépositaire!　　(IV, 3)

Similarly, Dorante explains that even if one of his lies is detected, it can only turn out to his advantage:

> J'aurai déjà gagné chez elle quelque accès;
> Et loin d'en redouter un malheureux succès,
> Si jamais un fâcheux nous nuit par sa présence,
> Nous pourrons sous ces mots être d'intelligence.　　(I, 6)

---

[1] He repeats the same words in Act IV, scene 1.

When Dorante's lies land him in an awkward situation, Cliton observes:

> Vous en avez sans doute un plus heureux succès,
> Et vous avez gagné chez elle un grand accès;
> Mais je suis ce fâcheux qui nuis par ma présence,
> Et vous fais sous ces mots être d'intelligence.   (III, 6)

Repetition as an effective retort is used by Lucrèce in the same play. The two girls are wrangling, both denying that they feel anything approaching love for Dorante. Why, then, did you listen to his compliments, asks Lucrèce?

> Curiosité pure, avec dessein de rire
> De tous les compliments qu'il aurait pu me dire,

answers Clarice. And that is precisely why I read his letter, says Lucrèce:

> Je fais de ce billet même chose à mon tour;
> Je l'ai pris, je l'ai lu, mais le tout sans amour:
> Curiosité pure, avec dessein de rire
> De tous les compliments qu'il aurait pu m'écrire.   (IV, 9)

There is comedy of situation, too. In *La Veuve* (II, 2–3), Philiste, having bribed the nurse to influence her mistress in his favour, overhears her running him down; he taxes her with this infidelity, and she quickly retorts that this *is* the best way to win her mistress over. Similarly, in *L'Illusion comique*, Matamore overhears Clindor wooing Isabelle on his own behalf instead of for Matamore. In *Le Menteur*, Alcippe appears just as Dorante has described to Cliton how he killed him in a duel. Dorante makes love to Clarice, thinking that she is Lucrèce, and each lady thinks that he is addressing her.

Some of the standard types of comic situation analysed by Bergson are to be found in Corneille. There is the Jack-in-the-Box, for example — the almost mechanical repetition of an action. In *La Suivante*, Daphnis, wishing to have Florame to herself, keeps sending Amarante away on flimsy pretexts, and Amarante keeps coming back just a little too soon. In *La Place Royale*,

Cléandre keeps trying to go and see Angélique, but each time Phylis calls him back until her brother has had time to become engaged to Angélique, when she dismisses him curtly. In *Le Menteur*, Cliton keeps interrupting his master (I, 3), and — in a scene of delicate comedy, not unreminiscent of Musset's *Il faut qu'une porte soit ouverte ou fermée* — Clarice keeps saying 'Mon père va descendre' or denying it, according to whether she wishes to cut short or prolong her interview with Alcippe. The situation of the biter bit is common, too. In *La Veuve*, Alcidon thinks he is deceiving Doris and is himself being taken in by her (II, 5); the nurse is trapped into confessing her own villainy (IV, 6); and Alcidon, who thinks that he is deceiving Célidan, is himself the victim (V, 3 and 9). In *La Suivante*, Théante, who has introduced Florame to Amarante in order that Florame might take Amarante off his hands and free him to woo her mistress, Daphnis, finds that Florame, too, is after Daphnis. In *Le Menteur*, Cliton tells Dorante how just it would be if Lucrèce were to deceive him as he deceives her; in fact, immediately afterwards, she does.

Finally, there is comedy of character in the comedies of Corneille. A good deal of the humour in them springs from the hypocrisy of the characters, from the contrast between words and deeds. In *La Suivante*, there is an amusing contrast between what Florame thinks about Amarante and what he says to her (II, 2–3); and in Act IV, scene 6, Théante persuades Florame to fight a duel, but changes his tune when he finds that he is expected to act as second. In *La Galerie*, Hippolyte and Célidée are discussing their love affairs, when they are interrupted.

> Nous causions de mouchoirs, de rabats, de dentelles,
> De ménages de fille, (IV, 10)

says Hippolyte with ready wit. In *L'Illusion*, Matamore's boasts contrast with his cowardice, which is finally laid bare.

The comedy of character that we find in Molière is not fully developed in Corneille, but it is there in germ. Amarante in *La Suivante* and Alidor in *La Place Royale* are interesting character studies, though scarcely comic characters;[1] but these plays are not comedies of character in the same way as those of Molière. *L'Illusion comique*, with Matamore, comes nearer to the comedy of character, and the two *Menteur* plays, with the inventiveness and glibness of Dorante and the materialism of his valet, come very close to it. In *La Suite du Menteur*, incidentally, the scene in which the gallantry of the master, Dorante, is contrasted with the vulgarity of the servant, Cliton, uses a technique which Molière exploited later.

Corneille's comedies, then, without resembling Molière's, provoking smiles more often than open laughter, nevertheless contain many of the elements out of which Molière was to construct his plays.

Though we have, for the sake of clarity, discussed separately the baroque, realistic, and comic elements of Corneille's plays, it should be emphasized that these are not in fact separate. Many baroque features, such as double-entendre and hypocrisy, lend themselves to comic treatment and can easily become comic. There is, too, an inherent affinity between realism and comedy, presumably because everyday reality is the antithesis of romance and heroism. Glimpses of ordinary people leading ordinary lives often produce a comic effect on the stage or in a film, and in the seventeenth century realism is closely associated with parody of the heroic or idyllic novel.

§ 5 *Evolution*

If the comedies of Corneille have a general family resemblance, each differs from the others and has some original features of its own; and, if one examines them in turn, one can trace a certain evolution.

The first five comedies are social comedies of the type we have studied in *Mélite*, and all deal with lovers prevented by some obstacle from marrying. *La Veuve*, as Corneille points out in the *Examen*, is superior in plot to *Mélite*, though it resembles it

---

[1] Rivaille maintains that they are.

closely:[1] in both plays a poor man is in love with a wealthy woman; in both he has a sister whose lover is his rival; and in both a rival attempts by a trick to prevent him from marrying the lady. An abduction, however, has replaced the false letters of *Mélite*, a step in the direction of greater truth to life, and the improbabilities of *Mélite* have been eliminated. Moreover, the obstacle to the happiness of the lovers is no longer a purely material one: before Alcidon carries off Clarice, Philiste's happiness was delayed by his own diffidence and his reluctance to declare his love. *La Veuve* is further remarkable for the delicately delineated pair of lovers, Philiste and Clarice, and the delightful character of Florange 'qui ne paraît point' — a device used again by Corneille in *La Suivante* (in which Florame's sister, Florise, though often mentioned, never appears), and with great effect in *La Mort de Pompée*.

In *La Galerie du Palais*, Corneille takes a further step in the direction of realism by substituting a *suivante* for the nurse, and by adding the racy scenes set in the Galerie du Palais from which the play takes its name.[2] The plot is similar to those of the previous plays, though this time the situation is reversed: instead of two men making love to one woman, we have here two women who are rivals for the affections of one man. The plot, however, is more natural than in the earlier plays, and for the first time the fifth act, as Corneille notes in the *Examen*, is really essential to the action. For the first time, moreover, the obstacle to the happiness of the lovers is purely psychological: Célidée is not quite sure whether she really wants to marry Lysandre or not and resolves to test his constancy.

La Suivante is Corneille's first regular comedy. It has the same basic plot as the others — with two men in love with one woman,

---

[1] 'Les différences de présentation sont si grandes entre les deux comédies, tandis que leurs sujets sont si proches, qu'il ne serait pas déraisonnable de se demander si Corneille, dans *La Veuve*, n'a pas voulu reprendre sa première œuvre et la corriger, conformément à ses nouvelles préoccupations.' (Rivaille)

[2] Lovers similarly meet in a shop and fall in love in Sorel's *Francion*. — In Act IV, there is a reminiscence of the pastoral, however. Aronte shows Lysandre, Célidée and Dorimant conversing together, to make him believe that Célidée is in love with Dorimant. This device is found in the pastorals, e.g. Mairet's *Sylvie*.

and two women in love with one man into the bargain — but is distinguished from the others by the hypocrisy and misunderstandings which form its theme, by the central character, the *suivante* Amarante, and by its ending, which comes close to tragedy.

La Place Royale is the *Galerie* in reverse: instead of a woman hesitating to marry her lover, we have a lover hesitating to marry his mistress. The main interest in this play, a psychological one, is in the character of the hero, Alidor, in the conflict between his desire for freedom and his love for Angélique, and in the underlying theme that inconstancy is a more practical philosophy than fidelity. The sufferings of Angélique remind one a little of those of Rosine in Musset's *On ne badine pas avec l'amour* — which might well be the title of this play. Once again the ending is close to tragedy.

With *L'Illusion comique* there comes a change. Hitherto the plot has centred round two lovers crossed in love, but the main interest of this play is elsewhere. Its two stock characters, the magician and the boasting soldier, make it something of a throw back to an earlier kind of play, and Matamore's boasting speeches develop, but with amazing virtuosity, the vein of fancy that we find in the mad scenes of *Mélite*. Nevertheless, with its mixture of tones and genres, of burlesque and heroic, of comedy and tragedy, of realism and fancy, with the extraordinary variety of styles and the skilful construction reaching its climax in the carefully prepared eulogy of the theatre at the end, *L'Illusion* is a highly original work, 'une fantaisie shakespearienne,' as Faguet calls it, unique amongst Corneille's plays and in French literature. Finally, in the two *Menteur* plays, Corneille adapts Spanish plays and moves in the direction of character comedy.

Very varied, often witty and amusing, containing many touches of delicate psychology and some well-observed and original characters, full of realism of various kinds and yet with a strong vein of fancy and imagination, Corneille's comedies deserve to be far more widely known — repay reading and rereading, indeed, far more than many better known French comedies.

Chapter Five

THE TRAGEDIES FROM *CLITANDRE* TO *PERTHARITE*

Corneille's tragedies[1] oscillate between two tendencies — on the one hand, a romantic love of adventure and gallantry, and, (on the other, a love of realism, of historical and political subjects.) These two tendencies are not incompatible and are often found together, though in varying proportions. They co-exist, indeed, already in the comedies, which have plots akin to those of the pastoral taking place in a realistic setting.

Immediately after Corneille's first play, *Mélite*, he wrote a tragi-comedy, *Clitandre*, which, with its complex plot — Corneille himself says that it needs to be seen twice to be understood — and its multiplicity of incidents, is an example of the romantic, rather than the realistic, tendency. It shows an ambush, fights, masked assassins, a woman disguised as a man, attempted murder and rape, the ravisher's eye being put out by the intended victim with a hairpin, and a storm. It is not without interest, and there is a pleasing love scene (V, 3) and some attractive descriptions of nature (I, 1, IV, 2–3). The play does not obey the unities and, as Corneille points out in the *Examen*, suffers from the same defect as *Mélite*, the fifth act lacking action.

[1] For the sake of brevity, the word 'tragedies' is used to cover tragi-comedies, *comédies héroïques*, and machine plays, as well as tragedies. For want of an exact equivalent to the French word *romanesque*, the adjective 'romantic' has been used.

Clitandre was followed by four more comedies, a tragedy (*Médée*), another comedy (*L'Illusion comique*), and a second tragi-comedy (*Le Cid*). *La Place Royale*, perhaps the least comic of Corneille's comedies, is sometimes regarded as an indication that Corneille was beginning to turn naturally to tragedy — just as many critics have seen Matamore's speeches in *L'Illusion* as a first essay in the heroic style, a kind of parody of *Le Cid* before it was written. But all this is hypothetical, and it is likely that Corneille was merely following the trend of the times — that he turned to tragedy because the success of Mairet's *Sophonisbe* (1634) had infused new life into the genre.

Corneille's first tragedy, *Médée*, is an adaptation of Seneca's *Medea*. Corneille himself tells us that in turning to a new genre, he had not the courage to trust to his own unaided powers: 'pour m'élever à la dignité du tragique, je pris l'appui du grand Sénèque [. . .]'[1] Corneille imitates some of the scenes of his model and follows the Latin text closely in them; but the changes he makes in adapting the ancient play to seventeenth-century taste are interesting for what they reveal of his conception of tragedy at this early stage of his career. They serve three purposes. Some are clearly dictated by the need to expand the original into a five-act play. Corneille, for example, unlike Seneca, makes Créuse appear on the stage; he introduces the confidants, Pollux and Cléone; and, more important, by giving Jason a rival for the hand of Créuse in the person of Ægée, he adds a subplot.

Another group of changes serves to adapt the play to seventeenth-century ideas. In the interests of *vraisemblance*, Corneille removes some of the improbabilities of Seneca's play — in particular, the imprudence of Créon and Créuse in accepting Médée's gift of the dress which consumes them. In Corneille's play, Créuse asks Jason to obtain Médée's dress, which she admires, for her in exchange for a good turn she has done Médée, instead of merely accepting it as a gift; and Créon, suspicious of any gift from Médée, makes a female prisoner try it on first. The dénouement is thus better motivated. Further, Médée's nurse

---

[1] *Epître* prefixed to *Le Menteur*.

becomes a *suivante*, and Médée performs her enchantments in her private room instead of in the public square. In the interests of *bienséance*, we are not shown Médée killing her children, though Créon and Créuse come on to the stage to die.

A third group of changes is even more interesting. Corneille decreases the amount of rhetoric and heightens the dramatic interest of his play. He alters the characters of the protagonists, and makes Médée more resolute and strong-willed, and Jason more fickle than in Seneca, in whose play there are no allusions to Jason's previous desertion of Hypsipyle. Moreover, Corneille introduces an element of suspense and something of that alternation of hopes and fears which is characteristic of him. In Act IV, scene 3, for instance, there is some prospect of a happy ending, when Créon thinks that all is well and that Médée is appeased and decides that another woman shall try on the dress before his daughter wears it. In other words, although the content of *Médée* is unoriginal, Corneille's play already has the form and technique of Corneille's later plays.

Le Cid is, of course, a land-mark, both in Corneille's career and in the history of the seventeenth-century French theatre. It is usually regarded as the first great tragedy of the period, though in fact it is a tragi-comedy and was not called a tragedy until 1648.[1] It set the pattern for subsequent drama by its combination of regularity with a concentrated dramatic action following logically from the initial situation,[2] the interest of which lies mainly in the psychological conflict in the minds of the main characters. In this play, Corneille finds himself. He has again adapted a model — Guilhem de Castro's *Las Mocedades del Cid* — but he has handled it with freedom and mastery, and his adaptation is an original creation.

Le Cid represents a successful fusion of the two tendencies mentioned above, the realistic and the romantic, and perhaps owes its particular appeal precisely to that fusion. On the one hand, it is a stirring, exciting play of love and heroism, set in

[1] But the distinction was not hard and fast.
[2] Except that the Moorish attack is fortuitous.

medieval Spain and dealing with a legendary, rather than a historical, subject. Moreover, the subject of the play is love, the fortunes of a pair of young lovers on whom love and family obligations make incompatible demands; the conclusion of the play is the triumph not of duty but of love;[1] and the play expresses the courtly ideal:

> L'infamie est pareille, et suit également
> Le guerrier sans courage et le perfide amant.   (III, 6)

On the other hand, there is a great deal of realism of various kinds. There is psychological realism: the main interest of the play lies in the realistically portrayed conflict in the minds of the characters. Moreover, the political problem in the play is a central problem of Corneille's own age — the problem of order and disorder, of the conflict between the authority of the monarch and the independence and lawlessness of a feudal aristocracy. Finally, Corneille displays one of his most remarkable qualities, mastery of dialogue. *Le Cid* is full of excellent discussions: the characters are good debaters, quick-witted, and the rapidity of their thrust and parry in argument, their ability to find solid reasons to support their arguments, make their discussions very stimulating and satisfying intellectually, while at the same time Rodrigue and Chimène give moving expression to their dilemma and reach emotional heights which Corneille had not achieved before.

Le Cid gave rise to a prolonged controversy. The play, briefly, was criticized for falling short of the classical ideal in a number of ways: not only were there changes of scene, but these were not always clearly marked; the Infante was an episodic character, inessential to the action; the multiplicity of events strained the unity of time; and Chimène was considered to have acted improperly in receiving Rodrigue and in agreeing to marry him. The result of these criticisms, which were endorsed by the Academy, was to cause Corneille to reflect on the principles of his

---

[1] Corneille's later disclaimer in the *Discours* is not to be taken too seriously: 'Dans le *Cid* même, qui est sans contredit la pièce la plus remplie d'amour que j'aie faite, le devoir de la naissance et le soin de l'honneur l'emportent sur toutes les tendresses qu'il inspire aux amants que j'y fais parler.'

art and to be more scrupulous henceforth in conforming to them
— though, as the *Discours* show, he was never servile to Aristotle. The *Querelle du Cid* seems also to have discouraged him:
Corneille, wrote Chapelain to Balzac on January 15, 1639,

> est ici depuis deux jours [. . .] Il ne fait plus rien, et Scudéry a du
> moins gagné cela, en le querellant, qu'il l'a rebuté du métier, et lui a
> tari sa veine. Je l'ai autant que j'ai pu, réchauffé et encouragé à se
> venger, et de Scudéry et de sa protectrice, en faisant quelque nou-
> veau *Cid* qui attire encore les suffrages de tout le monde, et qui
> montre que l'art n'est pas ce qui fait la beauté; mais il n'y a pas
> moyen de l'y résoudre; et il ne parle plus que de règles et que des
> choses qu'il eût pu répondre aux académiciens, s'il n'eût point craint
> de choquer les puissances, mettant au reste Aristote entre les auteurs
> apocryphes lorsqu'il ne s'accommode pas à ses imaginations.

Moreover, an unusually long interval elapsed between the first
performance of *Le Cid* and that of Corneille's next play, *Horace*.[1]
It may also be that the quarrel decided Corneille to turn to tragedy,
the genre in which his two main adversaries, Mairet and Scudéry,
had made their reputation.

Be that as it may, *Horace* breaks new ground in a number of
ways. It is a tragedy, like *Médée*, not a tragi-comedy, like
Clitandre and *Le Cid*; and it treats a subject taken from Roman
history — a source on which Corneille here drew for the first
time,[2] but which was to be his chief source henceforth. It obeys
the rules more strictly than *Médée* and *Le Cid* — the action takes
place easily in a day, and the scene is a single room — though the
unity of action is, perhaps, not strictly observed, since the murder
of Camille and the trial of Horace for it to some extent represent a
separate action. It is also a highly dramatic play, in which suspense
is skilfully maintained and hopes and fears alternate throughout.

Corneille has, in fact, introduced into tragedy the technique of
tragi-comedy: there are signs of this development already in

[1] Since Corneille was already working on his new play in 1637, the delay may be in part
due to other causes. The diminution of income caused by the appointment of a second
holder of his legal office in 1638 must have been disturbing and involved him in an attempt
to get the new appointment quashed; his father died in 1639; and there was a rising in
Normandy the same year, which affected Rouen.

[2] Possibly with the aim of outdoing Scudéry and Mairet, his critics in the *Querelle du Cid*,
both of whom had written plays on Roman subjects.

Médée, but it is complete in *Horace*. It is interesting to see that for Scudéry the difference between tragedy and tragi-comedy is precisely that the latter gives rise to suspense:

> La tragédie composée selon les règles de l'art, ne doit avoir qu'une action principale [. . .]; et l'argument en devant être tiré de l'histoire ou des fables connues selon les préceptes qu'on nous a laissés, *on n'a pas dessein de surprendre le spectateur*, puisqu'il sait déjà ce qu'on doit représenter: mais il n'en va pas ainsi de la tragi-comédie; car bien qu'elle n'ait presque pas été connue de l'antiquité, néanmoins puisqu'elle est comme un composé de la tragédie et de la comédie, et qu'à cause de sa fin elle semble même pencher plus vers la dernière, il faut que le premier acte dans cette espèce de poème, embrouille *une intrigue qui tienne toujours l'esprit en suspens*, et qui ne se démêle qu'à la fin de tout l'ouvrage.

Another indication of the fusion of the two genres is that *Horace*, as Herland has pointed out, is the first tragedy to contain a pair of young lovers and a rival, a situation common enough in tragi-comedy and the pastoral, as well as in Corneille's own comedies.

There are few signs of the romantic side of Corneille in this play, which discusses two problems, both previously found in *Le Cid* — the conflict between the demands of the state and personal loyalties, between love and patriotism; and the conflict between the lawlessness of the individual and the authority of the state. The play is a study in patriotism: each character has a slightly different attitude to the first of the two problems, from the unquestioning devotion to the state of Horace, through his father, Sabine and Curiace (in all three of whom the claims of the state conflict in differing degrees with those of humanity), to the revolt of Camille. Camille provides the link between the two problems, for her attitude offends her brother, Horace, who — like the count who slaps Don Diègue and Rodrigue who challenges the count to a duel, in *Le Cid* — takes the law into his own hands and kills her.

Cinna, which follows *Horace*, is the first completely regular tragedy of Corneille. It observes the unities strictly — and not merely the unities of time and place, narrowly interpreted, but the unity of action, strictly observed for the first time. It is, too, the first tragedy in which a sovereign is a central figure, and the first political play of Corneille. Both *Le Cid* and *Horace* deal with a political problem, but it is overshadowed by the moral problem. *Cinna* is essentially a political play dealing with three separate questions. First, it is a study in conspiracy — which is, after all, a form of the problem of *Le Cid* and *Horace*: the conflict between the right of the individual to private vengeance and the authority of the state. Only here, the desire for vengeance is directed against the head of the state, and what is stressed is the selfishness of the motives of the conspirators. Second, the question of the best form of government, monarchy or republic, is debated at length in Act II. The third problem is one discussed by Machiavelli in the *Prince*: when the prince has seized power, how should he consolidate his position? By conciliating his subjects rather than by oppression, is Corneille's answer. Auguste has already tried the other policy, that of exterminating his enemies, but it has failed, and he is still surrounded by enemies. At the end of the play, however, he wins over Cinna and Emilie by his clemency.

Polyeucte again breaks new ground, by treating the subject of martyrdom and religion. On the other hand, though *Le Cid*, *Horace*, *Cinna* and *Polyeucte* are all in some way original, there is a certain continuity, a certain progression from one to the other, that has often been pointed out. *Le Cid* depicts the conflict between the emotions of the individual and family loyalties; *Horace* the conflict between love or family ties and patriotism; *Cinna* the victory of humanity over *raison d'état*. *Polyeucte* continues the progression by depicting the conflict between human love and the love of God.

Polyeucte, often regarded as Corneille's masterpiece, is certainly one of his greatest achievements. It shows the progress of the newly wedded and newly converted Polyeucte from baptism to martyrdom and the struggle in him between his love for his wife and his religion. It contains a number of finely drawn and skilfully contrasted characters, representing different attitudes to religion (as those of *Horace* represent different attitudes to the demands of the state) — the fervent neophyte, Polyeucte; the Christian,

Néarque, whose fervour has waned; the prejudiced pagan, Stratonice; the enlightened, sceptical pagan, Sévère; the two pagans miraculously converted, Pauline and Félix; — representing, too, different levels of humanity — the sublimity of the martyr; the nobility of Pauline and Sévère; the mixture of self-interest, short-sightedness and affection of Félix. There is, too, the intensely human and poignant situation of Pauline, torn between her love for her former suitor, Sévère, and her loyalty to the husband she has accepted in obedience to her father. And the action takes place against a magnificently suggested historical background — the old age giving place to the new — the pagan Empire gradually becoming permeated with the new religion of Christianity. All these strands, skilfully woven together, make *Polyeucte* a great play.

*   *   *

La Mort de Pompée is very different again. Like *Cinna*, it is a political play, and expresses Corneille's attitude to a problem treated by Machiavelli. Here, the theme — a fundamental question of perennial interest — is that of the maxims of conduct which government should adopt, whether it should follow a realistic policy of self-interest at the expense of gratitude and loyalty, or whether its guiding principles should be the same as those of the individual — honour, generosity, and uprightness.[1] Not only is the play like *Cinna* in being political and anti-Machiavellian, it resembles *Cinna*, too, in dealing, as most of Corneille's plays do henceforth, with characters of royal rank and the struggle for power and in treating a Roman subject. It is, indeed, largely a glorification of Rome, full of the poetry of the Roman character as Corneille conceived it, and has been called 'le plus magnifique tableau de politique et d'histoire qui soit sorti de la main de Corneille.'[2]

On the other hand, *Pompée* is in many ways unlike its predecessors. Unlike them, it shows no conflict *within* the characters.

---

[1] This problem had already been touched upon in *Polyeucte*, in the person of Félix.
[2] Dorchain.

Such conflicts become rarer after *Polyeucte*, and the interest of the next group of plays tends to be centred more in the relations between the characters and in their intrigues. It has been pointed out, too, that in some respects *Pompée* is a return to the tragedy of Corneille's predecessors, in that it contains no young lovers crossed in love, glorifies Roman virtue, deals with the death of a great hero, and gives a good deal of space to the lamentations of Pompée's widow. It has, indeed, been called Corneille's least Cornelian play.[1] The romantic element creeps in, in the love of César and Cléopâtre:[2]

> chaque jour ses couriers [says Cléopâtre]
> M'apportent en tribut ses vœux et ses lauriers.
> Partout, en Italie, aux Gaules, en Espagne,
> La fortune le suit, et l'amour l'accompagne.
> Son bras ne dompte point de peuples ni de lieux
> Dont il ne rende hommage au pouvoir de mes yeux;
> Et de la même main dont il quitte l'épée,
> Fumante encore du sang des amis de Pompée,
> Il trace des soupirs, et d'un style plaintif
> Dans son champ de victoire il se dit mon captif.   (II, 1)

In one respect, too, *Pompée* harks back to Corneille's comedies: like Florange in *La Veuve*, Pompée, though an important character in the play, does not appear at all.

Pompée is a magnificent play, with some admirable scenes — the council scene (I, 1) and the narratives of the death of Pompée and the arrival of César (II, 2, III, 1), for instance. The splendid narrations give the play something of an epic grandeur, and Corneille is justly proud of the splendour of his verse: 'Pour le style, il est plus élevé en ce poème qu'en aucun des miens, et ce sont, sans contredit, les vers les plus pompeux que j'aie faits.'

---

[1] L. Herland, 'Les éléments précornéliens dans "La Mort de Pompée" de Corneille', in *Revue d'Histoire Littéraire*, 1950.

[2] But Professor R. C. Knight points out that in practice his love does not affect his actions — he is unwilling to renounce further conquests in order to remain with Cléopâtre, and loath to forgive at her request ('Andromaque et l'ironie de Corneille', in *Actes du Premier Congrès Racinien*, 1962). Corneille's Caesar, incidentally, resembles Montaigne's. Montaigne describes him as amorous, but as subordinating love to ambition. 'Ses plaisirs ne lui firent jamais dérober une seule minute d'heure, ni détourner un pas des occasions qui se présentaient pour son agrandissement.'   (*Essais*, Book II, Chapter 33.)

After *La Mort de Pompée*, Corneille wrote two comedies, *Le Menteur* and *La Suite du Menteur*, and then returned to tragedy with *Rodogune*, his own favourite amongst his plays:

> Cette préférence est peut-être en moi un effet de ces inclinations aveugles qu'ont beaucoup de pères pour quelques-uns de leurs enfants plus que pour les autres; peut-être y entre-t-il un peu d'amour-propre, en ce que cette tragédie me semble être un peu plus à moi que celles qui l'ont précédée, à cause des incidents surprenants qui sont purement de mon invention, et n'avaient jamais été vus au théâtre; et peut-être enfin y a-t-il un peu de vrai mérite qui fait que cette inclination n'est pas tout à fait injuste [. . .]   (*Examen*)

Corneille's opinion is fully justified: *Rodogune* is a fine play and superbly constructed.[1] It is also very different from its predecessors. Whereas there had been little that was romantic in the plays from *Horace* to *Pompée*, *Rodogune* marks a return to that vein, or rather consists of a fusion of realism with a new kind of romantic interest. Realism is there in plenty, in the psychological insight, in the delicately delineated and admirably differentiated pair of brothers and the contrast between them and the two women for whom they feel affection, Rodogune and their mother, the wily, unscrupulous, ambitious, resolute Cléopâtre, who is a continuation of Médée. There is a political interest, too: *Rodogune* treats the same problem as *Pompée*. The immoral realism of Cléopâtre is contrasted with the uprightness of her sons and of Rodogune; and Cléopâtre, for all her shrewdness, never really understands the situation, because — like Félix in *Polyeucte* and Ptolomée and his advisers in *Pompée* — she never appreciates the different values and outlook of her adversaries. The basic situation, too, is an essentially human one, though found here in an extreme form: it is that of any son torn between his love for a woman of whom his mother disapproves and his loyalty to his mother. But at the same time there is a strong romantic element: we find it in the great liberties which Corneille takes with the historical facts; we find it in the intensely dramatic plot, in the extraordinary situation, and in the mysteries of the play — which is the elder of the two

---

[1] See below, chapter XI.

brothers and the rightful heir? who killed Séleucus? will Antiochus drink the poison which Cléopâtre has prepared for him or not? But we must not make too much of this last point. Given the situation and the characters, the action follows logically and inevitably; psychology is nowhere distorted; and the mysteries are not really important. As Tanquerey points out, the question which of the two brothers is the true heir is of so little importance that it is never answered, and the identity of the murderer of Séleucus is unknown to Antiochus but not to the audience. *Rodogune*, in fact, strikes a happy balance between the two tendencies. With its essential humanity, its psychological and political realism, and its intensely dramatic interest, it is certainly one of the peaks of Corneille's production.

Théodore, Corneille's next tragedy, is a return to the theme of martyrdom treated in *Polyeucte*. Though the play failed, it is, despite the general opinion of critics, an excellent play. The abbé d'Aubignac, in his *Pratique du Théâtre*, called it Corneille's masterpiece:

> C'est une pièce dont la constitution est très ingénieuse, où l'intrigue est bien conduite et bien variée, où ce que l'histoire donne, est fort bien manié, où les changements sont fort judicieux, où les mouvements et les vers sont dignes du nom de l'auteur.

And Jules Lemaitre wrote of it: 'Telle qu'elle est, je la trouve des plus intéressantes et, sinon égale au *Cid* et à *Polyeucte*, du moins supérieure à *Horace* et à *Cinna*.' Corneille, on the other hand, has little to say in defence of his play; but he is in a dilemma, as he points out:

> J'aurais tort de m'opposer au jugement du public: il m'a été trop avantageux en mes autres ouvrages pour le désavouer en celui-ci; et si je l'accusais d'erreur ou d'injustice pour *Théodore*, mon exemple donnerait lieu à tout le monde de soupçonner des mêmes choses tous les arrêts qu'il a prononcés en ma faveur.

Le Cid having been upheld by the public, despite the strictures of Scudéry and the Academy, Corneille cannot now impugn public taste, whose verdict on *Le Cid* he had accepted. It is, however, clear that he regards the judgment of the public on *Théodore* as unjust. In the *Epître dédicatoire*, he attributes the failure of the play to the prudery of the public, shocked by the references to a brothel; and, since d'Aubignac gives the same explanation, he is probably right. In the *Examen*, written long afterwards, he gives an additional reason, the weakness of the character of Théodore: 'une vierge et martyre sur un théâtre n'est autre chose qu'un Terme qui n'a ni jambes ni bras, et par conséquent point d'action.' But however true this may be, it does not seem to explain adequately the failure of the play, which, as Corneille mentions in the *Examen* to the *Suite du Menteur*, was successfully performed in the provinces. In any case, Théodore — unlike Polyeucte — is not an important figure in the play: she appears in only three acts, and even in one of those her appearance is brief.

The subject of the play, in fact, is not so much Théodore as the dramatic duel between Placide and his stepmother, Marcelle. Placide, the son of Valens, governor of Syria, loves Théodore; his stepmother, Marcelle, wants him to marry her own daughter, Flavie, who is dying of jealousy. Here Corneille is harking back to a theme of his early comedies, the wickedness of arranged marriages. He stresses the point in the *Examen*, where he criticizes

> l'opiniâtreté à faire des mariages par force, et à ne se point départir du projet qu'on en fait par un accommodement de famille entre des enfants dont les volontés ne s'y conforment point quand ils sont venus en âge de l'exécuter.

The stages of the duel are these. In an excellent scene, full of irony, Marcelle — since Placide loves Théodore and scorns Flavie — swears to have Théodore put to death, and Placide swears to have his revenge if she does. In Act II, Marcelle interviews Théodore and provokes her to an avowal of her Christianity. This scene (II, 4), incidentally, is the first example in a serious play of a kind of scene at which Corneille excels — that in which two women who hate each other are outwardly polite, their antagonism expressing itself through irony, until the mask falls and the hostility becomes overt. The well-meaning, weak-minded Valens, Placide's father and Marcelle's husband, decides that, instead of being put

to death, Théodore shall be punished for her religion by being sent
to a brothel. He believes that he is thus serving both the interests
of his son and those of his wife. Théodore, he thinks, will recoil
from such a fate; whereas, if she were put to death, he tells Marcelle, Placide would wreak vengeance on her:

> Chaque jour à ses yeux cette ombre ensanglantée,
> Sortant des tristes nuits où vous l'aurez jetée,
> Vous peindra toutes deux avec des traits d'horreur
> Qui feront de sa haine une aveugle fureur.   (II, 6)

Placide, in Act III, tries to persuade Théodore to marry him and
flee with him to Egypt, of which he has been made governor, and
on her refusal he pleads with Marcelle to spare Théodore.[1] Marcelle promises to help, on condition that Placide will visit Flavie.

In Act IV, which Corneille justly praises in his *Examen*,
Placide finds that Marcelle has tricked him. She has taken advantage of his visit to Flavie to accelerate Théodore's punishment: Théodore has been sent to a brothel. She is, however,
rescued by another suitor of hers, Didyme, a fellow-Christian,
who visits her in the brothel and changes clothes with her (this
episode is finely narrated). In Act V, Didyme is arrested; and
Placide, who now identifies his interests with those of Didyme,
tries to save him:

> Piqué contre Marcelle, il cherche à la braver,
> Et hasardera tout afin de le sauver.   (V, 1)

Didyme — like Polyeucte — expresses the wish that Théodore
will marry his rival. Flavie dies at this point, and Théodore, believing herself safe, not from death but from infamy, gives herself
up in order to try to save her rescuer. Valens stands by idly,
watching the duel between his son and his wife, who is determined to kill Théodore and avenge her daughter's death:

> laissons faire et Marcelle et Placide:
> Que l'amour en furie ou la haine en décide;
> Que Théodore en meure ou ne périsse pas,
> J'aurai lieu d'excuser sa vie ou son trépas,   (V, 7)

[1] This act is reminiscent in its structure of Act IV of *Rodogune*, in which Antiochus tries
to avert tragedy by appealing in turn to Rodogune and to Cléopâtre.

he says. His inaction has the outcome it deserves. Marcelle kills
Théodore and Didyme with her own hand, making it clear that
this is part of the struggle between herself and Placide:

> 'Viens, dit-elle, viens voir l'effet de son secours.'

She then stabs herself:

> 'Je n'ai pas résolu de mourir à ton choix,
> Dit-elle, ni d'attendre à rejoindre Flavie
> Que ta rage insolente ordonne de ma vie.'   (V, 8)

Placide commits suicide.

The characterization of the play is excellent — particularly
that of Marcelle, whose unscrupulousness and cruelty spring from
her love for her daughter — 'la maladie de Flavie, sa mort, et les
violences des désespoirs de sa mère qui la venge, ont assez de
justesse,' says Corneille — and that of the irresolute, scheming,
over-optimistic Valens, who in his attempts to be subtle is constantly overreaching himself. If the play has a weakness, it is that
pointed out by Corneille, with his usual perspicacity, in the
Examen: that, in a sense, the play could have ended with Théodore's escape, and that consequently the fifth act, like that of
Horace, might be considered superfluous: 'je ne sais s'il n'y a point
une duplicité d'action, en ce que Théodore, échappée d'un péril,
se rejette dans un autre de son propre mouvement.' But the return
of Théodore is well-motivated — as, indeed, is the whole action
of the play: the provocation of Théodore into declaring her
religion, Valens's suggestion of the form her punishment should
take, and Théodore's refusal of possible ways out (in any case, as
she says, Marcelle's vigilance would prevent any escape). *Théodore*, despite its failure in the seventeenth century, is one of the
best, not one of the worst, of Corneille's plays.

*   *   *

The next three plays, *Héraclius*, *Andromède* and *Don Sanche*,
are in the romantic vein and continue, in different ways, the trend
seen in *Rodogune*.

Théodore, an excellent play, failed; *Héraclius*, though it succeeded, is one of the least interesting of Corneille's tragedies. The romantic element is here excessive: the mystery of the identity of the two heroes — reminiscent of *The Gondoliers* — is here the centre of the plot, as it is not in *Rodogune*; and the letters from the tomb which solve it at the end strain credulity. *Héraclius*, with *Agésilas*, is the least historical of all Corneille's historical plays: it is, in fact, as Corneille says, 'une pièce d'invention sous des noms véritables.' Practically nothing in it is historical except the names of the characters. But its chief defect is not so much that it is romantic, as that it lacks humanity. Whereas *Rodogune* combines humanity with an interesting plot, *Héraclius* does not. Except that Phocas, the tyrant, who, like Auguste, is disillusioned with the throne he has won, becomes a moving figure when faced with the reluctance of the two young men to admit kinship with him, the characters are cast in too uniformly heroic a mould. Pulchérie is an Emilie without weakness; and neither Léontine, nor Martian, nor Héraclius, betray any human feeling. On the other hand, though the situation is romantic, it is treated in a realistic way. The theme — a political one, not dissimilar to that of Racine's *Athalie* — is the fall of a tyrant and a usurper, brought about by a plot on the part of the supporters of his predecessor; and the discussion about the right moment for the legitimate heir to reveal his identity (II, 2), and the study of the method by which the revolution is successfully accomplished, show Corneille's usual grasp of political realities.

Corneille's next play, *Andromède*, commissioned by Mazarin and performed in 1649 or 1650 with music by D'Assoucy and machines by Torelli, is a machine play. The subject is taken from Greek mythology, and there is plenty of the supernatural and of spectacle. We are here far from classicism. Each act is set in a different place. We see the gods and goddesses descending from the heavens, Nereids arising from the waves, and Neptune in his chariot on the sea; we see Persée slaying the monster which is about to devour Andromède chained to a rock; and the play ends with the spectacle of Cephée and Cassiope, Persée and Andromède,

I

being carried up into the heavens to become immortal. There is an opportunity for Corneille to make use of that rich vein of fancy so evident in some of his comedies. But the Greek world is adapted to seventeenth-century France and becomes both gallant and *précieux*. In two delightful scenes, Phinée's page serenades Andromède and one of Andromède's nymphs replies; Persée can turn a graceful compliment and explain to Cassiope that the punishment inflicted on her by the gods is just — they are punishing her, not for boasting of her daughter's beauty, but for marrying her to a mere mortal; and Andromède quizzes her nymphs on the subject of Persée. Moreover, much of the play is concerned with the contrast between the perfect lover, Persée, and the bad lover, Phinée. Persée is gallant, devoted, submissive, and does not wish to use any kind of pressure to win Andromède's love; he tells her to disregard the wishes both of her parents and of the gods:

> Ils vous donnent à moi, je vous rends à vous-même;
> Et comme enfin c'est vous, et non pas moi, que j'aime,
> J'aime mieux m'exposer à perdre un bien si doux,
> Que de vous obtenir d'un autre que vous.   (IV, 1)

He tells her, too, to disregard what he has done for her:

> L'excès de vos bontés pourrait en ma présence
> Faire à vos sentiments un peu de violence:
> Ce bras vainqueur du monstre, et qui vous rend le jour,
> Pourrait en ma faveur séduire votre amour;
> La pitié de vos maux pourrait même surprendre
> Ce cœur trop généreux pour s'en vouloir défendre;
> Et le moyen qu'un cœur ou séduit ou surpris
> Fût juste en ses faveurs, ou juste en ses mépris?
>   De tout ce que j'ai fait ne voyez que ma flamme;
> De tout ce qu'on vous dit ne croyez que votre âme;
> Ne me répondez point, et consultez-la bien;
> Faites votre bonheur sans aucun soin du mien:
> . . . .
> Je mourrai trop content si vous vivez contente.   (IV, 1)

In contrast, Phinée not only does not save Andromède, but does

not even commit suicide because of his inability to help her.
Moreover, he is prepared to win her by force:

> La force me rendra ce que ne peut l'amour.   (IV, 4)

With the splendour and magnificence of its setting, with the
metamorphoses, the fancy and the supernatural element, with the
variety of its verse, *Andromède* is a delightful play, full of grace
and charm, and an expression of a whole aspect of the seventeenth
century which we have not seen in previous tragedies.

In *Don Sanche*, which is in no way historical, Corneille returns
to Spain and recaptures something of the atmosphere of *Le Cid*.
The play is almost purely romantic: the hero is an adventurer
whose origins are mysterious — like Hugo's *Hernani*; and indeed
this is not the only resemblance between *Don Sanche* and Hugo's
play. The scene in which the Queen ennobles Don Sanche —

> Hé bien! seyez-vous donc, marquis de Santillane,
> Comte de Pennafiel, gouverneur de Burgos,   (I, 3)

— reminds one of *Hernani*:

> Allons! relevez-vous, duchesse de Segorbe,
> Comtesse Albatera, marquise de Monroy . . .

Carlos, the adventurer, is loved by the Queen, who, having to
choose a husband, commits the choice to him. The play has also
much in common with *Héraclius*: in both, the birth of the hero is
surrounded by mystery; in both, the rightful heir to the throne,
believed dead, is rumoured to be alive, though his identity is
unknown; in both, there is a suggestion of incest, in that a
character is in love with a girl whom he later finds to be his sister;
in both, the *voix du sang* occurs; in both, the identity of the hero
is revealed by letters written by his dead parents; and finally, in
both, we find the idea that personal qualities betray rank, that
merit is evidence of noble birth.[1] *Don Sanche* is not a tragedy:
Corneille coined for it the term *comédie héroïque*, which he employed again later to designate *Tite et Bérénice* and *Pulchérie*. By
comédie héroïque he means, as he says in the first *Discours*, a play

---

[1] This idea recurs in *Othon*, II, 2. It is also seen in Rotrou's *Saint Genest* (I, 3).

in which the characters are of royal rank, but in which they are in
no danger of losing their lives or of being banished. Another
original feature is that this play is the first of Corneille's matrimonial plays: it deals with a Queen torn between love of a subject
and the obligation of marrying in the interests of her country, and
closely resembles *Pulchérie* in situation. *Don Sanche* is an excellent, stirring, exciting play, full of love and jealousy, though the
shift of interest from the question of the Queen's marriage
(Acts I–III) to that of the identity of Don Sanche (Acts IV–V)
has been criticized; and Corneille, in his *Examen*, justly praises
the 'délicatesse des sentiments' of the second act.

With *Nicomède*, Corneille abandons romance[1] and turns to
reality, to Roman history and the study of political relationships,
in a simple play with little action. The interest here is not in the
conflict within the minds of the characters, but in the relationships between them and in the study of Roman policy:

> Mon principal but a été de peindre la politique des Romains au
> dehors, et comme ils agissaient impérieusement avec les rois leurs
> alliés; leurs maximes pour les empêcher de s'accroître, et les soins
> qu'ils prenaient de traverser leur grandeur, quand elle commençait à
> leur devenir suspecte à force de s'augmenter et de se rendre con-
> sidérable par de nouvelles conquêtes.

Roman policy, embodied in the person of the Roman ambassador,
Flaminius, is portrayed in masterly fashion. So, too, is the situation in the court of Prusias, whose second wife, Arsinoé, is
intriguing, with the help of Flaminius, to place her son, Attale,
who has been brought up in Rome, on the throne, to the detriment
of the rightful heir, Nicomède, the disciple of Hannibal and the
enemy of Rome. Two further points of interest are the very strong
vein of comedy in the play (to which we shall return later), and
the new conception of tragedy with which Corneille is here
experimenting. Corneille, never servile to Aristotle, is here trying
to purge the passions, not by pity and terror, but by admiration:

---

[1] The episode in which Attale, after rescuing Nicomède, gives him a diamond so that he
shall know his rescuer again, is conventional and romantic. In Hardy's *Cornélie* and
Rotrou's *Bélisaire*, both tragi-comedies, the person rescued gives his rescuer jewels or a
ring.

La tendresse et les passions, qui doivent être l'âme des tragédies, n'ont aucune part en celle-ci: la grandeur de courage y règne seule, et regarde son malheur d'un œil si dédaigneux qu'il n'en saurait arracher une plainte [...] Ce héros de ma façon sort un peu des règles de la tragédie, en ce qu'il ne cherche point à faire pitié par l'excès de ses malheurs; mais le succès a montré que la fermeté des grands cœurs, qui n'excite que de l'admiration dans l'âme du spectateur, est quelquefois aussi agréable que la compassion que notre art nous commande de mendier pour leurs misères.

(Au Lecteur)

This, of course, is not entirely new; *Don Sanche* is similar. But *Don Sanche*, a *comédie héroïque*, belonged to a different genre.

Pertharite continues *Nicomède* in many ways. The interest resides in the relationships and the intrigues of the characters rather than in psychological conflict. There are two situations of interest — the relationship between the usurper, Grimoald, and the widow of the late King, Pertharite;[1] and the relationship between the usurper, Grimoald, and the king he has dispossessed, when Pertharite, at first believed dead, is found to be alive and delivers himself into Grimoald's hands. Moreover, like *Nicomède*, the play ends with all the characters vying with one another in magnanimity. Despite some fine scenes, the play was a failure; and one cannot feel that the public was mistaken. It somehow fails to capture one's interest. Partly, perhaps, because it does deal with two situations — the relationship between Grimoald and Rodelinde has just reached an interesting crisis (Rodelinde has consented to marry Grimoald, *providing* he puts her son to death, and he has agreed), and one is curious to know what the outcome of this impossible situation will be, when Pertharite puts an end to it by returning. Partly, too, because the play — like *Héraclius* — lacks humanity. Rodelinde's insistence that Grimoald should put her son to death is powerfully reasoned, but does not quite carry conviction. Perhaps the most moving thing about the play is Corneille's own preface, which betrays the bitterness of his setback, and is a noble piece of prose:

[1] The situation in *Pertharite*, as was first pointed out in the eighteenth century, closely resembles that of Racine's *Andromaque* later.

La mauvaise réception que le public a faite à cet ouvrage m'avertit qu'il est temps que je sonne la retraite [. . .] Il vaut mieux que je prenne congé de moi-même que d'attendre qu'on me le donne tout à fait; et il est juste qu'après vingt années de travail, je commence à m'apercevoir que je deviens trop vieux pour être encore à la mode. [. . .] Cependant agréez que je joigne ce malheureux poème aux vingt et un qui l'ont précédé avec plus d'éclat; ce sera la dernière importunité que je vous ferai de cette nature: non que j'en fasse une résolution si forte qu'elle ne se puisse rompre; mais il y a grande apparence que j'en demeurerai là.

Years after, in the *Examen,* he wrote: 'Le succès de cette tragédie a été si malheureux, que pour m'épargner le chagrin de m'en souvenir, je n'en dirai presque rien.'

Chapter Six

FROM
OEDIPE TO *SURÉNA*

Corneille's retirement from the theatre was not permanent. Encouraged by the bounty of Foucquet, the surintendant des finances, he invited him to suggest a subject for a new tragedy. Of three subjects proposed by Foucquet, Corneille chose the subject of Oedipus, possibly because the legend, with its problem of the identity of the hero and its theme of incest, appealed to the author of *Héraclius* and *Don Sanche*. *Oedipe*, successfully performed at the Hôtel de Bourgogne in 1659, is a free adaptation of the plays on the same subject by Sophocles and Seneca, written, Corneille tells us, in two months, and interesting as showing how different the spirit of Corneille's tragedy is from that of the Greeks.

In adapting his originals, Corneille has the same objects as in *Médée*: to achieve greater *vraisemblance* by removing some of the improbabilities of Sophocles, to suit the play to the taste of the contemporary audience, and to fill out the inadequate material of the original. There are a number of things in Sophocles which — to seventeenth- and eighteenth-century French dramatists — seemed improbable, or at least to require explanation. Why does Laïus's servant say that Laius was killed by robbers, when in fact he was killed by one man? Sophocles offers no explanation; Corneille gives shame as his motive. Why was the murder of Laius not punished when it occurred? Corneille's Oedipe believes that he has in fact punished the murder, that the men he attacked were the brigands who had killed Laius. Why had Laius such a small escort? To a nation which conceived of a king as a person surrounded by pomp and ceremonial, it was incredible that a king should drive out in a coach with only two attendants. Corneille attempts to make it plausible:

> il voulut à mon sort [says Dircé] faire parler l'oracle;
> Mais comme à ce dessein la Reine mit obstacle,
> De peur que cette voix des destins ennemis
> Ne fût aussi funeste à la fille qu'au fils,
> Il se déroba d'elle, ou plutôt prit la fuite,
> Sans vouloir que Phorbas et Nicandre pour suite.   (II, 3)

Why did Phorbas not prevent the marriage of Oedipus and Jocasta? Because, says Corneille, he did not recover from his wounds for a year, by which time it was too late. How is it that the Theban shepherd and the Corinthian shepherd can recognize each other so easily after a lapse of twenty or thirty years? In Corneille, it is because they have seen each other nearly every year in the temple of Elide — an explanation which, like the dress in *Médée* which is harmless to anyone but Créuse, is perhaps no less improbable than what it is trying to explain. Moreover, Oedipus in Sophocles has been considered slow-witted for not realizing earlier who he is. Corneille avoids this difficulty in several ways. He suppresses the fact that Oedipus has been warned that he will kill his father and marry his mother; so that it cannot occur to him that he is the son of Laius of whom the same things have been prophesied. He suppresses, too, the scene in which Tiresias accuses Oedipus of having killed Laius; and, in any case, his *Oedipe*, convinced that he has already punished the murderers, can have no reason for consulting Laius. Corneille keeps Oedipe off the stage, too, for much of the play, and arranges for the various pieces of information to come, not to him, but to Jocaste. Moreover, for much of the play, Thésée is believed to be the missing son of Laius.

In the interests of the *bienséances*, Corneille turns the Theban shepherd into Phorbas, the servant of the king, the Corinthian shepherd into Iphicrate, *chef du conseil*, and Oedipe into a seven-teenth-century absolute monarch. The details of the death of Jocaste and the self-blinding of Oedipe are reduced, and Oedipe does not reappear after he has plucked out his eyes.

Finally, to give body to the play and to appeal to the con-temporary audience, Corneille added the 'heureux épisode' of Dircé and Thésée. Dircé is the daughter of Laïus and Jocaste, and is loved by Thésée, king of Athens. Corneille thus adds not merely a love interest, but a political interest as well. Dircé is the rightful heir of Laïus and her marriage will give her husband a claim to the throne, so that the choice of a husband for her is of vital importance to the usurper, Oedipe. Moreover, Corneille adds more events and an element of suspense. The shade of Laïus being conjured up (a detail taken from Seneca) says, ambiguously, that

> la fin de vos maux ne se fera point voir,
> Que mon sang n'ait fait son devoir.   (II, 3)

Dircé thinks that he means that she must give her life to save Thebes. It is rumoured, however, that Laïus's son still lives, and Thésée claims to be he and that Laïus's oracular statement refers to him; so that he and Dircé vie in wishing to be sacrificed. Then Oedipe recognizes Phorbas and is convicted of the murder of Laïus, and Thésée, as Laïus's outraged son, challenges him to a duel. Jocaste laments that she is torn between love for Oedipe and the obligation of punishing him as the murderer of her first husband.

The result of all these changes and additions, however, is that *Oedipe*, however good it may be, is not *Oedipus*. The sub-plot overshadows the main plot: the play opens and closes with Thésée and Dircé. Oedipe recedes into the background, and not only ceases to be a symbol of human destiny, but loses the sym-pathies of the audience. The appeal of the citizens to the King to help them and his sympathetic reply are omitted; and the fortitude of Corneille's Oedipe is a poor substitute for the moving lamen-tations of Sophocles's hero and his joy at being allowed to say farewell to his children. Instead of the human hero of Sophocles, we have Oedipe, a usurper and the obstacle to the marriage of

Dircé and Thésée, the main centre of interest; so that the play, ending as it does with the termination of the plague and the removal of the obstacle to the happiness of the lovers, can almost be said to end happily. Furthermore, in the middle of this play of fate, Corneille puts into the mouth of Thésée a noble — but surely misplaced — defence of human free-will (III, 5). In short, nothing remains of the universal human significance of Sophocles's play, which above all depicts a human being, the plaything of the gods, battered by a series of blows, one after the other.

In his next play, *La Toison d'Or*, commissioned by the marquis de Sourdéac and performed at his château in Normandy to celebrate the marriage of Louis XIV with Maria Theresa of Spain, Corneille again treats a Greek legend. Although Corneille's Greek plays are commonly believed to be inferior, the two machine plays at least have a good deal in them to appeal. It is perhaps because they do not fit in with preconceived notions about the nature of Corneille's genius that they are neglected; and it is precisely because they illustrate the variety of his work that they deserve attention. *La Toison*, another machine play, has something in common with *Andromède*: the vein of fancy reappears; the gods intervene in human affairs; and there is abundance of spectacle — Hypsipyle arrives in a shell, borne by dolphins and winds and accompanied by Tritons and mermaids; Absyrte appears in a cloud and puts to flight eight monsters who are threatening Hypsipyle; Médée flies through the air on a dragon and is unsuccessfully attacked by two winged argonauts. The settings are magnificent and include a country and town ravaged by war, a garden, a *palais d'horreur*, a forest, and the palaces of Aæte and of Venus, and that of the sun in the heavens. There is gallantry and *préciosité* in the speeches of Absyrte and of Jason — though, unlike Persée, Jason is not a perfect lover, but fickle and insincere.[1] Indeed, insincerity is the keynote of the play, and the conception of love embodied in it is more akin to that of Racine than to that usually associated with Corneille.[2]

[1] Is it a coincidence that the Don Juan theme was popular at this time?
[2] See below c hapter VIII.

After these two Greek plays, Corneille returned to Rome in a series of historical plays — *Sertorius, Sophonisbe, Othon, Attila*, and *Tite et Bérénice* — broken only by *Agésilas*.

Sertorius, performed at the Marais theatre, is a fine play and offers a number of new features. It is a political play, and shows Corneille evolving a new conception of tragedy, writing a more intellectual kind of play, in which, in the words of Saint-Evremond, 'il visait moins à émouvoir qu'à introduire dans le secret des cabinets et dans les replis du cœur.' 'Vous n'y trouverez ni tendresses d'amour, ni emportements de passions, ni descriptions pompeuses, ni narrations pathétiques,' writes Corneille in the preface, and adds that 'la politique [. . .] fait l'âme de toute cette tragédie'. Like *Cinna* it touches on the theme of conspiracy; it touches also on a new theme, the problem of civil war. But, above all, it deals with the complex relationships between people, the divergence between public interest and private inclination, the conflicting interests of different individuals, all of which have to be taken into account by a ruler if he is to govern successfully. Love and politics are more inextricably intermingled in *Sertorius* and the plays which follow it than in the earlier plays. In *Pompée*, the love of César and Cléopâtre is not essential to the main political theme; even that of Nicomède and Laodice is incidental to the main theme. But in *Sertorius*, the subject of the play is the problem of Sertorius, hesitating between Viriate and Aristie, wondering which match will best prevent the disruption of his army; and the jealousy of his lieutenant, Perpenna, which he does not succeed in allaying, is the direct cause of his downfall. *Sertorius*, in fact, is not so barren of emotion as Corneille's remarks suggest. It is the first play in which he sympathetically portrays an elderly lover, a figure who recurs in several subsequent plays; and it depicts a conflict within the breast of the hero. Indeed, the psychological conflict, which had become rare after *Polyeucte* (the Queen in *Don Sanche* is the chief exception), here reappears and is a regular feature of Corneille's plays henceforth, in the form of the conflict between love and royal responsibilities or *raison d'état*. *Sertorius* is a comparatively simple play: once the situation is explained, the characters make known their points of view and emotions, argue, discuss and negotiate; but there are no external events.

In *Sophonisbe*, performed at the Marais theatre, Corneille treats the subject chosen by Mairet thirty years earlier, and it is interesting to compare the two plays. Broadly speaking, there are four main differences. First, there is very little suspense in Mairet's play, whereas Corneille provides a constant series of alternating hopes and fears. Second, he adds another heroine, Eryxe, who is in love with Massinisse and consequently Sophonisbe's rival. This allows him to introduce some very fine scenes between the two jealous women. Third, his characters are different, and his psychology subtle and interesting. Syphax, like Sertorius, is an elderly lover; Sophonisbe, the implacable enemy of Rome, is not so much in love with Massinisse as possessive and jealous, eager to steal Eryxe's lover away from her; and Massinisse marries Sophonisbe because Eryxe, who loves him but is not sure of his affections, receives him coldly. Finally, Corneille's play is more historical and more political than Mairet's. The political situation is much more fully set forth and discussed and debated. In Corneille's play, which is more faithful to history, Sophonisbe marries Massinisse while her first husband, Syphax, is still alive, and Massinisse does not commit suicide at the end. What in Mairet is a simple story of unhappy love becomes in Corneille a complex study in human relationships.

Othon, a most interesting play, which will be studied in a subsequent chapter, is, of all this group, the one in which political intrigues are most important and the emotions most subdued. It was followed by *Agésilas*, which resembles it in some ways. Here again, the interest is largely political. There are three main political themes. One is the struggle between love and policy in a ruler, a theme already treated in *Sertorius* and taken up subsequently in *Attila*, *Tite et Bérénice*, and *Pulchérie*. Another is the problem of the relationship between a King and a too-powerful minister, from whom he withdraws his favour, thus causing him to conspire against him. Here, *Agésilas* continues *Othon*, which had depicted an Emperor whose power had all been usurped by his ministers. Another theme is that of marriage as an instrument of policy. Agésilas, hesitating between the woman he loves and the woman whom he ought to marry for political reasons, is in the same position as the heroes of *Sertorius*, and, later, of *Attila* and *Tite et Bérénice*. Since the woman Agésilas loves is a foreigner whom he cannot marry on that account, the play closely resembles *Tite et Bérénice*. But it is not only the marriage of the ruler that is involved in *Agésilas*, but the marriage of his subjects, too. Agésilas, King of Sparta, has an over-powerful minister, Lysander, of whom he wishes to become independent and whom he has begun to treat coldly. But Lysander has two daughters whom he is trying to marry so as to consolidate his position. They can, however, be married only with the consent of Agésilas, who withholds it on the grounds that what strengthens Lysander's position must of necessity weaken his own. Lysander is driven to conspire against Agésilas, who eventually resolves the problem by sacrificing his inclinations to his policy and marrying one of Lysander's daughters.

The play is a realistic political study. It stands apart from Corneille's other tragedies, however, in that it is the only one that treats a Greek historical subject, and the only one that is written in alexandrines interspersed with shorter, octosyllabic, lines. This innovation is probably an experiment in realism, since, in the *Examen* of *Andromède*, Corneille had quoted with approval Aristotle's opinion that the versification of a play should be as near to prose as possible, and argued that the use of shorter lines would achieve this better in France than the uniform use of the alexandrine:

Par cette même raison les vers de stances sont moins vers que les alexandrins, parce que parmi notre langage commun il se coule plus de ces vers inégaux, les uns courts, les autres longs, avec des rimes croisées et éloignées les unes des autres, que de ceux dont la mesure est toujours égale, et les rimes toujours mariées. [. . .] Mais l'usage en France est autre, à ce qu'on prétend, et ne souffre que les alexandrins à tenir lieu de prose. Sur quoi je ne puis m'empêcher de demander qui sont les maîtres de cet usage, et qui peut l'établir sur le théâtre, que ceux qui l'ont occupé avec gloire depuis trente ans [. . .]

The mixture of lines in *Agésilas*, though realistic in intention, gives the verse a tripping quality which, however suitable in a comedy like Molière's *Amphitryon* or a fanciful play like *Psyché* or the fables of La Fontaine, might seem out of place in a tragedy. But, in fact, *Agésilas* is not tragic in tone. The plot is complicated by the romantic love affairs of the two daughters of Lysander, Aglatide, betrothed to Spitridate, a Persian nobleman, and Elpinice, betrothed to Cotys, the King of Paphlagonia. But Spitridate has fallen in love with Elpinice, who returns his love. Spitridate tries to persuade Cotys to exchange mistresses, but Cotys really loves Spitridate's sister, Mandane, with whom Agésilas is in love, and insists that he will give up Elpinice only if Spitridate will allow him to marry Mandane. All this part of the play is romantic and more akin to the comedies of Corneille than to his tragedies, and the mixture of lines suits it well. Indeed, Aglatide is not unlike some of the heroines of the comedies:

> Je sais comme il faut vivre, et m'en trouve fort bien.
> La joie est bonne à mille choses,
> Mais le chagrin n'est bon à rien.   (II, 7)

The mixture of tones may be illustrated by saying that the two best scenes are Act III, scene 1, in which Lysander and Agésilas debate their conflicting interests, and Act IV, scene 2, in which Spitridate urges his sister Mandane to marry Agésilas (though she loves Cotys) so that he may be happy with Elpinice, and she banteringly reproaches him with his selfishness. In this scene, the kinship with the comedies is clear: the selfishness of Spitridate is that of Florame in *La Suivante*, and the sprightly Mandane reminds one of Doris in *Mélite*.

Agésilas is an attractive play, though it failed in the seventeenth century, no doubt because the style and the mixture of tones disconcerted the public. Everyone knows Boileau's epigram:

> Après *Agésilas*,
> Hélas!
> Après *Attila*,
> Holà!

That it is a condemnation of *Agésilas* is certain, though scholars are not agreed whether the second half means that after *Attila* Corneille should give up writing or critics stop carping. Be that as it may, *Attila*, first performed by Molière's company in March 1667, is a fine political and historical play, one of Corneille's best and most original. The basic situation is similar to that of *Sertorius*: like *Sertorius*, Attila is hesitating between two princesses, one of whom he loves, while the other is the more politic choice; and as in Sertorius each has another lover. Moreover, Attila, like Sertorius, eventually succumbs to his love. There is a certain family resemblance to *Othon*, too: Attila's different ways of tormenting his victims succeed one another in rapid succession like the proposed marriages in the earlier play. But there is much that is new in *Attila*. Act I, scene 2, is a magnificent political debate and a superb historical sketch; and the study of the crafty and cruel tyrant — an interesting variation on the amorous old man — and of the way in which his victims try to curry favour with him and intrigue against each other, is Corneille at his best.

*   *   *

Attila was followed by a silence of three years, broken by *Tite et Bérénice*. Racine's *Bérénice* was first performed at the Hôtel de Bourgogne on November 21, 1670, and Corneille's play a week later by Molière's company. Whether it was Henriette d'Angleterre, the English sister-in-law of Louis XIV, who suggested the subject to both, or whether one dramatist deliberately imitated the other, is of little importance;[1] but it is instructive to compare the two plays.

Corneille's play is not a tragedy, but a *comédie héroïque*, because there is here no question of the life or the state of the ruler being at stake; whereas Racine rejects this distinction:

[1] If one dramatist did copy the other, it seems more likely that Racine copied Corneille. *Tite et Bérénice* treats a theme which Corneille used continuously from *Sertorius* to *Pulchérie*, whereas *Bérénice* is exceptional in Racine's work. Moreover, Racine seems deliberately to have treated the same subject as a rival dramatist on previous occasions, and also to have attempted to outdo Corneille in some of his earlier tragedies (*Andromaque* uses the situation of *Pertharite*; *Mithridate* is reminiscent of *Nicomède*; and both *La Thébaïde* and *Britannicus* were written after Corneille had treated related subjects in *Oedipe* and *Othon*).

Ce n'est point une nécessité qu'il y ait du sang et des morts dans une tragédie; il suffit que l'action en soit grande, que les acteurs en soient héroïques, que les passions y soient excitées, et que tout s'y ressente de cette tristesse majestueuse qui fait tout le plaisir de la tragédie.

Corneille's plot is more complex than Racine's — inevitably, since, like Balzac and Stendhal, he is interested in the complexity of human relationships. He has added a second pair of lovers, Domitie, whom Tite is proposing to marry, and Domitian, his brother, and the interest lies in the intrigues of the characters: Domitie intrigues to marry Tite, in order to be Empress, and Bérénice and Domitian join forces to prevent her. Corneille's play is richer in *péripéties*, in reversals of the situation arousing interest and suspense, than Racine's, and it has a happy ending: although Tite and Bérénice separate, Bérénice is triumphant — her only aim had been to stop the marriage of Tite with Domitie, in which she has succeeded — and Domitie and Domitian marry. Moreover, both the political and the historical backgrounds are more elaborated in Corneille's play than in Racine's.[1]

Corneille's play is a good one, though not one of his best. The intrigues are not quite important or interesting enough for the play to rank with *Othon* or *Attila*; nor, as an expression of human emotion, can it rank with Racine's *Bérénice* or with Corneille's own next two plays.

Corneille treats the theme of the conflict of love and duty to the state far more movingly and effectively in *Pulchérie*, an excellent play which enjoyed considerable success, according to Corneille, at least.[2] It was performed, not by Molière's company, but at the Marais theatre:

Bien que cette pièce ait été reléguée dans un lieu où on ne voulait plus se souvenir qu'il y eût un théâtre, bien qu'elle ait passé par des bouches pour qui on n'était prévenu d'aucune estime, bien que ses principaux caractères soient contre le goût du temps, elle n'a pas

[1] See below, chapter X.
[2] Mme de Coulanges wrote to Mme de Sévigné on February 24, 1673 that '*Pulchérie* n'a pas réussi.' On the one hand, she might be regarded as a more impartial witness; on the other, Corneille is likely to have been better informed, and he was certainly not inclined to gloss over his failures.

laissé de peupler le désert, de mettre en crédit des acteurs dont on ne connaissait pas le mérite, et de faire voir qu'on n'a pas toujours besoin de s'assujettir aux entêtements du siècle pour se faire écouter sur la scène.

Pulchérie, another *comédie héroïque*, is a repetition of *Tite et Bérénice*, a rehandling of the theme of love and duty in a monarch, with the difference that we have here an Empress compelled to choose between two lovers, instead of an Emperor between two mistresses. Like *Tite*, Pulchérie, on being elevated to the throne, finds that rank brings obligations with it; she is thus no longer free to marry whom she pleases, even though the Senate leaves her free to choose a husband — just as in *Tite et Bérénice*, the Senate had approved the marriage of Tite and Bérénice. Pulchérie is torn between her love for Léon and her sense that it would be irresponsible to marry him, just as Tite is torn between Bérénice and Domitie. But there are many differences between the plays. Pulchérie has a simpler plot — interest is centred more on the main character. Moreover, whereas it was Bérénice who decided not to marry Tite, this time it is the Empress who makes the decision.

The problem in the play is the election of a new Emperor of Constantinople; Pulchérie, the sister of the late Emperor is to marry the newly elected Emperor. She loves Léon, who is one of the candidates, but, because of his youth and inexperience, a weak one. Léon, despite Pulchérie's love, thinks that his chance of being elected is weak and, at his sister's suggestion, has her elected Empress in her own right, convinced that she will choose him to be her husband. But Pulchérie feels — and the truth to life lies not only in the feeling itself, but in the fact that it is not so much spontaneous as implanted in her by a rival candidate — that now that she has the power to choose whom she will, she must use it responsibly. However much she loves Léon, therefore, she cannot take it upon herself to make one who is so young and untried her husband and coadjutor, especially as such a choice would lead to unrest in the Empire:

> Epargne à mon amour la douleur de te dire
> A quels troubles ce choix hasarderait l'empire:

K

Je l'ai déjà tant dit, que mon esprit lassé
N'en saurait plus souffrir le portrait retracé.
Ton frère [Léon] a l'âme grande, intrépide, sublime;
Mais d'un peu de jeunesse on lui fait un tel crime,
Que si tant de vertus n'ont que moi pour appui,
En faire un empereur, c'est me perdre avec lui.   (IV, 2)

Eventually she chooses an older candidate to be her husband in name only.

Another difference between *Pulchérie* and its predecessor is that in the former there is more sincere emotion and it is more openly expressed. Whereas Domitian in *Tite et Bérénice* makes love to Bérénice in order to make Tite jealous, Léon in *Pulchérie* refuses to do such a thing. And, in some very moving speeches, Léon and Martian express their love for Pulchérie, and Pulchérie hers for Léon. *Pulchérie* well deserved its success.

Suréna, the last play of all and one of the finest, has a good deal in common with *Pulchérie*. In both, the hero is a sympathetically portrayed elderly man, in love with a mistress whose rank is superior to his own. In both, though love and politics are inextricably intermingled, as in all the later plays, the love is expressed with greater poignancy than previously. Nevertheless, *Suréna* differs considerably from *Pulchérie*. The latter portrays the triumph of duty; the former, like *Le Cid*, the triumph of love. *Suréna*, too, a tragedy — unlike not only *Pulchérie*, which was a *comédie héroïque*, but most of Corneille's tragedies — has an unhappy ending. It is a tragedy in every sense of the word — a very simple, moving play, in which the situation allows of no solution, so that the play moves inevitably to a tragic outcome. In the centre is a pair of lovers whose love is secret. For political reasons, each must marry someone else. Their mutual love is stronger than their political obligations and they refuse to conform. Their love is discovered — as it must be — and Suréna is assassinated.

And yet, however tragic, the play harks back in some of its details to the early comedies of Corneille. Like them, it treats the problem of arranged or obligatory marriages:

Orode.   La seule politique est ce qui nous émeut;
         On la suit, et l'amour s'y mêle comme il peut . . .

    . . . .

Palmis.   Pardonnez-moi, Seigneur, si mon âme alarmée
         Ne veut point de ces rois, dont on n'est point aimée.   (III, 3)

Like *Agésilas*, it treats of the problem of the over-great subject, the subject whose services are so great that he has become an object of suspicion to the King. But whereas Agésilas solves the problem by marrying the daughter of Lysander, there is no solution in *Suréna*. Suréna, the general of King Orode, secretly loves Eurydice, the daughter of the King of Armenia whom he has defeated. Orode decides that, for political reasons, his son, Pacorus, who is loved by Suréna's sister, Palmis, shall marry Eurydice, and that Suréna shall marry his own (Orode's) daughter, Mandane — since Suréna can only cease to be a danger to the throne he has served too well if he is connected with it by marriage. Eurydice, however, receives Pacorus's addresses coldly, and Suréna rejects the hand of Mandane. Their mutual love is divined and discovered; they are placed under arrest; neither will yield. Suréna is sent into exile but assassinated as he leaves the palace.

It should be added that *Suréna* shows signs of the influence of Racine, not only in its simplicity and its tragic ending, but in some of its details. Pacorus is coldly received by Eurydice, as Roxane is by Bajazet. And as Roxane is led by this reception to suspect that Bajazet loves another woman and to obtain proof, first that Atalide loves Bajazet, and then that Bajazet loves Atalide, so Pacorus divines that he has a rival. Pacorus scrutinizes Eurydice's gestures like a character in Racine, and his efforts to surprise her secret remind us of Mithridate's to surprise Monime's. And as Monime refuses to marry Mithridate after he has tricked her into an avowal, so Eurydice refuses to marry Pacorus for his inquisitiveness. Suréna's reluctance to marry Mandane resembles Bajazet's to marry Roxane; and, as Atalide finally agrees to let Bajazet promise to marry Roxane, so Eurydice, at the end of the play, when it is too late, consents at last to save Suréna's life by

allowing him to marry Mandane. The death of Suréna is reminiscent of that of Bajazet. In both plays, the hero is in a room surrounded by guards; in both, he goes out and meets his death.[1]
Moreover, one or two of the speeches remind us of Racine.
Palmis declares her intention of being revenged on Pacorus for his
infidelity by remaining near him so as to fill him with remorse and
shame (III, 3), as Bérénice hopes that her suicide will arouse a
feeling of remorse in Titus. The opening of Act II, scene 2 —

> *Pacorus.*   Quoi? Madame, venir vous-même à ma rencontre!
> Cet excès de bonté que votre cœur me montre . . .
> *Eurydice.*   J'allais chercher Palmis,[2] que j'aime à consoler
> Sur un malheur qui presse et ne peut reculer.

— is not unlike the famous passage in *Andromaque*:

> *Pyrrhus.*   Me cherchiez-vous, Madame?
> Un espoir si charmant me serait-il permis?
> *Androm.*   Je passais jusqu'aux lieux où l'on garde mon fils.
> Puisqu'une fois le jour vous souffrez que je voie
> Le seul bien qui me reste et d'Hector et de Troie . . .

*   *   *

Looking back over the long series of Corneille's plays, one is
struck by a number of features. First, by the oscillation between
the romantic and the realistic to which we have referred above.
Then again, by the great variety of his plays. His works include
two tragi-comedies (*Clitandre* and *Le Cid*), three *comédies
héroïques* (*Don Sanche*, *Tite et Bérénice* and *Pulchérie*), three
machine plays (*Médée*, *Andromède* and *La Toison d'Or*), eight
comedies and sixteen tragedies. Of these last, two (*Polyeucte* and
Théodore) have martyrdom as their theme; one (*Oedipe*), like the
last two machine plays, has a subject drawn from Greek legend;
two (*Rodogune* and *Héraclius*) might be described as romantic
tragedies; and one (*Agésilas*) is an experiment which defies
classification. The remaining ten are historical and political

---

[1] But *Bajazet* owed something to *Othon*. In *Othon*, Plautine tells Othon to pay his
addresses to Camille, but feels jealous when he obeys; and Othon cannot make his hypocrisy convincing. This episode passed into *Bajazet*.
[2] Whom Pacorus has abandoned.

tragedies on a wide variety of subjects connected with Roman history, some with happy endings, others (such as *Horace* and *Suréna*) tragic in every sense of the word. Corneille is constantly trying to vary his manner, continually experimenting — and that this was a conscious aim is shown by the prefaces to *Nicomède* and to *Agésilas*. Every play has something new and original in it — some theme or some feature of style or treatment which differentiates it from all Corneille's other plays.

At the same time, there is a considerable degree of continuity in Corneille's work. It is seldom that an idea or feature appears once only: Corneille seems to like to exploit every new theme or situation at least twice. This characteristic can be seen already at the very beginning of his career. *La Veuve* is in many ways a repetition of *Mélite*, though it also differs greatly from it. As Eraste in *Mélite* introduces his inconstant friend, Tirsis, to Mélite and finds that Mélite prefers Tirsis to himself, so Théante in *La Suivante* introduces the inconstant Florame to Amarante with a similar result. Corneille first introduced a *suivante* into his comedies in *La Galerie*; a *suivante* was the main character of his next comedy. *La Galerie* is set in a real part of Paris; so is *La Place Royale*. Another original feature of *La Galerie* is that it contains a character who hesitates between freedom and the bonds of matrimony (Célidée); the idea is developed in Alidor in *La Place Royale*. *La Suivante* again contains a number of new features which occur subsequently. The rivalry of mistress and servant is repeated in *L'Illusion comique*, and in both the mistress triumphs because of her superior wealth. As Florame and Théante pay court to Amarante in order to have access to Daphnis, so Cléandre in *La Place Royale* woos Phylis in order to approach Angélique. Both *La Suivante* and *La Place Royale* show men who treat their womenfolk heartlessly and both end with a soliloquy — indeed, the imprecations of Amarante at the end of *La Suivante* are perhaps a development of those of the nurse which conclude *Mélite*. As Philiste in *La Veuve* overhears the nurse who is in his pay speaking unfavourably of him to her mistress, so Matamore in *L'Illusion* discovers his servant,

Clindor, wooing Isabelle on his own account instead of on behalf of his master.

This same characteristic is continued throughout Corneille's career. *Médée* deals with a magician and a fickle lover who uses love as a means to an end; *L'Illusion comique* contains a magician, too, and Clindor is in some respects a repetition of Jason. Moreover, Corneille later returned to Jason and Medea in *La Toison*. As the count in *Le Cid* takes the law into his own hands, so does Horace; indeed, *Horace* has been called — with a good deal of exaggeration — 'eine zweite verbesserte Auflage des Cid'.[1] Both *Horace* and *Polyeucte* contain a dream. Emilie in *Cinna* is reincarnated in Pulchérie in *Héraclius*. The martyrdom theme, first used in *Polyeucte*, recurs in *Théodore*; and the unwarranted mistrust by the realist, Félix, of the generous Sévère is repeated in *La Mort de Pompée*, in which Ptolomée unjustly mistrusts César. The futile Machiavellianism of Ptolomée and his counsellors resembles that of Cléopâtre in *Rodogune*. *Le Menteur* was followed by a sequel. In *Rodogune*, there is doubt which of the two princes is the elder; in *Héraclius*, there is doubt which of two men is the real Héraclius. The hen-pecked husband, Valens, in *Théodore*, reappears as Prusias in *Nicomède*, and both plays depict a duel between a stepson and his stepmother. Martian in *Héraclius* believes himself for a moment to be the brother of the girl he loves — so do Don Sanche and Thésée (in *Oedipe*). Both *Héraclius* and *Don Sanche* end with voices from the tomb revealing the secret. *Héraclius* opens with rumours of the return of the legitimate ruler — so do *Don Sanche* and *Pertharite*.

In the last period, *Oedipe* was followed by another play on a Greek legend, *La Toison*. The situation of *Sertorius* — which has been called a pastiche of *Pertharite*[2] — that of a ruler hesitating between two women, one of whom he loves and one of whom he feels he ought to marry for political reasons, is repeated in *Othon*, *Agésilas*, *Attila*, and *Tite et Bérénice*: there is a particu-

---

[1] Steinweg, who lists a large number of features which *Le Cid*, *Horace*, *Cinna* and *Polyeucte* have in common.
[2] May.

larly close resemblance between the situation of *Attila* and that of *Sertorius*. The ambitious Aglatide of *Agésilas*, who will marry only a King, is resuscitated in the person of Domitie in *Tite et Bérénice*; and there is a close resemblance in the situation of the two plays. Ildione in *Attila* plans to marry Martian and then murder him; Plautine in *Othon* had thought of marrying Martian and killing him. Many features of *Tite et Bérénice* are repeated in *Pulchérie* — the situation of a ruler called on to choose between love and abnegation; the wish of Bérénice that her lover, if he cannot marry her, should marry a wife of her choosing, is expressed also by Pulchérie (and by Eurydice in *Suréna*); Pulchérie, like Tite, finds that power brings responsibility. Finally, there is a family resemblance between *Pulchérie* and *Suréna*; moreover, in both, the idea is expressed that lack of heirs is no misfortune since they are often degenerate.[1]

In other words, a play of Corneille is almost always a combination of some original idea with a development of an idea used before. Corneille rarely uses an idea once only — though the most original features of *L'Illusion comique* and *Agésilas* are unique. In some cases, the repetition of several ideas or motifs in successive plays constitutes a real kinship between them — between *Rodogune* and *Héraclius*, *Le Menteur* and its sequel, *Héraclius* and *Don Sanche*, *Tite et Bérénice* and *Pulchérie*, and *Pulchérie* and *Suréna*, for example. Continuity and experiment are found in close contiguity throughout.

Finally, if Corneille's plays are not all equally good, very few are less than admirable, and none is without interest. Nothing could be more unjust than La Bruyère's remark:

Ses premières comédies sont sèches, languissantes, et ne laissaient pas espérer qu'il dût aller si loin, comme ses dernières font qu'on s'étonne qu'il ait pu tomber de si haut.

[1] Tite in *Tite et Bérénice* had previously said:
Pour revivre en des fils nous n'en mourons pas moins . . .   (V, 5)

PART III

---

*Aspects of Corneille's
Tragedies*

Chapter Seven

AFFINITIES
BETWEEN THE TRAGEDIES
AND THE COMEDIES

Corneille's comedies are comic, realistic, and contain baroque features. The purpose of the present chapter is to show that there is no clean break between the comedies and the tragedies, and that the tragedies likewise contain much that is baroque and much that is comic. Subsequent chapters will aim at showing that the tragedies continue the realism of the comedies.

§ 1 *Baroque elements in the tragedies*

Clitandre, Corneille's second play and his first attempt at a serious genre, is no less baroque than its predecessor, *Mélite*. It is, indeed, more baroque in form, since it lacks unity, and interest is divided between three groups of characters: the lovers, Rosidor and Caliste; the pair, Pymante and Dorise; and Clitandre.[1]

The subject matter and the style of the play are no less baroque: it is a play of violence and strong passions, hatred and jealousy. With typical baroque hyperbole, Pymante invokes the aid of Hell against his rival, Rosidor:

[1] It has been suggested that the shift of interest from the four lovers to Clitandre is the result of a political preoccupation, that Corneille, after he had begun the play, decided to turn it into a plea for the maréchal de Marillac. It seems unlikely that a dramatist should change his subject in the middle of a play like this. The shift of interest is the natural consequence of the need to explain how Clitandre came to be arrested for a crime he did not commit.

> Sortez de vos cachots, infernales furies,
> Apportez à m'aider toutes vos barbaries,
> Qu'avec vous tout l'enfer m'assiste en ce dessein,
> Qu'un sanglant désespoir me verse dans le sein.   (II, 1)

Dorise's anger, when she believes that Pymante has killed Rosidor similarly knows no bounds:

> Monstre de la nature, exécrable bourreau,
> Après ce lâche coup qui creuse mon tombeau
> D'un compliment moqueur ta malice me flatte,
> Fuis, fuis, que dessus toi ma vengeance n'éclate,
> Ces mains, ces faibles mains que vont armer les Dieux,
> N'auront que trop de force à t'arracher les yeux,
> Que trop à t'imprimer sur ce hideux visage
> En mille traits de sang les marques de ma rage.   (III, 3)

In a scene reminiscent of *King Lear*, Pymante attempts to rape Dorise, who puts out his eye with a hair-pin — all on the stage. Pymante swears vengeance; a storm breaks out, which Pymante identifies with his own emotions — again we are reminded of *Lear*:

> Je n'ai plus de penser qui n'en veuille à sa vie.
>
> . . . .
>
> Recourons aux effets, cherchons de toutes parts.
> Prenons dorénavant pour guides les hasards,
> Quiconque rencontré n'en saura de nouvelle
> Que son sang aussitôt me réponde pour elle,
> Et ne suivant ainsi qu'une incertaine erreur
> Remplissons tous ces lieux de carnage et d'horreur.
>   *Une tempête survient*
> Mes menaces déjà font trembler tout le monde,
> Le vent fuit d'épouvante, et le tonnerre en gronde,
> L'œil du Ciel s'en retire, et par un voile noir,
> N'y pouvant résister, se défend d'en rien voir;
> Cent nuages épais se distillant en larmes
> A force de pitié veulent m'ôter les armes:
> L'univers n'ayant pas de force à m'opposer
> Me vient offrir Dorise afin de m'apaiser.
> Tout est de mon parti, le Ciel même n'envoie
> Tant d'éclairs redoublés qu'afin que je la voie,
> Quelque part où la peur porte ses pas errants,

Ils sont entrecoupés de mille gros torrents.
O suprême faveur! Ce grand éclat de foudre
Décoché sur son chef le vient de mettre en poudre,
Ce fer s'il est ainsi me va tomber des mains,
Ce coup aura sauvé le reste des humains,
Satisfait par sa mort, mon esprit se modère,
Et va sur sa charogne achever sa colère.   (IV, 2)

Masks and disguise are an essential part of the plot. Pymante and his companions dress as peasants and don masks in order to waylay Rosidor; Dorise puts on man's attire:

Nous changeons bien d'habits, mais non pas de visages,
Nous changeons bien d'habits, mais non pas de courages
Et ces masques trompeurs de nos conditions
Cachent sans les changer nos inclinations.   (III, 3)

In these lines, à propos of her disguise, she shows her awareness of the fundamental baroque problem of the relationship between — or better, of the unrelatedness of — appearances and reality. But this theme dominates the whole play, which shows how Clitandre is made to appear guilty of a crime which he has not committed, and how he is falsely accused and wrongfully incarcerated:

L'apparence déçoit, et souvent on a vu
Sortir la vérité d'un moyen impourvu,
Bien que la conjecture y fût encor plus forte.   (III, 1)

His unjust arrest fills him with bewilderment:

Je ne sais si je veille, ou si ma rêverie
A mes sens endormis fait quelque tromperie,
Peu s'en faut dans l'excès de ma confusion
Que je ne prenne tout pour une illusion.   (III, 2)

When he finds himself in prison, he concludes that his senses must be deceiving him:

vous vous trompez, mes yeux,
Vous aviez autrefois des ressorts infaillibles
Qui portaient en mon cœur les espèces visibles,
Mais mon cœur en prison vous renvoie à son tour
L'image et le rapport de son triste séjour ...   (III, 2)

These are not the only baroque themes. The King comments on the weakness of human reason, which cannot distinguish between the appearance and the reality:

> Que souvent notre esprit trompé de l'apparence
> Règle ses mouvements avec peu d'assurance!
> Qu'il est peu de lumière en nos entendements,
> Et que d'incertitude en mes raisonnements! (V, 4)

The prince points out that jealousy easily gets the better of the reason:

> un ver de jalousie
> Jette souvent notre âme en telle frénésie
> Que la raison tombée en un aveuglement
> Laisse notre conduite à son dérèglement . . .[1] (V, 4)

The sense that fate rules human destinies —

> Destins, qui réglez tout au gré de vos caprices . . . (II, 1)

— and that fate is by nature paradoxical, is there too. It is paradoxical, as Dorise points out, that the hair-pin which betrayed her sex in spite of her disguise should turn out to be her means of defence. Rosidor, who is confined to his bed by his wounds, learns that his marriage must be postponed until he is better and comments:

> Que le sort a pour moi de subtiles malices!
> Ce lit doit être un jour le champ de mes délices,
> Et recule lui seul ce qu'il doit terminer,
> Lui seul il m'interdit ce qu'il doit me donner. (V, 3)

The same sense of paradox is evident in many lines of the play:

> Je ne t'ai méconnu qu'en songeant trop à toi. (I, 7)

> Tu me fais un outrage à force de m'aimer. (I, 7)

> Lui rendre contre moi l'impossible possible . . . (II, 1)

> Votre pâleur de teint me rougit de colère . . . (III, 1)

> Qu'il t'écouterait mieux s'il te chérissait moins. (III, 1)

---

[1] 'Si l'on se rappelle que le XVIIe siècle croyait à la génération spontanée et voyait dans le ver "*un insecte produit par la décomposition des chairs*" on comprendra mieux le sens de cette dernière image: la jalousie est engendrée par la corruption de l'âme.' (Crétin)

There is also a passage in which the vivid contrast of light and shade, so beloved of the baroque painters, is described. The sun is rising, and

> l'aube de ses rais
> A déjà reblanchi le haut de ces forêts.
> Si je me peux fier à sa lumière sombre
> Dont l'éclat impuissant dispute avecque l'ombre,
> J'entrevois le sujet de mon jaloux ennui . . .   (I, 1)

With its violent action shown on the stage, *Clitandre* is quite unclassical; indeed, in the preface, Corneille expresses his independence of the ancients:

> Il est vrai qu'on pourra m'imputer que m'étant proposé de suivre la règle des Anciens, j'ai renversé leur ordre, vu qu'au lieu des messagers qu'ils introduisent à chaque bout de champ pour raconter les choses merveilleuses qui arrivent à leurs personnages, j'ai mis les accidents mêmes sur la Scène. [. . .] Je me donne ici quelque sorte de liberté de choquer les Anciens, d'autant qu'ils ne sont plus en état de me répondre, et que je ne veux engager personne en la recherche de mes défauts. Puisque les sciences et les arts ne sont jamais à leur période, il m'est permis de croire qu'ils n'ont pas tout su, et que de leurs instructions on peut tirer des lumières qu'ils n'ont pas eues.

On the other hand, Corneille does obey the unities in the play, though he says in the preface that he does not consider them essential. Subsequently, his plays become more classical. In the *Epître* prefixed to *Médée*, his first tragedy, he still maintains an independent attitude towards the rules, but *Le Cid* which follows represents the fusion of baroque and classical, as Corneille himself more or less points out:

> Bien que ce soit celui de tous mes ouvrages réguliers où je me suis permis le plus de licence, il passe encore pour le plus beau auprès de ceux qui ne s'attachent pas à la dernière sévérité des règles [. . .]
> *(Examen)*

After the *Querelle du Cid*, Corneille becomes more and more classical; he observes the unities more rigorously, and the *bienséances* banish violence from the stage. Nevertheless baroque themes and characteristics never disappear entirely.

The theme of the falseness of appearances occurs over and over again. In *Le Cid*, Chimène takes Don Sanche to be the victor in the duel he has just fought with Rodrigue: he has in fact been vanquished. Horace seems to have been defeated by the Curiaces and to be running away: in reality, it is a stratagem, and he kills them all. Cinna exhorts his fellow conspirators to free Rome from the tyranny of Auguste; he also, by a curious paradox, dissuades Auguste from abdicating by means of cogent political arguments: but beneath these two conflicting attitudes is the real Cinna, in love with Emilie, and actuated only by selfish motives — only if he kills Auguste will she consent to marry him. Similarly, in *Théodore*, Valens suggests that Théodore should be sent to a brothel. He explains to Marcelle that to shame her in this way is the only means of killing Placide's love for her; but he tells his confidant that the real reason for his proposal is that he is convinced that Théodore will renounce her religion rather than her virtue. In the same play, Didyme, who appears to be the first client of Théodore in her brothel, turns out to be her rescuer.

Deliberate hypocrisy is not uncommon either. Félix feigns a wish to be converted in *Polyeucte*; Cléopâtre uses hypocrisy as a means of attaining her ends in *Rodogune*; and Marcelle in *Théodore* falsely promises to save Théodore if Placide will feign for Flavie the love he cannot feel. In *Othon*, nearly all the characters wear a mask and explain their actions differently in public and in private; even Othon's love for Plautine is merely a mask which has become the face.

Often, too, Corneille portrays a kind of virtuous hypocrisy, in which a character assumes a mask in order to conceal from the world his weakness or selfishness. Although Eryxe in *Sophonisbe*, when she finds that Massinisse is betrothed to Sophonisbe, affects indifference —

> Ce grand titre de roi, que seul je considère,
> Etend sur moi l'affront qu'en vous ils vont lui faire;
> Et rien ici n'échappe à ma tranquillité
> Que par les intérêts de notre dignité . . .

— it is clear, even from the sarcasm with which she ends the scene, that she is far from feeling the tranquillity she professes:

> Mais voici cet objet si charmant à vos yeux,
> Dont le cher entretien vous divertira mieux. (III, 2)

Irène, in *Pulchérie* — like Eryxe, and like Cloris in *Mélite* — is abandoned by her lover; and, like them, she tries to hide her suffering under a brave face:

> Puisque en vain je m'attache à qui ne m'aime pas,
> Il faut avec honneur franchir ce mauvais pas:
> Il faut, à son exemple, avoir ma politique,
> Trouver à ma disgrâce une face héroïque,
> Donner à ce divorce une illustre couleur,
> Et sous de beaux dehors dévorer ma douleur. (IV, 1)

Eurydice in *Suréna*, reproached by Palmis with her apparent indifference to Suréna's fate, replies:

> Pensez-vous qu'exposée à de si rudes coups,
> J'en soupire au dedans, et tremble moins que vous?
> Mon intrépidité n'est qu'un effort de gloire,
> Que, tout fier qu'il paraît, mon cœur n'en veut pas croire,
> Il est tendre, et ne rend ce tribut qu'à regret
> Au juste et dur orgueil qu'il dément en secret. (IV, 2)

In two of the last plays, the theme of false appearances is given a new twist. Domitie, in *Tite et Bérénice*, wants to marry Tite, because he is the Emperor, though she does not love him. When he tries to probe into her real feelings, she retorts that one should be content with appearances and not try to penetrate to what lies beneath:

> A l'amour vraiment noble il suffit du dehors;
> Il veut bien du dedans ignorer les ressorts . . . (V, 2)

This, in fact, is presumably what Polyeucte had done when he married Pauline, still in love with Sévère. The idea is carried a step further in *Suréna*. Eurydice, like Domitie, is destined to marry a prince she does not love, and she postpones her marriage with him precisely because he seeks to know her real feelings:

> Mais puisque vous m'avez arraché mon secret,
> Il n'est ni roi, ni père, il n'est prière, empire,
> Qu'au péril de cent morts mon cœur n'ose en dédire.   (II, 2)

A form of the problem of appearances and reality which occurs in the tragedies but not in the comedies is confusion of identity. We meet it in *Héraclius*, in *Don Sanche* and in *Oedipe*. *Héraclius* is very largely concerned with false appearances. Martian passes for Léonce, and for part of the play believes himself to be Héraclius; and Héraclius passes for Martian. People's actions are ambiguous: Léontine allows Martian to believe he is Héraclius, though she knows the truth; and Exupère, while seeming to be working against Héraclius, is really working for him. The sense of bewilderment is understandably strong in this play.

> Je ne sais qui je suis, et crains de le savoir;
> . . . .
> Je crains tout, je fuis tout; et dans cette aventure,
> Des deux côtés en vain j'écoute la nature,   (V, 2)

says Héraclius. Martian is no less perplexed:

> Voyez d'autre côté quelle est ma destinée,
> Madame: dans le cours d'une seule journée,
> Je suis Héraclius, Léonce, et Martian;
> Je sors d'un empereur, d'un tribun, d'un tyran.
> De tous trois ce désordre en un jour me fait naître,
> Pour me faire mourir enfin sans me connaître.   (V, 5)

Even Léontine, who is responsible for the imbroglio, is bewildered — like Amarante in *La Suivante*:

> Tout me confond, tout me devient contraire.
> Je ne fais rien du tout, quand je pense tout faire;
> Et lorsque le hasard me flatte avec excès,
> Tout mon dessein avorte au milieu du succès:
> Il semble qu'un démon funeste à sa conduite
> Des beaux commencements empoisonne la suite.   (II, 7)

In *La Toison d'Or*, Juno takes on the identity of Chalciope; and, both in that play and in *Médée*, Médée is an enchantress who can create illusions — yet another form of this same problem of appearance and reality. In *La Toison*, she changes a *palais doré* into a *palais d'horreur* — *Andromède*, too, is full of transformations and metamorphoses — and we are told that the apparent fertility of Colchos is merely one of her illusions:

> Ces climats désolés où même la nature
> Ne tient que de votre art ce qu'elle a de verdure,
> Où nos plus beaux jardins n'ont ni roses ni lis,
> Dont par votre savoir ils ne soient embellis . . .   (IV, 1)

The mutability of human things is a constant theme. At the beginning of *Le Cid*, Chimène has a foreboding that her happiness cannot endure:

> Un moment donne au sort des visages divers,
> Et dans ce grand bonheur je crains un grand revers.   (I, 1)

And later in the play, she and Rodrigue lament the fickleness of fortune:

> Rodrigue, qui l'eût cru? — Chimène, qui l'eût dit? —
> Que notre heur fût si proche et sitôt se perdît? —
> Que si près du port, contre toute apparence,
> Un orage si prompt brisât notre espérance?   (III, 4)

In *Horace*, Tulle reminds old Horace that

> Beaucoup par un long âge ont appris comme vous
> Que le malheur succède au bonheur le plus doux . . .   (V, 2)

The instability of human happiness, contrasted with the permanence of celestial bliss, is the theme of Polyeucte's meditations in prison (IV, 2). Pompée is an example of the uncertainty of fate:

> Ce déplorable chef du parti le meilleur,
> Que sa fortune lasse abandonne au malheur,
> Devient un grand exemple, et laisse à la mémoire
> Des changements du sort une éclatante histoire.   (I, 1)

The theme is taken up by Orode in *Suréna*:

> Mais sous le ciel tout change, et les plus valeureux
> N'ont jamais sûreté d'être toujours heureux.   (*Suréna*, III, 2)

Fickle lovers are, of course, less common in the tragedies than in the comedies, but they are not absent. Whereas Seneca's Jason is compelled by circumstances to desert Medea, Jason in both the plays of Corneille in which he figures is the embodiment of fickleness, and, like the characters in some of the comedies, he expresses the philosophy of inconstancy:

> Aussi je ne suis pas de ces amants vulgaires:
> J'accommode ma flamme au bien de mes affaires;
> Et sous quelque climat que me jette le sort,
> Par maxime d'Etat je me fais cet effort.   (*Médée*, I, 1)

The love of strong passions and abnormal emotions is evident from time to time. Hatred and revenge are the subject of *Médée*, while *Rodogune* deals with violent and unnatural conflicts: the tension reaches its climax in the fifth act, when Antiochus does not know whether to suspect his mother or his bride of having murdered his brother. Léontine in *Héraclius* seeks her revenge on Phocas by having him killed by his own son or by making him kill his son; and she tortures him cruelly by refusing to disclose which of the two young men is his son. Théodore is condemned to a brothel — one is reminded of *Pericles*; and the theme of incest is touched upon in *Héraclius*, *Don Sanche*, and *Oedipe* — indeed, it is the threat of an incestuous marriage which starts off the action in *Héraclius*. The admiration which *Nicomède* seeks to arouse is, perhaps, no less characteristic of baroque than the horror of *Rodogune* or *Héraclius*. Even a certain taste for the macabre appears occasionally — in the description of the death agonies of Créon and Créuse, for example:

> Loin de me soulager, vous croissez mes tourments:
> Le poison à mon corps unit mes vêtements,
> Et ma peau, qu'avec eux votre secours m'arrache,
> Pour suivre votre main de mes os se détache:
> Voyez comme mon sang en coule à gros ruisseaux.
> Ne me déchirez plus, officieux bourreaux . . .   (*Médée*, V, 3)

— or in such a couplet as:

> L'amour va rarement jusque dans un tombeau
> S'unir au reste affreux de l'objet le plus beau.
>
> (*Théodore*, I, 3)

It is perhaps strongest of all in *Attila*, in which the death of Attila is described with a wealth of detail.

In a general way, Corneille's plays are baroque by the emotions to which they appeal. The aim of baroque art, according to the Italian poet, Marino, is to 'far stupir'; and this Corneille does. His tragedies are full of surprises, of alternations of hopes and fears, of sudden reversals of the situation, which can be traced back both to the sense of the instability of human fortunes and to the desire to cause surprise.

The sense of the paradoxical nature of life never leaves Corneille. In *Le Cid*, Rodrigue's duty obliges him to kill his mistress's father, and Chimène ends by marrying the man who killed her father. In *Horace*, none but the three Horaces are chosen to fight the three Curiaces with whom they have strong family ties, and Horace wins glory by running away:

> Certes l'exemple est rare et digne de mémoire,
> De trouver dans la fuite un chemin à la gloire.   (IV, 2)

In *Cinna*, Auguste has achieved his ambition of becoming Emperor, only to find disillusionment; Cinna wishes to assassinate Auguste, and yet dissuades him from abdicating. In *Polyeucte* it is paradoxical that Félix, who has put Polyeucte to death to placate Sévère, should find that Sévère, so far from being pleased, is threatening to depose him, and should retain his position only by himself becoming a Christian. Cléopâtre brings out the paradox of the destiny of Pompée:

> Ce prince d'un sénat maître de l'univers,
> Dont le bonheur semblait au-dessus du revers,
> Lui que sa Rome a vu plus craint que le tonnerre,
> Triompher en trois fois des trois parts de la terre,
> Et qui voyait encore en ces derniers hasards
> L'un et l'autre consul suivre ses étendards;
> Sitôt que d'un malheur sa fortune est suivie,
> Les monstres de l'Egypte ordonnent de sa vie.
> On voit un Achillas, un Septime, un Photin,
> Arbitres souverains d'un si noble destin;
> Un roi qui de ses mains a reçu la couronne

> A ces pestes de cour lâchement l'abandonne.
> Ainsi finit Pompée; et peut-être qu'un jour
> César éprouvera même sort à son tour.   (*Pompée*, II, 2)

In the same play, Cornélie, Pompée's widow, though bent on killing César to avenge her husband's death ('O ciel, que de vertus vous me faites haïr!'), nevertheless saves his life.

In *Théodore*, Placide loves Théodore who does not return his love, and dislikes Flavie who loves him:

> Mon sort des deux côtés mérite qu'on le plaigne:
> L'une me persécute, et l'autre me dédaigne;
> Je hais qui m'idolâtre, et j'aime qui me fuit,
> Et je poursuis en vain, ainsi qu'on me poursuit.
> Telle est de mon destin la fatale injustice,
> Telle est la tyrannie ensemble et le caprice
> Du démon aveuglé qui sans discrétion
> Verse l'antipathie et l'inclination.[1]   (I, 1)

Héraclius, in order to save the life of Phocas's son, Martian, is compelled to tell Phocas that *he* is Martian and that Martian is Héraclius. Don Alvar in *Don Sanche* laments his lot: compelled by circumstances to fight a duel for the hand of Léonor, whom he does not love, he is effectively prevented, whether he wins or loses, from marrying Doña Elvire, whom he does love:

> Ni vaincu, ni vainqueur, je ne puis être à vous:
> Vaincu, j'en suis indigne, et vainqueur son époux;
> Et le destin m'y traite avec tant d'injustice,
> Que son plus beau succès me tient lieu de supplice.   (III, 1)

Rodelinde in *Pertharite* hates Grimoald for his virtues, and Eduige finds that success is failure:

> Et la Princesse alors par un bizarre effet,
> Pour l'avoir voulu roi, le perdit tout à fait.   (I, 1)

Sophonisbe marries Massinisse in order to prevent him from marrying Eryxe; but she thereby encompasses her own destruction

---

[1] Cf. Célidée's complaint:
> L'un et l'autre me fuit, et je brûle pour eux;
> L'un et l'autre t'adore, et tu les fuis tous deux.
>   (*Galerie du Palais*, IV, 8)

Hermia and Helena in the *Midsummer Night's Dream* could say exactly the same.

— and leaves Massinisse free to marry Eryxe. And what could be more paradoxical than a situation which leads a girl to tell her lover:

> Donnez-vous à Camille, ou je me donne à lui.   (*Othon*, IV, 1)

The sense of the impotence of human reason, if it is not directly touched upon, underlies many of the debates and discussions. In *Pompée*, for example, the King's advisers find equally cogent reasons in support of divergent policies; but, despite all their ratiocination, they fail either to agree or to find a satisfactory course of action. Similarly, the conflicting advice, powerfully reasoned, of their advisers leaves both Galba and Attila bewildered. In *Sophonisbe*, there is a fine scene in which Eryxe argues that peace is imminent and Sophonisbe that it is not. Both advance convincing reasons for their conviction, but, in fact, each is arguing that what is likely is what will best serve her own interests: reason is the slave of emotion.

There are baroque features in the style of the tragedies, too. The love of paradoxical antithesis continues:

> Croirait commettre un crime à n'en commettre pas.   (*Médée*, I, 1)
>
> Et punis-toi, Jason, de ne la punir pas.   (*Médée*, V, 7)
>
> Je travaille à le perdre, et le perds à regret ...   (*Le Cid*, I, 2)
>
> Ma plus douce espérance est de perdre l'espoir.   (*Le Cid*, I, 2)
>
> Se montre généreux par un trait de faiblesse ...   (*Pompée*, III, 1)
>
> Mais, las! contre mon feu mon feu me sollicite ...   (*Pompée*, IV, 3)
>
> Il ne vous trahissait que pour vous couronner ...   (*Héraclius*, V, 6)
>
> Ah! si je lui déplais à force de lui plaire,
> Si de son trop d'amour sa haine est tout le fruit,
> Alors qu'on la mérite, où se voit-on réduit?   (*Attila*, III, 2)

Oxymoron is frequent, too: 'cruels généreux', 'aimable inhumaine', 'ce rival si cher', 'ce généreux coupable', 'perfide généreux', 'pitié cruelle', 'trop aimable ennemie'.[1] The line:

---

[1] *Horace*, III, 2; *Cinna*, III, 3; *Rodogune*, IV, 1; *Théodore*, V, 1; *Héraclius*, V, 7; *Oedipe*, ‸, 1; *Tite et Bérénice*, III, 2.

Cette obscure clarté qui tombe des étoiles ...

(Le Cid, IV, 3)

is an example not merely of oxymoron but of the chiaroscuro beloved of baroque painters;[1] another occurs in *Horace*:

Pareille à ces éclairs qui dans le fort des ombres
Poussent un jour qui fuit et rend les nuits plus sombres,
Tu n'as frappé mes yeux d'un moment de clarté
Que pour les abîmer dans plus d'obscurité.   (III, 1)

Baroque conceits and metaphors are uncommon, but not entirely absent. A famous example is the passage in *Le Cid* in which Chimène speaks of her father's blood:

Ce sang qui tant de fois garantit vos murailles,
Ce sang qui tant de fois vous gagna des batailles,
Ce sang qui tout sorti fume encor de courroux
De se voir répandre pour d'autres que pour vous ...

. . . .

Son sang sur la poussière écrivait mon devoir;
Ou plutôt sa valeur en cet état réduite
Me parlait par sa plaie, et hâtait ma poursuite;
Et pour se faire entendre au plus juste des rois,
Par cette triste bouche elle empruntait ma voix.   (II, 8)

In similar vein we read in *Héraclius* that

Il n'avait que six mois; et lui perçant le flanc,
On en fit dégoutter plus de lait que de sang ...   (I, 1)

A baroque feature that is enduring in Corneille's verse is double-entendre. There are ambiguous oracles in *Horace* and *Oedipe*, and an ambiguous prophecy in *Andromède*; and frequently characters in the plays use expressions which seem to mean one thing and really mean the opposite. Martian, who is

---

[1] 'Est-ce un hasard si ce vers du *Cid* appartient à l'âge du *tenebroso* en peinture, bientôt nommé *clair-obscur*?' (Marcel Raymond). The description of the followers of Phinée after they have been turned to stone reminds us of baroque statues, full of movement: Bernini was fond of portraying just such transformations.

Je vois tous ces méchants en pierre transformés;
Mais l'un plein de fureur, et l'autre plein de crainte,
En porte sur le front l'image encore empreinte;
Et tel voulait frapper, dont le coup suspendu
Demeure en sa statue à demi descendu ...   *(Andromède,* V, 5)

really Héraclius, for example, tells Léonce, who is the real Martian:

> Je te connais, Léonce, et mieux que tu ne crois;
> Je sais ce que tu vaux, et ce que je te dois.
> Son bonheur est le mien, Madame; et je vous donne
> Léonce et Martian en la même personne . . .   (I, 4)

— lines which are not understood by his hearers in the sense in which he intends them.[1] Similarly, he tells Phocas:

> Perdez Héraclius, et sauvez votre fils,   (IV, 4)

— a remark which Phocas, unaware that his son and Héraclius were changed at birth, naturally misunderstands. *Héraclius* by its very nature is exceptionally rich in double-entendre. Exupère, who feigns treachery in order to serve his master the better, naturally uses it, too. In answer, for example, to the question,

> Quelque allégresse que vous fassiez paraître,
> Trouvez-vous doux les noms de perfide et de traître?

he replies:

> Je sais qu'aux généreux ils doivent faire horreur:
> Ils m'ont frappé l'oreille, ils m'ont blessé le cœur;
> Mais bientôt, par l'effet que nous devons attendre
> Nous serons en état de ne les plus entendre.   (III, 5)

He seems to mean that his success will silence his detractors; in fact, he means that he will throw off the mask and appear in his true colours. Massinisse, in *Sophonisbe*, addresses Eryxe in such ambiguous terms that Corneille felt himself obliged to explain to the reader:

Les protestations d'amour que semble lui faire Massinisse au commencement de leur premier entretien ne sont qu'un équivoque, dont le sens caché regarde cette autre reine. Ce qu'elle y répond fait voir qu'elle s'y méprend la première; et tant d'autres ont voulu s'y méprendre après elle, que je me suis cru obligé de vous en avertir.

---

[1] A similar example of double-entendre occurs in *Oedipe*, when Thésée hints to Jocaste that he is her lost son:

> Vous le connaissez donc? — A l'égal de moi-même. —
> De quand? — De ce moment. — Et vous l'aimez? — Je l'aime
> Jusqu'à mourir du coup dont il sera percé.   (III, 5)

Eryxe is herself a mistress of double-entendre:

> Votre félicité sera longtemps parfaite,
> S'ils la laissent durer autant que je souhaite,   (III, 3)

she tells her successful rival — a remark which reminds us that irony, so common in Corneille, is but another form of double-entendre.

§ 2 *Comedy in the tragedies*

It is not, perhaps, surprising to find baroque themes and features present in the tragedies as well as in the comedies; it is more extraordinary that the tragedies should continue the comedies in other respects.

Some of the characters of the comedies recur in the serious plays. The count in *Le Cid* is something of a *miles gloriosus*, not unreminiscent of Matamore:

> Tout l'Etat périra, s'il faut que je périsse.   (II, 2)

Emilie and Pauline, as Herland suggests, are two young girls from the comedies who have strayed into a tragedy; and in *Horace* Sabine and Camille debate a *question d'amour* — whether Camille, who is betrothed to Curiace, should suffer more or less than Sabine, who is actually married to Horace. Many of the men of the tragedies would be at home in a comedy — the irresolute and time-serving Félix of *Polyeucte*; the henpecked Valens of *Théodore*; and the weak and equally henpecked Prusias of *Nicomède*. Attila has something of the Alidor of *La Place Royale* in him:

> L'amour chez Attila n'est pas un bon suffrage;
> Ce qu'on m'en donnerait me tiendrait lieu d'outrage,
> Et tout exprès ailleurs je porterais ma foi,
> De peur qu'on n'eût par là trop de pouvoir sur moi.
> Les femmes qu'on adore usurpent un empire
> Que jamais un mari n'ose ou ne peut dédire.
> C'est au commun des rois à se plaire en leurs fers,
> Non à ceux dont le nom fait trembler l'univers.
> Que chacun de leurs yeux aime à se faire esclave;

> Moi, je ne veux les voir qu'en tyrans que je brave:
> Et par quelques attraits qu'ils captivent un cœur,
> Le mien en dépit d'eux est tout à ma grandeur.   (I, 2)

The untruthful, fickle and glib Jason of *La Toison* is reminiscent of Clindor in *L'Illusion comique*. Aspar in *Pulchérie* is a member of the same family: he is ready to marry Irène if her brother Léon is elected Emperor, equally ready to marry Justine if her father, Martian, becomes Emperor, no less ready to marry the Empress, Pulchérie:

> Il m'aime en apparence, en effet il m'amuse;
> Jamais pour notre hymen il ne manque d'excuse . . .
> . . . .
>   Son cœur suivra le sceptre en quelque main qu'il brille:
> Si Martian l'obtient, il aimera sa fille;
> Et l'amitié du frère, et l'amour de la sœur,
> Céderont à l'espoir de s'en voir successeur.   (I, 3)

One is reminded of some of the characters of the comedies — Philandre in *Mélite*, for example, or Théante in *La Suivante* — who pay their addresses to one mistress while hoping to marry another for her greater wealth; and the words with which Irène closes the first act might have been spoken equally well by Doris, or Cloris, or Amarante:

> Perfide, tu n'es pas encore où tu te penses,
> J'ai pénétré ton cœur, j'ai vu tes espérances,
> De ton amour pour moi je vois l'illusion;
> Mais tu n'en sortiras qu'à ta confusion.   (I, 5)

In her clear-sightedness and her ability to see through her lover, Irène resembles Cloris in *Mélite* — as she does also in her resolve to put a brave face on it when she is abandoned by him.

Many details of plot or structure in the tragedies remind us of the comedies. The constant passage from hope to foreboding of the tragic characters is anticipated by the sudden reversals of fortune, the sudden passage from joy or elation to disappointment in the comedies. The broken-backed structure of *Horace*, in which the hero faces two successive perils, is that of *La Place Royale*; and the false report that Horace has been defeated is not very different from the false report of the deaths of Mélite and Tirsis in *Mélite*, or from the way in which, in *L'Illusion*, the spectator is led to believe that Clindor has been faithless to Isabelle and has been assassinated by a jealous husband. Maxime, who betrays Cinna on finding that he is in love with Emilie, behaves like Eraste in *Mélite*, Alcidon in *La Veuve*, Théante in *La Suivante*, or Florame in *La Galerie du Palais*. When Polyeucte gives Pauline to Sévère, he is merely emulating Alidor in *La Place Royale*, who gives Angélique to his friend — no more successfully. Neither Pompée in *La Mort de Pompée*, nor Flavie in *Théodore* appear on the stage, though they play an important part in the action: Florange 'qui ne paraît point' anticipates them in *La Veuve*. *Théodore* deals very largely with a favourite theme of the comedies, one to which Corneille returns in *Suréna* — the wickedness or folly of marriages arranged by parents. Exupère who, in *Héraclius*, seems to be working against Héraclius but turns out to be on his side, recalls Damon in *La Suivante*. When Attale in *Nicomède* changes his allegiance in the course of the play, he is following the example of Célidan in *La Veuve*. In *La Toison d'Or*, a play of love intrigues, Absyrte resorts to a trick to win the love of Hypsipyle; he also exhorts his sister, Médée, to make Jason fall in love with her in order that Hypsipyle shall come to hate Jason and be more receptive to his own advances — just as Hippolyte in *La Galerie du Palais* schemes to make Lysandre's mistress appear unfaithful to him, so that jealousy may drive him into her (Hippolyte's) arms. Similarly, Domitian in *Tite et Bérénice* pays court to Bérénice in order to arouse the jealousy of his brother, Tite, and make him abandon his projected marriage with Domitie — just as Lysandre in *La Galerie* pays court to Hippolyte to make Célidée jealous. *Othon*, in which a large number of different matches are suggested, reminds us of *La Suivante*, though it goes far beyond *La Suivante*; and Othon, like Théante in *La Suivante*, loves one woman but pays court to another (not of his own free will, it is true). The *comédies héroïques*, *Don Sanche* and *Pulchérie*, and *Agésilas*, end, like the comedies, with the arrangement of several marriages. Finally, the vein of fancy that one finds in the mad scenes in *Mélite* or in the speeches of Matamore and Dorante, is continued in the machine plays, *Andromède* and *La Toison d'Or*.

So far, we have been concerned with characters, scenes and situations in the comedies which have their counterparts in the tragedies, without necessarily being in themselves comic — though, in fact, nearly all, if not comic, are of a kind normally associated with comedy rather than tragedy, and indeed of a kind which would normally be considered unsuited to the dignity of tragedy. But the tragedies are not merely reminiscent of the comedies in such details as these, they abound in elements either comic or verging on the comic. This indeed might be considered as yet another baroque feature in Corneille. A fondness for mixed genres is characteristic of the baroque age, and the mixture of tones, of comedy and tragedy, is akin to the mixture of speech, music and mechanical ingenuity in the machine play or opera.

Many scenes in the tragedies verge on the comic. In *Le Cid*, for example, Don Sanche comes to tell Chimène that he has been defeated; she jumps to the conclusion that he has defeated Rodrigue and does not even give him a chance to open his mouth and explain. In *Nicomède*, there is a scene (I, 2) in which Attale is talking with his elder brother, Nicomède, whom he has never seen. Nicomède knows Attale, but Attale does not know Nicomède, and his remarks are comically wide of the mark. When Prusias is easily taken in by his wife's show of affection, we are reminded of the similar scene in *Le Malade imaginaire*. In *La Toison*, Jason finds himself confronted by Médée, whom he is wooing, and Hypsipyle, whom he has abandoned (II, 4). In a later scene, he tries to appease Hypsipyle, but Médée appears and he is afraid lest she should have overheard him:

Trouvez donc les moyens de nous tirer d'ici.
La toison emportée, il agira, Madame,
Ce véritable amour qui vous donne mon âme;
Sinon . . . [Here Médée appears]
        Mais, Dieux! que vois-je? O ciel! je suis perdu,
Si j'ai tant de malheur qu'elle m'ait entendu.

In *Othon*, Martian threatens Plautine and tells her that she will never marry Othon. At that moment, Lacus enters and announces that Galba has consented to the marriage of Plautine with Othon. One is reminded of Dorante in *Le Menteur*, whose adversary arrives at the precise moment when Dorante is relating how he left him for dead. Othon, who intended to obtain the empire by marrying Camille, finds (III, 5) that he is betrothed to Camille but that the empire has been given to his rival, and he has to talk himself out of this difficult situation — exactly as Trissotin, at the end of *Les Femmes savantes*, believing Henriette to be poor, has to find pretexts for not marrying her.

Talking themselves out of difficult situations is a thing at which Corneille's characters excel. Jason, in *La Toison*, is told by Aæte that he would not have thought of marrying his daughter, Médée, had there been any other way of obtaining the golden fleece. The accusation is perfectly true; but with admirable resourcefulness, Jason manages to rebut it:

> C'est faire trop d'outrage à mon cœur enflammé.
> Dès l'abord je la vis, dès l'abord je l'aimai;
> Et mon amour n'est pas un amour politique
> Que le besoin colore, et que la crainte explique.
> Mais n'ayant que moi-même à vous parler pour moi,
> Je n'osais espérer d'être écouté d'un roi,
> Ni que sur ma parole il me crut de naissance
> A porter mes désirs jusqu'à son alliance.
> Maintenant qu'une reine a fait voir que mon sang
> N'est pas fort au-dessous de cet illustre rang,
> Qu'un refus de son sceptre après votre victoire
> Montre qu'on peut m'aimer sans hasarder sa gloire,
> J'ose, un peu moins timide, offrir, avec ma foi,
> Ce que veut une reine à la fille d'un roi.   (III, 1)

In *Tite et Bérénice*, Domitie is asked to say explicitly whether she prefers Tite or Domitian — just as Célimène in *Le Misanthrope* is asked to choose between Oronte and Alceste — and has to use her wits to avoid giving an answer.[1] Aspar, in *Pulchérie*, finds

---

[1] In a later scene (II, 6), after the return of Bérénice, the tables are turned, and it is she who is in the position of asking Tite to declare whether he loves her or Bérénice. The

himself in the awkward situation of having to explain to Irène and others how it is that, though he loves her, he can nevertheless consider marrying other ladies.

The tone of the dialogue is often homely, familiar, and down-to-earth: it is significant that eighteenth-century critics such as Voltaire and Batteux should find fault with many of Corneille's lines for their lowness and familiarity. The tone of Pauline's complaint that marriage has diminished her husband's affection is conversational:

> Tu vois, ma Stratonice, en quel siècle nous sommes:
> Voilà notre pouvoir sur les esprits des hommes;
> Voilà ce qui nous reste, et l'ordinaire effet
> De l'amour qu'on nous offre, et des vœux qu'on nous fait.
> Tant qu'ils ne sont qu'amants, nous sommes souveraines,
> Et jusqu'à la conquête ils nous traitent de reines;
> Mais après l'hyménée ils sont rois à leur tour.   (*Polyeucte*, I, 3)

This is not a tragic heroine speaking, but (except for the military metaphor (*conquête*)), an ordinary woman of any class. Many of the speeches of Pauline's father, Félix, are decidedly comic in tone — his pretence of being a Christian, for example, or his regrets on finding that Sévère, whom he would not accept as a son-in-law when he was poor, has become rich and influential:

> Ah! regret qui me tue
> De n'avoir pas aimé la vertu toute nue!
> Ah! Pauline, en effet, tu m'as trop obéi;
> Ton courage était bon, ton devoir l'a trahi.
> Que ta rébellion m'eût été favorable!
> Qu'elle m'eût garanti d'un état déplorable!   (I, 4)

Here, he comes as near as possible to blaming his daughter for having done what he asked her. He is comic, too, when he prides himself on his perspicacity and overreaches himself in his cunning, attributing to Sévère selfish motives which exist only in his own mind:

reversal of the situation is emphasized by the fact that Domitie uses a line in speaking to Tite which he had addressed to her in the earlier scene:
> Où porte votre cœur ce qu'il sent de plus tendre.   (II, 6)

It is significant that there are no comic elements in Racine's play.

> Mais un vieux courtisan est un peu moins crédule:
> Il voit quand on le joue, et quand on dissimule;
> Et moi j'en ai tant vu de toutes les façons,
> Qu'à lui-même au besoin j'en ferais des leçons.   (V, 1)

A colloquial bluntness of speech often has a comic effect. Paulin, in *Théodore*, tells Placide how Didyme entered the brothel where Théodore is confined:

>   loin de le blâmer,
> Je présume . . .
> *Placide.*   Ah! je sais ce qu'il faut présumer.
> Il est entré lui seul.   (IV, 3)

In *Pertharite*, Grimoald, impatiently waiting to hear how Rodelinde has received his proposal of marriage, is told that she listened to it calmly, and bursts out:

> Ah! c'est m'assassiner d'un discours inutile:
> Je ne veux rien savoir de sa tranquillité;
> Dis seulement un mot de sa facilité.   (II, 4)

Jason, in *La Toison*, argues that if Aæte gives him Médée and the fleece they will still be his, because Jason, as his son-in-law, will become 'une part de vous-même'. With blunt shrewdness, with that kind of commonsense that amuses us in Mme Jourdain, Aæte replies:

> Vous prenez un peu tard une mauvaise adresse:
> Nos esprits sont plus lourds que ceux de votre Grèce;
> Mais j'ai d'assez bons yeux, dans un si juste effroi,
> Pour démêler sans peine un gendre d'avec moi.
> Je sais que l'union d'un époux à ma fille
> De mon sang et du sien forme une autre famille,
> Et que si de moi-même elle fait quelque part,
> Cette part de moi-même a ses destins à part.   (III, 1)

The comic effect is heightened by the word play of the last line, which echoes Jason's words.

Both extreme gallantry and rudeness may have the same effect. In *Nicomède*, Act I, scene 2, Laodice neatly answers Attale's flowery compliments in much the same way as the heroines of the early comedies. Later, she expresses her real feelings with more directness:

> Votre importunité, que j'ose dire extrême ...   (III, 4)

Nicomède pays his brother a neat backhanded compliment, too:

> Vous avez de l'esprit, si vous n'avez du cœur.   (III, 6)

The opening scene of *La Toison* borders on the comic in the same way. Chalciope expresses her hope that Médée has not fallen in love with Jason. To this sisterly remonstrance, Médée retorts with sisterly candour:

> La remontrance est douce, obligeante, civile;
> Mais à parler sans feinte elle est fort inutile:
> Si je n'ai point d'amour, je n'y prends point de part;
> Et si j'aime Jason, l'avis vient un peu tard.

Irony and double-entendre, of both of which the baroque age was fond, are both capable of being used with comic effect, are perhaps both inherently comic. Irony is very common in Corneille. The count speaks ironically to Don Diègue in *Le Cid*:

> Instruisez-le d'exemple, et rendez-le parfait,
> Expliquant à ses yeux vos leçons par l'effet,   (I, 3)

—thus taunting the old man by reminding him that this is precisely what he can no longer do. Sabine uses irony to dissuade Horace and Curiace from fighting (II, 6),[1] and greets Horace with contemptuous irony after he has murdered his sister:

> A quoi s'arrête ici ton *illustre* colère?
> Viens voir mourir ta sœur dans les bras de ton père;
> Viens repaître tes yeux d'un *spectacle si doux*:
> Ou si tu n'es point las de ces *généreux* coups,
> Immole au *cher* pays des *vertueux* Horaces
> Ce reste malheureux du sang des Curiaces.
> Si prodigue du tien, n'épargne pas le leur ...[2]   (IV, 7)

---

[1] See below, p. 286. The irony in Corneille is very often overlooked. To my knowledge the only critic who has mentioned that this speech of Sabine's is ironical is H. Gehle ('Staat und Menschlichkeit. Gedanken über "Horace" von Pierre Corneille,' in *Die Neueren Sprachen*, 1954, p. 57).

[2] Similarly, Attila addresses his friends ironically as '*illustres* amis' (V, 4), emphasizing that they are, in fact, his slaves. Honorie's use of the epithet 'cher' is similar. If Attila

M

In *Pompée*, Cléopâtre alludes ironically to Ptolomée's reliance on his unworthy advisers:

> Photin vous vient aider à le bien recevoir:
> Consultez avec lui quel est votre devoir.   (II, 3)

Nicomède is particularly rich in irony, and if not all the examples that we have quoted are comic (though irony nearly always tends to be comic), there is no doubt that the general effect in *Nicomède* is comic. The hero makes great use of irony, whether he is admonishing Attale to be worthy of his Roman upbringing —

> Pour avoir tant vécu chez ces cœurs magnanimes,
> Vous en avez bientôt oublié les maximes.
> Reprenez un orgueil digne d'elle et de vous;
> Remplissez mieux un nom sous qui nous tremblons tous,
> Et sans plus l'abaisser à cette ignominie
> D'idolâtrer en vain la reine d'Arménie,
> Songez qu'il faut du moins, pour toucher votre cœur,
> La fille d'un tribun, ou celle d'un préteur . . .   (I, 2)

whether he is fencing verbally with his father — attributing his return to his affection for his father, and by his expressions of gratitude insinuating that thanks are due rather to himself —

> La seule ambition de pouvoir en personne
> Mettre à vos pieds, Seigneur, encore une couronne,
> De jouir de l'honneur de vos embrassements,
> Et d'être le témoin de vos contentements.
> Après la Cappadoce heureusement unie
> Aux royaumes du Pont et de la Bythinie,
> Je viens remercier et mon père et mon roi
> D'avoir eu la bonté de s'y servir de moi,
> D'avoir choisi mon bras pour une telle gloire,
> Et fait tomber sur moi l'honneur de sa victoire.[1]   (II, 2)

or whether he is opposing the Roman attempt to place Attale on the throne which ought to be Nicomède's:

persists in marrying her to Octar, she says, she will turn him against Attila; and she adds, as Octar enters:

> Ton rival entre, adieu, délibère avec lui,
> Si ce *cher* Octar m'aime, où sera ton appui.   (IV, 3)

[1] This is reminiscent of Cléopâtre in *Rodogune*, who tells her sons:

> Mon amour pour vous fit tout ce que je fis . . .   (II, 3)

> Attale a le cœur *grand*, l'esprit *grand*, l'âme *grande*,
> Et toutes les *grandeurs* dont se fait un *grand* roi;
> Mais c'est trop que d'en croire un Romain sur sa foi.
> Par quelque *grand* effet voyons s'il en est digne,
> S'il a cette vertu, cette valeur insigne:
> Donnez-lui votre armée, et voyons ces *grands* coups ...
>
> (II, 3)

He seems to infect the other characters by his example — Laodice, for instance:

> *Prusias.*   Reine, puisque ce titre a pour vous tant de charmes,
> Sa perte vous devrait donner quelques alarmes:
> Qui tranche du roi ne règne pas longtemps.
> *Laodice.*   J'observerai, Seigneur, ces avis *importants*;
> Et si jamais je règne, on verra la pratique
> D'une si *salutaire* et *noble* politique.
>
> (III, 1)

In Act II, scene 1, Araspe plays, with delicate irony, on Prusias's mistrust of his son:

> C'est ce que *de tout autre* il faudrait redouter,
> Seigneur, et qu'*en tout autre* il faudrait arrêter;
> Mais ce n'est pas pour vous un avis nécessaire:
> Le prince est vertueux, et vous êtes bon père.

Here one is reminded of Molière — on the one hand of Alceste's 'Je ne dis pas cela,' on the other of those fathers (Argante and Argan) who, being told 'vous êtes bon naturellement,' are provoked into replying, 'Je ne suis point bon, et je suis méchant quand je veux.'

Irony is by no means rare in the later plays. Aristie in *Sertorius* uses it very effectively in speaking to her faithless husband, who has divorced her and married another wife, Emilie:

> Je ne suis pas, Seigneur, d'une telle importance.
> D'autres soins éteindront cette ardeur de vengeance;
> Ceux de vous agrandir vous porteront ailleurs,
> Où vous pourrez trouver quelques destins meilleurs;
> Ceux de servir Sylla, d'aimer *son* Emilie,
> D'imprimer du respect à toute l'Italie,
> De rendre à votre Rome un jour sa liberté,
> Sauront tourner vos pas de quelque autre côté.

> Surtout *ce privilège acquis aux grandes âmes*
> *De changer à leur gré de maris et de femmes,*
> *Mérite qu'on l'étale aux bouts de l'univers,*
> *Pour en donner l'exemple à cent climats divers.*   (III, 2)

Even the great scene between Pompée and Sertorius — in which
irony is by no means lacking — has moments when the tone of
the dialogue becomes almost comic:

> P. De si hautes leçons, Seigneur, sont difficiles,
>   Et pourraient vous donner quelques soins inutiles,
>   Si vous faisiez dessein de me les expliquer
>   Jusqu'à m'avoir appris à les bien pratiquer.
> S. Aussi me pourriez-vous épargner quelque peine,
>   Si vous vouliez avoir l'âme toute romaine:
>   Je vous l'ai déjà dit.

Here, Pompée's hint that he may one day defeat Sertorius,
coming in contrast to the polite deference of his attitude, and
Sertorius's harping on his mysterious advice that Pompée should
have 'l'âme toute romaine' (the meaning of which is not explained
until later) would not be out of place in a comedy. Plautine in
Othon receives Martian's offer of marriage ironically, and when he
eulogizes the class of freedmen to which he belongs and which she
scorns, she says:

> Pardonnez donc, Seigneur, si je me suis méprise:
> Mon orgueil dans vos fers n'a rien qui l'autorise.
> Je viens de me connaître, et me vois à mon tour
> Indigne des honneurs qui suivent votre amour.   (II, 2)

Pulchérie, like *Nicomède*, is particularly rich in irony. Léon,
when Pulchérie tells him that she must marry whoever the Senate
elects as Emperor, replies:

> Qu'avez-vous à trembler? Quelque empereur qu'on nomme,
> Vous aurez votre amant, ou du moins un grand homme,
> Dont le nom, adoré du peuple et de la cour,
> Soutiendra votre gloire, et vaincra votre amour.
> Procope, Aréobinde, Aspar, et leurs semblables,
> Parés de ce grand nom, vous deviendront aimables,
> Et l'éclat de ce rang qui fait tant de jaloux,
> En eux, ainsi qu'en moi, sera charmant pour vous.   (I, 1)

The fifth line takes on all the more point if we remember that Léon is repeating Pulchérie's own words: earlier in the scene she had named his rivals: 'Procope, Gratian, Aréobinde, Aspar.' When Aspar refuses to help Irène's brother, Léon, to become Emperor so that he may marry Pulchérie, she tells him:

> Je suis plus raisonnable, et ne demande pas
> Qu'en faveur d'un ami vous descendiez si bas.
> Pylade pour Oreste aurait fait davantage;
> Mais de pareils efforts ne sont plus en usage;
> Un grand cœur les dédaigne, et le siècle a changé:
> A s'aimer de plus près on se croit obligé,
> Et des vertus du temps l'âme persuadée
> Hait de ces vieux héros la surprenante idée.   (I, 5)

He refers ironically in the same scene to 'ce *cher* frère,' and is himself later referred to as 'votre *cher* Aspar,' 'cet *illustre* Aspar'. There is a delicious scene in which Aspar, the lover of Irène, delicately hints that Martian might be elected Emperor and take a son-in-law (meaning himself). Martian, his daughter, Justine, and Aspar, all keep up the pretence that Aspar would not desert Irène, knowing that he would do it with alacrity.

> *M.* Il faudrait que ce gendre eût les vertus d'Aspar;
> Mais vous aimez ailleurs, et ce serait un crime
> Que de rendre infidèle un cœur si magnanime.
> *A.* J'aime, et ne me sens pas capable de changer;
> Mais d'autres vous diraient que pour vous soulager,
> Quand leur amour irait jusqu'à l'idolâtrie,
> Ils le sacrifieraient au bien de la patrie.
> *J.* Certes, qui m'aimerait pour le bien de l'Etat
> Ne me trouverait pas, Seigneur, un cœur ingrat,
> Et je lui rendrais grâce au nom de tout l'empire;
> Mais vous êtes constant; et s'il vous faut plus dire,
> Quoi que le bien public jamais puisse exiger,
> Ce ne sera pas moi qui vous ferai changer.   (II, 2)

One wonders which is more comic — the delicate innuendoes and irony, or the bluntness of the last line.

One type of comic scene in which irony is used with devastating effect is the scene between two jealous women, in which irony and

double-entendre alternate with blunt plain speaking, in which a
mask of icy, formal politeness does not hide the real vindictive-
ness beneath and is allowed to fall from time to time. Such scenes
are common in Corneille, and are hardly less comic than the scene
in *Le Misanthrope* between Célimène and Arsinoé. It is perhaps
significant that the first such scenes occur in a comedy (*La
Suivante*); but they occur in many of the tragedies from *Théodore*
to *Tite et Bérénice*.[1] Every remark in these scenes has a sting.
Unfortunately, they are too long to quote, and two short extracts
must suffice. Here is part of the interview between Hypsipyle and
Médée in *La Toison*:

> *H.* Je n'ai que des attraits, et vous avez des charmes.
> [This remark is less innocent than it looks. The
> word *charmes*, besides personal charms, means the
> charms of the sorceress: Hypsipyle is hinting that
> Médée can only attract Jason by her magic arts.]
>
> . . . .
>
> *M.* Il vous aima jadis?
> [hinting that his love for Hypsipyle is a thing of
> the remote past.]
> *H.*   Peut-être il m'aime encor,
> Moins que vous toutefois, ou que la toison d'Or.
> [a cutting suggestion that Jason is only interested
> in winning the golden fleece and sees Médée only
> as a means to an end.]
>
> . . . .
>
> Avec sincérité je dois vous avouer
> Que j'ai quelque sujet encor de m'en louer.
> *M.* Avec sincérité je dois aussi vous dire
> [Arsinoé and Célimène also affect sincerity.
> Médée's repetition of the phrase used by
> Hypsipyle shows that politeness is wearing thin.]
> Qu'assez malaisément on sort de mon empire,
> Et que quand jusqu'à moi j'ai permis d'aspirer,
> On ne s'abaisse plus à vous considérer.
> Profitez des avis que ma pitié vous donne.
> *H.* A vous dire le vrai, cette hauteur m'étonne.
> Je suis reine, Madame, et les fronts couronnés . . .

[1] E.g. *Théodore*, II, 4; *Pertharite*, I, 2, III, 2; *Sophonisbe*, I, 3, II, 3, III, 3; *Othon*, IV, 4;
Tite et Bérénice, III, 3.

> *M.* Et moi, je suis Médée, et vous m'importunez.
> [The mask of politeness drops, and Médée
> bluntly says what she thinks.] (III, 4)

One wonders why Péguy claims that Corneille's characters cannot wound each other's feelings. In *Attila*, Ildione tells Honorie that she, Honorie, is to marry Attila — but only because Ildione has refused him:

> Je vous rends à vous-même [she tells Attila], et ne puis rien de
>   plus;
> Et c'est à vous de faire accepter mes refus.
> *H.* Accepter ses refus! Moi, Seigneur?

This time one thinks of the village girl in one of Thomas Hardy's stories who, in similar circumstances, exclaims, 'What! take her leavings!'

Double-entendre is also used by Corneille with comic effect — indeed, it is difficult to distinguish clearly between irony and double-entendre. In *Nicomède*, the two adversaries, Arsinoé and Nicomède, converse: their remarks, outwardly friendly, have a sinister undertone:

> *A.* Ce qui vous amène?
> *N.*   Oui, Madame; et j'espère
> Que vous m'y servirez auprès du Roi mon père.
> *A.* Je vous y servirai comme vous l'espérez.
> *N.* De votre bon vouloir nous sommes assurés.
> *A.* Il ne tiendra qu'au Roi qu'aux effets je ne passe.
> *N.* Vous voulez à tous deux nous faire cette grâce?
> *A.* Tenez-vous assuré que je n'oublierai rien.
> *N.* Je connais votre cœur, ne doutez pas du mien. (I, 3)

A related comic device is talking at cross-purposes. This occurs already in *Horace*, when Valère talks of Horace's flight as glorious and Horace's father as disgraceful, not knowing that it was only a subterfuge (IV, 2); but there the comic effect is not strongly marked. It is clearer in *Nicomède*, when Arsinoé and Laonice discuss how the 'cause de nos maux' should be punished, each

believing herself to be in a position to punish the other (V, 6). In
Sertorius (IV, 3), Perpenna asks for Sertorius's help — meaning
his help to win the hand of Viriate. Sertorius affects to understand
his help to make peace with Sylla. Here there is no doubt about
the comic effect, because the misunderstanding is wilful: Sertorius is trying to avoid the ticklish question of Viriate, whom he
hopes to marry himself.

Repetition also sometimes produces a comic effect, especially
if it is used ironically or to tease, like the repetition of 'deux mots
de vérité' in *Nicomède*:

Nicomède.	Qu'ont-ils dit qui vous plaise, et que vous vouliez croire?
Arsinoé.	Deux mots de vérité qui vous comblent de gloire.
N.	Peut-on savoir de vous ces deux mots importants?
Araspe.	Seigneur, le Roi s'ennuie, et vous tardez longtemps.
N.	Je commence, Madame, enfin à vous entendre:
	Son amour conjugal, chassant le paternel,
	Vous fera l'innocente, et moi le criminel,
	Mais . . .
Ars.	Achevez, Seigneur, ce mais, que veut-il dire?
N.	Deux mots de vérité qui font que je respire.
Ars.	Peut-on savoir de vous ces deux mots importants?
N.	Vous les saurez du Roi, je tarde trop longtemps. (III, 7)

A similar, almost equally delicious, scene is that in which, in
Pulchérie, Aspar hints that a rising may take place, but refuses to
say who he thinks might head it (he has himself in mind):

> Le besoin de l'Etat est souvent un mystère
> Dont la moitié se dit, et l'autre est bonne à taire.

Pulchérie, who sees through Aspar, then tells him that Martian has
warned her against a secret enemy; but when, with consternation,
he asks who it is, she, in her turn refuses to say:

> Aspar, c'est un mystère
> Dont la moitié se dit, et l'autre est bonne à taire.   (IV, 3)

In *Sophonisbe*, Eryxe says to Sophonisbe:

> On ne m'avait pas dit qu'il fallût votre aveu.

With greater rudeness, Sophonisbe replies, in a line which is comic in its forceful, colloquial tone and its bluntness:

> Qu'on vous l'ait dit ou non, il m'importe assez peu.

But at the end of the scene, Eryxe manages to get her own back:

> Et d'ailleurs, s'il vous vient demander votre aveu,
> Soit qu'il l'obtienne, ou non, il m'importe fort peu.   (I, 3)

Repeating her own or other people's words, usually with a comic or semi-comic effect is a habit of Camille in *Othon*. At the beginning of Act II, scene 3, for example, she tells Lacus and Martian:

> Je vous rencontre ensemble ici fort à propos,
> Et voulais à tous deux vous dire quatre mots.

She then tells them some home-truths, and neatly rounds off the scene with the words:

> Voilà les quatre mots que j'avais à vous dire.
> Pensez-y.

In Act III, her father, Galba, having given his reasons for deciding to marry her to Pison, she gives hers for refusing, often cleverly repeating his very words and phrases. Galba, for example, had said that Rome

> ne peut souffrir, après cette habitude,
> Ni pleine liberté, ni pleine servitude.
> Elle veut donc un maître . . .

She uses this remark against him with great skill:

> Je crois tenir un peu de Rome où je suis née.
> Je ne demande point la pleine liberté,
> Puisqu'elle en a mis bas l'intrépide fierté;
> Mais si vous m'imposez la pleine servitude,
> J'y trouverai, comme elle, un joug un peu bien rude.

The comic or semi-comic devices enumerated occur in nearly all Corneille's plays, but more frequently and with more clearly marked comic effect, perhaps, in the later plays. In the later plays, indeed, the comic element is not just a question of occasional situations or passages; it is part of the very conception of the play.

In his last plays, Corneille seems to be moving towards a new kind of drama which is half way between tragedy and comedy. They aim at portraying realistically intrigues, usually turning on the marriage of a person of royal rank. Whereas most of Corneille's plays have a happy ending, in his later plays he often provides with a happy ending a subject which would not seem to admit of one, *Oedipe* and *Sophonisbe*, for example. Oedipe recedes into the background and is shown as the obstacle to the marriage of Dircé and Thésée, so that his death is merely the prelude to the wedding of the two lovers. Sophonisbe, too, is the obstacle to the union of Eryxe and Massinisse, and the play ends with the suggestion that in time Massinisse and Eryxe will come together. *Tite et Bérénice*, too, has a happy ending, all the more so if it is compared with Racine's *Bérénice*. Bérénice has gained her object, which was to stop Tite from marrying Domitie, and Domitie and Domitian are free to marry and to succeed to the throne.

Sometimes, too, the psychology of the later plays is that of comedy. In *Sophonisbe*, Eryxe loves Massinisse, but is not sure of his love, so she greets him coldly. Massinisse, feeling himself rebuffed, offers his hand to Sophonisbe. She, against her better judgment, accepts him in order to make sure that he will not marry Eryxe, and thereby encompasses her own destruction. This play, though it deals with the subject of Sophonisbe, has more in common with Molière than Mairet. Rousset has shown that the plot of *Tite et Bérénice* closely resembles that of the comedies.[1] And, as we have seen, from *Théodore* onward, *prises de bec* between two jealous women are a regular feature of Corneille's plays.

In short, Corneille does not make a clear-cut distinction be-

---

[1] 'Supposons le schéma suivant:

'Cléandre, amant d'Angélique, feint d'aimer Phylis; celle-ci, d'abord éprise de Doraste, le quitte aussitôt pour Cléandre, qui offre un meilleur parti; Cléandre se prend à son jeu, incline vers Phylis, puis regrette Angélique, de nouveau penche vers elle; Doraste, de son côté, amoureux de Phylis, feint d'aimer Angélique pour donner de la jalousie à Cléandre, le ramener vers Angélique et lui reprendre Phylis; dépit de Phylis, qui veut bien quitter, mais non pas qu'on la quitte; Cléandre continue à osciller tantôt vers Phylis, tantôt vers Angélique, avec une secrète préférence pour celle-ci, etc.

'Tout le monde croira reconnaître là le schéma type d'une comédie de Corneille telle qu'il en faisait au début de sa carrière; or, c'est la donnée de son *Tite et Bérénice*, une fois transposés les noms de Tite, Bérénice, Domitie et Domitian dans les noms de comédie Cléandre, Angélique, Phylis et Doraste.'   (J. Rousset)

tween comedy and tragedy: his conception of tragedy embraces comedy as well. His characters, given to teasing and irony, fond of using familiar language, sometimes comic in their blunt out-spokenness, their innuendoes, their double-entendre, and the contrast between their words and their inmost thoughts, are human and natural. And here is one difference between Corneille and Racine. Although comic touches occasionally occur in Racine, they are less frequent; and this is surely connected with the fact that, for Racine, a tragic character should be remote (*major e longinquo reverentia*). Corneille, on the other hand, brings tragedy and the tragic hero increasingly close to everyday life. It is significant that it was he who invented the term *comédie héroïque*.

Chapter Eight

THE REALISM OF CORNEILLE
(1)
CHARACTERS

Epithets derived from names of writers sometimes suffer a strange fate. Some are merely used with the sense of 'like or pertaining to the writer in question', as 'Shakespearean'. Others, however, take on a different shade of meaning and imply, not 'like the writer', but 'like some popular misconception of the writer'. The word 'Machiavellian', for instance, has acquired undertones and overtones of meaning which make the reading of *The Prince* something of a surprise to the reader who expects it to be 'Machiavellian'. 'Cartesianism' is only a part of Descartes, as 'marivaudage' is only a part of Marivaux. In the same way, the adjective 'Cornelian' has acquired implications, based on an over-simple, if not erroneous, interpretation of Corneille, which make it difficult to approach his plays with an open mind.

Corneille is often regarded as lacking in humanity, as the creator of a false psychology. Corneille, said La Bruyère in a famous phrase, 'peint les hommes comme ils devraient être.' 'Corneille est presque toujours hors de la nature,' wrote Voltaire. 'L'observation de la nature ne l'occupait point,' asserted Guizot. In more recent times, we find Faguet saying that 'rien ne ressemble moins à la vie que le théâtre de Corneille,' and Barrère that 'il a aimé l'humanité inhumaine'. His characters, it is said, are over-simplified, and get less and less convincing as time goes on:

Drama of this kind must, it is clear, lack many of the qualities which are usually associated with the dramatic art; there is no room in it for variety of character-drawing, for delicacy of feeling, or for the realistic presentation of the experiences of life. Corneille hardly attempted to produce such effects as these; and during his early years his great gifts of passion and rhetoric easily made up for the deficiency. As he grew older, however, his inspiration weakened; his command of his material left him; and he was no longer able to fill the figures of his creation with the old intellectual sublimity. His heroes and his heroines became mere mouthing puppets, pouring out an endless stream of elaborate, high-flown sentiments, wrapped up in a complicated jargon of argumentative verse. His later plays are miserable failures. (Lytton Strachey)

Corneille, indeed, has even come to be regarded as a moralist, a creator of supermen. The Cornelian hero is often described as a being whose will is capable of executing whatever course he has selected by the exercise of his reason and whose passions are rational; a magnanimous being, following the path of duty whatever temptations beset him, and fond of abnegation for its own sake. His essential nature, it is said, is expressed in lines such as:

> Je le ferais encor, si j'avais à le faire.[1]
> > (*Le Cid*, III, 4; *Polyeucte*, V, 3)

> Je suis maître de moi comme de l'univers . . .
> > (*Cinna*, V, 3)

> *Antiochus.* Le pourrez-vous, mon frère?
> *Séleucus.*   Ah! que vous me pressez!
> Je le voudrai du moins, mon frère, et c'est assez;
> Et ma raison sur moi gardera tant d'empire
> Que je désavouerai mon cœur, s'il en soupire.
> > (*Rodogune*, I, 3)

> Voilà quelle je suis, et quelle je veux être.[2]

The Cornelian hero has been seen as the dramatic equivalent of the *généreux* of Descartes, and Corneille has been described as 'le

---

[1] But this need not in itself denote strength. When Mme de Rênal in *Le Rouge et le Noir*, for instance, says, 'Je commettrais de nouveau ma faute si elle était à commettre,' it is rather a sign of weakness.

[2] This line is pronounced by four characters, in *Héraclius, Théodore, Pertharite* and *Sophonisbe*.

poète de la volonté,' 'professeur d'énergie nationale'. These views have been challenged by some recent writers, such as Bénichou and Nadal, for whom the Cornelian hero is motivated, not by virtue and reason, but by the passion for *gloire*, which makes him ambitious of heroism, magnanimity, or rank. Even this, however, does not clear Corneille of the imputation of lacking humanity; and, in any case, the older view is still current — even such a great Cornelian scholar as M. Couton talks of 'l'idée cornélienne de l'homme, éclairé par la raison, doué d'une volonté capable de dompter les passions.'

Now, Corneille began by writing comedies which, besides their comic elements, were distinguished by their use of baroque themes and characteristics and by realism of various kinds. Neither the baroque characteristics nor the comic elements disappeared from Corneille's work when he turned from tragedy to comedy, so that it would seem unlikely, on the face of it, that he abandoned his psychological realism and became a creator of supermen. Indeed, the presence of a comic element in his tragedies seems almost to be a guarantee of their realism. Certainly, in his theoretical writings, Corneille shows that he was no less concerned with realism in tragedy than in comedy:

> Le poème dramatique est une imitation, ou pour en mieux parler, un portrait des actions des hommes; et il est hors de doute que les portraits sont d'autant plus excellents, qu'ils ressemblent mieux à l'original. (*Troisième Discours*)

The same preoccupation with realism is evident in his views about the characters of tragedy:

> Le poète doit considérer l'âge, la dignité, la naissance, l'emploi et le pays de ceux qu'il introduit: il faut qu'il sache ce qu'on doit à sa patrie, à ses parents, à ses amis, à son roi; quel est l'office d'un magistrat, ou d'un général d'armée, afin qu'il puisse y conformer ceux qu'il veut faire aimer aux spectateurs, et en éloigner ceux qu'il leur veut faire haïr; car c'est une maxime infaillible que, pour bien réussir, il faut intéresser l'auditoire pour les premiers acteurs. (*Premier Discours*)

He is no less concerned with the *vraisemblance* of the action:[1] even in his first tragedy, *Médée*, he attempts to make the events more probable than they are in his original. As for style, he insists that it should be as natural as is compatible with writing in verse:

> Il y a cette différence pour ce regard entre le poète dramatique et l'orateur, que celui-ci peut étaler son art, et le rendre remarquable avec pleine liberté, et que l'autre doit le cacher avec soin, parce que ce n'est jamais lui qui parle, et que ceux qu'il fait parler ne sont pas des orateurs [. . .] le langage doit être net, les figures placées à propos et diversifiées, et la versification aisée et élevée au-dessus de la prose, mais non pas jusqu'à l'enflure du poème épique, puisque ceux que le poète fait parler ne sont pas des poètes.[2]   (*Premier Discours*)

His dislike of asides, his reluctance to let a monologue be over-heard by another character, his aversion from moral discourses and maxims of a general nature, his insistence that narrations must be introduced realistically or not at all, his blend of comedy and tragedy, and his invention of the *comédie héroïque* are all evidence of the same tendency. It is clear that Corneille's conception of tragedy by no means excludes realism.[3]

*   *   *

The Cornelian superman is certainly not to be found in the four most commonly read plays, *Le Cid*, *Horace*, *Cinna* and *Polyeucte*.

In *Le Cid*, what is exceptional is the situation, not the characters. Rodrigue obeys the claims of family honour and kills the Count, who has insulted his father; but he makes the point clearly that this is the only course open to him, since, whatever he does, he is bound to lose Chimène:

> Allons, mon bras, sauvons du moins l'honneur,
> Puisqu'après tout il faut perdre Chimène.   (I, 6)

---

[1] Too much should not be made of Corneille's saying, in the *Discours*, that 'les grands sujets [. . .] doivent toujours aller au delà du vraisemblable'. He means that tragedy cannot be made of everyday events. Racine and Shakespeare would not disagree.

[2] See above, p. 131.

[3] The realism of his mind is also evinced by his clear insistence that in some respects the stage and real life are different. 'Le stratagème d'Exupère, avec toute son industrie, a quelque chose un peu délicat, et d'une nature à ne se faire qu'au théâtre, où l'auteur est maître des événements qu'il tient dans sa main, et non pas dans la vie civile, où les hommes en disposent selon leurs intérêts et leur pouvoir.'   (*Examen* of *Héraclius*)

Once he has fought and killed the Count, there is no going back.
The initiative passes to Chimène — and, in fact, in Chimène, as
Corneille's critics pointed out in the *Querelle du Cid*, love is
stronger than duty.

She easily strays from the course of action she thinks she ought
to follow; her protestations of firmness cover up a fundamental
indecision and weakness. After every effort to do what she thinks
she ought, she makes, in reaction, increasingly greater concessions
to her love, until the final concession of all, the acceptance of the
marriage, is only the logical conclusion of the series.

She demands vengeance (II, 8). Subsequently, however, she
refuses Don Sanche's offer of summary justice (III, 2), admits that
she loves Rodrigue and is pursuing him unwillingly (III, 3), and,
in an interview with her lover, not merely refuses to kill him, but
confesses that she still loves him —

> Va, je ne te hais point. — Tu le dois. — Je ne puis.

— and that she does not want vengeance:

> Je ferai mon possible à bien venger mon père;
> Mais malgré la rigueur d'un si cruel devoir,
> Mon unique souhait est de ne rien pouvoir.   (III, 4)

When she hears of his exploits against the Moors, she immediately
asks:

> Mais n'est-il point blessé?   (IV, 1)

She then screws her courage up to the sticking-point once more
and goes to the King to demand vengeance again; but, believing
Rodrigue to be dead, she reveals her true feelings by fainting in
the King's presence (IV, 5). The duel between Rodrigue and Don
Sanche, Chimène's champion, is arranged, and the King tells her
that she must marry the victor; all she can say in protest is:

> Quoi! Sire, m'imposer une si dure loi!   (IV, 5)

Indeed, as Léonor points out, Chimène has chosen a weak
champion:

> Chimène aisément montre par sa conduite
> Que la haine aujourd'hui ne fait pas sa poursuite.
> Elle obtient un combat, et pour son combattant
> C'est le premier offert qu'elle accepte à l'instant:
> Elle n'a point recours à ces mains généreuses
> Que tant d'exploits fameux rendent si glorieuses;
> Don Sanche lui suffit ...   (V, 3)

From this moment on, her resistance grows weaker. In Act V, scene 1, she urges Rodrigue to fight and win her:

> Sors vainqueur d'un combat dont Chimène est le prix.
> Adieu: ce mot lâché me fait rougir de honte.

Later, she does, it is true, say to Elvire:

> Quand il sera vainqueur, crois-tu que je me rende?
> . . . .
> Mon honneur lui fera mille autre ennemis.   (V, 4)

But this is merely a momentary reaction: the King has already forbidden her to 'faire mille autre ennemis;' so that we cannot take the remark very seriously. Moreover, a few lines later, Elvire having suggested that perhaps Don Sanche might win and become her husband, she bursts out:

> Elvire, c'est assez des peines que j'endure,
> Ne les redouble point de ce funeste augure.
> Je veux, si je le puis, les éviter tous deux;
> Sinon, en ce combat Rodrigue a tous mes vœux.   (V, 4)

Mistakenly believing Don Sanche to be the victor, she publicly admits her love for Rodrigue (V, 6), and in the final scene she agrees to marry him:

> Rodrigue a des vertus que je ne puis haïr;
> Et quand un roi commande, on lui doit obéir.   (V, 7)

The Infante resembles Chimène: indeed, one of the functions of her rôle may well be to set another example of feminine subservience to passion by the side of Chimène and so lend credibility

to the portrayal.[1] Like Chimène, she is unable to master her love
for Rodrigue:

> A combien de soupirs
> Faut-il que mon cœur se prépare,
> Si jamais il n'obtient sur un si long tourment
> Ni d'éteindre l'amour, ni d'accepter l'amant!   (V, 2)

She hopes until the last that the marriage of Rodrigue and
Chimène will not take place: there is even a suggestion that she
would not hesitate to use foul means to prevent it:

> Si Rodrigue combat sous ces conditions,
> Pour en rompre l'effet, j'ai trop d'inventions.
> L'amour, ce doux auteur de mes cruels supplices,
> Aux esprits des amants apprend trop d'artifices.   (V, 3)

In *Horace*, there is only one possible 'Cornelian hero', Horace.
Curiace does his duty with reluctance; Sabine and Camille try to
deter their menfolk from fighting; and Camille is all love:

> Je le vois bien, ma sœur, vous n'aimâtes jamais;
> Vous ne connaissez point ni l'amour ni ses traits:
> On peut lui résister quand il commence à naître,
> Mais non pas le bannir quand il s'est rendu maître . . .
>
> . . . .
>
> Et quand l'âme une fois a goûté son amorce,
> Vouloir ne plus aimer, c'est ce qu'elle ne peut,
> Puisqu'elle ne peut plus vouloir que ce qu'il veut . . .   (III, 4)

She is, as Sarcey says, neither reasonable nor strong-willed, but
'une personne toute de premier mouvement, incapable de se
maîtriser elle-même, l'esclave de ses nerfs toujours agités'. Horace
alone masters his feelings and puts his duty to his country before
his personal affections. But is he a 'Cornelian hero'?

There is certainly no question of reason and will getting the
better of passion: the most that one can say is that one passion

---

[1] The rôle of the Infante has been much criticized. It may be true, as Scudéry said, that
Corneille put her in so as to give a part to the actress, Mlle Beauchâteau; but her presence
can be justified on literary grounds. (1) Her love for Rodrigue enhances our impression of
his worth, and makes the persistence of Chimène's love more credible. (2) The opposition
between her hopes and those of Chimène is dramatic: when Chimène rejoices, she is
unhappy; when Chimène is miserable, her hopes rise. (3) She provides a note of lyricism in
an intensely dramatic play.

gets the better of another — for Horace, in contrast to Curiace, cares very much more about his *gloire* than his duty. Moreover, it is very doubtful whether Horace is an ideal character. The play is clearly a study of a Roman patriot, but it is by no means certain that Corneille shares his point of view.[1] A man who, after seeing both his brothers killed, can remark:

> Quand la perte est vengée, on n'a plus rien perdu.   (IV, 5)

— who, having killed his wife's brothers, can greet her with the words:

> Sèche tes pleurs, Sabine, ou les cache à ma vue . . .
> . . . .
> Participe à ma gloire au lieu de la souiller.   (IV, 7)

— who, having just killed his sister's lover, can adjure her:

> Songe à mes trophées:
> Qu'ils soient dorénavant ton unique entretien.   (IV, 5)

and who kills her because she cannot control her anguish, seems, on the face of it, to be too lacking in humanity, too self-centred, to be an ideal character. Of course, we may like to think that Corneille admired him, even if we do not; but it is striking that, in taking the law into his own hands in this way, in avenging a personal insult by violence, he places himself on a level with the Count in *Le Cid*, and that no one in the play condones his action: Tulle in his closing speech condemns it explicitly. Curiace calls Horace 'barbare', —

> Mais votre fermeté tient un peu du barbare . . .   (II, 3)

— and reproaches him with his inhumanity:

> J'ai le cœur aussi bon, mais enfin je suis homme.   (II, 3)

[1] The question has been much discussed. The best study is Dr W. G. Moore's article on 'Corneille's "Horace" and the Interpretation of French Classical Drama' in the *Modern Language Review*, July 1939. 'I submit,' says Dr Moore, 'that there is literally no evidence of Corneille's opinion as to the merits of various passions.' C. R. François, in 'En relisant *Horace* ou les objections de la conscience' (*French Review*, 1954–5), and P. Newmark, in 'A New View of *Horace*' (*French Studies*, 1956) think that Corneille's sympathies lie with Curiace rather than with Horace; so does A. Adam, in his *Histoire de la littérature française au XVIIe siècle*, vol. I, p. 528. Herland, in his *Horace ou la naissance de l'homme*, argues unconvincingly that it is Horace who enjoys his creator's sympathies.

Camille also calls him 'barbare' (IV, 5), and Corneille seems to
share her attitude, for, in the *Examen*, he refers to the 'vertu
farouche' of his hero and calls him 'criminel'.[1] Moreover, the
tragedy opens with a statement that human weakness and
emotion are right and proper, which seems to strike the keynote
of the play:

> Approuvez ma faiblesse, et souffrez ma douleur;
> Elle n'est que trop juste en un si grand malheur:
> Si près de voir sur soi fondre de tels orages,
> L'ébranlement sied bien aux plus fermes courages;
> Et l'esprit le plus mâle et le moins abattu
> Ne saurait sans désordre exercer sa vertu.   (I, 1)

The exponents of this point of view dominate the middle of the
play. It is not easy to see Horace as the expression of Corneille's
ideal.

It is no easier to find a 'Cornelian hero' in *Cinna*. In Emilie, as
in the women of the two previous plays, love is the strongest
passion:

> J'aime encor plus Cinna que je ne hais Auguste,
> Et je sens refroidir ce bouillant mouvement
> Quand il faut, pour le suivre, exposer mon amant.   (I, 1)

In the following scene, she says:

> Mon esprit en désordre à soi-même s'oppose:
> Je veux et ne veux pas, je m'emporte et je n'ose;
> Et mon devoir confus, languissant, étonné,
> Cède aux rébellions de mon cœur mutiné . . .   (I, 2)

The truth of her words is borne out subsequently. In Act I,
scene 4, when Auguste sends for Cinna, she is filled with un-
reasoning apprehension: there is no real likelihood that the plot
has been discovered, and even Cinna calls her alarm a 'terreur
panique'. She urges him to flee, and only changes her mind when
she reflects that flight would be useless.

---

[1] In the dedicatory letter, Corneille calls Horace 'ce généreux Romain', but 'généreux'
may only mean 'brave'. 'Quelquefois *Généreux* signifie particulièrement, Vaillant, hardi
dans les combats.'   (*Dictionnaire de l'Académie Française*)

Cinna is a most interesting character study, but a most unheroic hero. He is a hypocrite and a liar, who makes eloquent speeches to his fellow-conspirators, urging them to kill Auguste and restore the glories of Republican Rome —

> Avec la liberté Rome s'en va renaître ...   (I, 3)

— and who says precisely the opposite to dissuade Auguste from abdicating —

> la liberté ne peut plus être utile
> Qu'à former les fureurs d'une guerre civile ...   (II, 1)

In neither case is he concerned in the least about the interests of Rome. He is full of illusions, about himself and his allies. The enthusiastic account he gives of his fellow-conspirators in Act I, scene 3 — the falsity of which is surely revealed by the absurd

> par un effet contraire,
> Leur front pâlir d'horreur et rougir de colère[1]

— is in marked contrast to that of Auguste in Act V, scene 1:

> Le reste ne vaut pas l'honneur d'être nommé:
> Un tas d'hommes perdus de dettes et de crimes,
> Que pressent de mes lois les ordres légitimes,
> Et qui désespérant de les plus éviter,
> Si tout est renversé, ne sauraient subsister.

As for himself, he tells Emilie that, if he is betrayed:

> Ma vertu pour le moins ne me trahira pas:
> Vous la verrez, brillante au bord des précipices,
> Se couronner de gloire en bravant les supplices,
> Rendre Auguste jaloux du sang qu'il répandra,
> Et le faire trembler alors qu'il me perdra.   (I, 4)

— a prophecy which his later conduct does not justify. When

---

[1] Couton, in his *Corneille*, p. 65, notes that Auguste expresses himself more simply than Cinna and Emilie, and observes that this contrast may be intended to suggest that the conspirators 'vivent dans une exaltation précaire', that their sincerity is not exempt from a certain 'gonflement factice'. E. Desjardins had anticipated him in *Le grand Corneille historien*, 1861, pp. 169–70. It is fair to add: (1) that the lines quoted are imitated from Statius: 'Sic variis manifesta notis — palletque rubetque — / Flamma repens' (*Achilleid*, I, 309–10); and (2) that, according to the *Anecdotes dramatiques* of Clément and La Porte, 1775, the actor Baron in playing the part of Cinna 'pâlit et rougit si rapidement que le feu et la vérité de son jeu lui concilièrent tous les suffrages'.

Auguste, having learned of the plot against his life, accuses Cinna of being involved in it, Cinna immediately denies it:

> Moi, Seigneur! moi, que j'eusse une âme si traîtresse;
> Qu'un si lâche dessein . . . (V, 1)

Above all, Cinna is exclusively motivated by self-interest, and 'ne forme qu'en lâche un dessein généreux'.[1] To kill Auguste is the only way to marry Emilie, and so Auguste must be killed — must not even be allowed to abdicate, because, if Auguste abdicates, though the freedom of Rome would be achieved, his marriage with Emilie would be impossible. But when Auguste promises him Emilie, he sees the possibility of getting Emilie without murdering Auguste and feels remorse as the result of Auguste's trust in him and generosity towards him. As the moment for action approaches, his purpose weakens and his hostility to Auguste diminishes. By Act III, scene 2, he has forgotten Auguste's crimes; by scene 3, Auguste has become a 'prince magnanime'; and by scene 4, he considers that it is honourable to be enslaved by Auguste. He is assailed by doubts and misgivings —

> On ne les sent aussi que quand le coup approche. (III, 2)

He is irresolute. When Emilie justly denounces him for succumbing to Auguste's promises —

> Je vois ton repentir et tes vœux inconstants:
> Les faveurs du tyran emportent tes promesses;
> Tes vœux et tes serments cèdent à ses caresses;
> Et ton esprit crédule ose s'imaginer
> Qu'Auguste, pouvant tout, peut aussi me donner.
> Tu me veux de sa main plutôt que de la mienne . . . (III, 4)

— he replies:

> J'obéis sans réserve à tous vos sentiments.

But by the end of the scene, finding that Emilie is intransigent and still expects him to fulfil his promises, he rails at her resentfully:

[1] III, 2. Cf. La Rochefoucauld: 'Nous aurions souvent honte de nos plus belles actions si le monde voyait tous les motifs qui les produisent.'

Eh bien! vous le voulez, il faut vous satisfaire

. . . .

Mais apprenez qu'Auguste est moins tyran que vous,
S'il nous ôte à son gré nos biens, nos jours, nos femmes,
Il n'a point jusqu'ici tyrannisé nos âmes . . .

Fortinbras says of Hamlet that

> he was likely, had he been put on,
> To have proved most royally.

Cinna, being put on, proves rather shabbily, and justifies Auguste's low opinion of him:

> Ta fortune est bien haut, tu peux ce que tu veux;
> Mais tu ferais pitié même à ceux qu'elle irrite,
> Si je t'abandonnais à ton peu de mérite.
> Ose me démentir, dis-moi ce que tu vaux,
> Conte-moi tes vertus, tes glorieux travaux,
> Les rares qualités par où tu m'as dû plaire,
> Et tout ce qui t'élève au-dessus du vulgaire.
> Ma faveur fait ta gloire, et ton pouvoir en vient . . .   (V, 1)

Auguste, like Cinna, is a most interesting study, but scarcely heroic. He has fulfilled his ambition by becoming Emperor, but found no satisfaction; he is tired of conspiracies and rebellions, of oppression and bloodshed, and thinks seriously of abdicating. The discovery of Cinna's plot brings his dissatisfaction to a head. He is inclined to punish Cinna and kill himself. His wife suggests that he might try a new policy, that of clemency; but he rejects her advice. The successive revelations of the complicity of Emilie and the treachery of Maxime strip him of his last illusions. In his complete disillusionment, his course at last becomes clear, and he forgives them all:

> Je suis maître de moi comme de l'univers.   (V, 3)

But if that is true, it is true for the first time in the play.

Why does Auguste choose to be merciful? The failure of his policy and the need to try another course is the obvious reason; but Corneille seems to mean us to believe that inspiration from above was the deciding factor. After rejecting his wife's advice, he says:

> Le ciel m'inspirera ce qu'ici je dois faire.[1]   (IV, 3)

Moreover, Emilie, learning that Cinna has been sent for, feels none of the alarm she had felt earlier (I, 3): something assures her that all will be well:

> Mon cœur est sans soupirs, mes yeux n'ont point de larmes,
> Comme si j'apprenais d'un secret mouvement
> Que tout doit succéder à mon contentement!   (IV, 4)

It is to the gods that she attributes the cessation of her hatred for Auguste (V, 3). Disillusionment and divine inspiration: we are far from reason and will.

Pauline, in *Polyeucte*, is of the same lineage as Chimène, the Infante, Camille and Emilie. In her, too, emotion is stronger than reason. We first see her unreasonably worried by a dream, not only one with apparently no possibility of fulfilment, but one which is itself unreasonable, since Sévère is the last man in the world to appear,

> La vengeance à la main, l'œil ardent de colère . . .   (I, 3)

Polyeucte talks of 'Pauline, sans raison dans la douleur plongée,' and adds that, to keep him at home,

> Elle oppose ses pleurs au dessein que je fais,   (I, 1)

a feminine, rather than a rational, line of argument. So far from being a purely rational being, she has a certain amount of amour-propre and possessiveness. Though she does not love Polyeucte — at the beginning of the play, at least — his love for her flatters her amour-propre, and her amour-propre is wounded if she thinks

---

[1] Cf.   Le ciel m'inspirera ce que je devrai faire.   (*Pulchérie*, I, 1)
> Et toutefois le ciel par les événements
> Fit voir qu'il approuvait ses justes sentiments.
> Du jaloux Gundebert l'ambitieuse haine,
> Fondant sur Pertharite, y trouva tôt sa peine.   (*Pertharite*, I, 1)

See L. Herland, 'Le pardon d'Auguste dans "Cinna",' in *La Table Ronde*, February 1961.

he no longer loves her. She is unhappy because Polyeucte leaves her and will not tell her his secret, and attributes the change in him to the effects of marriage (I, 2–3); and later she complains:

> Je te suis odieuse après m'être donnée!
>
> . . . .
>
> Tu préfères la mort à l'amour de Pauline!
> Va, cruel, va mourir: tu ne m'aimas jamais.   (IV, 3)

When she prevails on Sévère to do his best to save Polyeucte, even that 'parfait amant' remarks:

> vos douleurs avec trop de rigueur
> D'un amant tout à vous tyrannisent le cœur.   (IV, 6)

Her feminine, emotional nature betrays itself particularly in Act IV, scene 3, and in Act V, scene 3. Pauline feels a real affection for her husband; she has been filled with forebodings and fears on his account all day; she already thinks that marriage may have put an end to his love. In short, she is in a more or less hysterical state. And now, to crown everything, her husband not merely persists in his mistaken beliefs, but refuses to do anything to save himself. She at last loses control of herself and gives vent to her feelings:

> Cruel, car il est temps que ma douleur éclate . . .   (IV, 3)

In Act V, scene 3, she is stung — irrationally — by Polyeucte's bringing up her own words against her. Earlier, Pauline had told him, referring to her love for Sévère:

> Depuis qu'un vrai mérite a pu nous enflammer,
> Sa présence toujours a droit de nous charmer.   (II, 4)

Now, trying to persuade her to marry Sévère after his death, Polyeucte reminds her:

> Puisqu'un si grand mérite a pu vous enflammer,
> Sa présence toujours a droit de vous charmer.

And this taunt causes her to burst out:

> Que t'ai-je fait, cruel, pour être ainsi traitée . . .

She reminds him that she did violence to her feelings and over-came her love for Sévère in order to marry him, and suggests that it is time he made a sacrifice in his turn for her sake. To be wounded by being reminded of one's own words is intensely human, but not rational. The conversion of Pauline is entirely in keeping with her emotional nature.

One or two passages are sometimes quoted in support of the view that Pauline is rational:

> Ces surprises des sens que la raison surmonte . . .   (I, 3)

> jamais ma raison
> N'avoua de mes yeux l'aimable trahison.[1]   (I, 3)

> Et sur mes passions ma raison souveraine
> Eût blâmé mes soupirs et dissipé ma haine.   (II, 2)

The first two of these passages occur in Act I, scene 3, in which Pauline talks all the more complacently about her reason because she thinks that her love of Sévère, which is dormant, is dead; and she changes her tune considerably in the very next scene. The third quotation is particularly interesting. Pauline, at the begin-ning of her interview with Sévère — that interview which she has dreaded so much — tries to make it clear that she no longer loves him, that she loves her husband:

> Oui, je l'aime, Seigneur, et n'en fais point d'excuse.

She adds that, whatever husband her father had chosen, and even if Sévère had been never so suitable a match,

> J'en aurais soupiré, mais j'aurais obéi,
> Et sur mes passions ma raison souveraine
> Eût blâmé mes soupirs et dissipé ma haine.

This, she says, is what *would* have happened; she is not neces-sarily to be believed — any more than Cinna's opinion of what would happen if the conspiracy were betrayed is confirmed by the event. In fact, a touch of ironical reproach from Sévère melts her;

[1] This, in fact, merely means: 'I loved Sévère, but knew that my father would never consent to our marriage.'

she discards this attitude of cold disdain, and tells Sévère just how little power reason had over her, how much she has suffered and still suffers:

> si mon âme
> Pouvait bien étouffer les restes de sa flamme,
> Dieux, que j'éviterais de rigoureux tourments!
> Ma raison, il est vrai, dompte mes sentiments;
> Mais quelque autorité que sur eux elle ait prise,
> Elle n'y règne pas, elle les tyrannise;
> Et quoique le dehors soit sans émotion,
> Le dedans n'est que trouble et que sédition.[1]

Of Sévère, it is perhaps enough to quote a recent critic's opinion of him as 'weak and ineffectual'.[2] As for Polyeucte, he is more like the conventional conception of a Cornelian hero, in so far as he loses his life rather than betray his faith, despite the entreaties of his wife. But there are some reservations to be made. Polyeucte is a saint and a martyr, i.e. one in whom, by definition, worldly affections and considerations of personal safety come second to his religion. Any martyr would resemble Polyeucte; there is nothing peculiar to Corneille in such a portrait.[3] Moreover, his actions are the result of grace rather than of his own free will. Indeed, he wants to postpone his baptism, and it is only after he has been baptized that he is filled with fervour and zeal, with the desire to testify publicly to his new religion. Further, Polyeucte is certainly not rational, any more than Horace. The most

---

[1] She says much the same to her husband:

> Depuis qu'un vrai mérite a pu nous enflammer,
> Sa présence toujours a droit de nous charmer,
> Outre qu'on doit rougir de s'en laisser surprendre,
> On souffre à résister, on souffre à s'en défendre;
> Et bien que la vertu triomphe de ces feux,
> La victoire est pénible, et le combat honteux.   (II, 4)

> Vois, pour te faire vaincre un si fort adversaire,
> Quels efforts à moi-même il a fallu me faire;
> Quels combats j'ai donnés pour te donner un cœur
> Si justement acquis à son premier vainqueur ...   (V, 3)

[2] Dr R. A. Sayce in his edition of the play.
[3] L. Spitzer, in his 'Erhellung des "Polyeucte" durch das Alexiuslied' (*Archivum Romanicum*, vol. XVI, 1932), shows how closely Polyeucte resembles the medieval Saint Alexis. M. Couton, in an unpublished lecture, shows how closely *Polyeucte* follows the traditional pattern of plays about martyrs.

one can say is that he is torn between two passions, love for his wife and religious zeal, and that the latter triumphs over the former.

*   *   *

The first play in which characters who might be called 'Cornelian' appear is *Pompée*, where the magnanimity of Cléopâtre, Cornélie and César leads them to behave in unexpected ways. Cléopâtre, who loves César, urges her brother Ptolomée to fight for Pompée; César allows Cornélie, Pompée's widow to go free, even though she is resolved to overthrow him;[1] and Cornélie, whose chief desire is to avenge her husband's death, nevertheless gives César warning of a plot against his life.

'Cornelian' characters do in fact occur in Corneille, but chiefly in the plays from *Pompée* to *Pertharite* or *Oedipe*. In *Héraclius*, Martian and Héraclius vie in magnanimity, and the strong-minded Pulchérie, on learning that her lover is really her brother, is undismayed:

> Ce grand coup m'a surprise et ne m'a point troublée;[2]
> Mon âme l'a reçu sans en être accablée;
> Et comme tous mes feux n'avaient rien que de saint,
> L'honneur les alluma, le devoir les éteint.   (III, 1)

Pulchérie certainly verges on the inhuman: she is less concerned with her brother's fate than that he should not demean himself:

> Moi, pleurer! moi, gémir, tyran! J'aurais pleuré
> Si quelques lâchetés l'avaient déshonoré,
> S'il n'eût pas emporté sa gloire toute entière,
> Si quelque infâme espoir qu'on lui dût pardonner
> Eût mérité la mort que tu lui vas donner.   (III, 2)

She refuses to marry the son of the tyrant Phocas, because, if she did, filial duty would prevent her from hating him:

---

[1] César, however, is not a perfect character:
> Et forçant sa vertu d'être encor la maîtresse,
> Se montre généreux par un trait de faiblesse . . .   (III, 1)

He is not altogether sorry that Pompée is dead, though he is shocked that an Egyptian King should have dared to put a Roman to death. Moreover, his behaviour, as Cornélie points out, does consort with his interests. (See below, p. 206.)

[2] Cf.   Ma perte m'a surprise et ne m'a point troublée.   (*Cinna*, IV, 5)

It has been pointed out that her cry at the end of the play, 'Ah! vous êtes mon frère!' (V, 7), shows the intensity of her relief, the strength of her suppressed emotion.

Mais durant ces moments unie à sa famille,
Il deviendra mon père, et je serai sa fille:
Je lui devrai respect, amour, fidélité;
Ma haine n'aura plus d'impétuosité;
Et tous mes vœux pour vous seront mols et timides,
Quand mes vœux contre lui seront des parricides.   (III, 1)

In subsequent plays, Don Sanche, Nicomède and Laodice, Grimoald and Rodelinde, Dircé, Thésée and Oedipe show no sign of weakness. Rodelinde (in *Pertharite*) carries self-abnegation to the point of agreeing to marry Grimoald only if he puts her son to death. Dircé is prepared to die to save Thebes:

Je meurs l'esprit content, l'honneur m'en fait la loi . . .[1] (III, 1)

Her father's blood, she says,

ne peut trouver qu'on soit digne du jour,
Quand aux soins de sa gloire on préfère l'amour.   (III, 2)

As for Oedipe, after the discovery that he has killed his father and married his mother, he says:

Ce revers serait dur pour quelque âme commune;
Mais je me fis toujours maître de ma fortune.   (V, 2)

And we are told:

Parmi de tels malheurs que sa constance est rare!
Il ne s'emporte point contre un sort si barbare;
La surprenante horreur de cet accablement
Ne coûte à sa grande âme aucun égarement;
Et sa haute vertu, toujours inébranlable,
Le soutient au-dessus de tout ce qui l'accable.   (V, 7)

Even in this middle period, however, *Rodogune*, *Théodore*, and *Andromède* are exceptions. In *Rodogune*, the ambitious, crafty, and unscrupulous Cléopâtre, comparable with Lady Macbeth, might as well be called 'Shakespearean' as 'Cornelian'; and her two sons — a delicate portrayal of brotherly affection — alike, yet

---

[1] But she adds:

Mais j'aurais vécu plus contente,
Si j'avais pu vivre pour toi.   (III, 1)

admirably differentiated,[1] are certainly not 'Cornelian'. They are
unanimous in putting love before ambition, in preferring Rodogune to the throne and their own unity to either. In *Théodore*,
apart from the generosity with which Placide decides to succour
his rival, Didyme, who has rescued Théodore from ignominy,
and the contest between Didyme and Théodore in Act V, each
demanding to be martyred in place of the other, there is little that
is 'Cornelian'. The same is true of *Andromède*, in which the
heroine fears death:

> que la grandeur de courage
> Devient d'un difficile usage
> Lorsqu'on touche au dernier moment!
>
> . . . .
>
> Je pâme au moindre vent, je meurs au moindre bruit . . .
>
> (III, 1)

Moreover, there are reservations to be made even about the other
plays. Laodice and Nicomède show no sign of weakness; but
equally there is no sign either of any conflict between love and
duty; at no time have they to choose between each other and their
gloire. Grimoald, similarly, is virtuous and generous, but again
there is no question of any conflict.

Despite a common misconception,[2] the plays of the last period
contain few 'Cornelian' heroes and heroines, though there are
one or two, or at least one or two who show some 'Cornelian'
traits — such as Pompée, who, in *Sertorius*, destroys the letter
containing the names of the Romans in correspondence with his
enemy (a historical detail), or Viriate in the same play:

> Je sais ce que je suis, et le serai toujours,
> N'eussé-je que le ciel et moi pour mon secours. (V, 3)

In fact, in this last period, the internal conflict, which had been
relatively rare in the middle period, becomes common again and

[1] Antiochus, the less penetrating, cannot see through his mother, while his brother, the
loyal, unambitious, modest and sensitive Séleucus, does.
[2] E.g. 'A partir de [*Nicomède*], il n'y a plus chez les héros cornéliens d'obstacle intérieur;
ils vont sans hésitation, sereinement, facilement à l'acte qu'ils choisissent; ils se sacrifient,
ils meurent sans hésiter, sans sourciller.' (Lanson)

is resolved with more and more difficulty, and more and more frequently by the triumph of passion over duty.

All, then, is not false in the conventional conception of the Cornelian hero. Such characters are found in Corneille — magnanimous, strong-minded creatures, who put their duty or their *gloire* before their personal inclinations. But such characters are not found by any means in all the plays: they are found chiefly, almost exclusively, in the plays of the middle period. Moreover, even they do not entirely coincide with the conventional image of Corneille's heroes. There is in them all a strong element of emotion or passion — they are usually motivated, not by reason or duty, but by the passion for *gloire*, the desire for vengeance (Pulchérie in *Héraclius*), ambition, amour-propre, or the dislike of being subservient to another, of being second (Nicomède and Attale, Dircé who resents Oedipe's having usurped her throne and wants another, Sertorius, Pompée, Viriate, etc.). Nor is it true to describe these characters as 'les hommes comme ils devraient être'. Not only are they often far from ideal, but they are either men and women like the contemporaries of Corneille, or — if they outdo the men and women of Corneille's day — they show the influence of Corneille's conception of the character of Romans and Kings. For Corneille, like his contemporaries, regarded magnanimity as a Roman trait, and considered that Kings and Queens, more than their subjects, are obliged to master their inclinations.

Corneille's views on the obligations of persons of royal blood are constantly expressed from *Pompée* onwards:

> Plus la haute naissance approche des couronnes,
> Plus cette grandeur même asservit nos personnes;
> Nous n'avons point de cœur pour aimer ni haïr:
> Toutes nos passions ne savent qu'obéir.   (*Rodogune*, III, 3)

> Je sais ce que je suis, et ce que je me dois.
> > (Doña Elvire in *Don Sanche*, I, 1)

> Madame, je suis reine, et dois régner sur moi.
> > (Doña Isabelle in *Don Sanche*, I, 2)

Comptable de moi-même au nom de souveraine,
Et sujette à jamais du trône où je me voi,
Je puis tout pour tout autre et ne puis rien pour moi.

. . . .

... Tu verras avec combien d'adresse
Ma gloire de mon âme est toujours maîtresse.

(Doña Isabelle in Don Sanche, II, 1)

Et si je n'étais pas, Seigneur, ce que je suis,
J'en prendrais quelque droit de finir mes ennuis;
Mais l'esclavage fier d'une haute naissance,
Où toute autre peut tout, me tient dans l'impuissance;
Et victime d'Etat, je dois sans reculer
Attendre aveuglément qu'on me daigne immoler.

(Ildione in Attila, II, 6)

This is not to say that all these characters fulfil their obligations easily. Many, in fact, do not act in accordance with their principles, and there are plenty of undutiful princesses and weak or unvirtuous Kings in Corneille — Ptolomée, Prusias, and Eurydice and Orode (in *Suréna*), in whom mistrust and *raison d'état* overcome gratitude.

*   *   *

The identification of Corneille's heroes with the *généreux* of Descartes is not easy. The *généreux* controls his passions by means of the will using reason as its instrument; he is detached, aiming only at what it is in his power to achieve without the aid of external circumstances — such things as virtue, freedom, detachment. He is humble and esteems himself for nothing but self-mastery and will-power; he is not interested in *gloire* or ambition:

Ceux qui sont généreux en cette façon sont naturellement portés à faire de grandes choses, et toutefois à ne rien entreprendre dont ils ne se sentent capables; et pour ce qu'ils n'estiment rien de plus grand que de faire du bien aux autres hommes et de mépriser son propre intérêt, pour ce sujet ils sont toujours parfaitement courtois, affables et officieux envers un chacun. Et avec cela ils sont entièrement maîtres de leurs passions, particulièrement *des désirs*, *de la jalousie et de l'envie*, à cause qu'il n'y a aucune chose dont l'acquisition ne dépende pas d'eux qu'ils pensent valoir assez pour mériter d'être beaucoup souhaitée; et *de la haine* envers les hommes, à cause qu'ils les estiment tous; et de la peur, à cause que la confiance qu'ils ont en leur vertu les assure; et enfin *de la colère* à cause que, n'estimant que fort peu toutes les choses qui dépendent d'autrui, jamais ils ne donnent tant d'avantage à leurs ennemis que de reconnaître qu'ils en sont offensés.   (*Traité des Passions*, § 156)

The characters of Corneille are not usually subject to fear, but that is about the only respect in which they resemble the *généreux*. They are passionate, ambitious, egoistical, proud, amorous, subject to hatred, anger and jealousy; they are irrational, though they are good reasoners; above all, they are far from the philosophical detachment of the *généreux*.

They differ from the Cartesian character in another way: they are not usually rational in their love affairs. The conception of love as rational, as based on some positive quality (though it may only be good looks) in the loved one, is found in Descartes.

Lorsqu'on remarque quelque chose en une [person of the opposite sex] qui agrée davantage que ce qu'on remarque au même temps dans les autres, cela détermine l'âme à sentir pour celle-là seule toute l'inclination que la nature lui donne à rechercher le bien qu'elle lui représente comme le plus grand qu'on puisse posséder . . .   (§ 90)

The idea that love is based on 'mérite' does occur in Corneille, too — though it is important to realize that 'mérite' often means personal attractions, not moral worth:

Voyez-la donc, Seigneur, voyez tout son mérite . . .
                              (*Sophonisbe*, IV, 5)

This conception of love is first expressed in *La Galerie du Palais*:

Nous sommes hors du temps de cette vieille erreur
Qui faisait de l'amour une aveugle fureur,
Et l'ayant aveuglé, lui donnait pour conduite
Le mouvement d'une âme et surprise et séduite.
Ceux qui l'ont peint sans yeux ne le connaissaient pas;
C'est par les yeux qu'il entre et nous dit vos appas:
Lors notre esprit en juge; et suivant le mérite,
Il fait croître une ardeur que cette vue excite.   (III, 6)

o

But the speaker here is not sincere: he is paying court to a lady whom he does not love in order to arouse his mistress's jealousy. There are, however, examples in the tragedies of love based on rational grounds. Chimène and the Infante in *Le Cid* love Rodrigue because he is worthy of their love, and Pauline in *Polyeucte* fell in love with Sévère for his good qualities:

> Je l'aimai, Stratonice: il le méritait bien ...   (I, 3)

Carlos loves Doña Isabelle for her beauty:

> Lorsque je vois en vous les célestes accords
> Des grâces de l'esprit et des beautés du corps,
> Je puis, de tant d'attraits l'âme toute ravie,
> Sur l'heur de votre époux jeter un œil d'envie ...
> (Don Sanche, II, 2)

Laodice loves Nicomède because he is worthy of her:

> Vous devez le connaître; et puisqu'il a ma foi,
> Vous devez présumer qu'il est digne de moi.
> Je le désavouerais s'il n'était magnanime,
> S'il manquait à remplir l'effort de mon estime,
> S'il ne faisait paraître un cœur toujours égal.
> (Nicomède, V, 9)

Viriate's love for Sertorius (if it can be called love) is rational:

> Ce ne sont pas les sens que mon amour consulte:
> Il hait des passions l'impétueux tumulte;
> Et son feu, que j'attache aux soins de ma grandeur,
> Dédaigne tout mélange avec leur folle ardeur.
> J'aime en Sertorius ce grand art de la guerre
> Qui soutient un banni contre toute la terre;
> J'aime en lui ces cheveux tous couverts de lauriers,
> Ce front qui fait trembler les plus braves guerriers,
> Ce bras qui semble avoir la victoire en partage.
> L'amour de la vertu n'a jamais d'yeux pour l'âge:
> Le mérite a toujours des charmes éclatants;
> Et quiconque peut tout est aimable en tout temps.
> (Sertorius, II, 1)

But a different conception of love is much more common in Corneille — that of love as something quite irrational and instinctive. Isabelle, in *L'Illusion comique*, rejects the suitor favoured by her father on these grounds:

> Je sais qu'il est parfait,
> Et que je réponds mal à l'honneur qu'il me fait;
> Mais si votre bonté me permet en ma cause,
> Pour me justifier, de dire quelque chose,
> Par un secret instinct, que je ne puis nommer,
> J'en fais beaucoup d'état, et ne le puis aimer.
> Souvent je ne sais quoi que le ciel nous inspire
> Soulève tout le cœur contre ce qu'on désire,
> Et ne nous laisse pas en état d'obéir,
> Quand on choisit pour nous ce qu'il nous fait haïr.
> Il attache ici-bas avec des sympathies
> Les âmes que son ordre a là-haut assorties:
> On n'en saurait unir sans ses avis secrets;
> Et cette chaîne manque où manquent ses décrets.
> Aller contre les lois de cette providence,
> C'est le prendre à partie, et blâmer sa prudence,
> L'attaquer en rebelle, et s'exposer aux coups
> Des plus âpres malheurs qui suivent son courroux.   (III, 3)

Créuse, in *Médée*, rejects Ægée for similar reasons:

> Souvent je ne sais quoi qu'on ne peut exprimer
> Nous surprend, nous emporte, et nous force d'aimer;
> Et souvent, sans raison, les objets de nos flammes
> Frappent nos yeux ensemble et saisissent nos âmes.
>
> . . . .
>
> Je vous estimai plus, et l'aimai davantage.   (II, 5)

In this last line, Créuse makes a sharp distinction between love and esteem: one may love without esteem and esteem without love.[1] Mélisse, in *La Suite du Menteur*, sees love as the result of a heaven-created sympathy; for her, love precedes esteem:[2]

---

[1] Cf. Mme de Chevreuse. 'Elle nous a avoué, à Mme de Rhodes et à moi, que par un caprice, ce disait-elle, de la fortune, elle n'avait jamais aimé le mieux ce qu'elle avait estimé le plus, à la réserve toutefois, ajouta-t-elle, du pauvre Buckingham.'   (Retz)

[2] Cf. Thésée in *Oedipe*:

> Si vous avez aimé, vous avez su connaître
> Que l'amour de son choix veut être le seul maître;
> Que s'il ne choisit pas toujours le plus parfait,
> Il attache du moins les cœurs au choix qu'il fait;
> Et qu'entre cent beautés dignes de notre hommage,
> Celle qu'il nous choisit plaît toujours davantage.   (I, 2)

> Quand les ordres du ciel nous ont faits l'un pour l'autre,
> Lyse, c'est un accord bientôt fait que le nôtre:
> Sa main entre les cœurs, par un secret pouvoir,
> Sème l'intelligence avant que de se voir;
> Il prépare si bien l'amant et la maîtresse,
> Que leur âme au seul nom s'émeut et s'intéresse.
> On s'estime, on se cherche, on s'aime en un moment:
> Tout ce qu'on s'entre-dit persuade aisément;
> Et sans s'inquiéter d'aucunes peurs frivoles,
> La foi semble courir au-devant des paroles:
> La langue en peu de mots en explique beaucoup;
> Les yeux, plus éloquents, font tout voir tout d'un coup;
> Et de quoi qu'à l'envi tous les deux nous instruisent,
> Le cœur en entend plus que tous les deux n'en disent.[1]

Rodogune, like Créuse, separates love and esteem: of two young
princes, twin brothers, she loves one and not the other:

> Comme ils ont même sang avec pareil mérite,
> Un avantage égal pour eux me sollicite;
> Mais il est malaisé, dans cette égalité,
> Qu'un esprit combattu ne penche d'un côté.
> Il est des nœuds secrets, il est des sympathies
> Dont par le doux rapport les âmes assorties
> S'attachent l'une à l'autre et se laissent piquer
> Par ces je ne sais quoi qu'on ne peut expliquer.
> C'est par là que l'un d'eux obtient la préférence:
> Je crois voir l'autre encore avec indifférence;
> Mais cette indifférence est une aversion
> Lorsque je la compare avec ma passion.
> Etrange effet d'amour! Incroyable chimère!
> Je voudrais être à lui si je n'aimais son frère;
> Et le plus grand des maux toutefois que je crains,
> C'est que mon triste sort me livre entre ses mains.   (I, 5)

Placide complains of

> la tyrannie ensemble et le caprice
> Du démon aveuglé qui sans discrétion
> Verse l'antipathie et l'inclination.   (*Théodore*, I, 1)

---

[1] When Mademoiselle fell in love with Lauzun, she remembered these lines and sent for
a copy of Corneille's works. 'Je les appris par cœur, ils m'ont fait faire beaucoup de
réflexions depuis quelques années, et je regardais du côté de Dieu ce que la plupart des
hommes considèrent avec des sentiments profanes.'

Andromède, wondering why she should so suddenly transfer her affections from Phinée to her rescuer, Persée, is told that the gods are responsible: it is they who control our sympathies and antipathies (IV, 2).[1] Lysander in *Agésilas* is another who sees love as irrational, an 'aveugle sympathie' independent of beauty and 'vrai mérite' (II, 2). So are Spitridate in the same play (V, 3) and Domitian in *Tite et Bérénice* (II, 2).

Persée in *Andromède* sees love as irrational in another way: though he has no hope of marrying Andromède, he cannot stop loving her; a lover cannot think of the future:

> Vouloir que la raison règne sur un amant,
> C'est être plus que lui dedans l'aveuglement.
> Un cœur digne d'aimer court à l'objet aimable,
> Sans penser au succès dont sa flamme est capable;
> Il s'abandonne entier, et n'examine rien;
> Aimer est tout son but, aimer est tout son bien;
> Il n'est ni difficulté ni péril qui l'étonne.[2]   (I, 4)

Camille, in *Othon*, complains that love makes one believe what one wants to believe:

> Hélas! que cet amour croit tôt ce qu'il souhaite!
> En vain la raison parle, en vain elle inquiète,
> En vain la défiance ose ce qu'elle peut,
> Il veut croire, et ne croit que parce qu'il le veut.
> Pour Plautine ou pour moi je vois du stratagème,
> Et m'obstine avec joie à m'aveugler moi-même.[3]   (III, 1)

---

[1] In her case, however, esteem was a stepping-stone to love (IV, 2).

[2] Cf. Titus in Racine's *Bérénice*:
> Mon cœur se gardait bien d'aller dans l'avenir
> Chercher ce qui pouvait un jour nous désunir.
> Je voulais qu'à mes yeux rien ne fût invincible,
> Je n'examinais rien, j'espérais l'impossible.
> Que sais-je? j'espérais de mourir à vos yeux,
> Avant que d'en venir à ces cruels adieux.   (IV, 5)

[3] Domitian, in *Tite et Bérénice*, says that a lover never listens to reason:
> Qu'un salutaire avis fait une douce loi
> A qui peut avoir l'âme aussi libre que toi!
> Mais celle d'un amant n'est pas comme une autre âme:
> Il ne voit, il n'entend, il ne croit que sa flamme;
> Du plus puissant remède il se fait un poison,
> Et la raison pour lui n'est pas toujours raison.   (I, 3)

Albin, in *Tite et Bérénice*, expatiates on the essential selfishness of love:

> L'amour-propre est la source en nous de tous les autres:
> C'en est le sentiment qui forme tous les nôtres;
> Lui seul allume, éteint, ou change nos désirs:
> Les objets de nos vœux le sont de nos plaisirs.
> Vous-même, qui brûlez d'une ardeur si fidèle,
> Aimez-vous Domitie, ou vos plaisirs en elle?
> Et quand vous aspirez à des liens si doux,
> Est-ce pour l'amour d'elle, ou pour l'amour de vous? (I, 3)

This passage no doubt owes something to the *Maximes* of La Rochefoucauld, but the essential idea is contained already in *L'Illusion comique*:

> Ne me reproche plus ta fuite ni ta flamme:
> Que ne fait point l'amour quand il possède une âme?
> Son pouvoir à ma vue attachait tes plaisirs,
> Et tu me suivais moins que tes propres désirs. (V, 3)

Finally, in *La Toison d'Or*, written several years before Racine's *Andromaque*, there is a conception of love very close to that usually associated with Racine. Love in this play is an irrational, overriding passion, stronger than will or reason:

> Je veux ne t'aimer plus, et n'en ai pas la force, (II, 2)

says Médée. As in Racine, love changes easily into its opposite, hatred:

> Tout violent qu'il est, l'amour l'a[1] fait naître;
> Il va jusqu'à la haine, et toutefois, hélas!
> Je te haïrais peu, si je ne t'aimais pas.[2] (II, 2)

The action of the play is admirably summarized in a speech of Aæte, Médée's father, to her brother, Absyrte:

> Ah! que tu connais mal jusqu'à quelle manie
> D'un amour déréglé passe la tyrannie!

---

[1] I.e. her anger.
[2] Andromède's love for Phinée changes easily to hatred (IV, 2), and Camille, in *Othon*, says

> Du courroux à l'amour si le retour est doux,
> On repasse aisément de l'amour au courroux. (IV, 7)

Il n'est rang, ni pays, ni père, ni pudeur,
Qu'épargne de ses feux l'impérieuse ardeur.
Jason plut à Médée, et peut encore lui plaire;
Peut-être es-tu toi-même ennemi de ton père
Et consens que ta sœur, par ce présent fatal,[1]
S'assure d'un amant qui serait ton rival.
Tout mon sang révolté trahit mon espérance:
Je trouve ma ruine où fut mon assurance;
Le destin ne me perd que par l'ordre des miens,
Et mon trône est brisé par ses propres soutiens.   (V, 2)

If it seems rash to assert — as Lanson does, for example — that Corneille conceives of love as a rational preference based on merit, it is no less rash to say — as Lemaitre does — that *Le Cid* is the only play in which love gets the better of duty. In fact, it is remarkable how often in Corneille love triumphs over honour, ambition, duty, prudence, desire for revenge, and reason. This is already true of Alidor in *La Place Royale*. It is true, not only of Chimène and the Infante, of Camille and Emilie, of Médée in *La Toison*, but of most of the characters in the later plays.

*   *   *

Gloire is no more the mainspring of Corneille's characters than reason and will. In this respect, Corneille reflects the contradictory tendencies of his age[2] — his characters often talk of *gloire*, but they mean very different things by it, they do not always live up to their ideal, and many are not animated by a desire for *gloire* at all.

There are characters who are concerned above all with *gloire*. Cléopâtre, in *Pompée*, says of princes:

> Leur générosité soumet tout à leur gloire,   (II, 1)

— a remark which is certainly true of herself. For her, *gloire* consists of marrying César and becoming mistress of the world, but it must be achieved by honourable means; and, though she loves César, she wants her brother to treat Pompée magnanimously.

---

[1] The golden fleece.   [2] See above, pp. 15-19.

César is a kindred spirit, though it is interesting to see that the point is twice made that for him *gloire* and self-interest point the same way. On having Pompée's head presented to him, we are told:

> par un mouvement commun à la nature,
> Quelque maligne joie en son cœur s'élevait,
> Dont sa gloire indignée à peine le sauvait.　　　　　(III, 1)

And Cornélie points out that, in avenging Pompée, he is also serving his own interests — ensuring his own safety ('le Roi le veut perdre, et son rival est mort'), and defending Cléopâtre too. Laodice in *Nicomède*, similarly, knows no conflict between love and another passion. *Gloire* and love alike keep her faithful to Nicomède: Attale, his rival, is a subject, has not distinguished himself, and has been educated in Rome, so that to prefer him to Nicomède would be a 'frénésie'. The best example of a character for whom *gloire* is all-important is Horace, who puts *gloire* before *devoir*, in contrast to Curiace, who is primarily concerned with *devoir*.

> Contre qui que ce soit que mon pays m'emploie,
> J'accepte aveuglément cette gloire avec joie,

says Horace; whereas Curiace's attitude is different:

> Encor qu'à mon devoir je coure sans terreur,
> Mon cœur s'effarouche, et j'en frémis d'horreur ...　　(II, 3)

But Horace, as we have tried to show above, is in no sense an ideal character, and Sabine finds fault with him precisely because he is over-preoccupied with *gloire* to the exclusion of more human feelings:

> Prenons part en public aux victoires publiques;
> Pleurons dans la maison nos malheurs domestiques,
> Et ne regardons point des biens communs à tous,
> Quand nous voyons des maux qui ne sont que pour nous.
> Pourquoi veux-tu, cruel, agir d'une autre sorte?
> Laisse en entrant ici tes lauriers à la porte;
> Mêle tes pleurs aux miens.　　　　　　　　　　　(IV, 7)

To these characters, there are few others to add — Don Alvar and Don Sanche in *Don Sanche*, and Rodelinde in *Pertharite*, are the chief.

It is easier to find examples of characters who act in the interests of their *gloire*, but only after a struggle — though often *gloire* is not the only motive. Rodrigue, in *Le Cid*, fights and kills the father of Chimène, but there is a struggle within him, and the conflict is resolved only by the realization that, whether he avenges his father or not, he is bound to lose Chimène. Emilie is similarly torn between duty and *gloire*, on the one hand, and love for Cinna on the other. With her, one might associate Sévère, in *Polyeucte*, in whom there is no particular struggle, but whose motives are mixed. In deciding to try to save Polyeucte, he says:

> Et contentons ainsi, d'une seule action,
> Et Pauline, et ma gloire, et ma compassion.

For him, *gloire* is being worthy of Pauline:

> La gloire de montrer à cette âme si belle
> Que Sévère l'égale, et qu'il est digne d'elle ...   (IV, 6)

He is also motivated by honour — 'l'honneur m'oblige'.

Doña Isabelle in *Don Sanche* belongs to this group. Though *gloire* forbids her to marry except for *raison d'état*, she is deeply in love with Carlos, and her love influences her behaviour. She is so much preoccupied with Carlos that she gives him the responsibility of choosing a husband for her, and that her other suitors, not unreasonably, complain at one point: 'Toujours Carlos.' *Gloire* does not win easily in Doña Isabelle. Dircé, in *Oedipe*, despite the entreaties of her lover, Thésée, and her own regrets, is determined to die in obedience to the oracle, both to save her people and to achieve *gloire*. One is unworthy to live, she says,

> Quand aux soins de sa gloire on préfère l'amour.   (III, 2)

Nevertheless, she is regretful:

> Mais j'aurais vécu plus contente,
> Si j'avais pu vivre pour toi.   (III, 1)

Mandane, in *Agésilas*, though she loves someone else, is prepared reluctantly to marry Agésilas, partly because this is the means of saving her brother and herself, but partly out of *gloire*. Domitie, in *Tite et Bérénice*, is similarly torn between love for Domitian and the *gloire* of being Empress, as Pulchérie is between love for Léon and the *gloire* of making a responsible choice of a husband.

Other characters, after a struggle, do not follow their *gloire*. Chimène, for example, admits:

> Mon unique souhait est de ne rien pouvoir.   (III, 4)

For Othon, *gloire* means that he must remain faithful to Plautine and Plautine to him; but circumstances are too strong, and he agrees to pay court to Camille, as Plautine consents to marry Martian. In *Attila*, Honorie says firmly that she will not marry Valamir, who is merely a puppet-king:

> . . . rien ne m'est sensible à l'égal de ma gloire.   (II, 2)

But — like Doña Isabelle — she is jealous of the happiness of Ildione and Ardaric, and, what is more, she later offers the hand of Flavie to Octar if he will bring about her marriage with Valamir — a change of heart which Flavie points out. Tite is prepared to abdicate in order to marry Bérénice:

> Ma gloire la plus haute est celle d'être à vous.   (III, 5)

In other words, love matters more to him than *gloire*.

Cinna talks much of *gloire*, but his conception of it changes in the course of the play. In Act I, scene 3, he identifies *gloire* with the success of his conspiracy; two acts later, he tells Emilie that, after killing Auguste, he means to kill himself:

> Et par cette action dans l'autre confondue,
> Recouvrera ma gloire aussitôt que perdue.   (III, 4)

The murder of Auguste, from being *gloire*, has come to be its antithesis. One might class Félix with Cinna. For him, in Act III, scene 5, *gloire* means *not* sacrificing Polyeucte, whom he is tempted to put to death out of self-interest. In Act V, scene 4, *gloire* means shedding Polyeucte's blood and emulating the ancient Roman heroes, Brutus or Manlius. In fact, however, *gloire* is not his main motive. His decision to execute Polyeucte is due to self-interest, fear of Sévère, determination to carry out his *devoir* (his orders, the obligations of his official position), and revulsion from Polyeucte's new religion:

> sans l'horreur de ses derniers blasphèmes,
> Qui m'ont rempli soudain de *colère et d'effroi*,
> J'aurais eu de la peine à *triompher de moi*.   (V, 4)

His self-domination results from wrath and fear: there is almost a burlesque contrast here between his words and their meaning.

Then there are characters for whom *gloire* is entirely divorced from honour or morals. The Infante, in *Le Cid*, begins by combating her love for Rodrigue in the interests of her *gloire* (i.e. because he is her inferior in station); but when later she decides that his *gloire* is the equivalent of her rank, she says that she will stop at nothing to prevent the marriage of Rodrigue with Chimène:

> Pour en rompre l'effet, j'ai trop d'inventions.
> L'amour, ce doux auteur de mes cruels supplices,
> Aux esprits des amants apprend trop d'artifices.   (V, 3)

For Cléopâtre in *Rodogune* and Aspar in *Pulchérie*, *gloire* is merely the throne. When Jason, in *La Toison*, says 'Il y va de ma gloire' (III, 3), he means that for him *gloire* is the achievement of the golden fleece, and that he can only win it by paying his addresses to Médée, whom he does not love. For Vinius in *Othon*, *gloire* means power; and when he says that he is prepared to die for his *gloire*, he means that he will commit suicide in order to avoid serving an emperor who is hostile to him.

Finally, there is a very large group of characters who do not seem to be motivated by the desire for *gloire* — i.e. there is nothing in the play to suggest that this is the motive for their actions. In *Horace*, Sabine and Curiace talk of *devoir*, not *gloire*, and Camille cares for nothing but love. There is nothing in *Cinna* to suggest a desire for *gloire* as the motive for Auguste's clemency. Polyeucte is animated by religious fervour, by grace, by the desire for permanent happiness; and, when he uses the word *gloire*, he uses it — the context makes it clear — in the sense of 'heaven', a perfectly normal sense of the word in the seventeenth century.[1] Pauline uses the word *devoir* at least as much as the word *gloire*, and a convincing case has been made out for regarding her as a heroine of duty, the embodiment of the doctrines of the neo-stoical philosophers rather than of the *éthique de la gloire*.[2] What matters for her, whether she calls it *gloire* or *devoir*, is obedience to her father, and obedience and fidelity to her husband:

> Je l'aimai par devoir: ce devoir dure encore.   (III, 2)

For Séleucus and Antiochus in *Rodogune* — one of the plays in which the word *gloire* occurs least — love and their own unity are more important than anything else. It is true that Antiochus does once use the word, equating it with renunciation of the throne. Ptolomée and his advisers in *Pompée* care nothing for *gloire*: Ptolomée does say (III, 2) that he has 'immolé sa gloire' to César, but he seems at no time to have been deterred by the prospect of losing his *gloire*.

Gloire has little place in *Théodore*. Marcelle is animated by maternal love and the desire for vengeance. Valens's facile optimism leads him to a policy of masterly inactivity. At one point he does, it is true, claim that this will increase his *gloire* —

> cette illusion de ma sévérité
> Augmentera ma gloire et mon autorité,   (V, 7)

— but it is difficult to take this very seriously. Didyme rescues Théodore out of Christian zeal. Théodore herself says that martyrdom will ensure her *gloire*, and protests that the particular martyrdom chosen will endanger her *gloire*, and Placide is eager to save Théodore's *gloire*, which — since he loves her — is also

[1] '*Gloire*, signifie aussi, La béatitude dont on jouit dans le Paradis. *Les âmes qui jouissent de la gloire, de la gloire éternelle. un avant-goût de la gloire éternelle. la gloire que Dieu a préparée à ses élus.*' (*Dictionnaire de l'Académie*). Cf. Drelincourt's poem, *Sur le tombeau du fidèle*:

> L'Espérance et la Foi l'ont porté dans la Gloire . . .

[2] J. Maurens, 'Pauline amoureuse passionnée ou héroïne du devoir?' in *Annales publiées par la Faculté des Lettres de Toulouse*, February 1957.

his own; but it is hard to see *gloire* as the fundamental principle of either — Théodore is primarily a Christian, and Placide a lover.

The word *gloire* is not much used in *Héraclius*. Phocas, the tyrant, is not interested in *gloire*, and Héraclius wants the throne only in order to give it to Eudoxe. Pulchérie says that marriage with Phocas would be fatal to her *gloire*; but, whenever she shows fortitude or does anything more positive, she talks more of her *devoir*. She is chiefly actuated by hatred of the tyrant, which she carries to extremes: she is prepared to acknowledge a false claimant, and, though she will not marry Martian to save her brother, she professes her willingness to marry anyone who will kill Phocas. Léontine, though she is gratified by the *gloire* of having sacrificed her own son to save her Emperor's, is chiefly animated by the desire for vengeance. It is, perhaps, significant that the only character in the play who cares about *gloire* is Martian: he is eager to have the *gloire* of dying as Héraclius (who, of course, he is not).

Gloire is unimportant in subsequent plays. In *Nicomède*, uprightness, independence, magnanimity, *générosité* and *vertu* are contrasted with Machiavellian principles. We cannot take Arsinoé very seriously when she claims that her *gloire* is 'souillée' by the false accusations of two informers, since they are in her pay, and the whole thing is a ruse. In *Pertharite*, Grimoald only once uses *gloire* so as to suggest that he cares for it: love and virtue are his pre-eminent characteristics. Pertharite returns from his place of concealment, not to win *gloire*, but to have the pleasure of seeing his wife. Eduige, after wanting the *gloire* of marrying a king, decides that in the last resort she prefers virtue to rank, and *gloire* has no significance for the scheming, selfish Garibalde. It is true that the play ends with the line:

> ... des hautes vertus la gloire est le seul prix,

but (except in Rodelinde), it is virtue that is stressed in the play. In *Attila*, when Ardaric talks of dying to preserve his *gloire*, Ildione is unimpressed:

> Cette immortalité qui triomphe en idée
> Veut être, pour charmer, de plus loin regardée;
> Et quand à notre amour ce triomphe est fatal,
> La gloire qui le suit nous en console mal.   (IV, 6)

Léon in *Pulchérie* is moved only by love of the Empress, not by
ambition or *gloire*, and Martian by love, duty and virtue. In
Suréna, Eurydice, Orode and Suréna care little for *gloire*. Eurydice tries to conceal her feelings —

> Mon intrépidité n'est qu'un effort de gloire,
> Que, tout fier qu'il paraît, mon cœur n'en veut pas croire,
>   (IV, 2)

— but her behaviour is that of one for whom love is everything.
Gloire has little part in *Andromède*, *Oedipe*, *Sophonisbe*, *Sertorius*,
Othon and *Tite et Bérénice*.

The word *gloire* occurs frequently in Corneille's plays — some
thirty times in each play (much less in *Rodogune* and *Héraclius*) —
but too much must not be made of this. For one thing, not all the
uses of the word are significant — it occurs quite often in the
phrase 'faire gloire de', for example, which is an ordinary expression of the period for 'to be proud of', and sometimes, like the
word 'honneur', it merely means 'glory' in the sense in which the
word might be used to-day. Moreover, it is used in a variety of
contexts and with a variety of meanings. It may mean military
glory. Sometimes it is equated with honour and duty and virtue.
For Pulchérie in *Héraclius* it means fortitude. For Emilie in *Cinna*
it includes avenging her father and freeing Rome from a tyrant,
but does not exclude crime:

> Pour qui venge son père il n'est point de forfaits . . .   (I, 2)

When Sophonisbe says that she 'prend pour seul objet ma gloire
à satisfaire,' she means that *gloire* requires her to separate her
fortunes from those of her vanquished husband. Polyeucte uses
the word in the sense of Heaven. For Antiochus in *Rodogune* it
means giving up the throne. Théodore uses the word to mean
martyrdom and chastity. Elsewhere it means fidelity in love. It
may be used without any idea of duty or honour. For many, such

as Aspar, it means gaining a throne, or marrying a king. For Palmis in *Suréna* it means keeping one's lovers. Camille uses it in protest:

> C'est gloire de passer pour un cœur abattu,
> Quand la brutalité fait la haute vertu.   (*Horace*, IV, 4)

The variety of senses is admirably illustrated by a passage in *Agésilas*. Aglatide says that she wants the *gloire* of marrying a king, but Elpinice, with sisterly candour, points out that that is the only kind of *gloire* she wants, that the *gloire* of marrying a suitor of lesser rank in obedience to her father's wishes does not appeal to her:

> La gloire d'obéir à votre grand regret
> Vous faisait pester en secret . . .   (II, 6)

One wonders whether a word which can be used in so many senses can be a useful guide to the motivation of Corneille's characters. It can describe any aim or ambition, and is often very hard to distinguish from self-interest.

Even when characters are actuated by a desire for *gloire* without self-interest, they often have other motives as well. When they make sacrifices or renunciations, *gloire* is seldom, if ever, the motive. It is not for *gloire* that the Infante decides to let Chimène marry Rodrigue:

> Je me vaincrai pourtant, non de peur d'aucun blâme,
> Mais pour ne troubler pas une si belle flamme[1] . . .   (V, 3)

The supreme example of a sacrifice in Corneille is that of Rodelinde in *Pertharite*, and Rodelinde is one of the characters who talks most of her *gloire*; but when she proposes that Grimoald should kill her child, the word disappears from her vocabulary, and she justifies her proposition on severely practical grounds. Since the usurper is certain to put her son to death sooner or later, it is better that he should do it now, when he will show himself in

---

[1] Cf. Don Sanche, who, in the same play, similarly says:
> Perdant infiniment, j'aime encore ma défaite,
> Qui fait le beau succès d'une amour si parfaite.   (V, 6)

his true colours at the outset, and when his action may well be the signal for rebellion. Her attitude is not very human, but at least *gloire* has nothing to do with it. Agésilas, after a struggle, decides to marry Aglatide, though he prefers Mandane. The desire for *gloire* is not absent from his decision, but it is due mainly to more concrete motives. He has just learnt that Mandane loves another; he knows, and has just been reminded, that Mandane is not acceptable to Sparta; and he is aware that to marry Aglatide and contract an alliance with Lysander is the best means of consolidating his authority. Mandane, though she loves someone else, is prepared, reluctantly, to marry Agésilas, partly out of a desire for *gloire*, but also because this is the only means of saving her brother and herself. Bérénice leaves Tite because she has solid grounds for fearing that his safety would be endangered by marriage with her. Pulchérie renounces Léon, because marriage with him would endanger the Empire. If she marries Léon, Martian, the mainstay of her Empire, will go into retirement, and she is afraid both of weakening her Empire and of giving cause for revolts. Hence her determination to marry Léon only at the command of the Senate.

In short, although the word *gloire* is often on the lips of Corneille's characters, it covers a multitude of senses; and Corneille, in depicting the variety of motives which influence men and women, in depicting all kinds of men and women, from the noblest to the basest, reflects the complex reality both of his own age and of all others. His psychology is profoundly human.

* * *

There are, then, in Corneille, particularly in the plays of the middle period, magnanimous and intrepid characters, practically all of royal rank, who have a strong sense of their duty or the exigencies of their *gloire*. But they are much rarer than is generally supposed, much rarer than a cursory reading of the tragedies might lead one to suppose; for the characters of Corneille must not always be taken at their face value, and their words are not always plain statements of fact. Not only are they fond of using irony and double-entendre but they are often insincere. 'Il n'y a pas de théâtre,' says Rousset, 'dont les héros se mentent davantage les uns aux autres.'

Sometimes they delude themselves. Horace, on the point of murdering his sister, says:

> C'est trop, ma patience à la raison fait place . . .   (IV, 5

'Raison' of course may not mean 'reason' in the modern sense; it can also mean 'tout ce qui est de devoir, de droit, d'équité, de justice' (*Dictionnaire de l'Académie*). But there is nothing rational or just in Horace's murder of his sister: he is deluding himself in his passion. Very frequently the actions of Corneille's characters belie their words and make their self-deception clear. Doña Isabelle in *Don Sanche*, for all her talk of her duties as a princess, cannot help betraying to Don Sanche her love for him. Médée, in *La Toison*, says:

> Je suis prête à l'aimer, si le Roi le commande;
> Mais jusque-là, ma sœur, je ne fais que souffrir
> Les soupirs et les vœux qu'il prend soin de m'offrir.   (II, 2)

> Je ferai mon devoir, comme tu fais le tien.
> L'honneur doit m'être cher, si la gloire t'est chère:
> Je ne trahirai point mon pays et mon père . . .   (II, 2)

In fact, love is too strong for her:

> Silence, raison importune;
> Est-il temps de parler quand mon cœur s'est donné?   (IV, 2)

She betrays her father, and helps Jason to win the fleece:

> Du pays et du sang l'amour rompt les liens,
> Et les dieux de Jason sont plus forts que les miens.   (V, 5)

Nothing could be more apparently 'Cornelian' than some of Sophonisbe's lines:

> Je sais ce que je suis et ce que je dois faire,
> Et prends pour seul objet ma gloire à satisfaire.[1]   (III, 5)

> De tout votre destin vous êtes la maîtresse:
> Je la serai du mien . . .   (V, 4)

---

[1] She means that *gloire* requires that she should separate her fortunes from those of her vanquished husband — a somewhat personal interpretation of the word.

P

She tells Massinisse that she is only marrying him to avoid being taken in triumph to Rome (II, 4); she explains, too, that she is marrying him in order to gain an ally for her country:

> Il est à mon pays, puisqu'il est tout à moi.
> A ce nouvel hymen, c'est ce qui me convie,
> Non l'amour, non la peur de me voir asservie.   (II, 5)

But she is motivated neither by the desire for *gloire* nor by patriotism, but by love and jealousy:

> c'est pour peu qu'on aime, une extrême douceur
> De pouvoir accorder sa gloire avec son cœur;
> Mais c'en est une ici bien autre, et sans égale,
> D'enlever, et sitôt, ce prince à ma rivale,
> De lui faire tomber le triomphe des mains,
> Et prendre sa conquête aux yeux de ses Romains.   (II, 5)

> Ce n'était point l'amour . . .
> C'était la folle ardeur de braver ma rivale;
> J'en faisais mon suprême et mon unique bien.
> Tous les cœurs ont leur faible, et c'était là le mien.
> La présence d'Eryxe aujourd'hui m'a perdue;
> Je me serais sans elle un peu mieux défendue;
> J'aurais su mieux choisir et les temps et les lieux.
> Mais ce vainqueur vers elle eût pu tourner les yeux . . .   (V, 1)

Perpenna tells Sertorius:

> Oui, sur tous mes désirs je me rends absolu . . .
> J'en veux, à votre exemple, être aujourd'hui le maître.   (IV, 3)

He is probably speaking ironically; if not, he is deluding himself, as the course of the rest of the play shows. Honorie, in *Attila*, says:

> . . . rien ne m'est sensible à l'égal de ma gloire,   (II, 2)

but never lives up to her principles. Tite, in *Tite et Bérénice*, says, speaking of Domitie, 'Je veux l'aimer, je l'aime . . . .' But he has no such power over his emotions:

> Je souffrais Domitie, et d'assidus efforts
> M'avaient malgré l'amour, fait maître du dehors.
> La contrainte semblait tourner en habitude;
> Le joug que je prenais m'en paraissait moins rude . . .   (III, 5)

He also says (II, 1) that, if Bérénice were to come to Rome, he would still marry Domitie; but he is deceiving himself, as subsequent events show. Indeed, Tite admits that what he says and what he feels are two different things:

> Je sais qu'un empereur doit parler ce langage;
> Et quand il l'a fallu, j'en ai dit davantage;
> Mais de ces duretés que j'étale à regret,
> Chaque mot à mon cœur coûte un soupir secret;
> Et quand à la raison j'accorde un tel empire,
> Je le dis seulement parce qu'il le faut dire,
> Et qu'étant au-dessus de tous les potentats,
> Il me serait honteux de ne le dire pas.   (V, 1)

We have seen already how Corneille's characters often feign a calmness or indifference which they are far from feeling, like Eryxe. Similarly, they sometimes say one thing in public, for the sake of appearances, and another in private. Eryxe, for example, recognizes in public that 'l'hymen des rois doit être au-dessus de l'amour,' but in private she confesses that she does not share this view:

> Mais je suis au-dessus de cette erreur commune:
> J'aime en lui sa personne autant que sa fortune ...   (II, 1)

Pulchérie tells Léon that she loves him with a calm, rational love:

> Je vous aime, et non pas de cette folle ardeur
> Que les yeux éblouis font maîtresse du cœur,
> Non d'un amour conçu par les sens en tumulte,
> A qui l'âme applaudit, sans qu'elle se consulte,
> Et qui ne concevant que d'aveugles désirs,
> Languit dans les faveurs, et meurt dans les plaisirs.
> Ma passion pour vous généreuse et solide
> A la vertu pour âme, et la raison pour guide,
> La gloire pour objet ...   (I, 1)

But her real passion comes out in her confession to Irène:

> Léon seul est ma joie, il est mon seul désir ...[1]   (III, 2)

Sometimes, too, Corneille's characters are simply untruthful

---

[1] See below, p. 311.

or hypocritical. Chimène, when she faints on hearing that Rodrigue has been wounded, gives a false explanation of her emotion. Cinna denies his complicity in the plot against Auguste's life. Jason tells Aæte that his love for Médée is genuine:

> Et mon amour n'est pas un amour politique.   (III, 1)

But a few minutes later, he says precisely the opposite to Hypsipyle:

> entendez-le, Madame,
> Ce soupir qui vers vous pousse toute mon âme;
> Et concevez par là jusqu'où vont mes malheurs,
> De soupirer pour vous, et de prétendre ailleurs.   (III, 3)

Othon tells Camille:

> C'est votre intérêt seul qui fait parler ma flamme.   (III, 5)

In fact, he is only interested in obtaining the Empire. Suréna, when Orode asks him if he knows whom the princess Eurydice loves, does not answer truthfully.

In other words, to understand a character of Corneille — as of any other dramatist — it is not enough to consider isolated passages. What he says on one occasion, must be related with what he says elsewhere; what he says in public, must be taken in conjunction with what he says in private. Due allowance must always be made for irony, double-entendre and hypocrisy. Actions are a safer guide to character than words. Nor must the opinion of other characters in the play be overlooked — it is from Léonor that we learn that Chimène has chosen the weakest champion possible. We must beware, above all, of taking lines out of their context. One or two examples of the way in which this can distort the meaning have been encountered already. Here is one more. Sophonisbe's line,

> Sur moi, quoi qu'il en soit, je me rends absolue,   (V, 1)

is often quoted as an instance of the strength of will of Corneille's characters. Looked at in its context it is less convincing. In fact, it merely means that Sophonisbe is determined to commit suicide;

and the rest of the speech shows that she is less resolute than that
single line suggests. She continues:

> Contre sa[1] dureté j'ai du secours tout prêt,
> Et ferai malgré lui moi seule mon arrêt.
>   Cependant de mon feu l'importune tendresse
> Aussi bien que ma gloire en mon sort s'intéresse,
> Veut régner en mon cœur comme ma liberté;
> Et n'ose l'avouer de toute sa fierté.
> Quelle bassesse d'âme! ô ma gloire! ô Carthage!
> Faut-il qu'avec vous deux un homme la partage?
> Et l'amour de la vie en faveur d'un époux
> Doit-il être en ce cœur aussi puissant que vous?   (V, 1)

Although Corneille is almost always his best critic, what he
says about his plays in his *Discours* and *Examens* is not *always* a
safe guide to their interpretation. Of Sophonisbe, for example, he
says this:

> Je lui prête un peu d'amour, mais elle règne sur lui, et ne daigne
> l'écouter qu'autant qu'il peut servir à ces passions dominantes qui
> règnent sur elle, et à qui elle sacrifie toutes les tendresses de son
> cœur, Massinisse, Syphax, sa propre vie.   (*Avis au lecteur*)

As has been shown above, the text of the play contradicts him.
Sophonisbe is less single-minded than this passage suggests; she
herself admits that her downfall is the result of her jealousy and
her desire to spite her rival.

*   *   *

Corneille's characters are not, then, remarkable for will-power
or self-mastery. Moreover, if they often lack the will to carry out
what they conceive to be their duties, will-power sometimes
occurs divorced from any moral sense at all. Cléopâtre, in *Rodogune*, is the supreme example of a strong, immoral or amoral,
character; but Médée (in *Médée*) and Arsinoé are her sisters, and
Dircé in *Oedipe* is not strikingly dutiful.

Not only are Corneille's characters unable to master their
passions, but they are far from ideal in other respects. Weak or

---

[1] Scipio's.

vacillating or mediocre characters are not rare in Corneille. The King in *Le Cid*; Cinna, Auguste and Maxime in *Cinna*; Félix in *Polyeucte*, irresolute, pusillanimous, worldly and selfish; the vacillating Ptolomée of *Pompée* and his Machiavellian advisers; Antiochus and Séleucus in *Rodogune*; the indulgent but weak Valens in *Théodore*, who is dominated by his wife, allows her to act for him, and will not intervene even between her and his son; Prusias in *Nicomède*, timid, dominated by *his* wife, devoid of gratitude to his son, whom he mistrusts and who, he fears, is scheming to supplant him; Attale in the same play; the selfish Garibalde of *Pertharite*, who says:

> Je t'aime, mais enfin je m'aime plus que toi,   (II, 2)

and who is Grimoald's evil counsellor, who is responsible for Grimoald's love for Rodelinde, and who persuades Grimoald to threaten the life of Rodelinde's son because he wants Grimoald to be hated: none of these is ideal; some are ordinarily human, others more than ordinarily weak and selfish.

Of the characters in the later plays, the same is true. In *La Toison d'Or*, there is Jason, the fickle opportunist, untruthful but possessed of a quick, subtle brain, for whom love is a means to an end, and who is prepared to make love to any woman if it suits his interests. There is Médée, who betrays her father for love, and who is jealous, violent, and cruel:

> Je ne croirai jamais qu'il soit douceur égale
> A celle de se voir immoler sa rivale . . .   (IV, 3)

There is her brother, Absyrte, for whom love takes precedence over every other consideration, who does not hesitate, with Médée's help to play a trick on Hypsipyle to make her love him, and who roundly declares:

> Et je ne suis pas homme à servir mon rival . . .   (V, 1)

There is Hypsipyle, too, who, devoid of any amour-propre, pursues her faithless lover, Jason, cannot resolve to give him up —

> Prince, vous savez mal combien charme un courage
> Le plus frivole espoir de reprendre un volage,

De le voir malgré lui dans nos fers retombé,
Echapper à l'objet qui nous l'a dérobé,
Et sur une rivale et confuse et trompée
Ressaisir avec gloire une place usurpée,   (II, 5)

— implores him to return to her, and finally marries someone else.

Sertorius opens with the words of Perpenna:

D'où me vient ce désordre, Aufide, et que veut dire
Que mon cœur sur mes vœux garde si peu d'empire?

— words which characterize not only Perpenna, but almost everyone else in the play. Aristie asks:

Qu'importe de mon cœur, si je sais mon devoir?   (I, 3)

but her state of mind is not so simple as that. Although her husband, Pompée, has divorced her and remarried, she cannot overcome her love for him:

je hais quelquefois,
Et moins que je ne veux et moins que je ne dois.   (III, 2)

She offers her hand to Sertorius from resentment, jealousy and wounded amour-propre. Love, in Sertorius himself, is stronger than political prudence. He decides to marry Viriate, whom he loves himself, to Perpenna, his lieutenant, in order to avoid dissensions in his army, but he lacks strength to carry out his resolution:

Je m'étais figuré que de tels déplaisirs
Pourraient ne me coûter que deux ou trois soupirs;
Et pour m'en consoler, j'envisageais l'estime
Et d'ami généreux et de chef magnanime;
Mais près d'un coup fatal, je sens par mes ennuis
Que je me promettais bien plus que je ne puis.   (IV, 1)

He tries to evade discussing the matter with Perpenna, in order to avoid committing himself. It is by no means certain that he is telling the truth when he says to Perpenna:

Non, je vous l'ai cédée, et vous tiendrai parole.
Je l'aime, et vous la donne encor malgré mon feu . . .[1]   (IV, 3)

[1] Viriate says that he would not have married her without Perpenna's consent (V, 4).

Certainly, the arguments he uses to dissuade Perpenna from marrying Viriate do not all appear to be sincere: it seems unlikely, for example, that Viriate would treat with her enemies if Sertorius were to keep his promise to Perpenna. It is because Sertorius cannot convince Perpenna of his sincerity that he is assassinated. Perpenna plots against Sertorius from envy and jealousy; yet in so doing he is conscious that he is doing wrong. He murders Sertorius, but his deed fills him with remorse.

Othon is by no means an ideal character. His love for Plautine originated in self-interest (like the love of Rastignac for Delphine de Nucingen in *Le Père Goriot*). Though it has become genuine, he agrees to relinquish her, albeit reluctantly. Having paid court to Camille, Galba's niece, in order to gain the Empire, he finds himself engaged to the princess but excluded from the succession, and has to try to dissuade her from marrying him, but without daring to confess the truth. He is hypocritical, virtuous under a good emperor, depraved under a bad one. Plautine, who urges Othon to make love to Camille, cannot help being jealous when he does so (like Atalide in *Bajazet*, later). Her father, Vinius, is another Félix, eager above all to maintain his power. Galba describes him thus:

> Voyez ce qu'en un jour il m'a sacrifié:
> Il m'offre Othon pour vous, qu'il souhaitait pour gendre;
> Je le rends à sa fille, il aime à le reprendre;
> Je la veux pour Pison, mon vouloir est suivi;
> Je vous mets en sa place, et l'en trouve ravi;
> Son ami se révolte, il presse ma colère;
> Il donne à Martian Plautine à ma prière . . .   (V, 1)

Galba is weak. Camille, his niece, is intelligent and shrewd, but jealous and vindictive. She is determined to marry Plautine, her rival in Othon's affections, to Martian, whom Plautine loathes, in order to be revenged upon her; and, when Othon places himself at the head of a revolt, she says:

> Allons presser Galba pour son juste supplice
>
> . . . .
> Du courroux à l'amour si le retour est doux,
> On repasse aisément de l'amour au courroux.   (IV, 7)

In *Agésilas*, Cotys, who is betrothed to Elpinice but does not love her, refuses to give her up to Spitridate:

> Je serai malheureux, vous le serez aussi.   (I, 4)

Spitridate is equally selfish in proposing to his sister that she should overcome her love for Cotys and marry Agésilas in order that he should be happy with Elpinice. Agésilas himself says:

> ... Je ne suis pas assez fort
> Pour triompher de ma faiblesse.   (III, 4)

Attila is a most interesting study. He is an able politician, excelling rather at sowing dissension amongst his enemies than at military conquest, shrewd and suspicious, wily and cruel. He devises one scheme after another to torment the wretched kings and princesses in his power, playing with them like a cat with mice. But he is at the same time irresolute, and allows love to get the better of political prudence. Though Honorie is the more suitable match, he cannot overcome his preference for Ildione:

> Moi qui veux pouvoir tout, sitôt que je vous voi,
> Malgré tout cet orgueil, je ne puis rien pour moi.   (III, 2)

Ildione and Honorie do not love Attila, but they are jealous of his favour and speak spitefully to each other. Honorie is particularly interesting. In situation, and to some extent in character, she resembles Racine's Hermione. She is unbalanced, and lacks self-control; jealousy makes her mean and spiteful. In a fit of pique, she refuses Attila, and, against her principle that a puppet-king is unworthy of her, agrees to marry Valamir. Wounded by Ildione's taunts, she seeks an unworthy revenge by betraying to Attila Ildione's love for Ardaric and suggesting that she should be made to marry a subject. She imprudently betrays the secret of her own love for Valamir:

> Que n'ai-je donc mieux tu que j'aimais Valamir!
> Mais quand on est bravée et qu'on perd ce qu'on aime,
> Flavie, est-on si peu maîtresse de soi-même?   (IV, 2)

She sinks her pride and asks Attila to marry her.

Domitie, in *Tite et Bérénice*, finds that her ambition to be Empress is not strong enough to overcome her love for Domitian:

> Si l'amour quelquefois souffre qu'on le contraigne,
> Il souffre rarement qu'une autre ardeur l'éteigne;
> Et quand l'ambition en met l'empire à bas,
> Elle en fait son esclave, et ne l'étouffe pas.
> Mais un si fier esclave ennemi de sa chaîne,
> La secoue à toute heure, et la porte avec gêne,
> Et maître de nos sens, qu'il appelle au secours,
> Il échappe souvent, et murmure toujours.
> Veux-tu que je te fasse un aveu tout sincère?
> Je ne puis aimer Tite, ou n'aimer pas son frère;
> Et malgré cet amour, je ne puis m'arrêter
> Qu'au degré le plus haut où je puisse monter.
> . . . .
> Hélas! plus je le vois, moins je sais que lui dire.
> Je l'aime, et le dédaigne, et n'osant m'attendrir,
> Je me veux mal des maux que je lui fais souffrir.   (I, 1)

She cannot prevent herself from feeling jealous when she sees Domitian paying court to Bérénice; though, on the other hand, when she thinks that Tite prefers Bérénice, her pride is hurt and she wants to be revenged on him. Corneille's Tite, unlike Racine's Titus, is weak and vacillating —

> Maître de l'univers sans l'être de moi-même . . .   (II, 1)

— and is prepared to abdicate to win Bérénice. His brother, Domitian, is not magnanimous. Finding Domitie determined to marry Tite, he expresses the wish that Bérénice would return and prevent the marriage and exults in her discomfiture:

> Que je verrais, Albin, ma volage punie,
> Si de ces grands apprêts pour la cérémonie,
> Que depuis si longtemps on dresse à si grand bruit,
> Elle n'avait que l'ombre, et qu'une autre eût le fruit!
> Qu'elle serait confuse! et que j'aurais de joie!   (I, 3)

For Eurydice and Suréna, love is the only thing that matters.

> Je veux, sans que la mort ose me secourir,
> Toujours aimer, toujours souffrir, toujours mourir,

says Eurydice, and Suréna echoes her words:

> où dois-je recourir,
> O ciel! s'il faut toujours aimer, souffrir, mourir.   (I, 3)

For Suréna,

> le moindre moment d'un bonheur souhaité,
> Vaut mieux qu'une si froide et vaine éternité.   (I, 3)

There is nothing rational about Eurydice, who is all fears and jealousy, and who touchingly strikes up a friendship with Suréna's sister, as a way of being near him vicariously. Though her duty requires her to marry Pacorus, not only does she not love him, but she makes no pretence of doing so, reminds him that he has loved another, postpones her marriage with him, and does not conceal that she loves someone else. Nor can she bring herself to allow Suréna to obey the king and marry Mandane, so that she is directly responsible for his death. Pacorus, too, is another character who cannot master his love: Suréna tells him:

> l'amour jaloux de son autorité,
> Ne reconnaît ni rois ni souveraineté.
> Il hait tous les emplois où la force l'appelle:
> Dès qu'on le violente, on en fait un rebelle;
> Et je suis criminel de n'en pas triompher,
> Quand vous-même, Seigneur, ne pouvez l'étouffer!   (IV, 4)

Palmis is yet another:

> *Pacorus.* Ah! vous ne m'aimez plus.
> *Palmis.*   Je voudrais le pouvoir,
> Mais pour ne plus aimer que sert de le vouloir?   (II, 3)

The women of Corneille are often spiteful, jealous and possessive. Doña Isabelle, who suspects that Don Sanche loves Doña Elvire, is determined that if she cannot marry him herself, her rival shall not be happier than she. If she should have to marry Doña Elvire's brother, she says:

> devenant par là reine de ma rivale,
> J'aurai droit d'empêcher qu'elle ne se ravale,
> Et ne souffrirai pas qu'elle ait plus de bonheur
> Que ne m'en ont permis ces tristes lois d'honneur.
>
> (*Don Sanche*, III, 6)

If Don Sanche must marry someone else, it must be a woman she has chosen for him, not one he has chosen himself:

> Qu'il souffre autant pour moi que je souffre pour lui ...   (III, 6)

Mandane, in *Agésilas*, expresses similar views; so do Bérénice and Eurydice. Sophonisbe is more openly possessive:

> Un esclave échappé nous fait toujours rougir.   (I, 2)

Albin, in *Tite et Bérénice*, discourses in general terms on this feminine characteristic:

> Seigneur, telle est l'humeur de la plupart des femmes.
> L'amour sous leur empire eût-il rangé mille âmes,
> Elles regardent tout comme leur propre bien,
> Et ne peuvent souffrir qu'il leur échappe rien.
> Un captif mal gardé leur semble une infamie:
> Qui l'ose recevoir devient leur ennemie;
> Et sans leur faire un vol on ne peut disposer
> D'un cœur qu'un autre choix les force à refuser:
> Elles veulent qu'ailleurs par leur ordre il soupire,
> Et qu'un don de leur part marque un reste d'empire.   (IV, 4)

Several of Corneille's heroines, besides Domitie, illustrate his remarks.

*   *   *

Corneille's portrayal of human nature, then, is much more varied and subtle than is often supposed. His characters are for the most part unable to subdue their passions by their reason or their will; relatively few place honour or duty before inclination. They are not supermen or ideal creatures, but real men and women. Nearly all have their moments of weakness and indecision; nearly all have human faults and weaknesses. Above all, they are more complex in their motivation than they are often considered to be.

They are very varied. There are some strong characters, with some of the traits we think of as 'Cornelian', though they are far less numerous than is often imagined, and are by no means always virtuous. But such characters are relatively few and untypical, and confined to a certain number of plays. By their side are to be found a host of ordinary or weak or erring characters. Corneille's plays, indeed, constitute a wonderful and varied gallery of portraits. In *Polyeucte*, for example, we have Polyeucte, Sévère, Pauline, and Félix, all different types of humanity, admirably differentiated one from the other. To take another example, in *Nicomède* Corneille gives us — by the side of the self-confident, honourable, plain-speaking, tactless, ironical Nicomède and his feminine counterpart, Laodice — the wily Arsinoé, ambitious for her son, Attale, rather than for herself, adept at winding round her little finger her husband, the timid, mistrustful, uxorious Prusias. There are, too, the admirably portrayed diplomat, Flaminius, shrewd and subtle, skilfully concealing the iron hand beneath the velvet glove, making his will known by reasoned advice and hints, an excellent ambassador, and Attale, the brother of Nicomède, young and inexperienced, somewhat *précieux*, but intelligent and endowed with sound instincts, so that he gradually learns to distinguish between the world as he has been brought up to believe that it is and the world as it really is. Or, ranging over the whole work of Corneille, Rodrigue, Horace, Curiace, Auguste, Cinna, Polyeucte, César, Don Sanche, Nicomède, Othon, Martian and Suréna are not the same type of hero, any more than Chimène, Camille, Sabine, Pauline, Cléopâtre, Rodogune, Laodice, Dircé, Sophonisbe, Camille (in *Othon*), Ildione, Honorie, Pulchérie or Eurydice are one type of heroine. Maxime, Garibalde and Perpenna are three quite different types of weak character or villain. Again, Corneille shows many different types of older men — the count and Don Diègue, old Horace, Félix, Valens, Prusias, Vinius, Attila, Martian, and Suréna have little in common.

Corneille is excellent, too, at depicting family life. There is great variety in his fathers, for example: Don Diègue and old Horace, both affectionate and proud of their sons, but the former a little out of sympathy with his son's inner conflict, Félix, Valens, Prusias, Aæte . . . . Two deserve a particular mention: Phocas, in *Héraclius*, suffering because neither of the two young men will acknowledge him as father; and Martian, in *Pulchérie*, guessing the secrets of his daughter's heart and betraying his own in a touching scene. Then the mothers: Marcelle, in *Théodore*, full of fierce, maternal affection; Arsinoé, in *Nicomède*, like her a good mother but a bad stepmother; Jocaste, in *Oedipe*, who, though she has remarried, is thoughtful for her daughter's welfare; Cléopâtre, in *Rodogune*, devoid of any affection for her sons; Cassiope, in *Andromède*, whose excessive maternal pride has brought misfortune to her country and her daughter. Perhaps Corneille is at his best in portraying the relationships between brothers and sisters. Leaving aside the comedies, we think of the sisterly bickering of Chalciope and Médée; of the delicate affection between Antiochus and Séleucus in *Rodogune*; of the dawning affection between the two half-brothers, Nicomède and Attale; of Mandane, in *Agésilas*, resisting the entreaties of her brother, Spitridate, who wants her to marry Agésilas, whom she does not love, so that Agésilas may let him be happy with Elpinice; of the eagerness of Irène in *Pulchérie* to help Léon; of the loyalty and affection of Palmis in *Suréna*. It is clear that no attempt to reduce Corneille's characters to a single formula can do justice to the range and variety of his characterization.

Nor is there any evidence that Corneille wrote with the object of inculcating a moral lesson of any kind. He himself, in the *Discours*, expressly denies that drama should have a moral aim; and it is difficult to feel that in any play we are being shown ideal characters on whom Corneille wishes us to model ourselves. Let us rather say, with Vedel: 'Il reste aussi invisible derrière son œuvre que Shakespeare.' The truth is surely that Corneille was concerned with studying human nature, with portraying different types of men and women, of fathers and sons and mothers and daughters, of lovers and their mistresses, of kings and tyrants and diplomats and politicians, of soldiers and adventurers, with studying their behaviour in different situations, their problems, their sufferings. Indeed, a contemporary anecdote, recently unearthed by Professor Lough, shows us a Corneille who — like Balzac — closely identified himself with his characters:

M'a dit[1] qu'étant à table avec M. l'Abbé de Cerisy, M. de Corneille, et avec d'autres honnêtes gens à Rouen, M. Corneille qu'était assis auprès de lui à mi-repos, lui donna un coup de poing sur l'épaule avec un cri, qui fut suivi de paroles, qui témoignèrent assez qu'il songeait ailleurs: Ah! que j'ai de la peine à faire mourir cette fille! Comme il avait surpris la compagnie, il fut obligé à dire la vérité, et en les demandant pardon, il les assurait, qu'il n'était propre pour la conversation, et qu'il ne saurait s'empêcher rêver sur quelqu'une de ses comédies qu'il avait sur les mains, et qui fut l'occasion de ses paroles.[2]

[1] These are Martin Lister's notes of a conversation he had had with a M. de la Mothe in 1665: hence the odd French.

[2] J. Lough, 'Comment travaillait le grand Corneille,' in the *Revue de la Société d'Histoire du Théâtre*, 1950. The following note is also of interest: 'Que ce fut de façon de M. de Corneille quand il pensait à travailler à quelqu'une de ses pièces de théâtre, de se mettre au lit, et de se faire couvrir avec plusieurs grosses couvertures afin de s'échauffer et de se faire suer. Après qu'il y eut demeuré quelques moments en cet état-là, en sortant de lit, il demanda à écrire.' Bonnegarde, in his *Dictionnaire historique et critique*, 1771, says, of Estoile: 'Lorsqu'il voulait travailler dans le jour, il faisait fermer les fenêtres de sa chambre, et apporter de la lumière. On a dit la même chose du grand *Corneille*.'

Chapter Nine

THE REALISM OF CORNEILLE
(2)
CORNEILLE AND HIS AGE

In the previous chapter, an attempt was made to show that the characters of Corneille are varied and complex and universal in their truth and interest. The object of the present chapter is to show that Corneille's characters, whether 'Cornelian' or not, and his plots and situations, however apparently romantic, reflect the atmosphere of the age in which he wrote.

§ 1 *Characters*

In so far as the characters of Corneille are marked by pride, fortitude, and stoicism, they are like many of his contemporaries, as they were described in the first chapter. Even Corneille's women, who have been unjustly criticized, are very much of their age. Médée or Cléopâtre (in *Rodogune*) might be compared in real life to Christina of Sweden, who had her secretary assassinated at Fontainebleau, or the poisoner, Mme de Brinvilliers. Pulchérie, in *Héraclius*, was quoted above as an example of extreme fortitude:

Ce grand coup m'a surprise et ne m'a point troublée . . .

But parallels can be found in real life. Anne of Austria, compelled to dismiss Mazarin, her minister and favourite, possibly her

husband, displayed as much strength of mind as Pulchérie on learning that her lover was her brother:

> Le Cardinal étant donc résolu de partir, il vint chez la Reine le soir de ce jour sixième de février. Elle lui parla longtemps devant tout le monde, dans la créance que vraisemblablement ce serait la dernière fois qu'elle le verrait. Nous qui étions présentes à cette conférence, et moi comme les autres, ne pûmes apercevoir aucune altération dans son visage. Sa gravité ne l'abandonna point. Son cœur, qui était touché sans doute, de colère, de haine, de pitié, de douleur, et de dépit, ne laissa rien voir au dehors de tous ces sentiments; et jamais je ne l'ai vue plus tranquille qu'elle le parût alors. [. . .]
>
> La Reine, après que le Cardinal fut parti, demeura le reste du soir à s'entretenir de choses indifférentes. Elle parut la même qu'elle avait accoutumée d'être. Ceux qui l'observèrent, et nous même, en fûmes étonnés; car il était impossible d'attribuer sa constance à son insensibilité. Aussi, doit-on dire à sa louange, pour satisfaire simplement à la vérité, que dans toutes les grandes occasions, nous l'avons toujours vue recevoir d'un visage égal les peines qui sont accoutumées de troubler tous les autres.[1]   (Mme de Motteville)

If we reflect that, on the stage, a character cannot just be calm, he must let the audience know that he is calm, we have here a reasonably close equivalent in real life of Pulchérie's speech.

The *grande Mademoiselle* is more Cornelian than many characters in Corneille: indeed, she is several different heroines of Corneille rolled into one. She was a woman of action, who, during the Fronde, entered Orléans at the head of an army and defended it against the royal armies, who, later, when the royalists attacked Paris and her father, Gaston d'Orléans, was feigning illness, took command and defended the Porte Saint-Antoine, and who was not afraid to face the mob and quell a riot. Laonice, who stirs up the populace in *Nicomède*, has something of Mademoiselle in her.

---

[1] Cf. 'Voilà un endroit où la Princesse Marguerite [of Savoy, who was being considered as a match for Louis XIV] acquit beaucoup d'estime et de gloire, et beaucoup de louanges de la Reine même; car, soit que le Roi ne la regardât pas, soit qu'il lui parlât, elle demeura toujours égale en toutes ses actions, vivant civilement avec tous, mais ne montrant point se soucier de plaire. Comme les liaisons que le Cardinal avait prises avec Made de Savoie étaient grandes, que ce voyage fait à la face de toute l'Europe était de lui-même un grand engagement, et qu'elle pressait la Reine et le ministre de la satisfaire, il y avait des jours qu'il semblait que ce mariage allait bien et d'autres où par les ressorts de la Reine et de Pimentel il paraissait rompu; mais *ni le bien ni le mal ne se voyait point sur le visage de la Princesse Marguerite, et sa noble fierté ne l'abandonna jamais.*'   (Mme de Motteville)

Mademoiselle, too, was determined to marry only a King — like Rodogune, or Dircé, or Aglatide, or Honorie, or Domitie:

> Je n'oublierai jamais que je me dois un roi.[1]
>
> (*Rodogune*, IV, 1)

Just as Oedipe is faced with the problem of disposing of Dircé in marriage, so Anne of Austria and Louis XIV had trouble with Mademoiselle. She set her heart upon marrying the Emperor, scorned the Prince of Wales (then in exile in France), and was for a time banished from court for refusing to marry the King of Portugal. Eventually — like the Infante, Doña Elvire, Camille (in *Othon*), Pulchérie (in *Pulchérie*), and Eurydice — she fell in love with a gentleman far beneath her in rank. In a passage which reminds one of some of these heroines, she relates how she tried in vain to conquer her love:

> Il me souvient qu'après avoir fait de sérieuses réflexions sur ce que tout le monde dirait de mon affaire, et sur les dégoûts que je pourrais trouver dans ce mariage, je résolus de ne plus parler à M. de Lauzun qu'avec une tierce personne, et je voulais m'éloigner des occasions de le voir, afin de me l'ôter de la tête. J'avais commencé à tenir cette conduite, je ne lui tenais plus que des discours indifférents; je m'aperçus que je ne savais ce que je lui disais, que je n'arrangeais pas trois mots qui eussent une suite de bon sens; et plus je cherchais à le fuir, plus j'avais envie de le voir. Madame, qui était de ses amies, et qui m'avait témoigné être des miennes, me parlait souvent de son mérite. Je fus tentée mille fois de lui ouvrir mon cœur, afin qu'elle me dît bonnement ce que je devais faire, et de quelle manière elle me conseillerait de me conduire. Je n'étais pas en état de le pouvoir faire de moi-même, puisque je faisais toujours le contraire de ce que je voulais chercher à faire; ce que j'avais projeté la nuit, je ne pouvais l'exécuter le jour. Voilà une manière de vie et de démêlé que j'avais cent fois le jour avec moi-même. Après avoir songé à l'impossibilité de m'ôter cela de la tête, et aux obstacles que j'y pouvais trouver, et que j'eus bien surmonté tout ce qu'on en pourrait dire, je me vis dans une nécessité absolue de prendre une résolution.

Eventually, she confessed her love to M. de Lauzun. Louis XIV at first consented to the match, then forbade it and imprisoned

---

[1] Maria Theresa, asked by the mother superior of the Val-de-Grâce if she had not shown particular favour to any young man at her father's court, replied: 'Mais non, ma Mère, il n'y avait pas de roi.'

Lauzun. Mme de Sévigné vividly describes her despair; but she would not give way — any more than Eurydice — and at last bought Lauzun's freedom by giving her estates to the King's illegitimate son, the duc du Maine.

There are, in Corneille's plays, plenty of unheroic characters, weak, cowardly, or dominated by their passions. There are plenty of counterparts to them in the seventeenth century, such as the irresolute duc de Longueville, and, above all, Mademoiselle's father, the pusillanimous, vacillating, unreliable Gaston d'Orléans, who had a habit of feigning illness whenever circumstances became too much for him and he had a difficult decision to make. Retz says of him, in a passage which makes us think of Félix:

> L'irrésolution de Monsieur était d'une espèce toute particulière. Elle l'empêchait souvent d'agir, quand même il était le plus nécessaire d'agir; elle le faisait quelquefois agir, quand même il était le plus nécessaire de ne point agir.

§ 2 *Plots and situations*

If Corneille's characters, weak or strong, men or women, have their counterparts in the seventeenth century, so, too, have the events and situations of his plays, however apparently romantic.

The assassination of Sertorius or Suréna reminds one that murder was a not uncommon political weapon in the seventeenth century. Concini, the minister of Maria de' Medici, was murdered. Cinq-Mars suggested to Louis XIII that Richelieu should be murdered. Ferdinand II had Wallenstein murdered. Christina of Sweden caused her favourite, Monaldeschi, to be murdered at Fontainebleau. The account of the death of Suréna may, Couton suggests, owe something to the assassination in 1621 of the count of Villa-Mediana, who was the rival of the King of Spain. The King ordered him to withdraw from court:

> Au lieu de suivre l'ordre du Roi, le Comte va au palais avec une enseigne à son chapeau, où il y avait un diable dans les flammes avec ce mot, qui se rapportait à lui:

Mas penado, menos arrepentido.[1]

Le Roi, irrité de cela, le fit tuer dans le Prade d'un coup de mousquet qu'on lui tira dans son carrosse, et puis on cria: *Es por mandamiento del Rey.* (Tallemant)

Political intrigues and rivalry between the ministers of the sovereign, such as those depicted in *Pompée* or *Othon*, were a feature of the life of the court of Anne of Austria and of Louis XIV. Revolts and revolutions occur in *Héraclius*, in *Don Sanche*, and in *Nicomède*; they were common enough in France and abroad in this age. In consequence, usurpers such as Grimoald or Phocas, and members of deposed royal families living in foreign courts were no less a feature of the period than of Corneille's plays. Marie de Gonzague, Queen of Poland, was forced by a Swedish invasion to take refuge in Silesia in 1665; the Count Palatine was driven out of his Kingdom during the Thirty Years War; the family of Charles I took refuge in France; Henry IV was King for years before he could enter his capital; Louis XIV, Anne of Austria and Mazarin were compelled to leave Paris during the Fronde; Christina of Sweden, after her abdication, lived in France and Italy. Pompée taking refuge at the court of Ptolomée, Rodogune living at the court of Cléopâtre, Pulchérie at that of Phocas, Doña Elvire at that of Doña Isabelle, Laonice at that of Prusias, Rodelinde at that of Grimoald, Eryxe at that of Sophonisbe, Honorie and Ildione at that of Attila — are reminiscent of many seventeenth-century figures.

The problem of the overgreat subject, treated in *Nicomède*, in *Agésilas*, and in *Suréna*, is a seventeenth-century problem. Lysander, in *Agésilas*, a king-maker with more power than the King, is a kind of Richelieu or Mazarin or Foucquet:

> tirant toute à vous la suprême puissance,
> Vous me laissez des titres vains.
> On s'empresse à vous voir, on s'efforce à vous plaire;
> On croit lire en vos yeux ce qu'il faut qu'on espère;

[1] The more he is in torment, the less he repents. Kings and subjects were rivals in love in France, too — e.g. Henry IV. Lauzun, the rival of Louis XIV for the good graces of Mme de Monaco, betrayed his jealousy by stamping on her hand one day, and was sent to the Bastille.

On pense avoir tout fait quand on vous a parlé.
Mon palais près du vôtre est un lieu désolé;
Et le généralat, comme le diadème
M'érige sous votre ordre en fantôme éclatant,
En colosse d'Etat qui de vous seul attend
    L'âme qu'il n'a pas de lui-même,
    Et que vous seul faites aller
Où pour vos intérêts il le faut étaler.   (III, 1)

Nicomède or Suréna, all-powerful generals whose influence in the state alarms Prusias and Orode, call to mind Wallenstein or Condé. Of Condé's arrest, Mme de Motteville says that Mazarin 'crut que ce qu'il devait au Roi, et ce qu'il se devait à lui-même, l'obligeaient de mettre des bornes à la puissance de ce prince, qui n'en voulait plus avoir sur aucun sujet.'

In *Héraclius*, in *Rodogune*, in *Don Sanche*, we are shown mysteries of birth, characters not knowing whose children they really are. Nothing could be more romantic; and yet these things were not unknown in the seventeenth century. It was an age of considerable sexual licence, when many distinguished figures, including Henry IV of France, had considerable illegitimate progeny, besides their lawful issue. Tallemant tells of a certain Lisette, for example, who claimed to be the illegitimate daughter of Henry IV and the Princesse de Conti. About the time of *Héraclius*, the Rohan case caused a great sensation in France. Mme de Rohan gave birth secretly to a son — legitimate or illegitimate. Mme de Rohan's own daughter had the child stolen away and brought up in Holland, lest he should be passed off as legitimate and succeed to the Rohan estates. Eventually, the mother traced her son, recovered him, and claimed that he was a legitimate child and the rightful heir to the property. His claims were opposed by Condé, and supported by the parlement; but he was killed, during the Fronde, before the case could be decided. In a passage which would not be out of place in *Don Sanche*, Mme de Motteville says of him:

Malgré sa jeunesse, qui n'était pas encore fort éloignée de l'enfance, il y fit des merveilles de sa personne, et donna tant de preuves de sa

valeur, qu'il laissa dans le monde cette créance de lui, que s'il
n'était fils du Duc de Rohan, ce grand capitaine, il l'était du moins
d'une personne de qualité, qui sans doute ne manquait ni de grandeur, ni de courage. Il faut que les conquérants fassent plus que le
commun des autres hommes: il savait déjà qu'il avait à combattre,
non seulement pour la gloire, mais encore pour acquérir un père, un
nom, des parents, de grandes terres, et de la fortune; et, surtout, pour
fuir une honteuse destinée.

Don Sanche is an adventurer of obscure birth — a romantic
figure, but also a common enough type in an age when many men
made their way in the world by their wits or their swords. One
thinks of ministers of state like Concini or Mazarin, of soldiers
like Bernard of Saxe Weimar, Johann von Werth, Wallenstein.
Tallemant tells of one Roussel, who started life as a servant and
was successively Russian ambassador in Sweden and Swedish
ambassador in Holland and in Constantinople. Gourville, the
servant of La Rochefoucauld, passed into the employment of
Mazarin, of Foucquet and of Condé, became very wealthy, was
employed on various diplomatic missions, and lived on intimate
terms with the ministers of Louis XIV and the highest French
society.

Cinna is reminiscent of the age of Richelieu, with its frequent
conspiracies against the King and his all-powerful minister.
Emilie has many counterparts in real life, and the blend of conspiracy and love is characteristic of the period. Mazarin told Don
Luis de Haro:

> Les nôtres [i.e. women] [...] soit prudes, soit galantes, soit vieilles,
> jeunes, sottes ou habiles, veulent se mêler à toutes choses. Une femme
> de bien ne coucherait pas avec son mari ni une coquette avec son
> galant s'il ne leur avait parlé ce jour-là d'affaires d'Etat; elles veulent
> tout voir, tout connaître, tout savoir et, qui pis est, tout faire et tout
> brouiller. Nous en avons trois entre autres, la duchesse de Longue-
> ville, la duchesse de Chevreuse et la Princesse Palatine qui nous
> mettent tous les jours en plus de confusion qu'il n'y en eut jamais à
> Babylone.

Like Cinna, Chalais was induced to join the party of malcontents by his passion for Mme de Chevreuse.[1] Cinq-Mars conspired out of love for Marie de Gonzague:

> par ce sentiment il entra dans de grands desseins qui le firent périr, et se laissa flatter [. . .] de l'espérance qu'il deviendrait Connétable, et qu'avec cette qualité et l'éclat de sa faveur, il pourrait être digne mari de la fille d'un souverain.   (Mme de Motteville)

La Rochefoucauld took part in the Fronde from love of Mme de Longueville; and Cardinal de Retz admits to being tempted to love both Mme de Longueville and Mme de Bouillon. On her side, Mme de Longueville was drawn into politics by love; so was Mme de Chevreuse, of whom Retz writes:

> Si elle fût venue dans un siècle où il n'y eût point eu d'affaires, elle n'eût pas seulement imaginé qu'il y en pût avoir. Si le prieur des Chartreux lui eût plu, elle eût été solitaire de bonne foi. M. de Lorraine, qui s'y attacha, la jeta dans les affaires; le duc de Buckingham et le comte de Holland l'y entretinrent; M. de Châteauneuf l'y amusa. Elle s'y abandonna, parce qu'elle s'abandonnait à tout ce qui plaisait à celui qu'elle aimait.

War and politics were associated with love no less than conspiracy. The Duke of Buckingham provides an example both of this, and of a subject in love with a queen (*Don Sanche*, *Pulchérie*, *Suréna*). Buckingham met Anne of Austria when he went to Paris to marry, as proxy for his royal master, Charles I, Henriette de France, sister to Louis XIII. He fell in love with her. Having escorted the new Queen of England as far as Calais, he invented a pretext to leave her and return to Paris.

> Après avoir parlé de sa chimérique négociation, il alla chez la Reine, qu'il trouva au lit assez seule [. . .] elle fut surprise de ce que tout librement il vint se mettre à genoux devant son lit, baisant son drap avec des transports si extraordinaires qu'il était aisé de voir que sa passion était violente, et de celles qui ne laissent aucun usage de raison à ceux qui en sont touchés.   (Mme de Motteville)

---

[1] '*Cinna* présente une conspiration de style Louis XIII: par l'importance des femmes et de l'amour; par les secrets mal gardés; parce que les mobiles personnels et familiaux se joignent aux raisons politiques jusqu'à rendre indiscernables le désir d'un changement de régime et l'exercice de la vendetta; par l'imprévoyance des lendemains; par un véritable snobisme de la conspiration (v. 1207–1208).'   (Couton, *Corneille*, pp. 68–9)

The Queen was too embarrassed to speak, but one of her women
bade Buckingham rise, such behaviour not being customary in
France. He resisted, saying that he was not a Frenchman.

> Puis s'adressant à la Reine, lui dit tout haut les choses du monde les
> plus tendres; mais elle ne lui répondit que par des plaintes de sa
> hardiesse, et sans peut-être être trop en colère lui ordonna sévère-
> ment de se lever et de sortir. Il le fit [. . .]   (Mme de Motteville)

The English expedition against La Rochelle was undertaken —
or so it was believed in France — in order that Buckingham might
have a chance of returning to Paris to negotiate a peace treaty. On
arriving at the île de Ré,

> il prit un gentilhomme de Xaintonge, nommé Saint-Surin, homme
> adroit et intelligent et qui savait fort bien la Cour. Il lui fit mille
> civilités, et lui ayant découvert son amour, il le mena dans la plus
> belle chambre de son vaisseau. Cette chambre était fort dorée; le
> plancher était couvert de tapis de Perse, et il y avait comme une
> espèce d'autel où était le portrait de la Reine, avec plusieurs flam-
> beaux allumés. Après, il lui donna la liberté, à condition d'aller dire à
> M. le Cardinal qu'il se retirerait et livrerait La Rochelle, en un mot,
> qu'il offrait la carte blanche, pourvu qu'on lui promît de le recevoir
> ambassadeur en France.   (Tallemant)

After this, there is nothing improbable in the love of César for
Cléopâtre in *Pompée*, or in his finding time to write to her in the
midst of his campaigns.

Marriage was an important instrument of policy — in real life,
as in Corneille. Condé feared the marriage of Luynes's niece to
the duc de Retz, 'ce qui eût attiré toute l'affection dudit duc de
Luynes de leur côté, et peut-être éloignée de messieurs le prince et
duc de Guise.' He therefore tried to arrange that she should marry
Bassompierre. Mlle de Pont-de-Courlay was married to Combalet
in order to ensure the friendship of Luynes and Richelieu. The
great Condé opposed the marriage of Mazarin's two nieces to
Candale and Vendôme because these political alliances would have
strengthened Mazarin's position and made him less dependent on
Condé. Condé himself incurred the hostility of the court because
he married the young duc de Richelieu secretly to Mme du Pons

in order to gain control of Le Havre. Condé himself, as duc d'Enghien, though in love with Mlle du Vigean, was compelled to marry Richelieu's niece, Mlle de Maillé-Brézé.

In these circumstances, the conflict of love and duty or ambition, as we find it in the Infante, in Doña Isabelle, in Sertorius, in Attila, in Tite, in Pulchérie, and in Eurydice, was bound to arise. Louis XIV renounced Marie Mancini, Mazarin's niece, though he was very much in love with her. Princesses, compelled to marry one man while loving another, suffered deeply. Mademoiselle was unhappy when she was separated from Lauzun, though she, at least, was not required to marry anyone else. In 1679, Marie-Louise, daughter of Henriette d'Angleterre, was married to Charles II, King of Spain, though she had hoped to marry her cousin, the Dauphin. More touching is the case of Mademoiselle's half-sister, Marguerite d'Orléans. In 1661, though deeply in love with Prince Charles of Lorraine, she was married to Prince Cosimo of Tuscany (later Cosimo III). She was desperately unhappy, all the more so since her husband was quite unworthy of her. After a long and unhappy life of matrimonial discord, she eventually left Tuscany and returned to France in 1674.

Polyeucte reflects the religious sentiment of the seventeenth century. Eager for martyrdom, the hero causes a public scandal by breaking the idols in the temple, an action far in excess of anything his duty requires, and renounces his wife, whom he comes to regard as an obstacle to his own salvation. All these traits are characteristic of the period. We have already seen how some of the missionaries in Canada aspired to be martyred. Excess of zeal was common, too. M. Le Maître, when Saint-Cyran recommended that he should speak to no women, resolved to speak to no one at all. Many people regarded earthly affections as an obstacle to their salvation. Pascal thought that the duty of a Christian was to love 'sans attache'. The Norman, M. de Renty, when his wife was dying, in 1643, felt that her death would be a great loss, but on the other hand the idea of sacrificing to God what he loved most dearly filled him with such joy that 'si la bienséance ne m'empêchait, je la ferais éclater au dehors, et en donnerais des témoignages publics'. M. de Pontchâteau, who remarked that God had killed two men to save him (Richelieu and the Cardinal Archbishop of Lyons, who had both wanted to heap ecclesiastical preferment on him), added, when a woman whom he hoped to marry, died: 'Dieu a tué cette femme par-dessus le marché, pour me sauver encore.' Sœur Marie-Claire of Port-Royal was deeply attached to her sister, mère Angélique, but, being told by the Bishop of Langres that it would be better if she did not speak to her sister, did not address a single word to her for several years. Mère Angélique herself excluded her father from Port-Royal on the famous *journée du guichet*, between which and *Polyeucte* Sainte-Beuve drew an elaborate parallel. Mme de Sévigné's grandmother, Mme de Chantal, who founded the Visitandines, and Mme Martin, who went to Canada in 1639, both left their children in order to become nuns.

Pauline, too, has her counterparts in the seventeenth century. The princesse de Conti, though she preferred M. de Candale, had been compelled to marry the prince de Conti. Her husband was converted all of a sudden and was eager that she should be converted, too; but his efforts merely irritated her and made her regard religion as a rival in his affections. But one day in 1657 (she was then 19), she was suddenly converted in her turn and, sending for her husband, she said to him: 'Je crois que Dieu m'a changée. Je vous prie de m'envoyer M. l'abbé de Ciron' [his confessor]. She then went to excesses of austerity.

Even some of the episodes in Corneille's plays can be paralleled in real life. In *Le Cid*, we have a duel and a single combat. Duels were common enough; even single combats were not unknown. M. de Vitry, for example, claimed the estate of the comte de Chasteau-Vilain; the dispute reached such a pitch that, in 1624, the Count asked the King for permission to meet Vitry in single combat. After Don Diègue's quarrel with the Count in *Le Cid*, five hundred gentlemen offered him their help. Similarly, in 1611, the comte de Soissons and the prince de Conti, his brother, quarrelled. M. de Guise, sent to patch up the quarrel, passed in front of the hôtel de Soissons. The comte de Soissons was offended and sent for his friends. 'Alors les amis de M. de Guise accoururent à l'hôtel de Guise en telle foule,' says Bassompierre, 'qu'il s'y trouva plus de mille gentilshommes.' Even the scene in which Rodrigue urges Chimène to kill him with her own hand can be matched in the life of the time. Tallemant records two similar incidents. La Calprenède, the novelist, presented his unkind mistress 'a hundred times' with his sword so that she might kill him. A M. de Marcognet, who loved Mme d'Alincourt, contrived to find himself alone with her in her apartment one day and took advantage of the situation:

> Il lui fit après toutes les satisfactions qu'on peut s'imaginer. Elle le menaçait de le faire poignarder: 'Il ne faut point d'autre main que la vôtre pour cela,' lui dit-il, 'Madame'; et lui présentant un poignard: 'Vengez-vous vous-même, et je vous jure que je mourrai très content.' Durant ces tendres paroles, il se rapprocha d'elle et trouva à la vérité un peu moins de résistance. Enfin à la troisième, elle se laissa fléchir, il obtint son pardon, et la quatrième fut le sceau de leur amitié.

The false rumours put about in some of Corneille's plays were also sometimes used in real life in order to gauge the state of public opinion. In 1613, M. le Prince wanted to be made governor of the Château Trompette.

> On fit premièrement courir le bruit, par la cour, que la Reine lui avait donné cette capitainerie pour voir comme cela serait reçu pour disposer la chose: comme en ces derniers temps on en avait ainsi usé, de faire prévenir par des bruits faux les choses que l'on a envie de faire.   (Bassompierre)

Corneille has been criticized for the meeting of Pompée and Sertorius in the latter's camp; and no doubt the unity of place is partly responsible. But such meetings were not out of keeping with the customs of the age. In 1620, the Cardinal de Guise, who was in the service of the Queen Mother, sent a message to the headquarters of Bassompierre, who was on the other side, asking him to give him supper. He even presented himself at the gates, but found them closed against him. During the Fronde, Mademoiselle, on her way back from Orleans, which she had been governing and defending for her father against the royal troops, visited

Turenne's camp and was received by him and his army with every mark of respect. Similarly, after they had been fighting, the maréchal d'Hocquincourt was invited over by Condé for a chat. During the Fronde, too, La Rochefoucauld, in hiding in Paris, paid secret visits to Mazarin under a safe-conduct; their trust was mutual. Mme de Motteville says:

> J'ai ouï dire au Duc de la Rochefoucauld, que le Cardinal venant seul leur ouvrir la porte, il aurait pu facilement le tuer, et qu'il avait souvent admiré sa confiance, et le hasard où il se mettait, se livrant au meilleur ami qu'eût alors M. le Prince et Madame de Longueville. Le Ministre, de même, l'aurait pu faire arrêter.

In 1658, when Condé was fighting for the Spaniards against France, he fell ill and asked the Queen to send him Guénaut, one of the court physicians. 'Elle le fit partir avec soin, et le Ministre y contribua de tout son pouvoir, pour montrer à ce grand Prince,' says Mme de Motteville, 'que leur malheur, et non sa haine, les tenait séparés.'[1]

§ 3 *Topical allusions*

It has been suggested that many of Corneille's plays allude to characters or events of his own day. Here we are clearly on dangerous ground, since, even if some of Corneille's situations resemble those of real people in the France of his day, we cannot be sure that he had them in mind. Nevertheless, it is worth summarizing the topical allusions which have been noticed in his plays, because they do at least prove the close similarity between Corneille's plays and the life of his period.

Clitandre has been construed as a plea for the maréchal de Marillac, who was in the service of Gaston d'Orléans, and who was arrested by order of Richelieu and condemned to death, after the *Journée des Dupes*.

In a general way, it has been suggested that *Le Cid*, *Horace* and *Cinna* were written in support of the policy of Richelieu, of authority against individualism. It has been stated that *Le Cid* is a

---

[1] Hector similarly visits the Greek camp in *Troilus and Cressida*.

defence of Anne of Austria, whose position as wife of Louis XIII and daughter of a King of Spain resembled Chimène's. *Le Cid* has also — and with much more probability — been thought to reflect the alarms of the year 1636, when the Spaniards captured Corbie and threatened Paris itself, and the relief of France when Corbie was again wrested from them. Indeed, it has been claimed that the account of Rodrigue's struggle against the Moors is closely based on the actual events of the recapture of Corbie.

Horace has been seen as another reflection of the war with Spain. It has, further, been suggested that Sabine, torn between loyalty to her husband's country and her own, is another reflection of Anne of Austria, and that one of Sabine's speeches is particularly topical, that in which she expresses her wish that Rome, instead of fighting Alba, would turn her attention to other enemies:

> Je voudrais voir déjà tes troupes couronnées,
> D'un pas victorieux franchir les Pyrénées.
> Va jusqu'en l'Orient pousser tes bataillons;
> Va sur les bords du Rhin planter tes pavillons . . .   (I, 1)

Cinna has been seen as a dramatization of the conspiracy of Chalais (1626), as an attempt to persuade Richelieu to be lenient in suppressing the riots which had occurred in Normandy — and in particular in Corneille's native town, Rouen — in 1639, and as a glorification of Richelieu.

Polyeucte has been seen as topical. The question of Grace was in the air, Jansen's *Augustinus* having been published in Rouen and Paris in 1641 and subsequently denounced in Paris and condemned in Rome. It has also been thought to allude to the *querelle du pur amour* — a controversy whether one should do good from pure love of God or whether it is legitimate to act from fear of Hell and desire for Heaven. Corneille, according to this interpretation, comes down on the latter side, since Polyeucte hopes for heavenly reward. The play has also been seen as a reference to the conversion of Antoine Le Maître, and a detailed (if unconvincing) parallel has been drawn between Polyeucte and Néarque on the one hand, and Le Maître and Saint-Cyran on the other.

La Mort de Pompée has been interpreted as an attack on Richelieu (in the person of the ministers of Ptolomée), and as a plea to
Louis XIII, Richelieu being dead, to govern himself instead of
relying on another Richelieu.

Don Sanche has been seen as an apology for Anne of Austria
and Mazarin, who, like Carlos in the play, was an adventurer and
a man of low origins; and the person of rank, to whose opposition
Corneille attributes the failure of the play, has been thought to be
Condé.

In 1649, the five propositions drawn from the *Augustinus* were
denounced in the Sorbonne, and a passage in *Andromède* may
allude to this:

> Le ciel, qui mieux que nous connaît ce que nous sommes,
> Mesure ses faveurs au mérite des hommes . . .   (V, 2)

Nicomède has been thought to reflect the atmosphere of the
Fronde. There is a general resemblance between the situation in
the play and that of France. Arsinoé under the control of the
Roman ambassador, Flaminius, recalls Anne of Austria under the
influence of her minister, the Roman Mazarin. Mademoiselle tells
us that the arrest of Nicomède made Corneille's audiences think
of the arrest of Condé, Conti and Longueville:

> Rien n'est si véritable qu'un vers de Nicomède, qui est une tragédie
> de Corneille, qui fut mise au jour aussitôt après la liberté de M. le
> Prince, en laquelle il y a,
>
>> Quiconque entre au Palais porte sa tête aux Rois.

Couton suggests that the Zénon and Métrobate episode may be
based on the *témoins à brevets*, false witnesses employed by the
royal government.

The subject of *Pertharite* may have been chosen because of its
resemblance to the state of affairs in England at the time — Pertharite in hiding after his defeat resembles Charles II, who had
fled in disguise after the battle of Worcester and passed through
Rouen. Both Grimoald and Cromwell are usurpers. Couton
suggests that, since Condé was threatening to become a French
Cromwell, the play is an admonishment to him to submit.

Oedipe is another usurper, and Thésée's speech on free will (III, 5) is often thought to have been inserted because the Jansenist controversy was then at its height. Dircé's lines to Thésée —

> Il faut qu'en vos pareils les belles passions
> Ne soient que l'ornement des grandes actions,[1]   (I, 1)

— have been seen as advice to Louis XIV to give up Marie Mancini.

La Toison d'Or was performed to celebrate the marriage of Louis XIV and Maria Theresa of Spain, and it has been suggested that the theme of the play — the achievement of peace through a royal marriage — alludes to that event.[2]

Sertorius is said to be full of allusions to the Fronde, and to have been written as a compliment to Louis XIV on the magnanimity he had shown to those who had opposed him during that war. The resemblance of Sylla to Mazarin, of Pompée to Louis XIV, and of Sertorius to Condé has been remarked. It has also been claimed that the scene between Pompée and Sertorius is based on the conference between Mazarin and Don Luis de Haro, which preceded the Treaty of the Pyrenees (1659).

Othon has been seen both as a compliment to Louis XIV for governing by himself and as a warning to him not to let the power pass out of his own hands. The first interpretation has seventeenth-century authority. Tallemant writes:

Corneille a lu par tout Paris une pièce qu'il n'a pas encore fait jouer. C'est le couronnement d'Othon. Il n'a pris ce sujet que pour faire continuer les gratifications du Roi en son endroit; car il ne fait préférer Othon à Pison par les conjurés qu'à cause, disent-ils, que Othon gouvernera lui-même et qu'il y a plaisir à travailler sous un

---

[1] Lélius's speech to Sophonisbe —

> Vous parlez tant d'amour qu'il faut que je confesse
> Que j'ai honte pour vous de voir tant de faiblesse,   (IV, 3)

— and Agésilas's speech,

> Il faut vaincre un amour qui m'était aussi doux,   (V, 6)

— have been similarly interpreted as admonitions to Louis XIV.

[2] The theme would seem rather to be the omnipotence of love. Neither Jason nor Médée much resemble Louis XIV or his queen, and one may doubt whether they would have felt flattered by the comparison.

prince qui tienne lui-même le timon; d'ailleurs ce dévot y coule quelques vers pour excuser l'amour du Roi.[1]

According to the *Bolæana*,

Corneille avait affecté d'y faire parler trois ministres d'état, dans le temps où Louis XIV n'en avait pas moins que Galba, c'est-à-dire Messieurs Le Tellier, Colbert, et de Lionne.

Couton suggests that Agésilas represents Louis XIV, and Lysander, the over-powerful minister, either Condé or Foucquet. Be that as it may, there can be no doubt that, in *Attila*, the passage in Act II, scene 5, describing the French King, Mérouée, and his son, is a magnificent evocation of Louis XIV and the Dauphin.

Tite et Bérénice — like Racine's *Bérénice* — has often been taken to allude to the separation of Louis XIV and Marie Mancini. Adam sees in it a warning to Louis XIV and his brother, who had quarrelled in 1670, of the dangers of dissension between brothers.

Pulchérie has been thought to refer to the love of Mademoiselle for Lauzun and their separation. In April 1672, the maréchal de Bellefonds was disgraced for refusing to serve under Turenne, and two other marshals followed his example. There is a passage in *Pulchérie* which may allude to this affair:[2]

> *Aspar.*   Cependant nous voyons six généraux d'armée,
> Dont au commandement l'âme est accoutumée,
> Viendront-ils recevoir un ordre souverain
> De qui l'a jusqu'ici toujours pris de leur main?
> Seigneur, il est bien dur de se voir sous un maître,
> Dont on le fut toujours, et dont on devrait l'être.

---

[1] The lines are usually identified as the following:

> Si l'injuste rigueur de notre destinée
> Ne permet plus l'espoir d'un heureux hyménée,
> Il est un autre amour dont les vœux innocents
> S'élèvent au-dessus du commerce des sens.
> Plus la flamme en est pure et plus elle est durable;
> Il rend de son objet le cœur inséparable;
> Il a de vrais plaisirs dont ce cœur est charmé,
> Et n'aspire qu'au bien d'aimer et d'être aimé.

(I, 4)

[2] This has not, so far as I know, been previously pointed out.

Martian. Et qui m'assurera que ces six généraux
        Se réuniront mieux sous un de leurs égaux?
        Plus un pareil mérite aux grandeurs nous appelle,
        Et plus la jalousie aux grands est naturelle.   (III, 2)

None of these parallels between the plays of Corneille and the events of the period can be proved to have been intended by Corneille; some of these interpretations contradict each other; some are highly improbable. It is most unlikely that Corneille wrote to advise his rulers, but not at all inconceivable that he sometimes slipped into his plays a passage which might call to mind some contemporary event. One may, however, safely conclude that Corneille, while writing of the events of Greek or Roman history or legend, seldom lost sight of his own age; that whether he consciously intended to refer to contemporary events and characters or not, he was strongly influenced in his choice of subjects by the world around him; that, in short, as Lanson puts it, 'il pense le passé dans les formes et les conditions du présent.'

§ 4 *Style*

Even the language of Corneille's characters reflects that of the period, and one encounters, not infrequently, in the memoirs of the time, remarks in prose which remind one strongly of Corneille's verse. Mademoiselle, for example, being reproached by her father with her heroics at the Porte Saint-Antoine, replied:

Je ne crois pas vous avoir plus mal servi à la porte St. Antoine qu'à Orléans: ces deux actions si reprochables je les ai faites par votre ordre, *si elles étaient à recommencer je les ferais encore,*[1] parce que mon devoir m'y obligerait, je ne pouvais pas me dispenser de vous obéir et de vous servir; si vous êtes malheureux, il est juste que je partage votre disgrâce et votre mauvaise fortune; quand je ne vous aurais pas servi je ne laisserais pas d'y participer: ainsi à mon sens il vaut mieux avoir fait ce que j'ai fait, que de pâtir pour n'avoir rien fait: je ne sais ce que c'est d'être héroïne, *je suis d'une naissance à ne jamais rien faire que de grand et d'élevé*; on appellera cela comme on

[1] Cf. 'Je ne me repentis pas un moment de ce que j'avais fait, parce que je fus persuadé et que le devoir et la bonne conduite m'y avaient obligé. Je m'enveloppai pour ainsi dire dans mon devoir'. . .   (Retz) ·

R

voudra, pour moi j'appelle cela suivre mon inclination, et aller mon chemin, je suis née à n'en pas prendre d'autres.

We are reminded, not only of the tone of some of the speeches in Corneille, but of the ideas of his characters, of

Je le ferais encor, si j'avais à le faire,

of the sense of duty of some of his heroes, of the notion that high birth is equivalent to nobility of character.

Bussy relates how Mlle de Romorantin overcame her love for him in language that frequently reminds us of Corneille. Finding that he was making no progress in her affections, Bussy decided to transfer his attentions to another woman.

Cela fit de la peine à mademoiselle de Romorantin, et sa gloire ne la put empêcher de me le faire connaître; je lui avouai sincèrement le parti que j'avais pris; elle me dit que jusque-là elle avait eu meilleure opinion de mon courage, et mille autres choses piquantes, et, dans son dépit, elle me témoigna plus d'amour qu'elle n'avait fait dans le temps que j'en méritais davantage. Je voulus faire une légère tentative pour voir si en revenant je serais le bienvenu, mais elle me dit bien fièrement qu'un cœur était indigne d'elle, qui au sortir de ses mains s'était profané un moment au service d'une petite dame de province, de sorte qu'elle acheva de me faire résoudre à m'abandonner de l'autre côté. Cependant la crainte que sa haine ne m'attirât celle de sa mère et de son père, m'obligea de lui dire toutes les douceurs dont je me pus aviser, et entre autres que la passion que j'avais pour elle ne me sortirait jamais du cœur, et que le désespoir me faisait porter ailleurs des demandes qu'elle n'avait pas voulu écouter: 'Allez, allez, mon cousin, me dit-elle en rougissant, souvenez-vous que le peu de douceurs que vous aviez près de moi valait mieux que les douceurs que vous allez chercher; au reste, ajouta-t-elle, *ne craignez point ma haine, je suis trop glorieuse pour vous faire du mal; au contraire, je serai dans vos intérêts plus hardiment que je n'y ai jamais été.* — Ah! mademoiselle, lui dis-je, quelles douceurs me dites-vous là! j'aimerais mieux vous voir en cette rencontre de la colère que cette espèce de bonté! — Oh! pour de la colère contre vous, mon cousin, me répliqua-t-elle, vous m'en dispenserez, s'il vous plaît, je n'en aurai jamais, tant que vous ne ferez que des choses qui me seront aussi indifférentes que celles-là.' Et en achevant ces mots elle me quitta sans attendre ma réponse.

There we are reminded of some of Corneille's characters (Eryxe, for example), trying to overcome their love in the interests of their *gloire*, apparently succeeding, but achieving victory over the expression of the emotion, rather than over the emotion itself. We recall, too, the magnanimity of a Sévère or a Placide, serving a mistress who prefers another.

A little later, dancing with Bussy after he had just fought a duel, Mlle Romorantin told him that she would like to tread on his adversary's foot, since there was nothing worse she could do:

> 'Vous mériteriez pourtant que je m'offrisse à lui contre vous, mais, après tout, bon sang ne peut mentir, je ne vous hais point. ['Va, je ne te hais point.'] [. . .] — Mais, mademoiselle, lui dis-je, n'y a-t-il plus de retour à la miséricorde? je ne suis pas encore trop dégagé. — Non, il n'y en a plus, me répondit-elle, brusquement, car je le suis, moi, et si je ne l'étais, je ferais les derniers efforts pour l'être.' Elle me dit cela d'un air à me fermer la bouche. ['Et sur mes passions ma raison souveraine'. . .]

She then struck up a friendship with Bussy's new mistress (one thinks of Eurydice and Suréna's sister):

> Enfin la gloire n'a jamais mieux triomphé de l'amour que dans le cœur de mademoiselle de Romorantin, car assurément elle m'avait aimé, et il y avait si peu, que le temps n'avait pu encore faire cet effet-là, il fallait que ce fût la raison. Il y avait pourtant des moments *où elle se démentait par des petites attaques qu'elle me donnait, mais elle reprenait bientôt cet air de douceur qui marque l'indifférence.*

Chapter Ten

THE REALISM OF CORNEILLE
(3)
HISTORY AND POLITICS

C orneille's interest in politics and his treatment of history
provide further evidence of the realistic cast of his mind.

§ 1 *Politics in Corneille*

The political interest of Corneille's plays is fourfold. In many
of his plays there are political scenes; many of them depict
political intrigues; several treat a political theme; and from them
there emerges a political philosophy, which, one is tempted to
say, is that of their author.

Corneille has not his master in the composition of political
scenes: they are one of the great beauties of his tragedies. Sometimes general principles are debated, sometimes courses of action
— though it is difficult to divide Corneille's political scenes into
two distinct categories, since so often the choice of a course of
action depends on the general principle which seems most
applicable. One of the best discussions of general principles is the
great scene in *Cinna*, when Auguste's enquiry whether or not he
should abdicate leads to a full discussion between Cinna and
Maxime of the comparative merits of republic and monarchy. One
example may illustrate the interest of this scene. In the speech of
Maxime which begins,

Oui, Seigneur, dans son mal Rome est trop obstinée . . .

and in Cinna's reply, Corneille gives both a survey of Roman history and a discussion of general principles. Whereas Maxime begins with the historical argument and then proceeds to the general principle, Cinna deals first with the general principle and then gives his opposing argument drawn from history — an example of that love of chiasmus which is characteristic of Corneille. In thirty-one lines, not only does Corneille manage to evoke the whole course of Roman history, but he gives us the basic theory of Montesquieu's *Esprit des Lois* (that constitutions necessarily vary from country to country, though Corneille does not specify that this is a matter of climate), and adds in addition the argument that nations evolve and necessarily change their constitutions to adapt themselves to altered circumstances. This short passage is an excellent example of the vigour and concision, the evocative power, and the grasp of general principles which are characteristic of his debates. And, moreover, the whole scene is intensely dramatic, not only because we find Cinna urging the opposite point of view from that which we should have expected him to take and are curious to know why, but because the whole course of the action depends on the decision of Auguste.

As examples of the type of scene which is concerned more with the solution of a practical problem, one might quote the opening scene of *Pompée*, in which Ptolomée and his advisers are discussing what to do with Pompée, who, having been defeated by César, has cast himself on their mercy; or the last scene of *Pertharite*, in which Grimoald explains how embarrassing it is to have Pertharite in his power; or the scene in *Othon* (V, 2) in which Galba debates with his counsellors the best way to suppress Othon's rising; or the scene in *Agésilas* (III, 1), in which Lysander asks Agésilas to sanction the marriage of his daughters, and Agésilas refuses on the grounds that this will increase the power of Lysander who is too powerful already; or the scene in *Attila* (I, 2), in which Attila asks the two subject kings to decide whether he should marry the Gallic or the Roman princess. One

of the finest of such scenes is the great scene in which Sertorius
tries to persuade Pompée to leave Sylla and join him. Here is part
of Pompée's reply:

> Lorsque deux factions divisent un empire,
> Chacun suit au hasard la meilleure ou la pire,
> Selon l'occasion ou la nécessité
> Qui l'emporte vers l'un, ou vers l'autre côté.
> Le plus juste parti, difficile à connaître,
> Nous laisse en liberté de nous choisir un maître;
> Mais quand ce choix est fait, on ne s'en dédit plus.
> J'ai servi sous Sylla du temps de Marius,
> Et servirai sous lui tant qu'un destin funeste
> De nos divisions soutiendra quelque reste.
> Comme je ne vois pas dans le fond de son cœur,
> J'ignore quels projets peut former son bonheur:
> S'il les pousse trop loin, moi-même je l'en blâme;
> Je lui prête mon bras sans engager mon âme;
> Je m'abandonne au cours de sa félicité,
> Tandis que mes vœux sont pour la liberté;
> Et c'est ce qui me force à garder une place
> Qu'usurperaient sans moi l'injustice et l'audace,
> Afin que, Sylla mort, ce dangereux pouvoir
> Ne tombe qu'en des mains qui sachent leur devoir.
> Enfin je sais mon but, et vous savez le vôtre.   (III, 1)

This is a noble expression — which no doubt owes something to
Corneille's experience of the Fronde — of the difficulty of choosing a course, when both sides (as so often happens) have some
right on their side, and of the wisdom of sticking to the party one
has chosen, once the choice is made.

In all these debates, one is struck by the ability of Corneille to
construct an argument — he himself praises the 'solidité du
raisonnement' of *Rodogune* and says that *Othon* has 'un peu de bon
sens dans le raisonnement'. This 'solidité du raisonnement' is a
source of great intellectual satisfaction to the reader or spectator.
Such is Corneille's skill that, in his discussions, each speaker in
turn convinces us that he is right and that his opponent must now
be silenced; we are left with a conviction of the complexity of the
problems involved, and of the inability of the human reason

unaided to find any definitive solution. Similar close, subtle reasoning is found in the political discussions in the memoirs of the period (in Retz, for example). One is struck, too, by Corneille's understanding, both of the general principles of policy, and of the motives and tactics of politicians — a feature which impressed Corneille's contemporaries, and has continued to impress later ages. The maréchal de Grammont said that Corneille's plays 'méritent d'être conservées dans le cabinet des rois,' and remarked, after seeing *Othon*, 'Corneille est le bréviaire des rois'. Louvois said that Corneille could only be understood by an audience of ministers, and Turenne, after seeing *Sertorius*, asked: 'Où donc Corneille a-t-il appris l'art de la guerre?'[1] Napoleon — no mean judge — who said: 'Je l'eusse fait prince, premier ministre,' also said:

> Celui-ci a deviné la politique et, formé aux affaires, c'eût été un homme d'Etat . . . Ce ne sont pas ses vers que j'admire le plus, mais son grand sens, sa grande connaissance du cœur humain, la grande profondeur de sa politique. [. . .] La raison d'Etat a remplacé chez les modernes le fatalisme des anciens; Corneille est le seul des poètes français qui ait senti cette vérité.

These debates are characteristic of Corneille. If we compare his *Sophonisbe*, for example, with that of Mairet, this is one of the striking differences. In his version of the subject, Corneille adds a scene (I, 3) in which Sophonisbe and Eryxe discuss the prospects of peace and war, a council scene (I, 4) in which Sophonisbe persuades her husband, Syphax, to continue the war, another in which Syphax after his defeat warns Lélius of the danger of Sophonisbe's influence on Massinisse (IV, 2), and another in which Lélius warns Massinisse of the danger of marrying Sophonisbe (IV, 3). None of these is in Mairet's play, in which, indeed, Lélie is no more than the confidant of Massinisse. The contrast shows both Corneille's interest in political details and his love of political discussions.

[1] 'Ce qui frappait Turenne, c'est la justesse des expressions, c'est l'adresse avec laquelle Corneille sait substituer à la vague phraséologie des poètes tragiques de son temps les termes propres à chaque profession. Jamais il n'y a manqué.' (Marty-Laveaux)

Corneille is remarkable, too, for the solidity with which he
depicts the political aspects of his plays. He fills in the political
backgrounds in a convincing manner, and excels at depicting
intrigues in a way that reminds us of Balzac and Stendhal. He
shows the complicated relationships between the characters, the
way in which the pattern of their relationships changes from time
to time as changed circumstances alter the balance of power, and
the way in which these relationships and changes affect the fate of
individuals.

To illustrate the solidity of his backgrounds, *Sophonisbe* might
serve as an example. In Act I, scenes 3 and 4, in debating what will
happen and what to do, Sophonisbe, Eryxe and Syphax give full
details of the political situation. The Romans have offered peace:
will Syphax, and should Syphax, accept it?

Soph. Il faut l'aveu de Rome, et que d'autre côté
       Le sénat de Carthage accepte le traité.
Er.   Lélius le propose; et l'on ne doit pas croire
       Qu'au désaveu de Rome il hasarde sa gloire.
       Quant à votre sénat, le Roi n'en dépend point.
Soph. Le Roi n'a pas une âme infidèle à ce point:
       Il sait à quoi l'honneur, à quoi sa foi l'engage;
       Et je l'en dédirais, s'il traitait sans Carthage.

   · · · · · · · · · · · · · · · · ·

       On ne voit point d'ici ce qui se passe à Rome.
       En ce même moment peut-être qu'Annibal
       Lui fait de nouveau craindre un assaut fatal,
       Et que c'est pour sortir enfin de ces alarmes
       Qu'elle nous fait parler de mettre bas les armes.   (I, 3)

Soph.   Jouissez de la paix qui vous vient d'être offerte,
       Tandis que j'irai plaindre, et partager sa perte:
       J'y mourrai sans regret, si mon dernier moment
       Vous laisse en quelque état de régner sûrement;
       Mais Carthage détruite, avec quelle apparence
       Oserez-vous garder cette fausse espérance?
       Rome, qui vous redoute et vous flatte aujourd'hui,
       Vous craindra-t-elle encor, vous voyant sans appui,
       Elle qui de la paix ne jette les amorces
       Que par le seul besoin de séparer nos forces,
       Et qui dans Massinisse, et voisin, et jaloux,

Aura toujours de quoi se brouiller avec vous?
Tous deux vous devront tout. Carthage abandonnée
Vaut pour l'un et pour l'autre une grande journée.
Mais un esprit aigri n'est jamais satisfait
Qu'il n'ait vengé l'injure en dépit du bienfait.
Pensez-y: votre armée est la plus forte en nombre;
Les Romains ont tremblé dès qu'ils en ont vu l'ombre;
Utique à l'assiéger retient leur Scipion;
Un temps bien pris peut tout: pressez l'occasion.
De ce chef éloigné la valeur peu commune
Peut-être à sa personne attache leur fortune;
Il tient auprès de lui la fleur de leurs soldats.
En tout événement Cyrthe vous tend les bras;
Vous tiendrez, et longtemps, dedans cette retraite.
Mon père cependant répare sa défaite,
Hannon a de l'Espagne amené du secours;
Annibal vient lui-même ici dans peu de jours.
Si tout cela vous semble un léger avantage,
Renvoyez-moi, Seigneur, me perdre avec Carthage:
J'y périrai sans vous; vous régnerez sans moi.   (I, 4)

None of this is to be found in Mairet's play.

Perhaps the best example of Corneille's ability to depict complicated intrigues is *Othon*. Corneille, rightly, had a high opinion of this play: 'Cette pièce égale ou passe la meilleure des miennes [. . .] vous y trouverez quelque justesse dans la conduite, et un peu de bon sens dans le raisonnement.' It is a great play, a political play, the interest of which is almost entirely intellectual — 'la plus abstraite, la plus tendue, la plus sévère de ses tragédies,' says Dorchain. It is a study of the essence of political life, or at least of that side of politics which is the struggle for power, as opposed to the making of policy. It takes up the theme of Pompée, that of bad advisers:

Quand le monarque agit par sa propre conduite,
Mes pareils sans péril se rangent à sa suite:
Le mérite et le sang nous y font discerner;
Mais quand le potentat se laisse gouverner,
Et que de son pouvoir les grands dépositaires
N'ont pour raison d'Etat que leurs propres affaires,
Ces lâches ennemis de tous les gens de cœur

> Cherchent à nous pousser avec toute rigueur,
> A moins que notre adroite et prompte servitude
> Nous dérobe aux fureurs de leur inquiétude.   (I, 1)

But in this play — unlike *Pompée* — the bad advisers are divided
amongst themselves, which provides a further theme:

> Qu'un prince est malheureux quand de ceux qu'il écoute
> Le zèle cherche à prendre une diverse route,
> Et que l'attachement qu'ils ont au propre sens
> Pousse jusqu'à l'aigreur des conseils différents!   (V, 2)

In *Othon*, love has little part: love and marriage are chiefly a
means of furthering political ends.

> Je puis dire qu'on n'a point encore vu de pièce où il se propose tant
> de mariages pour n'en conclure aucun. Ce sont intrigues de cabinet
> qui se détruisent les unes les autres.

The play is masterly: the 'bon sens dans le raisonnement' is
particularly noteworthy — the skill with which Corneille makes
his characters find convincing arguments in favour of policies
which in fact they are advocating exclusively from self-interest, to
use general principles as a cloak for selfish ends.

The subject of the play is the struggle for power between the
three ministers of the Emperor Galba, Vinius on the one hand,
Lacus and Martian on the other. Galba has a niece, Camille, and
intends the man he chooses to be her husband to succeed him as
Emperor. There are two possible candidates, Othon and Pison,
the latter a man of virtue but insignificant. Camille herself prefers
Othon, but he loves Vinius's daughter, Plautine. Othon's love
for Plautine, though it has become sincere, was originally a matter
of self-preservation:

> Je vis qu'il était temps de prendre mes mesures,
> Qu'on perdait de Néron toutes les créatures,
> Et que demeuré seul de toute cette cour,
> A moins d'un protecteur j'aurais bientôt mon tour.
> Je choisis Vinius dans cette défiance;
> Pour plus de sûreté j'en cherchai l'alliance.
> Les autres n'ont ni sœur ni fille à me donner;
> Et d'eux sans ce grand nœud tout est à soupçonner.   (I, 1)

Martian and Lacus are trying to persuade Galba to make Pison his son-in-law, since Othon would naturally favour Vinius; and Vinius realizes that, if they are successful, he, Othon and Plautine will be quickly put to death. In order that they may survive, he urges Othon to pay court to Camille:

> Si vous manquez le trône, il faut périr tous trois.   (I, 3)

Plautine encourages Othon to obey her father; he goes and makes love unconvincingly to Camille, while Plautine suffers pangs of jealousy.[1]

A new element in the situation is revealed when Martian tells Plautine that he loves her and will give his support to Othon if she will marry him. Lacus, however, warns him that Camille might become a kind of Mrs Proudie, influencing her husband, Othon, and that this match would put an end to the alliance of Lacus and Martian:

> Vous seriez mon ami, mais vous seriez son[2] gendre;
> Et c'est un faible appui des intérêts de cour
> Qu'une vieille amitié contre un nouvel amour.
> Quoi que veuille exiger une femme adorée,
> La résistance est vaine ou de peu de durée;
> Elle choisit ses temps, et les choisit si bien,
> Qu'on se voit hors d'état de lui refuser rien.   (II, 4)

Galba now chooses Pison to succeed him. Camille tells him that she loves Othon, and Galba decides to give the Empire to Pison and Camille to Othon, who arouses Camille's ire by backing out of this agreement in an amusing scene. The only salvation for Vinius, Plautine and Othon now is for Othon to appease Camille or to become Emperor; either he must marry Camille, or Plautine must marry Martian.

> Donnez-vous à Camille, ou je me donne à lui,   (IV, 1)

says Camille. Taken from its context, this line looks like an example of absurd renunciation for its own sake, but it is nothing of the kind. It is the exact expression of the reality of the situation;

---

[1] *Bajazet* owes a good deal to these scenes in *Othon.*   [2] Vinius's.

only one or the other of these two courses can save Vinius and Othon from death.

> *Othon.*   En concevez-vous bien toute l'ignominie ?
> *Plautine.* Je n'en puis voir, Seigneur, à vous sauver la vie.
>
> (IV, 1)

At this point a third course becomes possible. The army rises, in a well-motivated and well-prepared revolt, against Galba and Pison. Vinius persuades Othon to place himself at its head; but to make sure that he will be safe whatever happens, he consents to the marriage of Plautine and Pison — proposed by Galba in order to try to bring about the unity of his three ministers. There is, incidentally, a magnificent scene between the two rivals for Othon's hand, Camille and Plautine, the climax of which is Plautine's superb line:

> Aux unes on se donne, aux autres on se vend.   (IV, 4)

Martian, however, dissuades Galba from giving Plautine to Pison, and Camille tells Martian that *she* will marry Pison if he (Martian) will force Plautine to marry *him*. This intricate situation is finally resolved by the success of the revolt.

This study in political realism is certainly relevant to the age of Corneille, as we realize if we recall the intrigues of the Fronde on the one hand — the ever-shifting kaleidoscope of the relations between the court and Condé and Gaston d'Orléans and Retz and the parlement and the Frondeurs — and the importance of marriage as an instrument of policy on the other. The relevance of Corneille's play to his age is emphasized by such passages as the description of court life —

> Un homme tel que moi jamais ne s'en détache;
> Il n'est point de retraite ou d'ombre qui le cache;
> Et si du souverain la faveur n'est pour lui,
> Il faut, ou qu'il périsse, ou qu'il prenne un appui.   (I, 1)

— or that of the rôle of ministers under a strong monarch (such as Louis XIV):

> Sous un tel souverain nous sommes peu de chose;
> Son soin jamais sur nous tout à fait ne repose:

> Sa main seule départ ses libéralités;
> Son choix seul distribue Etats, et dignités.   (II, 4)

Corneille was not interested exclusively in bringing ancient Rome to life; and indeed several pages of the memoirs of Retz remind us of the atmosphere of *Othon*.

In his plays, too, Corneille often deals with a political problem. One of the chief problems, to which he returns several times, is that of the over-great subject — a topic which was certainly not without contemporary relevance. It is treated in *Nicomède*, in *Agésilas*, and in *Suréna*. It occurs in a somewhat different form in *Pertharite* and in *Oedipe*. In the first of these plays, Grimoald does not know what to do with Pertharite, whose country he has occupied and whose person he has captured:

> Madame, cependant mettez-vous en ma place:
> Si je le reconnais, que faut-il que j'en fasse?
> Le tenir dans les fers avec le nom de roi,
> C'est soulever pour lui ses peuples contre moi.
> Le mettre en liberté, c'est le mettre à leur tête,
> Et moi-même hâter l'orage qui s'apprête.
> Puis-je m'assurer d'eux et souffrir son retour?
> Puis-je occuper son trône et le voir dans ma cour?
> Un roi, quoique vaincu, garde son caractère:
> Aux fidèles sujets sa vue est toujours chère;
> Au moment qu'il paraît, les plus grands conquérants,
> Pour vertueux qu'ils soient, ne sont que des tyrans;
> Et dans le fond des cœurs sa présence fait naître
> Un mouvement secret qui les rend à leur maître.
>   Ainsi mon mauvais sort a de quoi me punir
> Et de le délivrer, et de le retenir.   (V, 2)

In *Oedipe*, Oedipe does not know how to dispose of the hand of Dircé, whose throne he has usurped. She resents his usurpation, and wants to marry a king, Thésée. But Oedipe is unwilling to consent to this match and wants her to marry Æmon. Dircé understands his reasons perfectly:

>   Politique partout.
> Si la flamme d'Æmon en est favorisée,
> Ce n'est pas qu'il l'estime, ou méprise Thésée;
> C'est qu'il craint dans son cœur que le droit souverain

> (Car enfin il m'est dû) ne tombe en bonne main.
> Comme il connaît le mien, sa peur de me voir reine
> Dispense à mes amants sa faveur ou sa haine,
> Et traiterait ce prince ainsi que ce héros,
> S'il portait la couronne ou de Sparte ou d'Argos.   (II, 2)

It is interesting — and significant — that Corneille has introduced a political interest into *Oedipe*.

Pompée treats a more general problem, that of the principles of
political conduct, of expediency, self-interest, and Machiavellianism, as opposed to honour, uprightness and loyalty. As in
Cinna, Corneille is anti-Machiavellian. Ptolomée and his advisers
come to grief because, however shrewd and subtle they may be,
there are always elements in the situation of which they are
ignorant and ignorance of which is fatal to their plans, and because they cannot understand the mentality of those who differ
from them. They are unaware of the love of César and Cléopâtre,
so that their decision to kill Pompée, taken in ignorance of a major
factor in the situation, is mistaken. They try to make good their
blunder by adopting a new course of action, based this time on a
misconception of the character of César. They then decide to
assassinate César — and fail, because they confide in Cornélie
without taking her character into account. Finally, Ptolomée
meets his death because he thinks César's attempt to save his life
is a trick. Political realists are condemned because they are not
realistic; they are in a constant state of bewilderment.

> Seigneur [says Photin], cette surprise est pour moi merveilleuse;
> Je n'en sais que penser, et mon cœur étonné
> D'un secret que jamais il n'aurait soupçonné,
> Inconstant et confus dans son incertitude,
> Ne se résout à rien qu'avec inquiétude.   (I, 4)

Since a dramatist puts different ideas into the mouths of his
characters, and since those ideas are to some extent dictated by the
situation in which those characters find themselves, there must
always be something arbitrary about deciding which of the views
expressed are those of the dramatist. Moreover, it is not primarily
for his political views that we read Corneille. Nevertheless, this

chapter would be incomplete without a brief outline of what the ideas of this poet, who clearly took an unusual interest in politics, appear to be.

Corneille has little sympathy with democratic or republican ideals. Cinna comes off best in the debate with Maxime, and the play ends with an enthusiastic speech by Livie in favour of monarchy. The people are on the whole referred to in disparaging terms[1] — old Horace calls them 'le peuple stupide', and Oedipe denies them the right to try to get rid of unpopular kings:

> ce n'est pas au peuple à se faire justice:
> L'ordre que tient le ciel à lui choisir des rois
> Ne lui permet jamais d'examiner son choix;
> Et le devoir aveugle y doit toujours souscrire,
> Jusqu'à ce que d'en haut on veuille s'en dédire.   (V, 1)

Kings are divine:

> C'est toi qui règles les Etats,
> C'est toi qui départs les couronnes,

says the sun to Jupiter at the end of *La Toison*. Cinna suggests that even usurpers govern by divine right: Heaven, he says, 'se met du parti de ceux qu'il fait régner'. Livie agrees, though perhaps she is not altogether impartial:

> Tous ces crimes d'Etat qu'on fait pour la couronne,
> Le ciel nous en absout alors qu'il nous la donne . . .
>
> (*Cinna*, V, 2)

The judgments of Kings are divinely inspired, according to Camille in *Horace*:

> Ces mêmes Dieux à Tulle ont inspiré ce choix;
> Et la voix du public n'est pas toujours leur voix;
> Ils descendent bien moins dans de si bas étages
> Que dans l'âme des rois, leurs vivantes images,
> De qui l'indépendante et sainte autorité
> Est un rayon secret de leur divinité.   (III, 3)

[1] It is true that in *Don Sanche*, Doña Léonor says:

> Quoi que vous présumiez de la voix populaire,
> Par de secrets rayons le ciel souvent l'éclaire:
> Vous apprendrez par là du moins les vœux de tous,
> Et quelle opinion les peuples ont de vous.   (IV, 2)

Kings must be respected: even an elderly King in love must not be mocked:

> Un vieillard amoureux mérite qu'on en rie;
> Mais le trône soutient la majesté des rois
> Au-dessus du mépris, comme au-dessus des lois.
> On doit toujours respect au sceptre, à la couronne.
>
> (*Médée*, II, 4)

No violence must be used against them, of course. 'M'attaquer n'est pas un léger attentat,' says the prince in *Clitandre* (IV, 5). This is insisted upon in *Oedipe*. In Corneille's play, Oedipe's crime is not that he killed a man, but that he murdered a king:

> Mégare, tu sais mal ce que l'on doit aux rois.
> Un sang si précieux ne saurait se répandre
> Qu'à l'innocente cause on n'ait droit de s'en prendre;
> Et de quelque façon que finisse leur sort,
> On n'est point innocent quand on cause leur mort.　　(II, 3)
>
> Mais jamais sans forfait on ne se prend aux rois;
> Et fussent-ils cachés sous un habit champêtre,
> Leur propre majesté les doit faire connaître.　　(IV, 2)

This last quotation suggests that kings are different in kind from their subjects, an idea which recurs elsewhere. In *Médée*, we learn that their strength does not decline with age:

> Les rois ne perdent point les forces avec l'âge.　　(II, 5)

Time and time again in *Don Sanche* the point is made that royal blood must betray itself in behaviour and appearance, and that, if Don Sanche is outstanding among men, it must be because he is of royal blood.

Kings have duties as well as privileges. In *Agésilas*, the distinction is made between the arbitrary despotism of Persia and the monarchy of Greece, the former being condemned.

> La Grèce a de plus saintes lois,
> Elle a des peuples et des rois
> Qui gouvernent avec justice:
> La raison y préside, et la sage équité;
> Le pouvoir souverain par elles limité
> N'y laisse aucun droit de caprice.　　(II, 1)

Kings must render justice:

> je ferai justice:
> J'aime à la rendre à tous, à toute heure, en tout lieu.
> C'est par elle qu'un roi se fait un demi-dieu ...   (V, 2)

says Tulle in *Horace*. They must be prepared to sacrifice their lives for the welfare of their subjects,[1] and they must subordinate their passions to the obligations of their rank. Tite and Pulchérie (in *Pulchérie*) find that power brings with it a sense of responsibility. Kings must above all beware of bad advisers. As long as they follow their own inclinations they can do no wrong:

> Les princes ont cela de leur haute naissance:
> Leur âme dans leur sang prend des impressions
> Qui dessous leur vertu rangent leurs passions.
> Leur générosité soumet tout à leur gloire:
> Tout est illustre en eux quand ils daignent se croire;
> Et si le peuple y voit quelques déréglements,
> C'est quand l'avis d'autrui corrompt leurs sentiments.
>
> (*Pompée*, II, 1)

Ptolomée in *Pompée* comes to grief because he follows a policy of expediency on the advice of his counsellors. *Othon* shows how, if the king trusts his ministers too far, self-interest reigns supreme: the ministers aim only at their own aggrandisement, and work against each other.

Corneille, like Montaigne, is opposed to Machiavellianism in politics. Expediency is not a safe principle, because one's views are often based on a misinterpretation of the situation. Félix mistakenly mistrusts Sévère, Ptolomée César, Prusias Nicomède, and all three act wrongly because they have misjudged the situation. All three, in fact, illustrate Retz's maxim: 'l'on est plus souvent dupe par la défiance que par la confiance.' The only safe guide to political conduct is to behave honourably; any other principle is tyranny:

> Porte, porte aux tyrans tes damnables maximes:
> Je hais l'art de régner qui se permet des crimes.
> De quel front donnerais-je un exemple aujourd'hui

[1] *Oedipe*, II, 4.

s

Que mes lois dès demain puniraient en autrui?
Le pouvoir absolu n'a rien de redoutable
Dont à sa conscience un roi ne soit comptable.

(*Pertharite*, II, 3)

In all this, Corneille is of his age and country. These are the
ideas and preoccupations of his time. Whereas some of the
libertin writers favoured the Machiavellian approach to politics,
Corneille belongs to that tradition of French political thought
which held that the king should be absolute, but that he should
use his power wisely and in the interests of his people, but without prescribing constitutional safeguards. In an age in which anything else but a monarchical constitution was virtually unthink-
able, opposition tended to justify itself on the grounds that it was
directed, not against the monarch, but against his advisers. On
the death of Louis XIII, Corneille wrote a poem condemning
Louis for having given Richelieu a free hand; and during the
Fronde the rebels insisted time after time that their quarrel was
not with the Queen Regent or with the King, but with Mazarin
alone.

§ 2 *Corneille's treatment of history*

There is realism, too, in Corneille's fidelity to history, in the
excellence of his historical backgrounds, and in particular in the
stress on the political aspects of his historical subjects.

Too much must not be made of the first point. Corneille
sometimes makes very free with history — *Rodogune* and *Héraclius* are, of course, the supreme examples: in the latter, particularly, Corneille has whittled away all the historical facts until
practically nothing remains but the names of the characters. These
are exceptions, but at no time does Corneille consider the rigid
observance of historical truth necessary to a dramatist, no doubt
rightly. In his *Discours* and *Examens*, he maintains that historical
events may be altered or details added to them, providing the
events are not so well known that the spectator would notice the
distortion of history, and recommends that the hero should be

relieved of crimes he may have committed. In practice he prolongs the life of Sylla and alters historical facts so that Antiochus is not guilty of the death of Cléopâtre, nor Héraclius of that of Phocas, nor Nicomède of that of Prusias. Moreover, the situations of his plays sometimes owe much to his invention. Sévère in *Polyeucte* is unhistorical, and the real Attila did not hesitate between Ildico and Honoria; nor did these last prefer two other kings.

On the other hand, Corneille treated history with more respect than the theorists considered necessary. D'Aubignac, for instance, thought that the poet had the right to change, not merely details, but the main events; and Corneille sometimes incurred adverse criticism for his adherence to historical fact. The Academy found fault with the dénouement of *Le Cid*, and thought that, if Chimène was to marry Rodrigue, the Count should turn out not to be dead after all, or not to be her real father. Similarly, d'Aubignac objected to the murder of Camille in *Horace*, and suggested that Camille should have rushed on to her brother's sword. In *Sophonisbe*, unlike Mairet, Corneille allows Sophonisbe to marry Massinisse while her first husband, Syphax, is still alive, and was apparently criticized for the character of his heroine.

Saint-Evremond praised Corneille because he 'fait mieux parler les Grecs que les Grecs, les Romains que les Romains, les Carthaginois que les citoyens de Carthage ne parlaient eux-mêmes'. Perhaps the modern reader, accustomed to the local colour of the Romantics, and aware that what the characters of Corneille and Racine are speaking is seventeenth-century French, is inclined to under-estimate the historical aspect of these writers. Certainly, the historical accuracy of the characters of *Polyeucte* has been praised, and Corneille seems to have made a serious attempt to portray César and Cléopâtre in *Pompée*, Sophonisbe, and Attila, as they were. His César, like Montaigne's, is amorous, but does not allow his amours to interfere with his conquests. His Cléopâtre is less passionate than ambitious, a conception which has been defended by historians. According to Saint-Evremond, his *Sophonisbe* failed to please precisely because Corneille gave his heroine her 'véritable caractère', and Corneille himself says of her:

> J'aime mieux qu'on me reproche d'avoir fait mes femmes trop
> héroïnes, par une ignorante et basse affectation de les faire ressembler
> aux originaux qui en sont venus jusqu'à nous, que de m'entendre
> louer d'avoir efféminé mes héros par une docte et sublime com-
> plaisance au goût de nos délicats, qui veulent de l'amour partout, et
> ne permettent qu'à lui de faire auprès d'eux la bonne ou mauvaise
> fortune de nos ouvrages.   (*Au Lecteur*)

It is clear, too, that Corneille has taken pains to put on the stage
the real Attila, except that, as he puts it, he 'retranche la pluralité
des femmes'. Brutal, violent, choleric, cruel, crafty, shrewd, preferring diplomacy to battles, Corneille's hero, despite the
seventeenth-century language, is not just a conventional seventeenth-century stage tyrant; and it is significant that Corneille has
retained the historical death by haemorrhage,[1] however much this
might conflict with the *bienséances*.

Perhaps the best statement of Corneille's attitude to history is
the preface to *Othon*, where he prides himself at one and the same
time on his fidelity to history and on the freedom with which he
treats it:

> Je n'en ai encore mis aucune sur le théâtre à qui j'aie gardé plus de
> fidélité, et prêté plus d'invention. Les caractères de ceux que j'y fais
> parler y sont les mêmes que chez cet incomparable auteur [Tacite],
> que j'ai traduit tant qu'il m'a été possible. J'ai tâché de faire paraître
> les vertus de mon héros en tout leur éclat, sans en dissimuler les
> vices, non plus que lui; et je me suis contenté de les attribuer à une
> politique de cour, où, quand le souverain se plonge dans les dé-
> bauches, et que sa faveur n'est qu'à ce prix, il y a presse à qui sera de
> la partie. J'y ai conservé les événements, et pris la liberté de changer
> la manière dont ils arrivent, pour en jeter tout le crime sur un
> méchant homme, qu'on soupçonna dès lors d'avoir donné des ordres
> secrets pour la mort de Vinius, tant leur inimitié était forte et
> déclarée.

Corneille's historical backgrounds are excellent. He treats a
wide variety of periods, particularly of Roman history, from its
beginnings in *Horace*, to its decline in *Attila*. *Pulchérie* deals with
the Byzantine Empire, and *Pertharite* with Italy after the break-

---

[1] *Not* nose-bleeding, but a cerebral haemorrhage due to failure to bleed from the nose.
(See *Attila, Au Lecteur*.)

up of the Roman Empire. Corneille is particularly fond of depicting a clash — between the present and the past, the last Republicans and the new Imperial Rome in *Cinna*, paganism and Christianity, the old religion and the new, in *Polyeucte* and *Théodore*, the declining might of Rome and the rising power of the barbarians and the Franks, in *Attila*; or between Rome and another state, Alba in *Horace*, Carthage in *Sophonisbe*; or between two Roman factions (*Sertorius*). In *Pompée*, there is not merely the conflict between two Roman factions, that of Pompée and that of César, but also the sharp contrast between Rome and Egypt. There are some magnificent historical narratives and tableaux in Corneille — one of the finest is the contrast drawn between the declining might of Rome and the rising power of France in *Attila* (I, 2).

But what interests Corneille most is the political aspect of his historical subjects. *Nicomède*, for example, is a masterly study of Roman policy, of the way in which Rome dealt with the semi-independent countries outside its borders, as *Cinna* is a masterly study of conspiracy and dictatorship. The political aspect is more fully developed in *Tite et Bérénice*, a significant difference, than in Racine's play on the same subject. Racine's play is less historical — indeed, he forgot that Bérénice was a Jewess and made her exclaim 'Dieux!' until the abbé Villars pointed out his error. Racine uses historical details more for their evocative power than for their political significance — to enhance the proportions of his characters and give them heroic stature. Hence he evokes the Jewish wars (in which, incidentally, he makes Titus owe much to Antiochus and nothing to Bérénice), stressing the heroic exploits of his characters and the destruction and desolation caused by the war; hence, too, he evokes the pomp of Titus:

> De cette nuit, Phénice, as-tu vu la splendeur? . . .

Corneille, on the other hand, gives a much fuller picture of the background. He makes the Senate meet to discuss the eruption of Vesuvius; he refers to the wars against the Jews; he introduces Domitian and Domitie, and makes the latter relate the story of her life; he discusses the character of the Senate; and he stresses that Bérénice is a Jewess and a monotheist. In all this, he brings out the political aspects of the historical situation.

Corneille's play is a political one. Domitian, Tite's brother, is trying to prevent his mistress, Domitie, from marrying Tite, and Bérénice is called to Rome by his confidant, Albin, as one means of doing this: she is, in fact, a pawn in the game. At the end, the lovers separate for political considerations. Domitie has claims on the throne, and Domitian is ambitious and has already headed a rising; so that their union will be a direct threat to Tite, unless they are his heirs. This is one reason why Tite cannot marry Bérénice, quite apart from the Roman prejudice against queens, on which Corneille lays less stress than Racine. On the other hand, Tite not only loves Bérénice, but owes her a deep debt of gratitude for her help against the Jews (it is for this reason that the Jewish wars are mentioned). Moreover, the Senate sanctions the marriage of Tite and Bérénice; but it is a degenerate and capricious body, and little reliance can be placed on its opinions. It is because Bérénice fully appreciates the situation and sees that her marriage with Tite would endanger his throne and his life that she departs.[1]

Corneille, in other words, is always conscious of the complexity of human relationships; he likes to show the individual in society, and the interaction of the individual and of society. This is but another aspect of his realism. One is tempted to think that it is from realism that he does not like love to play too much part in tragedy:

> J'ai cru jusques ici [he wrote to Saint-Evremond] que l'amour était une passion trop chargée de faiblesses pour être la dominante dans une pièce héroïque; j'aime qu'elle y serve d'ornement, et non pas de corps, et que *les grandes âmes ne la laissent agir qu'autant qu'elle est compatible avec de plus nobles impressions.*

---

[1] Comparing *Nicomède* with *Mithridate*, E. Desjardins writes: 'La politique du héros de Corneille se retrouve dans celle du héros de Racine, de Mithridate lui-même, mais les causes de l'agrandissement de Rome, les vues du Sénat, la suite de ses conseils, la portée des enseignements politiques que comporte un pareil sujet, tout cela n'est que timidement et incidemment exposé. Les amours des quatre personnages principaux occupent toute la scène et attachent exclusivement le spectateur. [. . .] Les ennemis de Mithridate ne sont pas plus des Romains que s'ils étaient nés sur les bords de la Seine.' (*Le grand Corneille historien*, 1861, pp. 97–8)

Is not that a way of saying that, while love is important, there are other preoccupations in life? Besides living our personal life, we have our part to play in society, responsibilities towards society and towards others. Literature concentrates perhaps too much on love and too little on the other aspects of life: with Corneille, who depicts not only men and women, but men and women in society, the balance is to some extent redressed.

Chapter Eleven

FORM

§ 1 *Aspects of Corneille's technique*

Corneille's plays afford many different kinds of pleasure. Not least is the satisfaction which comes from form, from the appreciation of the way in which the poet handles his material, arranges and distributes it, the consciousness that behind the play is an orderly and artistic mind.

One obvious feature of Corneille's plays is that they are dramatic. The plays of Corneille's predecessors seldom are. They sometimes show startling events on the stage — in Hardy's *Scédase*, two young men rape two sisters and throw their bodies down a well — but are not necessarily very interesting. At best, they show successive episodes of a narrative; too often they consist of long successions of laments. From the very beginning, Corneille understood the importance of arousing suspense. He maintains the spectator's interest by making him wonder what is going to happen next; he leaves the issue in doubt; he shows unexpected reversals of the situation. But though the spectator may be surprised, the changes or events which cause his surprise are always probable and always skilfully prepared and motivated.

It is interesting to compare Corneille's treatment of a subject with that of a contemporary; and two possible comparisons suggest themselves — that of Corneille's *Sophonisbe* with Mairet's, and that of his *Tite et Bérénice* with Racine's *Bérénice*.

The difference between Corneille's play and Mairet's is striking. Mairet's play arouses no suspense; on the contrary, everything turns out as it is predicted that it will. In Act I, Syphax foretells that the loves of Sophonisbe and Massinisse will end unhappily, and hopes and expects to die in battle; Sophonisbe, too, foresees that the outcome of her love for Massinisse cannot be a happy one. In Act II, Sophonisbe expects Syphax to be defeated, and is troubled by forebodings and bad dreams. Syphax is duly defeated and killed, but, even when it is arranged that Sophonisbe is to marry Massinisse, she is troubled with more forebodings of evil. In Act IV, the arrival of Scipio gives rise to further forebodings. In other words, from the very start of the play, the reader or spectator knows that the outcome will be unhappy. There is no suspense, except that, for a moment in Act III, we wonder whether Massinisse will fall in love with Sophonisbe.

Very different is Corneille's play, in which hopes and fears alternate up to the last. To start with, we do not even know that the Carthaginians and the Romans will fight. The play opens with hopes of peace, and Sophonisbe and Eryxe debate whether peace is likely or not, and which of them Massinisse prefers. Sophonisbe, however, persuades Massinisse to continue the war. The battle is fought and Syphax is defeated. But a new question arises. Whom does Massinisse love, Sophonisbe or Eryxe? Eryxe discusses the matter with her confidante, and expects that her position and Sophonisbe's will now be reversed. Massinisse appears, and, in an ambiguous scene (II, 2), seems to offer his crown to Eryxe, who gloats over Sophonisbe. Immediately afterwards, however, she understands her error: Massinisse asks Sophonisbe to marry him. Act III raises three questions in the mind of the spectator: what will the Romans think of this marriage? what will Eryxe and Massinisse say to each other when they meet? and what will Syphax and Sophonisbe say to each other when *they* meet? In Act IV, Syphax warns the Romans against Sophonisbe, who is arrested. Lélius condemns the marriage of Massinisse and

Sophonisbe, but Massinisse still hopes that Scipio will be favourable. Even in Act V, the issue is in doubt until the end. Sophonisbe refuses to accept the poison sent to her by Massinisse (V, 2); then she announces her intention of allowing the Romans to take her captive to Rome (V, 4). Lélius sends Lépide to Sophonisbe to cheer her with hopes that Rome may be lenient to her and to try to bring about a reconciliation between her and Syphax. Finally, Sophonisbe commits suicide; but Corneille has left us in doubt up to the end whether she would.

Racine, of course, learnt from Corneille, and, in his *Bérénice*, hopes and fears do alternate — not in the two main protagonists, Titus and Bérénice, but in Antiochus, who loves Bérénice, whose love is hopeless as long as Titus intends to marry her, but whose hopes revive when it seems that Titus means to send her away. He says himself:

> Tous mes moments ne sont qu'un éternel passage
> De la crainte à l'espoir, de l'espoir à la rage.

But Racine's play contains fewer alternations of hopes and fears, fewer *péripéties* and surprises, than Corneille's. In *Tite et Bérénice*, interest is maintained throughout. Domitian loves Domitie, whom Tite is about to marry; but Domitian's confidant, Albin, hints that Bérénice, whom Tite has formerly loved, may be in Rome. In Act II, scene 1, Tite expresses the belief that Bérénice no longer loves him, though he has not forgotten her. In scene 2, Domitian asks Tite to give up Domitie, and in scene 3, she is asked to choose between the brothers. In scene 4, Bérénice is announced, and she appears in the following scene. Act III opens with the spectacle of Domitian paying court to Bérénice, in order to try to arouse Tite's jealousy. This scene is thus adequately motivated. It is also well prepared, since Domitie had told him earlier, 'Quittez qui vous quitte' (I, 2), and Tite had said, 'Epousez Bérénice' (II, 2). In scene 3, Domitie salutes Bérénice as the future Empress, and, at the end of the act, Tite tells Bérénice that he will not marry Domitie. In Act IV, Bérénice asks Domitian to influence the Senate in her favour. In the following scene, however,

Domitie asks him to help *her* to marry Tite; he retorts by threatening to marry Bérénice unless Domitie will marry him. Domitian then plays upon Tite's jealousy by asking him to let him (Domitian) marry either Domitie or Bérénice. Once again, in Act V, the outcome remains uncertain right up to the end. Tite is undecided, and sees Domitie and Bérénice in turn. The Senate (influenced by the friends of Domitian) asks Tite to marry Bérénice. Finally, however, Bérénice makes up her mind to depart.

In structure, *Tite et Bérénice* and *Sophonisbe* are fairly representative of their author. A typical play of Corneille contains a constant succession of ups and downs, of hopes alternating with fears, of reversals of the situation.[1] Indeed, Corneille has been criticized for being too exclusively interested in surprise and dramatic effect. That he is interested in these things is undeniable; but he stated unequivocally in a letter to M. de Zuylichem that, besides surprise, he was aiming at 'quelque chose de plus solide,' and his plays bear him out. He never achieves surprise at the expense of psychological truth. Moreover, some of his plays lack this characteristic feature. There are few surprises in *Pompée*, for example — or at least, if surprise is felt, it is not by the audience so much as by Ptolomée and his advisers; for, in this superbly constructed play, the thread of interest is provided by the constant inability of Ptolomée and his counsellors to understand either the circumstances or the characters with whom they have to deal, so that they are continually taken unawares. There are few alternations of hope and fear in *Pulchérie* and none in *Suréna*.

Too much has been made of Corneille's love of complexity. It is true that, in the preface to *Clitandre*, he writes:

Il faut néanmoins que j'avoue que ceux qui n'ayant vu représenter *Clitandre* qu'une fois, ne le comprendront pas nettement, seront fort excusables, vu que les narrations qui doivent donner le jour au reste y sont si courtes, que le moindre défaut, ou d'attention du spectateur, ou de mémoire de l'acteur, laisse une obscurité perpétuelle en la suite, et ôte presque l'entière intelligence de ces grands mouvements

[1] Camille admirably summarizes the alternations of *Horace*:

Vit-on jamais une âme en un jour plus atteinte
De joie et de douleur, d'espérance et de crainte, etc.   (IV, 4)

dont les pensées ne s'égarent point du fait, et ne sont que des raisonnements continus sur ce qui s'est passé.

He says much the same about *Héraclius*:

> J'ai vu de fort bons esprits, et des personnes des plus qualifiées de la cour, se plaindre de ce que sa représentation fatiguait autant l'esprit qu'une étude sérieuse. Elle n'a pas laissé de plaire; mais je crois qu'il l'a fallu voir plus d'une fois pour en remporter une entière intelligence.
> (*Examen*)

It is true, too, that *Sophonisbe* and *Tite et Bérénice* are more complex than the corresponding plays of Mairet and Racine. But *Clitandre* and *Héraclius* are extreme cases; and, indeed, even in *Héraclius*, the situation is simple enough — what is fatiguing is the continual need to remember that Héraclius is Martian and Martian is Léonce. Most of Corneille's plays are far less complex, and some extremely simple. *Le Cid*, *Horace*, *Cinna*, and *Polyeucte* are all comparatively simple, and they are not exceptional. *Pompée* can briefly be analysed thus: In Act I, news of the arrival of Pompée after Pharsala causes Ptolomée and his advisers to discuss what course of action they should adopt. In Act II, Pompée is murdered, and César arrives. In Act III, César appears on the stage, and so does Pompée's widow, Cornélie. In Act IV, Ptolomée and his advisers conspire against César, and Cornélie warns him of their plot, which is frustrated in Act V. The essential action of *Nicomède* is slight: Nicomède refuses to let Attale have his throne (Act II); Laodice refuses to let him have hers by marrying him (Act III); Nicomède is arrested (Act V) and set free by a revolt stirred up by Laodice. In *Pulchérie*, all that happens is that Pulchérie is made Empress, decides that she cannot marry Léon (whom she loves) and will marry no one else, and resolves the situation by contracting a *mariage blanc* with Martian. The simplest of all is *Suréna*: Act I: exposition. Act II: Eurydice is reluctant to marry Pacorus. Act III: Suréna is reluctant to marry Mandane. Act IV: Orode and Pacorus guess the truth, that Suréna and Eurydice love each other. Suréna refuses to give up Eurydice; Eurydice refuses to give up Suréna. Act V: assassination of Suréna.

Corneille's mind seems to have a natural love of order and balance, of contrast and symmetry. This is evident in the basic situations of his plays. In *L'Illusion comique*, for example, there is a serving-maid (Lyse) who loves a serving-man (Clindor), but whose love is not returned. In contrast, the master (Matamore) loves the mistress (Isabelle), but his love is not returned. The man-servant loves and is loved by the mistress. Here, we have both parallelism and contrast. The pattern is this:

Man (Clindor) ⟵————— Maid (Lyse)

Master (Matamore) ————⟶ Mistress (Isabelle)[1]

In *Le Cid*, there is a pair of lovers, Rodrigue and Chimène, each of whom has an unsuccessful rival:

Infante ——⟶ Rodrigue ⟵⟶ Chimène ⟵—— Don Sanche

Polyeucte provides us with a similar situation. In the centre is a married couple (Polyeucte and Pauline). Pauline has a lover, Sévère, whom she loves still; Polyeucte has no other mistress, but deserts Pauline for God:

Sévère ⟵⟶ Pauline ⟵⟶ Polyeucte ——⟶ God

Othon and *Suréna* reproduce the same basic pattern:

Camille ——⟶ Othon ⟵⟶ Plautine ⟵—— Martian

Mandane ---⟶ Suréna ⟵⟶ Eurydice ⟵—— Pacorus[2]

In *Horace*, Horace is married to Sabine, while Sabine's brother is engaged to Horace's sister. Here, there is symmetry, too, in the points of view they express: Horace and Camille represent two opposite extreme attitudes, while Curiace and Sabine express more moderate views.

⎧ Horace (extreme) ⟵⟶ Sabine (moderation) ⎫
⎩ Camille (opposite extreme) ⟵⟶ Curiace (moderation) ⎭

---

[1] The symbol ——⟶ is used to indicate love; the symbol - - - - -⟶ to denote an inclination or a proposed marriage. The situations of Racine do not present the same symmetry. The most common situation in a tragedy of Racine is:

A ⟵⟶ B ⟵—— C

[2] The symmetry is not complete, since Suréna's sister, Palmis, loves Pacorus.

Don Sanche has an elaborate, but still symmetrical pattern. Don
Alvar loves Doña Elvire, who loves Don Sanche, who loves Doña
Isabelle, to whose hand Don Manrique and Don Lope aspire:

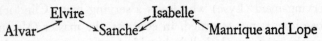

Sertorius and *Attila* share the same basic pattern. Sertorius hesitates between Viriate and Aristie, though his preference is for
Viriate. Viriate is loved by Perpenna, and Aristie by Pompée:

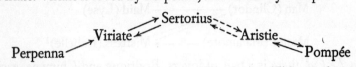

Similarly, Attila is hesitating between Honorie and Ildione, though
his preference is for Ildione. Ildione is loved by Ardaric, and
Honorie by Valamir:

In *Attila*, though, a new element enters in, that of contrast.
Ildione and Honorie are alike in being possible matches for Attila.
On the other hand, they are placed in sharp contrast, for Honorie
represents the weakness and decay of the Roman Empire, whose
glory is in the past, and Ildione the growing strength and brilliant
future of France. In *Tite et Bérénice*, the situation is again symmetrical, but in a different way. We have two pairs of lovers, Tite
and Bérénice on the one hand, and Domitie and Domitian on the
other. Tite, however, is thinking of marrying Domitie, and
Domitie is willing to marry Tite. To balance this, Domitian pays
court to Bérénice:[1]

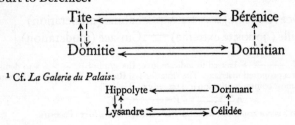

[1] Cf. *La Galerie du Palais*:

It is not, however, in the basic relationships of the characters alone that we find symmetry, but also in the structure of the plays. Corneille is very fond of showing parallel scenes, in which sometimes the second repeats the first, sometimes contrasts sharply with it. In *La Galerie du Palais*, for example, we twice see the shopkeepers in the Galerie: the first time they are conversing amicably together, the second time they are quarrelling. In *La Veuve*, Clarice is jealous because Philiste has been too much interested in his conversation with two ladies, Belinde and Chrysolite (I, 5). Later, Philiste is jealous in his turn, because Clarice owes her deliverance, and therefore her gratitude, to another. She reproaches him with his jealousy; he tells her that he is merely following her example, and reminds her of the Belinde and Chrysolite episode (V, 7). In one scene of *Horace*, we hear of the flight of Horace; in another, his victory is narrated. Act II of *Suréna* deals with Eurydice's reluctance to marry Pacorus; Act III, with Suréna's unwillingness to marry Mandane.

Attila is largely constructed on this principle:

> *Act I.* Attila, forced to choose between Honorie and Ildione, consults Valamir and Ardaric. Each tries to persuade Attila to marry the mistress of the other. Attila tells the two kings that they must see that one princess rejects him.

> *Act II.* { Valamir sees Honorie, who refuses to reject Attila.
> { Ardaric sees Ildione, who refuses to reject Attila.

> *Act III.* { Attila sees Ildione, whom he loves; she agrees to reject him.
> { Attila sees Honorie, whom he does not love; she rejects him.

(Here there is a double contrast. Both princesses do what they had refused to do in Act II; Ildione, whom he prefers but thinks it imprudent to marry, rejects him in obedience to his own wishes, whereas Honorie, whom he has decided to marry, rejects him out of wounded pride, because Ildione has rejected him already.)

Act IV. {
At the end of Act III, Attila learns that Honorie loves Valamir.

At the beginning of Act IV, Attila learns that Ildione loves Ardaric.
}

{
Attila tells Ardaric that he may marry Ildione if he kills Valamir.

Attila (off stage) tells Valamir that he may marry Honorie if he kills Ardaric.
}

The above summary may suggest an arbitrary series of scenes, but they are very carefully motivated. Attila is a wily and cautious monarch who, having to choose between two princesses of different countries, wishes to marry one without incurring the hostility of the other nation. Hence, in the first place, he resorts to the stratagem of seeking the advice of his satellite kings, so that the responsibility of rejecting one princess may fall on them. The council scene in Act I is fully consistent with the character of Attila. When the kings fail to agree and this plan fails, he is naturally led to suggest that they should find means of persuading one of the princesses to reject his hand. Equally naturally, they fail; neither of the princesses can accept the responsibility of rejecting the alliance of such a powerful monarch as Attila. At this point occurs the only *péripétie* of the play. A report of the death of Aétius arrives from Rome, making the Roman alliance politically more attractive. Attila himself asks Ildione to reject him. She reluctantly agrees, but ruins Attila's scheme by taunting Honorie, telling her that she must accept her 'refus'. Honorie, a proud and hasty princess, riled by the insult, not only refuses to marry Attila, but admits that she loves Valamir and betrays the secret love of Ildione and Ardaric for each other. Attila is stung by the discovery that both princesses prefer someone else to him, and that his two satellites are his rivals. Hence his cruel offer to the two kings, that whichever kills the other shall marry his mistress — an offer which he has no intention of carrying out. Only the death of Attila can resolve the situation. Ildione, whom he loves, wins him back, with the object of killing him on their wedding night. Their marriage is arranged, but Attila dies of a haemorrhage. Both Ildione's intention of killing Attila and his death, incidentally, have been carefully prepared earlier in the play.

Another feature to notice in any play of Corneille's is the great variety of scenes it contains. Emotional scenes, scenes of joy, disillusionment, foreboding, grief, wounded pride; scenes of discussion, discussion of general principles or of a course of action, council scenes, arguments, quarrel scenes, with cutting irony, sly ambiguous digs, wounding remarks; scenes of narrative — all play their part and set each other off.

The best way to illustrate Corneille's mastery of technique is to study a play in detail. Corneille himself praises the technique of two of his plays particularly, *Polyeucte* and *Rodogune*. Of the former he writes: 'A mon gré, je n'ai point fait de pièce où l'ordre du théâtre soit plus beau et l'enchaînement des scènes mieux ménagé.' Many critics have praised the mastery of this play. Two features, in particular, have been admired, deservedly — the ascending movement of the play, the way in which the interest is gradually transferred from earth to heaven, Polyeucte carrying the other characters of the play (Néarque, Pauline, Félix) after him; and the way in which the two plots are connected. It is the return of Sévère which provides the occasion for the religious ceremony at which Polyeucte smashes the idols, and it is the presence of Sévère which causes Félix to deal so harshly with his son-in-law.

Sévère [writes the abbé Batteux] est un personnage de la pure invention du poète; il peut servir d'exemple dans l'art de mêler le vrai avec le faux.

Quoique personnage épisodique, il est l'âme de toute l'action. Il change l'attachement de Pauline pour Polyeucte en vertu sublime, et la vertu de Polyeucte en prodige. Il ajoute à la politique craintive de Félix un degré d'activité nécessaire à l'action: enfin il joint à tant d'exemples de vertus, celui d'une probité généreuse et vraiment romaine, en prenant le parti de Polyeucte contre lui-même et contre Félix. On oubliait de dire que c'est lui encore qui fournit l'occasion d'un sacrifice éclatant qui met Polyeucte dans le cas du martyre.

T

But Corneille speaks with even greater enthusiasm of *Rodogune*:

> Elle a tout ensemble la beauté du sujet, la nouveauté des fictions, la force des vers, la facilité de l'expression, la solidité du raisonnement, la chaleur des passions, les tendresses de l'amour et de l'amitié; et cet heureux assemblage est ménagé de sorte qu'elle s'élève d'acte en acte. Le second passe le premier, le troisième est au-dessus du second, et le dernier l'emporte sur tous les autres. (*Examen*)

§ 2 *Rodogune*

Corneille's great achievement is to have created a tragedy which is intensely dramatic and whose interest is psychological. *Rodogune* is an excellent example. Given the situation and the characters, the whole action follows logically, necessarily, inexorably; and yet, at the same time, the spectator is kept continually in suspense. The interest is centred entirely in the characters and the situation, not in the action: indeed, until Act V, there is no action whatsoever. The play is admirably constructed; the structure is simple, clear, logical, symmetrical:

Act I. Exposition.

Act II. Cléopâtre appeals to the brothers: he who kills Rodogune shall rule.

Act III. Rodogune appeals to the brothers: he who kills Cléopâtre shall be her husband.

Act IV. Cléopâtre puts her scheme into action.

Act V. Cléopâtre's scheme fails.

Suspense is skilfully created and maintained throughout the play. It begins straight away. The play opens with a mystery: we learn that Cléopâtre is about to declare which of her two sons is the elder, and that the elder, whichever it is, is to marry Rodogune. A *coup de théâtre* takes place in the middle of the act, however. Antiochus says that he is about to offer his brother the kingdom in exchange for Rodogune; but, before he can make his offer, Séleucus forestalls him with the proposal that Antiochus should have the crown and Séleucus Rodogune. At the end of Act I,

Rodogune is filled with forebodings, and her confidante tries to reassure her; Rodogune says that she loves one of the two brothers, without naming him. Thus, at the end of the first act, the spectator is curious about three things: who is the eldest brother and the destined husband of Rodogune? whom does Rodogune love? and what is Cléopâtre really like, who is right about her, Rodogune or her confidante?

Cléopâtre herself opens the second act. One of the questions is answered: Cléopâtre reveals her true character, her hatred and fear of Rodogune, her lust for power, and her intention of using the secret of the order of her sons' birth for her own ends. The act ends with a new mystery. Séleucus speaks of a 'beau dessein' (II, 4): what is it? We learn what Séleucus's plan is in the third act. It is that whichever brother is loved by Rodogune shall be king and marry Rodogune, and that the other shall renounce all claim to the throne. Rodogune's reply provides a *coup de théâtre*: she will marry whichever of the brothers kills Cléopâtre. The end of the act leaves us wondering what the outcome of this impossible situation can be. Act IV ends with Cléopâtre disclosing her intention of killing both her sons, so that suspense is carried over into Act V.

In Act V, we learn that Cléopâtre has killed Séleucus and means to poison Rodogune and Antiochus, so that suspense is created from the very outset. How does she propose to do it? Will she succeed? And this suspense is skilfully maintained. The poisoned cup is brought; Antiochus is about to drink, when he is interrupted by a messenger bringing news of the death of his brother and repeating his last words. This message creates further suspense: we expect Cléopâtre to be named, but she is not; Séleucus, before he died, had merely time to warn his brother to beware of 'une main qui nous fut bien chère'. Antiochus hesitates: does this mean Cléopâtre or Rodogune? He tries to commit suicide; Cléopâtre accuses Rodogune and Rodogune Cléopâtre; Antiochus nearly drinks the poisoned cup; Cléopâtre drinks it and dies.

Thus, throughout the play, the tension rises until it reaches its peak in Act V. At the same time, however, Corneille skilfully alternates moments of tension with moments of tranquillity within each act. Act I is beautifully balanced. It is in three parts:

(1) Scene 1. Exposition (first part)   Tranquillity

(2) Scenes 2–3:

    (a) Offer of Antiochus   Rising tension

    (b) Offer of Séleucus

    (c) Lament of the brothers

    (d) Antiochus's proposal (love must   Climax
        be stronger than brotherly affec-
        tion

    (e) Séleucus's counter-proposal (let   Falling tension
        brotherly affection be stronger
        than love; let them take an oath
        of friendship)

(3) Scenes 4–5. Exposition (second part)   Tranquillity
    and Rodogune scene   (but note of
                                                    foreboding)

The shape of the act may be represented diagrammatically thus:

The first four acts all conform roughly to this pattern. The second part of Act I falls, it will be noticed, into three subdivisions: in the first, Antiochus and Séleucus make identical proposals; in the third, they make contrasting proposals.

Act II is similarly in three parts:

(1) Scenes 1–2. Cléopâtre soliloquizes and   Rising tension
    converses with Laonice

(2) Scene 3. Cléopâtre's interview with her
    sons (the long narrative provides a
    moment of calm; then comes her   Climax
    dramatic offer)

(3) Scene 4. The brothers' conversation   Comparative
                                                    tranquillity

One might represent this act diagrammatically thus:

Act III again falls into three parts:

(1) Rodogune explains her situation and formulates her plan	Rising tension
(2) Interview between Rodogune and the brothers	Climax
(3) Conversation between the brothers	Comparative tranquillity

This act duplicates the preceding one, with Rodogune substituted for Cléopâtre. It may be represented diagrammatically thus:

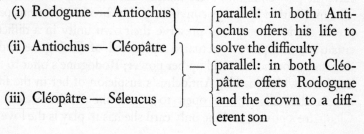

Act IV follows the same basic pattern, and is again in three parts:

(1) Rodogune and Antiochus meet. We learn that Rodogune loves Antiochus, but will not forego her vengeance	
(2) Cléopâtre sees Antiochus and Séleucus in turn	Tension rises as we suspect Cléopâtre of some deep design and falls when we see that Séleucus is not taken in
(3) Cléopâtre soliloquizes and says that she will kill both her sons	Tension rises steeply

There is a good deal of parallelism between the different parts of this act. We have three conversations:

(i) Rodogune — Antiochus
(ii) Antiochus — Cléopâtre } — parallel: in both Antiochus offers his life to solve the difficulty

(iii) Cléopâtre — Séleucus } — parallel: in both Cléopâtre offers Rodogune and the crown to a different son

Symmetry and parallelism play a great part in this play. It is
there in the basic situation. Two brothers, owing loyalty and
affection to their mother, love the same woman: the brothers are
united by strong ties of affection, whereas their mother and their
mistress feel implacable hatred for each other:

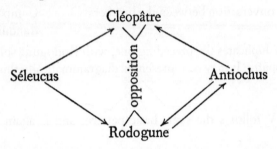

It is there in the structure. In the first act, the explanatory narrative is divided into two halves, one occurring at the beginning,
the other at the end of the act. In between, we have two parallel
offers by Antiochus and Séleucus, and then two contradictory
proposals by Antiochus and Séleucus. Acts II and III are parallel;
so are the scenes of Act IV. In Act V, Cléopâtre accuses Rodogune
of the murder, and Rodogune accuses Cléopâtre. There is symmetry even in the arrangement of the characters on the stage; for,
in Act V, we find the following stage direction:

> Ici Antiochus s'assied dans un fauteuil, Rodogune à sa gauche, en
> même rang, et Cléopâtre à sa droite, mais en rang inférieur, et qui
> marque quelque inégalité. Oronte s'assied aussi à la gauche de
> Rodogune, avec la même différence [. . .]

However dramatic the play, however elaborate the formal structure, the play combines these things with truth to human nature.
The motivation is always convincing. The brothers' various proposals are all attempts to preserve their own unity in a difficult
situation; Cléopâtre is actuated by hatred of Rodogune and a
determination not to yield up her power; Rodogune's offer to the
brothers, which justifies Antiochus's suspicion of her in the fifth
act, is the only course open to her — she is defenceless in
Cléopâtre's power, and the only card she has to play is the love of

Cléopâtre's two sons for her. Moreover, though the situation is an extreme one, it is a common enough one; men torn between their mother and their sweetheart or wife are not unknown in real life. Only, Corneille brings out all the latent potentialities of such a situation. Similarly, though Cléopâtre is an extreme character, Corneille himself stresses her essential truth:

> Il est peu de mères qui voulussent assassiner ou empoisonner leurs enfants de peur de leur rendre leur bien, comme Cléopâtre dans *Rodogune*; mais il en est assez qui prennent goût à en jouir, et ne s'en dessaisissent qu'à regret et le plus tard qu'il leur est possible. Bien qu'elles ne soient pas capables d'une action si noire et si dénaturée que celle de cette reine de Syrie, elles ont en elles quelque teinture du principe qui l'y porta, et la vue de la juste punition qu'elle en reçoit leur peut faire craindre, non pas un pareil malheur, mais une infortune proportionnée à ce qu'elles sont capables de commettre.
>
> (*Second Discours*)

Chapter Twelve

THE POETRY OF
CORNEILLE

§ 1 *Formal qualities in Corneille's verse*

Corneille's speeches are no less carefully constructed than his plays, his acts and his scenes. To take an example at random Sabine's speech in *Horace*, II, 6 —

> Non, non, mon frère, non; je ne viens en ce lieu . . .

is built up in a logical manner and exploits every possible variation of its theme, like a movement of a symphony of Beethoven. Sabine, the wife of Horace and the sister of Curiace, is trying, by her wits, to stop the two men from fighting. She is not expostulating with them, since they are beyond reason; she is trying to show them their inhumanity by a *reductio ad absurdum* of their position. Her speech falls into five parts: (1) I do not mean to deter you, but to suggest a way by which you may legitimately fight each other. Here, she is, of course, speaking, not seriously, but ironically:

> Votre sang est trop *bon*, n'en craignez rien de lâche,
> Rien dont la *fermeté* de ces *grands* cœurs se fâche:
> *Si ce malheur illustre ébranlait l'un de vous,*
> *Je le désavouerais pour frère ou pour époux.*

The ironical intention of the speech as a whole is brought out by Camille's remark: 'Courage! ils s'amollissent.' She is, as it were, standing at the ring-side, appreciating the effectiveness of her sister-in-law's tactics. (2) If one of you kills me, the other can then avenge my death. (Sabine, of course, is not seriously offering her life; this is her way of making her point.) (3) Possible objections are put forward and answered: it is the inhumanity of your combat which makes it glorious; very well, then, be inhuman and kill me. The climax here is marked by three parallel lines:

> Commencez par sa sœur à répandre son sang,
> Commencez par sa femme à lui percer le flanc,
> Commencez par Sabine à faire de vos vies
> Un digne sacrifice à vos chères patries . . .

(4) Another argument is put forward: I cannot live if one of you kills the other; if you will not kill me now, I shall kill myself later, so you may as well do it now. (5) Yet another argument appears: if you do not kill me now, I shall interpose myself between you, and you will have to kill me before you can begin to fight.

At times, we are reminded of a medieval disputation. Maxime, for instance, in *Cinna*, begins one of his speeches, in the great discussion scene, thus:

> Oui, *j'accorde* qu'Auguste a droit de conserver
> L'empire où sa vertu l'a fait seule arriver,
> Et qu'au prix de son sang, au péril de sa tête,
> Il a fait de l'Etat une juste conquête;
> *Mais que* sans se noircir, il ne puisse quitter
> Le fardeau que sa main est lasse de porter,
> *Qu'*il accuse par là César de tyrannie,
> *Qu'*il approuve sa mort, *c'est ce que je dénie.*

Anyone who has had the good fortune to hear a medieval disputation will recognize the formulae: 'That . . . I grant; that . . . I deny.'

The discussion scenes as a whole are organized on the same logical principle. The great scene in *Sertorius* (III, 1), for instance, falls into three parts. (1) Pompée tries to win over Sertorius. (2) The climax is Sertorius's line:

> Rome n'est plus dans Rome, elle est toute où je suis,

— which occurs in the middle speech of the scene. (3) Sertorius tries to win over Pompée.

Besides logical structure, Corneille's verse is marked by a love
of formal patterns. The love of symmetry and contrast, the
balance of like and like or the opposition of like and unlike, is as
evident in his verse as in the composition of the plays as a whole.
His lines are often symmetrical.

> Je mis, au lieu de moi, Chimène en ses liens . . .
>> (*Le Cid*, I, 2)

> L'obscurité vaut mieux que tant de renommée.
>> (*Horace*, II, 3)

In these two lines, there is rhythmical symmetry (2 4 2 4, 4 2 2 4)
together with a contrast in sense. Often the balance or opposition
of the two halves is exact:

> En l'une je suis fille, en l'autre je suis femme.
>> (*Horace*, III, 1)

> Quel prix de mon amour! Quel fruit de mes travaux!
>> (*Polyeucte*, II, 2)

> Que de pensers divers! que de soucis flottants!
>> (*Héraclius*, IV, 3)

The fondness for stichomythia is another form of the love of
antithesis. Already in *Mélite*, we find Mélite and the nurse rapidly
countering each other's arguments:

> *M.* Le bien ne touche point un généreux courage.
> *N.* Tout le monde l'adore, et tâche d'en jouir.
> *M.* Il suit un faux éclat qui ne peut m'éblouir.
> *N.* Auprès de sa splendeur toute autre est trop petite.
> *M.* Tu le places au rang qui n'est dû qu'au mérite.
> *N.* On a trop de mérite étant riche à ce point, etc.   (IV, 1)

The same love of balance is evident in the composition of
whole speeches. Sabine owes allegiance to both camps, and her
soliloquy in Act III, scene 1, again falls into five parts: (1) A
preamble: in this difficult situation, some decision must be reached.
(2) Let me try to rejoice in the victory of one side or the other: I
belong to both. (3) No: this is a delusion. (4) Whichever side
wins, I am bound to suffer: I belong to both. (5) Conclusion:

animadversions on the gods. The contrast between the two opposing attitudes of parts (2) and (4) is emphasized by the repetition in (4) of words, phrases and whole lines of (2):

(2) Songeons pour quelle cause, et non par quelles mains;
Revoyons les vainqueurs, sans penser qu'à la gloire
Que toute leur maison reçoit de leur victoire;
Et sans considérer aux dépens de quel sang
Leur vertu les élève en cet illustre rang,
Faisons nos intérêts de ceux de leur famille:
En l'une je suis femme, en l'autre je suis fille,
Et tiens à toutes deux par de si forts liens,
Qu'on ne peut triompher que par les bras des miens.

(4) Je songe par quels bras, et non pour quelle cause,
Et ne vois les vainqueurs en leur illustre rang
Que pour considérer aux dépens de quel sang.
La maison des vaincus touche seule mon âme:
En l'une je suis fille, en l'autre je suis femme,
Et tiens à toutes deux par de si forts liens,
Qu'on ne peut triompher que par la mort des miens.

Perhaps the best example of this kind of formal pattern is Aristie's speech in *Sertorius*. Pompée, who has divorced Aristie and married Emilie, tells his former wife that he still loves her. She says:

Sortez de mon esprit, ressentiments jaloux;
Noirs enfants du dépit, ennemis de ma gloire,
Tristes ressentiments, je ne veux plus vous croire.
Quoi qu'on m'ait fait d'outrage, il ne m'en souvient plus:
Plus de nouvel hymen, plus de Sertorius;
Je suis au grand Pompée; et puisqu'il m'aime encore,
Puisqu'il me rend son cœur, de nouveau je l'adore:
Plus de Sertorius. Mais Seigneur, répondez;
Faites parler ce cœur qu'enfin vous me rendez.
Plus de Sertorius. Hélas! quoi que je die,
Vous ne me dites point, Seigneur: 'Plus d'Emilie.'
    Rentrez dans mon esprit, jaloux ressentiments,
Fiers enfants de l'honneur, nobles emportements;
C'est vous que je veux croire; et Pompée infidèle
Ne saurait plus souffrir que ma haine chancelle:
Il l'affermit pour moi. Venez, Sertorius;

> Il me rend toute à vous par ce muet refus.
> Donnons ce grand témoin à ce grand hyménée;
> Son âme, toute ailleurs, n'en sera point gênée:
> Il le verra sans peine, et cette dureté
> Passera chez Sylla pour magnanimité.   (III, 2)

Here we have a similar structure to the speech of Sabine just quoted. It is in three parts: (1) Pompée loves me. I am happy and need not marry Sertorius. (2) The idea of Sertorius reminds me that Pompée has married Emilie and said nothing of divorcing her. (3) Pompée does not love me. I am unhappy. The third part is full of verbal reminiscences of the first part, repetitions (*jaloux ressentiments*) and antitheses (*sortez — rentrez; noirs enfants du dépit — fiers enfants de l'honneur — je ne veux plus vous croire — c'est vous que je veux croire*). In neither case is stylization incompatible with genuine emotion.

A feature of which Corneille is extremely fond is repetition. Sometimes a word is repeated:

> Pleurez, pleurez mes yeux, et fondez-vous en eau!
>   (*Le Cid*, III, 2)
> Je sais des souverains la raison souveraine.
>   (*Tite et Bérénice*, V, 4)

Often the repetition is rather more elaborate, and produces a variety of effects. In *Polyeucte*, the repetition of the word *voir* produces suspense:

> *Fabian.* Vous la *verrez*, Seigneur.
> *Sévère.*   Ah! quel comble de joie!
>   Cette chère beauté consent que je la *voie!*
>   . . . .
>   Puis-je tout espérer de cette heureuse *vue?*
> *F.*   Vous la *verrez*, c'est tout ce que je vous puis dire.
> *S.*   D'où vient que tu frémis, et que ton cœur soupire?
>   Ne m'aime-t-elle plus? *Eclaircis-moi ce point.*
> *F.*   M'en croirez-vous, Seigneur? Ne la *revoyez* point . . .
> *S.*   *Voyons-la*, Fabian; ton discours m'importune . . .
>   . . . .
> *F.*   Non, mais encore un coup ne la *revoyez* point.

S.   Ah, c'en est trop, enfin *éclaircis-moi ce point*;
            As-tu *vu* des froideurs quand tu l'en as priée.
F.   Je tremble à vous le dire, elle est . . .
S.   Quoi?
F.   Mariée.

                                            (II, 1)

In *Pompée*, the repetition of the word *fuir* produces an effect of hopelessness and despair:

> César n'est pas le seul qu'il *fuie* en cet état:
> Il *fuit* et le reproche et les yeux du sénat,
> . . . .
> Il *fuit* Rome perdue, il *fuit* tous les Romains,
> A qui par sa défaite il met les fers aux mains;
> Il *fuit* le désespoir des peuples et des princes . . .
> . . . .
> Auteur des maux de tous, il est à tous en butte,
> Et *fuit* le monde entier écrasé sous sa chute.   (I, 1)

One of the most elaborate of such repetitions is in the great scene in *Sertorius* (III, 1), in which Sertorius thrice mysteriously advises Pompée to have 'l'âme toute romaine'. This triple repetition, and the constant use of the words *Rome* and *romain* throughout by both speakers, lead up to the climax, Sertorius's famous line:

> Rome n'est plus dans Rome, elle est toute où je suis.

In *Attila*, the rhyme *Attila-jusque-là* is used three times to stress Attila's ferocity. In *Suréna*, the repetition of the word *murmure* gives an effect of sad hopelessness:

Pacorus.   M'aimez-vous?
Eurydice.   Oui, Seigneur, et ma main vous est sûre.
P.   C'est peu que de la main, si le cœur en murmure.
E.   Quel mal pourrait causer le murmure du mien,
      S'il murmurait si bas qu'aucun n'en apprît rien?   (II, 2)

In discussions, speakers often pick up and play on each other's words — this may sharpen the opposition of their ideas, attitudes or feelings; or it may crystallize a scene round one or two words. In *Suréna*, IV, 3, for example, the repeated use by both speakers of the words *confident* and *confidence* is most effective: it is by this means that Pacorus makes it clear that he has guessed Eurydice's secret, and that Eurydice gives him to understand that she knows that he knows. Camille and Plautine use the words *empire* and *Pison* as a means of taunting each other: both love Othon, but Plautine is to marry Pison and be empress, while Camille has lost the empire without gaining Othon.

> *C.* Lorsque Galba vous donne à Pison pour épouse . . .
> *P.* Il n'est pas encor temps de vous en voir jalouse.
> *C.* Si j'aimais toutefois ou l'empire ou Pison,
> Je pourrais déjà l'être avec quelque raison.
> *P.* Et si j'aimais, Madame, ou Pison ou l'empire,
> J'aurais quelque raison de ne m'en pas dédire.
> Mais votre exemple apprend aux cœurs comme le mien
> Qu'un généreux mépris quelquefois leur sied bien.
> *C.* Quoi? l'empire et Pison n'ont rien pour vous d'aimable?
> (IV, 4)

Often a phrase or line is repeated, either by the character who pronounced it first, or by another. Repetition by a character of his own words may bring out conflicting attitudes in his own breast (like Sabine's *En l'une je suis femme, en l'autre je suis fille* — *En l'une je suis fille, en l'autre je suis femme*) or to insist upon a point. In *Polyeucte*, II, 1, Sévère twice asks Fabian: 'Eclaircis-moi ce point,' and twice says that he only wants to 'la voir, soupirer, et mourir'. Early in the same play, Polyeucte tells his wife:

> Je vous aime,
> Le ciel m'en soit témoin, cent fois plus que moi-même;
> Mais . . . (I, 2)

The remark is left unfinished, but it is taken up and completed later when Polyeucte tells Pauline:

> Je vous aime,
> Beaucoup moins que mon Dieu, mais bien plus que moi-même.
> (IV, 4)

In *Pulchérie*, Pulchérie in one scene twice emphasizes her predicament by saying:

> Je suis impératrice, et j'étais Pulchérie. (III, 1)

Repetition of words by a second character may clinch a point. Prusias, in *Nicomède*, tells Attale that he needs the support of Rome:

> En perdant son appui tu ne seras plus rien. (IV, 4)

In the following scene, Flaminius repeats:

> Que perdant son appui vous ne serez plus rien,
> Que le Roi vous l'a dit, souvenez-vous-en bien.

Usually the effect of the repetition is more subtle. In the first scene of *Polyeucte*, Néarque urges Polyeucte not to postpone his baptism; he will soon be back with his wife:

> Dans une heure au plus tard vous essuierez ses larmes . . .

In the following scene, Polyeucte tells Pauline:

> Dans une heure au plus tard je reviens en ce lieu,

a repetition which has the effect of showing Polyeucte's dependence on Néarque at this stage. In *Pertharite*, Eduige tells Garibalde how she means to treat Grimoald, who has transferred his affections to Rodelinde:

> Je veux qu'il se repente, et se repente en vain,
> Rendre haine pour haine, et dédain pour dédain.
> Je veux qu'en vain son âme, esclave de la mienne,
> Me demande sa grâce, et jamais ne l'obtienne,
> Qu'il soupire sans fruit; et pour le punir mieux,
> Je veux même à mon tour vous aimer à ses yeux. (II, 1)

Later, Garibalde betrays this confidence to Grimoald, the baseness of his treachery being emphasized by the fact that he reports her very words:

> Elle veut, il est vrai, vous rappeler vers elle;
> Mais pour faire à son tour l'ingrate et la cruelle,
> Pour vous traiter de lâche, et vous rendre soudain
> Parjure pour parjure, et dédain pour dédain.
> Elle veut que votre âme, esclave de la sienne,
> Lui demande sa grâce, et jamais ne l'obtienne:
> Ce sont ses mots exprès; et pour vous punir mieux,
> Elle me veut aimer, et m'aimer à vos yeux:
> Elle me l'a promis. (IV, 1)

Often the repetition brings out the evolution in a character's feelings. In *Le Cid*, the Infante tells Léonor that she is encouraging the match between Rodrigue and Chimène because she loves Rodrigue:

> Si l'amour vit d'espoir, il périt avec lui . . .   (I, 2)

Later, Léonor congratulates the Infante on the peace of mind which she must now feel, since Rodrigue will either be killed by Don Sanche or marry Chimène:

> Si l'amour vit d'espoir, et s'il meurt avec lui,
> Rodrigue ne peut plus charmer votre courage.   (V, 3)

Here, the repetition serves to bring out the essential weakness and illogicality of the Infante, who is not pleased with the turn events have taken, and whose love for Rodrigue is stronger than ever. Similarly, in *Polyeucte*, when Polyeucte urges Pauline to marry Sévère after his death, repeating the words she had used earlier (II, 4) —

> Puisqu'un si grand mérite a pu vous enflammer,
> Sa présence toujours a droit de vous charmer:
> Vous l'aimiez, il vous aime . . .   (V, 3)

— the words no longer chime in with her feelings (loyalty to her husband is uppermost) and seem like a taunt. Plautine tells Othon that they must beware of Camille:

> Où ne portera point un si juste courroux
> La honte de se voir sans l'empire et sans vous?   (IV, 1)

She urges him to appease Camille by marrying her. Othon objects that this, for him, is the worst possible fate and, by neatly repeating Plautine's words, brings out the parallel between his lot and Camille's:

> Subissons de Lacus toute la tyrannie,
> Avant que me soumettre à cette ignominie.
> J'en saurai préférer les plus barbares coups
> A l'affront de me voir sans l'empire et sans vous.

Frequently repetition marks the reversal of a situation. Camille is in despair because she sees no hope of marrying Curiace:

> Cher amant, n'attends plus d'être un jour mon époux;
> Jamais, jamais ce nom ne sera pour un homme
> Qui soit ou le vainqueur, ou l'esclave de Rome. (*Horace*, I, 2)

At that moment, Curiace bursts in:

> revoyez un homme
> Qui n'est ni le vainqueur ni l'esclave de Rome . . .

Circumstances have altered and the threatened battle is not to take place. Néarque, at the beginning of *Polyeucte*, urges Polyeucte not to postpone his baptism because of his wife's presentiments: duty to God must come first.

> Comme rien n'est égal à sa grandeur suprême,
> Il faut ne rien aimer qu'après lui, qu'en lui-même,
> Négliger, pour lui plaire, et femme, et biens, et rang,
> Exposer pour sa gloire et verser tout son sang. (I, 1)

In Act II, scene 6, the situation is reversed. Polyeucte is eager to go to the temple and publicly overthrow the heathen idols; Néarque tries to deter him, and Polyeucte brings up his own words against him:

> Il faut (je me souviens encor de vos paroles)
> Négliger, pour lui plaire, et femme, et biens, et rang,
> Exposer pour sa gloire et verser tout son sang.

Earlier, Néarque was the leader; now the situation has changed and Polyeucte has taken first place. In *Rodogune*, Laonice reassures Rodogune, telling her that she is misjudging Cléopâtre, from whom she has nothing to fear:

> La paix qu'elle a jurée en a calmé la haine.
>
> . . . .
>
> A présent que l'amour succède à la colère,
> Elle ne vous voit plus qu'avec des yeux de mère . . .
>
> . . . .
>
> Le Roi souffrirait-il d'ailleurs quelque surprise? (I, 5)

But Cléopâtre reveals her true feelings by offering to proclaim

u

king whichever of her sons murders Rodogune; and Rodogune
reminds Laonice of her own words:

> Voilà comme l'amour succède à la colère,
> Comme elle ne me voit qu'avec des yeux de mère,
> Comme elle aime la paix, comme elle fait un roi,
> Et comme elle use enfin de ses fils et de moi.
>
> . . . .
>
> Ah, que ma défiance en jugeait beaucoup mieux!
> Tu le vois, Laonice.   (III, 1)

In *Sophonisbe*, each reversal of the situation is marked by the same
phrase. At the beginning of Act II, scene 3, Eryxe tells her rival:

> Tout a changé de face,
> Madame, et les destins vous ont mise en ma place.

In the following act, Eryxe has to confess:

> Une seconde fois tout a changé de face,
> Madame, et c'est à moi de vous quitter la place.   (III, 3)

Finally, Sophonisbe has to admit herself vanquished:

> Une troisième fois mon sort change de face,
> Madame, et c'est mon tour de vous quitter la place. (V, 4)

Another use of repetition is to bring out conflicting points of
view, as in the scene between Rodrigue and Chimène:

> R. Car enfin, n'attends pas de mon affection
>   Un lâche repentir d'une bonne action.
>
> . . . .
>
> C. Car enfin, n'attends pas de mon affection
>   De lâches sentiments pour ta punition.
>   De quoi qu'en ta faveur notre amour m'entretienne,
>   Ma générosité doit répondre à la tienne . . .
>
> . . . .
>
> R. De quoi qu'en ma faveur notre amour t'entretienne,
>   Ta générosité doit répondre à la mienne . . .   (III, 4)

In this kind of repetition, the words are often repeated with a
significant variation. In *Horace*, Curiace, learning that Horace has
been chosen as the Roman champion, remarks:

> Je vois trop dans ce choix ses funestes projets,
> Et me compte déjà pour un de vos sujets.

Horace retorts that *he* will rather kill himself than live subject to Alba:

> Et du sort envieux quels que soient les projets,
> Je ne me compte point pour un de vos sujets. (II, 1)

News is then brought that Curiace is to fight on behalf of Alba.

> Notre malheur est grand; il est au plus haut point;
> Je l'envisage entier, mais je n'en frémis point;
> Contre qui que ce soit que mon pays m'emploie,
> J'accepte aveuglément cette gloire avec joie . . .
> . . . .
> Albe vous a nommé, je ne vous connais plus,

says Horace. Curiace uses the very expressions of Horace to indicate his own, very different, feelings:

> Je vous connais encore, et c'est ce qui me tue;
> Mais cette âpre vertu ne m'était pas connue,
> Comme notre malheur elle est au plus haut point:
> Souffrez que je l'admire et ne l'imite point. (II, 3)

Photin, in *Pompée*, recommends that Pompée should be put to death:

> Qui punit le vaincu ne craint point le vainqueur.

On the contrary, says Achillas, Pompée should be spared:

> Qui n'est point au vaincu ne craint point le vainqueur. (I, 1)

Barcée tells Eryxe that she has nothing to fear since Massinisse owes her his hand: 'Il vous la doit, Madame.' Eryxe retorts: 'Il me la doit, Barcée;' but changes the meaning by adding:

> Mais que sert une main par le devoir forcée?
> (*Sophonisbe*, II, 1)

In *Othon*, Albiane tells Camille, who is trying to save Othon, that, however annoyed with Othon she may be, her anger is not irrevocable:

> Du courroux à l'amour le retour serait doux.

Immediately, however, news arrives that Othon's revolt has succeeded and that he has been proclaimed Emperor; and Camille observes:

> Puisqu'Othon veut périr, consentons qu'il périsse,
> Allons presser Galba pour son juste supplice.
> Du courroux à l'amour si le retour est doux,
> On repasse aisément de l'amour au courroux. (*Othon*, IV, 6)

Repetition may be used reproachfully, rather than to score a point in debate. Médée overhears Jason telling Hypsipyle that he loves her and is only wooing Médée from self-interest:

> entendez-le, Madame,
> *Ce soupir qui vers vous pousse toute mon âme;*
> *Et concevez par là jusqu'où vont mes malheurs,*
> *De soupirer pour vous, et de prétendre ailleurs.*
> Il me faut la toison . . .
> . . . .
> Pour faire ma conquête il faut que je me donne,
> Que pour l'objet aimé j'affecte des mépris,
> Que je m'offre en esclave, et *me vende à ce prix.*
> (*La Toison*, III, 3)

Later, Médée uses his own words to reproach him with his perfidy:

> Explique, explique encor ce soupir tout de flamme
> Qui *vers ce cher objet poussait toute ton âme,*
> Et fais-moi *concevoir jusqu'où vont tes malheurs*
> De *soupirer pour elle et de prétendre ailleurs.*
> Redis-moi les raisons dont tu l'as apaisée,
> Dont jusqu'à me braver tu l'as autorisée:
> Qu'il te faut la toison pour revoir tes parents,
> Qu'a ce prix je te plais, qu'*à ce prix tu te vends.* (IV, 4)

Othon tries to dissuade Camille from marrying him: if she were to see another occupying her place on the throne, she would be unable to control her resentment — like Poppæa:

> Le ciel vous a fait l'âme et plus grande et plus belle;
> Mais vous êtes princesse, et femme enfin comme elle.

But Camille understands that Othon is no longer interested in marrying her without the empire:

> Vous n'aimez que l'empire, et je n'aimais que vous.
> N'en appréhendez rien, je suis femme, et princesse,
> Sans en avoir pourtant l'orgueil ni la faiblesse ...
>
> (*Othon*, III, 5)

Repetition may provide a neat retort, even when there is no question of an argument. Honorie tells Flavie that she must marry Attila, otherwise Ildione will:

> Et le sang des Césars, qu'on adora toujours,
> Ferait hommage au sang d'un roi de quatre jours!
>
> (*Attila*, II, 1)

Later, Honorie promises Flavie's hand in marriage to Octar if he will enable her to marry Valamir. This reversal of attitude causes Flavie to ask:

> le chagrin de vous voir préférée,
> Etouffe-t-il la peur que marquaient vos discours
> De rendre hommage au sang d'un roi de quatre jours? (IV, 2)

Similarly, when Domitie — who had earlier advised Domitian, 'Quittez qui vous quitte' — is taken aback to find her lover at Bérénice's feet, he neatly points out:

> Vous m'avez commandé de quitter qui me quitte,
> Vous le savez, Madame, et si c'est vous trahir,
> Vous m'avouerez aussi que c'est vous obéir.
>
> (*Tite et Bérénice*, III, 2)

Repetition may also be used ironically. Félix tells Polyeucte:

> Je te parle sans fard, et veux être chrétien.

He urges Polyeucte to dissimulate until Sévère has departed; on which Polyeucte observes:

> Félix, c'est donc ainsi que vous parlez sans fard?

Polyeucte refuses, and Félix loses his temper, saying that in punishing Polyeucte he would be avenging both himself and his gods. Polyeucte replies:

> Quoi? vous changez bientôt d'humeur et de langage!
> Le zèle de vos Dieux rentre en votre courage!
> Celui d'être chrétien s'échappe, et par hasard
> Je vous viens d'obliger à me parler sans fard! (*Polyeucte*, V, 2)

Marcelle accuses Placide of loving an unworthy object:

> Il est digne de vous, d'une âme vile et basse.

In that case, retorts Placide, your daughter, Flavie, had better stop loving me, and you are wrong to want her to marry me:

> Ne blâmez que Flavie: un cœur si bien placé
> D'une âme vile et basse est trop embarrassé;
> D'un choix qui lui fait honte il faut qu'elle s'irrite,
> Et me prive d'un bien qui passe mon mérite. (*Théodore*, I, 2)

Flaminius tells Nicomède that he will give Attale a kingdom 'sans rien prendre sur vous'. He goes on to say that this can easily be done if Attale marries Laodice, Nicomède's betrothed.

> Voilà le vrai secret de faire Attale roi,
> Comme vous l'avez dit, sans rien prendre sur moi,
> (*Nicomède*, II, 3)

comments Nicomède ironically.

Two repetitions which do not fall into the categories mentioned deserve to be noticed. After Bérénice's return, Domitie asks Tite if he proposes to marry her or Bérénice. Tite answers:

> Dans le trouble où je suis
> Me taire, et vous quitter, c'est tout ce que je puis.
> (*Tite et Bérénice*, II, 6)

In the following scene, Domitie says to her confidante:

> Se taire, et me quitter! Après cette retraite
> Crois-tu qu'un tel arrêt ait besoin d'interprète?

And again:

> Mais pour toute réponse il se tait et me quitte,
> Et tu ne peux souffrir que mon cœur s'en irrite! (II, 7)

Domitie's double repetition of Tite's words shows how much they are preying on her mind. When, at the end of a scene, Suréna repeats words used earlier by Eurydice, 'toujours aimer, souffrir, mourir' (I, 3), the repetition serves to emphasize the hopelessness of the situation in which they find themselves and the unhappiness which can be its only outcome.

A feature often found in repetitions is chiasmus. Don Diègue inquires who will be bold enough to be Chimène's champion against Rodrigue:

> Qui serait ce vaillant, ou bien ce téméraire?
> Je suis ce téméraire, ou plutôt ce vaillant,   (*Le Cid*, IV, 5)

answers Don Diègue. There are several examples in *Horace* alone:

> En l'une je suis femme, en l'autre je suis fille …
> En l'une je suis fille, en l'autre je suis femme …   (III, 1)

> D'Albe avec mon amour j'accordais la querelle:
> *Je soupirais pour vous en combattant pour elle,*
> Et s'il fallait encor que l'on en vînt aux coups,
> *Je combattrais pour elle en soupirant pour vous.*   (I, 3)

> Vos deux frères et vous. — Qui? — Vous et vos deux frères.
>   (II, 2)

> Que *les hommes, les Dieux, les démons et le sort*
> Préparent contre nous un général effort!
> Je mets à faire pis, en l'état où nous sommes,
> *Le sort, et les démons, et les Dieux, et les hommes.*   (II, 3)

There is a somewhat similar example to this last in *Nicomède* (triple repetition with inversion):

> *Prusias.*   Seigneur, vous pardonnez aux chaleurs de *son âge*;
>   *Le temps et la raison* pourront le rendre sage.
> *Nic.*   *La raison et le temps* m'ouvrent assez les yeux,
>   Et *l'âge* ne fera que me les ouvrir mieux.   (II, 3)

'L'empire ou Pison,' says Camille; 'ou Pison ou l'empire,' answers Plautine. 'Vous êtes princesse et femme,' says Othon; 'je suis femme, et princesse,' replies Camille. The love of formal patterns is very strong in Corneille.

Another form it takes is a love of parallelism, of series of lines or speeches beginning in the same way or constructed on the same pattern. Parallelism may occur within one speech or between the speeches of two characters. Parallelism of the first kind usually produces a lyrical effect:

> On en a vu l'effet, lorsque ta fausse mort
> Fit dessus tous mes sens un véritable effort,
> On en a vu l'effet quand te sachant en vie
> De revivre avec toi je pris aussi l'envie,
> On en a vu l'effet lorsqu'à force de pleurs
> Mon amour, et mes soins aidés de mes douleurs
> Ont fléchi la rigueur d'une mère obstinée . . .
>
> *(Mélite*, V, 4)

> L'amour apprit ensemble à nos cœurs à brûler,
> L'amour apprit ensemble à nos yeux à parler,
> Et sa timidité lui donna la prudence
> De n'admettre que nous en notre confidence.
> Ainsi nos passions se dérobaient à tous,
> Ainsi nos feux secrets n'avaient point de jaloux . . .
>
> *(Clitandre*, V, 2)

> Pour le trône cédé, cédez-moi Rodogune,
> Et je n'envierai point votre haute fortune.
> Ainsi notre destin n'aura rien de honteux,
> Ainsi notre bonheur n'aura rien de douteux . . .
>
> *(Rodogune*, I, 3)

> Sanche, fils d'un pêcheur, et non d'un imposteur,
> De deux comtes jadis fut le libérateur;
> Sanche, fils d'un pêcheur, mettait naguère en peine
> Deux illustres rivaux sur le choix de leur reine;
> Sanche, fils d'un pêcheur, tient encore en sa main
> De quoi faire bientôt tout l'heur d'un souverain;
> Sanche enfin, malgré lui, dedans cette province,
> Quoique fils d'un pêcheur, a passé pour un prince.
>
> *(Don Sanche*, V, 5)

Parallelism serves several purposes. It introduces a note of lyricism; it emphasizes the idea or emotion expressed; it gives the impression of a character lingering nostalgically on a tender thought, dwelling on a memory or a wished-for solution, harbouring deep resentment. The most elaborate example is, perhaps,

Camille's speech in *Horace* — which is also an example of repetition. Horace urges Camille not to lament for Curiace:

> Et préfère du moins au souvenir d'un homme
> Ce que doit ta naissance aux intérêts de Rome.

Camille takes up this last word and makes it the starting-point of a series of imprecations:

> Rome, l'unique objet de mon ressentiment!
> Rome, à qui vient ton bras d'immoler mon amant!
> Rome qui t'a vu naître, et que ton cœur adore!
> Rome enfin que je hais parce qu'elle t'honore!

A series of parallel wishes follows:

> Puissent tous ses voisins ensemble conjurés
> Saper ses fondements encor mal assurés!
> Et si ce n'est assez de toute l'Italie,
> Que l'Orient contre elle à l'Occident s'allie;
> Que cent peuples unis des bouts de l'univers
> Passent pour la détruire et les monts et les mers!
> Qu'elle-même sur soi renverse ses murailles,
> Et de ses propres mains déchire ses entrailles!
> Que le courroux du ciel allumé par mes vœux
> Fasse pleuvoir sur elle un déluge de feux!

The last wish of all is another series of parallel remarks:

> Puissé-je de mes yeux y *voir* tomber ce foudre,
> *Voir* ses maisons en cendre, et tes lauriers en poudre,
> *Voir* le dernier Romain à son dernier soupir,
> Moi seule en être cause, et mourir de plaisir.[1]   (IV, 5)

In one scene, at least, parallelism provides the climax. Rodogune very cautiously introduces her proposal to the two brothers. She speaks for twenty-five lines, reminding them of the present and the past, before disclosing what this preamble is leading up to.

---

[1] Cf. Chimène's speech about her father's blood. Cf., too:

> Je sais aimer, Seigneur, je sais garder ma foi,
> Je sais pour un amant faire ce que je dois,
> Je sais à son bonheur m'offrir en sacrifice,
> Et je saurai mourir si je vois qu'il périsse;
> Mais je ne sais point l'art de forcer ma douleur
> A pouvoir recueillir les fruits de son malheur.   (*Othon*, IV, 3)

Suddenly, she tells them: Cléopâtre must be put to death. Both her proposal and the reaction of the brothers are expressed in three sets of parallel statements:

> Vous devez la punir si vous la condamnez;
> Vous devez l'imiter, si vous la soutenez.
> Quoi? cette ardeur s'éteint! L'un et l'autre soupire!
> J'avais su le prévoir, j'avais su le prédire ...
>
> (*Rodogune*, III, 4)

Parallel speeches uttered by different characters seem to be most suitable when both are lamenting a common misfortune or are debating. Examples of the first kind occur in *Le Cid* —

> Rodrigue, qui l'eût cru? — Chimène, qui l'eût dit.   (III, 4)

— in *Polyeucte* (II, 2), and in *Rodogune*:

Sél. Quoi? l'estimez-vous tant?
Ant.   L'estimez-vous moins?
S. Elle vaut bien un trône, il faut que je le die.
A. Elle vaut à mes yeux tout ce qu'en a l'Asie.
S. Vous l'aimez donc, mon frère?
A.   Et vous l'aimez aussi ...

. . . .

Ah, déplorable prince!
S.   Ah, destin trop contraire!
A. Que ne ferais-je point contre un autre qu'un frère?
S. O mon cher frère! O nom pour un rival trop doux!
Que ne ferais-je point contre un autre que vous?
A. Où nous vas-tu réduire, amitié fraternelle?
S. Amour, qui doit ici vaincre de vous ou d'elle?
A. L'amour, l'amour doit vaincre, et la triste amitié
Ne doit être à tous deux qu'un objet de pitié ...

. . . .

S. Il faut encor plus faire, il faut qu'en ce grand jour
Notre amitié triomphe aussi bien que l'amour ...   (I, 3)

S. Est-il une constance à l'épreuve du foudre
Dont ce cruel arrêt met notre espoir en poudre?
A. Est-il un coup de foudre à comparer aux coups
Que ce cruel arrêt vient de lancer sur nous?   (II, 4)

The other use of parallel speeches is diametrically opposed.

Instead of agreement, there is sharp disagreement, the extent of which is emphasized by the similarity in the expression contrasting with the divergence in the meaning.

> *S.* C'est ou d'elle ou du trône être ardemment épris,
> Que vouloir ou l'aimer ou régner à ce prix.
> *A.* C'est d'elle et de lui tenir bien peu de compte,
> Que faire une révolte et si pleine et si prompte.
>
> (*Rodogune*, III, 5)

> *Héraclius.* Je vous rends votre fils, je lui rends sa naissance.
> *Phocas.* Tu me l'ôtes, cruel, et le laisses mourir.
> *H.* Je meurs pour vous le rendre, et pour le secourir.
> *P.* C'est me l'ôter assez que ne vouloir plus l'être.
> *H.* C'est vous le rendre assez que le faire connaître.
> *P.* C'est me l'ôter assez que me le supposer.
> *H.* C'est vous le rendre assez que vous désabuser.
>
> (*Héraclius*, V, 3)

> *Spitridate.* Hélas! considérez ...
> *Mandane.*   Considérez vous-même ...
> *S.*   Que j'aime, et que je suis aimé.
> *M.*   Que je suis aimée, et que j'aime.
>
> (*Agésilas*, IV, 2)

A slightly different use occurs in *Don Sanche*. The Queen tells the two claimants to her hand that whichever marries her must give his sister to Carlos. They reply that both sisters are promised already.

> *D. Isabelle.*   A qui, don Lope?
> *D. Manrique.*   A moi, Madame.
> *D. Isabelle.*   Et l'autre?
> *D. Lope.*   A moi.
>   (III, 4)

Here the parallelism gives a sense of unanimity, of solidarity: the two noblemen are united against the Queen and Don Carlos.[1]

---

[1] Sometimes the ideas may be repeated in different words, e.g.

> *Néarque.* J'abhorre les faux Dieux.
> *Pol.*   Et moi, je les déteste.
> *N.* Je tiens leur culte impie.
> *P.*   Et je le tiens funeste.
> *N.* Fuyez donc leurs autels.
> *P.*   Je les veux renverser.
>
> (*Polyeucte*, II, 6)

§ 2 *Imaginative and sensuous elements in Corneille's verse*

So far, we have considered the qualities of Corneille's verse which appeal to the intellect — though both repetition and parallelism can intensify emotion. But this is only one side of Corneille, whose language appeals to the imagination, the senses, and the emotions as well.

It has been said that poetry is language charged with meaning, a definition which Corneille illustrates admirably. He can pack a wealth of meaning into a simple, concise line:

> Albe vous a nommé, je ne vous connais plus.
>
> (*Horace*, II, 3)
>
> Elle a lieu de me craindre, et je crains cette crainte.
>
> (*Rodogune*, I, 5)

He makes great use of analogy[1] to give force to his lines, creating a new expression on the analogy of an existing one, e.g. *éteindre un tumulte* on the analogy of *éteindre un feu* (*Nicomède*, V, 1). The use of the name of a part of the body to denote its function gives rise to some very striking effects:

> Et c'est mal démêler le cœur d'avec le front ...
>
> (*Rodogune*, IV, 5)
>
> C'est vous qui sous le joug traînez des cœurs si braves ...
>
> (*Sertorius*, III, 1)
>
> Afin que, Sylla mort, ce dangereux pouvoir
> Ne tombe qu'en des mains qui sachent leur devoir.
>
> (*Sertorius*, III, 1)

Metaphors and personifications play a great part, too: in the following couplet, there are both:

> L'estime et le respect sont *de justes tributs*
> Qu'aux plus fiers ennemis *arrachent les vertus*.
>
> (*Sertorius*, III, 1)

Often Corneille gives energy to his verse by revivifying a dead metaphor. We talk of the head of the state, for example, without remembering that this is a metaphor; for Corneille, a head implies a body:

[1] Vuillard has studied this in detail.

A moins que d'une tête un si grand corps chancelle.

> (*Othon*, III, 3)

L'empire est à donner, et le sénat s'assemble
Pour choisir une tête à ce grand corps qui tremble,
Et dont les Huns, les Goths, les Vandales, les Francs,
Bouleversent la masse et déchirent les flancs.

> (*Pulchérie*, I, 1)

Very often, too, Corneille's verse has the evocative power, the expressive harmony, that comes from the marriage of sound and sense, from the use of alliteration and assonance. Take, for example, the narrative of the death of Pompée (*Pompée*, II, 2):

D'un des pans de sa robe il couvre son visage,
A son mauvais destin en aveugle obéit,
Et dédaigne de voir le ciel qui le trahit . . .

The repetitions of v's, d's, l's and s sounds in these lines give a musical effect. A few lines further on, we come to the passage:

Aucun gémissement à son cœur échappé
Ne le montre, en mourant, digne d'être frappé:
Immobile à leurs coups, en lui-même il rappelle
Ce qu'eut de beau sa vie, et ce qu'on dira d'elle . . .

The repetition of the m's, interwoven with r's and l's, the recurrence of p's at the end of each of the three lines, the predominance of narrow vowel sounds (i, é, ê) and nasals, all help to convey the dignity and melancholy of the scene described. A little later, we come to the lines:

On descend, et pour comble à sa noire aventure,
On donne à ce héros la mer pour sépulture,
Et le tronc sous les flots roule dorénavant
Au gré de la fortune, et de l'onde, et du vent.

This time it is r's, l's, v's which provide the framework. Another good example occurs in Cléopâtre's speech which follows:

Ce prince d'un sénat maître de l'univers,
Dont le bonheur semblait au-dessus du revers,
Lui que sa Rome a vu plus craint que le tonnerre,
Triompher en trois fois des trois parts de la terre . . .

The last line, with its t's and r's, its a's and wa sounds, is a
glorious expression of triumph, like a trumpet call. Here is one
further example from *Pompée*:

> Et son sort que tu plains te doit faire penser
> Que ton cœur est sensible, et qu'on peut le percer.

. . . .

> Ne crois pas que jamais tu puisses à ce prix
> Récompenser sa flamme ou punir ses mépris . . .   (IV, 1)

Pompée is not an exception. Here are one or two examples of
assonance and alliteration from other works:[1]

> Et je pourrai souffrir qu'un amour suborneur
> Sous un lâche silence étouffe mon honneur!   (*Le Cid*, III, 3)

> Souffrons-nous moins tous deux pour soupirer ensemble?
>   (*Suréna*, I, 3)

> Tout fléchit sur la terre, et tout tremble sur l'onde;
> Et Rome est aujourd'hui la maîtresse du monde.
>   (*Nicomède*, III, 2)

> Si pour le couronner j'ai fait un noble effort,
> Dois-je en faire un honteux pour jouir de sa mort?
> Je me privais de lui sans me vendre à personne,
> Et vous voulez, Seigneur, que son trépas me donne,
> Que mon cœur, entraîné par la splendeur du rang,
> Vole après une main fumante de son sang;
> Et que de ses malheurs triomphante et ravie,
> Je sois l'infâme prix d'avoir tranché sa vie!
> Non, Seigneur: nous aurons même sort aujourd'hui;
> Vous me verrez régner ou périr avec lui:
> Ce n'est qu'à l'un des deux que tout ce cœur aspire.
>   (*Othon*, IV, 3)

Others will be encountered in the next section.

§ 3 *A brief anthology*

There are many kinds of pleasure to be derived from Corneille's verse — pleasure from its logical structure and careful

---

[1] Other examples will be found in Crétin, Freudemann and Grammont — and, of
course, in Corneille. Grammont studies in detail Sévère's speech in *Polyeucte*, V, 6: 'Père
dénaturé, malheureux politique,' etc.

form, and from its harmonies; pleasure from the stirring or moving narratives, from the great political debates and the *solidité du raisonnement*; pleasure from the arguments and quarrels and irony. There are, too, what Mme de Sévigné calls 'ces tirades qui font frissonner'. But Corneille can also move us by his tenderness, by his ability to give expression to the ordinary human emotions. The aim of these few pages is to illustrate this aspect of his poetry.

There are, in Corneille, plenty of expressive lines, lines which appeal to the imagination or the emotions, which evoke a mood or a sentiment without directly expressing it.

> Je cherche le silence et la nuit pour pleurer.
>
> (*Le Cid*, III, 4)

(This line owes a good deal to alliteration, to the predominance of l's and r's.)

> Cette obscure clarté qui tombe des étoiles ...
>
> (*Le Cid*, IV, 3)

(So does this to the repetition of the t's and of the k and s sounds.)

> Au gré de la fortune, et de l'onde, et du vent.[1]
>
> (*Pompée*, II, 2)
>
> Que pouvait-elle faire et seule et contre tous.
>
> (*Rodogune*, I, 1)
>
> Vous n'aimez que l'empire, et je n'aimais que vous.
>
> (*Othon*, III, 5)
>
> Il est doux de revoir les murs de la patrie ...
>
> (*Sertorius*, III, 1)
>
> Notre adieu ne fut point un adieu d'ennemis.
>
> (*Suréna*, I, 1)
>
> Non, je ne pl*eu*re point, *M*ada*m*e, *m*ais je *m*eurs.
>
> (*Suréna*, V, 5)

Corneille, except in *Clitandre*, has little to say about nature;[2]

---

[1] Cf. Wordsworth:
> Roll'd round in earth's diurnal course
> With rocks and stones and trees.

[2] In *Rodogune*, there is the description of the place where Séleucus's body was found:
> Je l'ai trouvé, Seigneur, au bout de cette allée,
> Où la clarté du ciel semble toujours voilée.   (V, 4)

but it may be worth quoting one passage from *Clitandre* to show that he was capable of nature poetry:

> L'haleine manque aux vents, et la force à l'orage,
> Les éclairs indignés d'être éteints par les eaux
> En ont tari la source et séché les ruisseaux,
> Et déjà le soleil de ses rayons essuie
> Sur ces moites rameaux le reste de la pluie,
> Au lieu du bruit affreux des foudres décochés
> Les petits oisillons encore demi-cachés
> Poussent en tremblotant, et hasardent à peine
> Leur voix qui se dérobe à la peur incertaine
> Qui tient encor leur âme, et ne leur permet pas
> De se croire du tout préservés du trépas.   (IV, 3)

Corneille touches on many different aspects of love. Here is a young girl thinking of her lover; Camille has been assured by an oracle that she will be united with Curiace:

> Je pris sur cet oracle une entière assurance,
> Et comme le succès passait mon espérance,
> J'abandonnai mon âme à des ravissements
> Qui passaient les transports des plus heureux amants.
> Jugez de leur excès: je rencontrai Valère,
> Et contre sa coutume, il ne put me déplaire,
> Il me parla d'amour sans me donner d'ennui:
> Je ne m'aperçus pas que je parlais à lui;
> Je ne lui pus montrer de mépris ni de glace:
> Tout ce que je voyais me semblait Curiace;
> Tout ce qu'on me disait me parlait de ses feux;
> Tout ce que je disais l'assurait de mes vœux.[1]   (*Horace*, I, 2)

[1] Cf. the somewhat similar passage in *Mélite*:

> cette volage évite ma rencontre,
> Ou si malgré ses soins le hasard me la montre,
> Si je puis l'aborder, son discours se confond,
> Son esprit en désordre à peine me répond,
> Une réflexion vers le traître qu'elle aime
> Presques à tous moments le ramène en lui-même
> Et tout rêveur qu'il est, il n'a point de soucis
> Qu'un soupir ne trahisse au seul nom de Tirsis
> Lors par le prompt effet d'un changement étrange
> Son silence rompu se déborde en louange,
> Elle remarque en lui tant de perfections,
> Que les moins avisés verraient ses passions,
> Sa bouche ne se plaît qu'en cette flatterie,
> Et tout autre propos lui rend sa rêverie.   (II, 1)

Another Camille, a princess, cannot help betraying her secret inclinations:

> A ne vous rien celer,
> { Sortant d'avec Galba, j'ai voulu lui parler:
> { J'ai voulu sur ce point pressentir sa pensée;
> J'en ai nommé plusieurs pour qui je l'ai pressée.
> A leurs noms, un grand froid, un front triste, un œil bas,
> M'ont fait voir aussitôt qu'ils ne lui plaisaient pas;
> Au vôtre elle a rougi, puis s'est mise à sourire,
> Et m'a soudain quitté sans me vouloir rien dire.
> C'est à vous qui savez ce que c'est que d'aimer,
> A juger de son cœur ce qu'on doit présumer.   (*Othon*, I, 2)

(The alliterations are very striking and effective here: especially the p's of the second, third and fourth lines, the f's and r's of the fifth, the s and z sounds throughout, the v's and k's at the end.)

Pulchérie loves Léon passionately, but cannot marry him:

> Léon seul est ma joie, il est mon seul désir;
> Je n'en puis choisir d'autre, et n'ose le choisir:
> Depuis trois ans unie à cette chère idée,
> J'en ai l'âme à toute heure, en tous lieux, obsédée;
> Rien n'en détachera mon cœur que le trépas,
> Encore après ma mort n'en répondrais-je pas;
> Et si dans le tombeau le ciel permet qu'on aime,
> Dans le fond du tombeau je l'aimerai de même.
> Trône qui m'éblouis, titres qui me flattez,
> Pourrez-vous me valoir ce que vous me coûtez?
> Et de tout votre orgueil la pompe la plus haute
> A-t-elle un bien égal à celui qu'elle m'ôte?[1]

> (*Pulchérie*, III, 2)

(Here again, the sound effects contribute to the poetry of the lines. S's and z's predominate in the first four lines, p's in the next two; m's and t's in the two following couplets and l's in the last one. The assonance of the line —

> P*ou*rrez-*vou*s me *v*aloir ce que *vou*s me c*oû*tez?

— is striking.)

---

[1] Cf. Byron:
> There's not a joy the world can give like that it takes away . . .

In the same play, Martian, an elderly general, tells his daughter
that he has fallen in love with Pulchérie:

J'aime, et depuis dix ans ma flamme et mon silence
Font à mon triste cœur égale violence:
J'écoute la raison, j'en goûte les avis,
Et les mieux écoutés sont le plus mal suivis.
{ Cent fois en moins d'un jour je guéris et retombe;
{ Cent fois je me révolte, et cent fois je succombe:
Tant ce calme forcé, que j'étudie en vain,
Près d'un si rare objet s'évanouit soudain!

. . . .

Pour ne prétendre rien, on n'est pas moins jaloux,
Et ces désirs, qu'éteint le déclin de la vie,
N'empêchent pas de voir avec un œil d'envie,
Quand on est d'un mérite à pouvoir faire honneur,
Et qu'il faut qu'un autre âge emporte le bonheur.
Que le moindre retour vers nos belles années
Jette alors d'amertume en nos âmes gênées!
'Que n'ai-je vu le jour quelques lustres plus tard!
Disais-je; en ses bontés peut-être aurais-je part,
Si le ciel n'opposait auprès de la princesse
A l'excès de l'amour le manque de la jeunesse;
De tant et tant de cœurs qu'il force à l'adorer,
Devais-je être le seul qui ne pût espérer?'
        J'aimais quand j'étais jeune, et ne déplaisais guère,
Quelquefois de soi-même on cherchait à me plaire,
Je pouvais aspirer au cœur le mieux placé;
Mais, hélas! j'étais jeune, et ce temps est passé.
Le souvenir en tue, et l'on ne l'envisage
Qu'avec, s'il le faut dire, une espèce de rage;
On le repousse, on fait cent projets superflus:
Le trait qu'on porte au cœur s'enfonce d'autant plus;
Et ce feu, que de honte on s'obstine à contraindre,
Redouble par l'effort qu'on se fait pour l'éteindre.

. . . .

Je m'attachais sans crainte à servir la princesse,
Fier de mes cheveux blancs, et fort de ma faiblesse;
Et quand je ne pensais qu'à remplir mon devoir,
Je devenais amant sans m'en apercevoir.
Mon âme, de ce feu nonchalamment saisie,
Ne l'a point reconnu que par ma jalousie:

⎧Tout ce qui l'approchait voulait me l'enlever,
⎩Tout ce qui lui parlait cherchait à m'en priver;
　Je tremblais qu'à leurs yeux elle ne fût trop belle;
　Je les haïssais tous, comme plus dignes d'elle,
　Et ne pouvais souffrir qu'on s'enrichît d'un bien
　Que j'enviais à tous, sans y prétendre rien.
　　　Quel supplice d'aimer un objet adorable,
　Et de tant de rivaux se voir le moins aimable!
　D'aimer plus qu'eux ensemble, et n'oser de ses feux,
　Quelques ardents qu'ils soient, se promettre autant qu'eux!
　On aurait deviné mon amour par ma peine,
　Si la peur que j'en eus n'avait fui tant de gêne.
　L'auguste Pulchérie avait beau me ravir,
　J'attendais à la voir qu'il la fallût servir:
　Je fis plus, de Léon j'appuyai l'espérance,
　La princesse l'aima, j'en eus la confiance,
　Et la dissuadai de se donner à lui
　Qu'il ne fût de l'empire ou le maître ou l'appui.
　Ainsi, pour éviter un hymen si funeste,
　Sans rendre heureux Léon, je détruisais le reste;
　Et mettant un long terme au succès de l'amour,
　J'espérais de mourir avant ce triste jour.
　　　Nous y voilà, ma fille, et du moins j'ai la joie
　D'avoir à son triomphe ouvert l'unique voie.
　J'en mourrai du moment qu'il recevra sa foi,
　Mais dans cette douceur, qu'ils tiendront tout de moi.
　　　J'ai caché si longtemps l'ennui qui me dévore,
　Qu'en dépit que j'en aie, enfin il s'évapore:
　L'aigreur en diminue à te le raconter.　　　(*Pulchérie*, II, 1)

We have Fontenelle's authority for believing that Corneille put
something of himself into Martian. His daughter, in the same
scene, tells her father how she has fallen in love with Léon. Here
is a passage in which she explains how it was that his passion for
Pulchérie did not disturb her:

　　'Quelque obstacle imprévu rompra de si doux nœuds,
　　Ajoutais-je; et le temps éteint les plus beaux feux.'
　　C'est ce que m'inspirait l'aimable rêverie
　　Dont jusqu'à ce grand jour ma flamme s'est nourrie;
　　Mon cœur, qui ne voulait désespérer de rien,
　　S'en faisait à toute heure un charmant entretien.

Qu'on rêve avec plaisir, quand notre âme blessée
Autour de ce qu'elle aime est toute ramassée!
Vous le savez, Seigneur, et comme à tous propos
Un doux je ne sais quoi trouble notre repos:
Un sommeil inquiet sur de confus nuages
Elève incessamment de flatteuses images,
Et sur leur vain rapport fait naître des souhaits,
Que le réveil admire et ne dédit jamais.
    Ainsi, près de tomber dans un malheur extrême,
J'en écartais l'idée en m'abusant moi-même . . .   (II, 1)

A baroque idea, and a baroque image.

There are many other scenes and passages one would like to quote. Not least is the delightful scene in *Clitandre* (V, 3), in which Caliste visits her lover, Rosidor, who is in bed with his wounds, and with whom she is shortly to be united. Their trials are over, and they can give themselves up to badinage and the contemplation of their future happiness. Faguet claims that *Psyché*[1] contains 'les plus beaux vers d'amour qui aient peut-être jamais été écrits en langue française'. There is, too, the scene in which Eryxe tells Massinisse, who is going to marry her rival, Sophonisbe, that she is not jealous, but cannot help gradually betraying her jealousy (*Sophonisbe*, III, 2). This is too long to quote, but here is Sophonisbe discussing Eryxe with her confidante. Herminie thinks that Eryxe is not jealous, but Sophonisbe knows better:

H. Je voudrais qu'elle vît un peu plus son malheur,
    Qu'elle en fît hautement éclater la douleur,
    Que l'espoir inquiet de se voir son épouse
    Jetât un plein désordre en son âme jalouse,
    Que son amour pour lui fût sans bonté pour vous.
S. Que tu te connais mal en sentiments jaloux!
    Alors qu'on l'est si peu qu'on ne pense pas l'être,
    On n'y réfléchit point, on laisse tout paraître;
    Mais quand on l'est assez pour s'en apercevoir,
    On met tout son possible à n'en laisser rien voir.
    Eryxe qui connaît et qui hait la faiblesse
    La renferme au-dedans, et s'en rend la maîtresse,

[1] Nothing has been said of *Psyché* (1671) in this book, since it was devised by Molière and only in part versified by Corneille.

Mais cette indifférence où tant d'orgueil se joint
Ne part que d'un dépit jaloux au dernier point,
Et sa fausse bonté se trahit elle-même
Par l'effort qu'elle fait à se montrer extrême:
Elle est étudiée, et ne l'est pas assez
Pour échapper entière aux yeux intéressés.

(Sophonisbe, II, 5)

Sophonisbe may be a Carthaginian princess, but she has served her apprenticeship in a seventeenth-century salon.

Let us conclude — as Corneille did — with *Suréna*. Eurydice relates the dawn of her love for Suréna:

Tous deux, ainsi qu'au Roi, me rendirent visite,
Et j'en connus bientôt le différent mérite.
L'un, fier et tout gonflé d'un vieux mépris des rois,
Semblait pour compliment nous apporter des lois;
L'autre, par les devoirs d'un respect légitime,
Vengeait le sceptre en nous de ce manque d'estime.
L'amour s'en mêla même; et tout cet entretien
Sembla m'offrir son cœur, et demander le mien.
Il l'obtint, et mes yeux que charmaient sa présence
Soudain avec les siens en firent confidence;
Ces muets truchements surent lui révéler
Ce que je me forçais à lui dissimuler;
Et les mêmes regards qui m'expliquaient sa flamme
S'instruisaient dans les miens du secret de mon âme.
Ses vœux y rencontraient d'aussi tendres désirs:
Un accord imprévu confondait nos soupirs,
Et d'un mot échappé la douceur hasardée
Trouvait l'âme en tous deux persuadée.

(I, 1)

(Once again, in the latter half of this passage the effect of the words is enhanced by the predominance of s and z sounds. M's and l's become appropriately frequent in the lines:

Ces muets truchements surent lui révéler
Ce que je me forçais à lui dissimuler;
Et les mêmes regards qui m'expliquaient sa flamme
S'instruisaient dans les miens du secret de mon âme.)

Like Martian, Eurydice is jealous.

Je suis jalouse.

. . . .

Orode fait venir la princesse sa fille;
Et s'il veut de mon bien enrichir sa famille,
S'il veut qu'un double hymen honore un même jour,
Conçois mes déplaisirs: je t'ai dit mon amour.
      C'est bien assez, ô ciel! que le pouvoir suprême
Me livre en d'autres bras aux yeux de ce que j'aime:
Ne me condamne pas à ce nouvel ennui
De voir tout ce que j'aime entre les bras d'autrui.

. . . .

Quand on a commencé de se voir malheureuse,
Rien ne s'offre à nos yeux qui ne fasse trembler:
La plus fausse apparence a droit de nous troubler;
Et tout ce qu'on prévoit, tout ce qu'on s'imagine,
Forme un nouveau poison pour une âme chagrine.

. . . .

La princesse est mandée, elle vient, elle est belle;
Un vainqueur des Romains n'est que trop digne d'elle.
S'il *l*a voit, s'i*l l*ui par*l*e, et si *l*e Roi *l*e veut . . .
J'en dis trop; et déjà tout mon cœur qui s'émeut . . .

In a touching passage in the same scene Eurydice describes how, being unable to see Suréna, she has made friends with his sister as a means of being near him vicariously:

N'osant voir Suréna, qui règne en ma pensée,
Et qui me croit peut-être une âme intéressée,
Tu vois quelle amitié j'ai faite avec sa sœur:
Je crois le voir en elle, et c'est quelque douceur,
Mais légère, mais faible, et qui me gêne l'âme
Par l'inutile soin de lui cacher ma flamme.
Elle le sait sans doute, et l'air dont elle agit
M'en demande un aveu dont mon devoir rougit:
Ce frère l'aime trop pour s'être caché d'elle.
N'en use pas de même, et sois-moi plus fidèle;
Il suffit qu'avec toi j'amuse mon ennui.
Toutefois tu n'as rien à me dire de lui
Tu ne sais ce qu'il fait, tu ne sais ce qu'il pense.
Une sœur est plus propre à cette confiance:
Elle sait s'il m'accuse, ou s'il plaint mon malheur,
S'il partage ma peine, ou rit de ma douleur,
Si du vol qu'on lui fait il m'estime complice,
S'il me garde son cœur, ou s'il me rend justice.

CONCLUSION

AFTER writing comedies which, besides being light-hearted and amusing, were characterized by their close observation of reality, Corneille wrote tragedies which reflect many aspects of seventeenth-century French life and contain a pronounced vein of comedy.

Because so many of his plays are called tragedies, it is sometimes asked whether they are in fact 'tragic'. The question is scarcely relevant. It is important to approach any author without preconceived notions, and Corneille is likely to prove most rewarding if we judge him by his own standards without expecting him to have a conception of tragedy which was not that of his age. In the seventeenth century, the distinction between comedy and tragedy was rather different from that existing in the minds of most of us to-day. We expect a comedy to be funny and a tragedy to depict the sufferings of a hero who is the victim of destiny or of circumstance or of some flaw in his own character. A tragedy for us is a play like *Oedipus* or *Antigone*, *Hamlet* or *Macbeth*, *Andromaque* or *Phèdre*. For the seventeenth-century Frenchman, however, the distinction was one of subject matter and of social class rather than of *Weltanschauung*. A tragedy, as Corneille tells us in the first of his *Discours*, dealt with persons of royal rank[1] in danger of losing their lives or their states, or of banishment. A play which dealt with less exalted members of society, or which depicted noble personages exposed to lesser dangers (such as that of being crossed in love), was a comedy. Hence, on the one hand, Thomas Corneille's *Les Illustres Ennemis* and Molière's *Dom Garcie de Navarre* are entitled comedies, though the latter contains none of the wit and humour we associate with its author, and the former is a complicated play about love, honour and vengeance. Hence, on the other hand, many of the tragedies even of Racine, whom we

[1] 'Eminent' or 'illustrious' would be more accurate than 'royal'. Corneille's Roman heroes are, of course, not kings.

tend to regard as a genuinely tragic poet, have happy endings and contain little that is tragic.[1]

Some of Corneille's plays are tragic in the narrower, modern, sense of the word. *Horace*, for instance, is a tragedy of character: the same motives lead the hero to win a heroic victory and to commit a shameful crime immediately afterwards. The irreconcilable passions of the two implacable adversaries in *Théodore* allow no hope of a solution, just as, in *Suréna*, there can be no compromise between love and political prudence. There are elements of this kind of tragedy in other plays: Sertorius's love and Sophonisbe's jealousy are their undoing. Nevertheless, with some exceptions, Corneille's tragedies, on the whole, end happily and are tragedies in the seventeenth-century sense of the word rather than tragic according to the modern view. This is, of course, in no sense a condemnation of Corneille. We do not deplore the fact that Molière did not write tragedies, or enquire whether or not Balzac is tragic — and, as we have seen, Corneille, whose plays so often verge on the comic, and who is deeply interested in man in society, in man with ambitions and duties and responsibilities, in rivalries and complex relationships, has a good deal in common with Molière and Balzac. The relevant question is not whether Corneille's plays are or are not tragic, but whether, whatever they are called, they are good and interesting.

This is the question which the present study has attempted to answer. It has tried to show that Corneille, in dealing with the characters and problems of his own age, has also raised problems of perennial interest and depicted characters of universal validity. It has tried, above all, to show the great diversity of his work — the great variety of types of play that he wrote, the subtlety of his portrayal of character and the range of his studies of human passion, the variety of tones within his plays, the variety and

---

[1] *Alexandre, Mithridate, Iphigénie* and *Esther* have happy endings; so has *Athalie*. The unhappy ending of *Bajazet* is not inherent in the play and is largely the result of chance. The whole question of the nature of seventeenth-century tragedy has been admirably treated by Professor R. C. Knight in his article, 'A Minimal Definition of Seventeenth-Century Tragedy', in *French Studies*, October 1956.

flexibility of his verse. As another Norman, Barbey d'Aurevilly, once remarked: 'Ce qu'il y a de plus rare dans ce monde, ce n'est pas le talent, quoiqu'il soit assez rare, mais c'est la *variété dans le talent.*'

SELECT BIBLIOGRAPHY

Adam (A.), *Histoire de la littérature française au XVIIe siècle*, vols I, II and IV, Paris, 1948–1954.

Barrière (P.), 'Le lyrisme dans la tragédie de Corneille,' in *Revue d'Histoire Littéraire*, 1928, pp. 23–38.

Bénichou (P.), *Morales du grand siècle*, Paris, 1948.

Boorsch (J.), 'L'invention chez Corneille. Comment Corneille ajoute à ses sources,' in *Essays in Honor of Albert Feuillerat*, Yale Romanic Studies, vol. XXII, 1943, pp. 115–128.

'Remarques sur la technique dramatique de Corneille,' in *Studies by Members of the French Department of Yale University*, ed. Feuillerat, Yale University Press, 1941, pp. 101–162.

Brasillach (R.), *Pierre Corneille*, Paris, 1938.

Couton (G.), *Corneille*, Paris, 1958.

Corneille et la Fronde, Théâtre et politique il y a trois siècles, Clermont Ferrand, 1951.

Réalisme de Corneille. Deux études: La Clef de Mélite. Réalités dans Le Cid, Paris, 1953.

La Vieillesse de Corneille, Paris, 1949.

Crétin (R.), *Les Images dans l'Oeuvre de Corneille*, Paris, 1927.

Lexique comparé des Métaphores dans le théâtre de Corneille et de Racine, Caen, 1927.

Dorchain (A.), *Corneille*, Paris, 1918.

Freudemann (E. R.), *Das Adjektiv und seine Ausdruckswerte im Stil Racines dargestellt an einem Stilvergleich Racine-Corneille*, Berlin, 1941.

Grammont (M.), *Le Vers français*, Paris, 1937.

Herland (L.), *Corneille par lui-même*, Paris, 1954.

Horace ou Naissance de l'Homme, Paris, 1952.

Lancaster (H. C.), *A History of French Dramatic Literature in the Seventeenth Century*, 9 vols, Baltimore, 1929–1942.

Lanson (G.), *Esquisse d'une histoire de la tragédie française*, Paris, 1927.

Corneille, Paris, n.d. (1895).

May (G.), *Tragédie cornélienne, tragédie racinienne. Etude sur les sources de l'intérêt dramatique*, Urbana, 1948.

Nadal (O.), *Le sentiment de l'amour dans l'œuvre de Pierre Corneille*, Paris, 1948.

Neukomm (Gerda), *Formwerdung und Formzerfall bei Pierre Corneille*, Zürich, 1941.

Péguy (Charles), *Victor-Marie, comte Hugo*, Cahiers de la Quinzaine, 1911.

Rivaille (L.), *Les Débuts de Pierre Corneille*, Paris, n.d. (1936).

Roaten (D.), *Structural Forms in the French Theater, 1500–1700*, Philadelphia, 1960.

Roques (M.), *Etudes de littérature française*, Lille, 1949.

Rousset (J.), *La littérature de l'âge baroque en France*, Paris, 1953.

Schérer (J.), *La Dramaturgie classique en France*, Paris, n.d.

Schlumberger (J.), *Plaisir à Corneille*, Paris, 1936.

Steinweg (C.), *Kompositionsstudien zum Cid, Horace, Cinna, Polyeucte. Ein Beitrag zur Geschichte des französischen Dramas*, Halle, 1905.

Tanquerey (F. J.), 'Le Héros cornélien,' in *Revue des Cours et Conférences*, July 15 and 30, 1934, pp. 577–594, 687–696.

    Le Romanesque dans le Théâtre de Corneille, Paris, 1939.

    'La technique de la composition dans les tragédies de Corneille et de Racine,' in *Revue des Cours et Conférences*, 1939–1940, First Series, pp. 225–236, 315–324, 549–561, Second Series, pp. 47–52, 136–143, 279–288.

Vedel (V.), *Deux Classiques français vus par un critique étranger*, Paris, 1935.

Vuillard (L.), 'De l'analogie dans la langue de Corneille,' in *Revue de Philologie française et de littérature*, vol. XXX, 1917–1918, pp. 97–129, and vol. XXXI, 1919, pp. 43–76.

INDEX OF PLAYS

PRINTED IN GREAT BRITAIN
BY ROBERT MACLEHOSE AND CO. LTD
THE UNIVERSITY PRESS, GLASGOW